The Past in the Present

AN INTRODUCTION TO ARCHAEOLOGY

Travis W. Stanton | Kenichiro Tsukamoto

Kendall Hunt
publishing company

Cover images provided by Sabrina Simon and Kenichiro Tsukamoto.

Kendall Hunt
publishing company

www.kendallhunt.com
Send all inquiries to:
4050 Westmark Drive
Dubuque, IA 52004-1840

Published in the United States of America

Dedicated to our families:

Karla, Charlie, and Sophie

and

Cheiko

Contents

Acknowledgments

The following people commented on this manuscript whole or in part and/or whose clarifications and suggestions contributed to the content:

Traci Ardren (University of Miami), Nic Barth (University of California Riverside), Andrea Cucina (UADY), Christine Gailey (University of California Riverside), Sang-Hee Lee (University of California Riverside), Leonardo López Luján (Templo Mayor, INAH), Karl Taube (University of California Riverside), and Vera Tiesler (UADY).

The following people were instrumental in gaining access to imagery:

Traci Ardren (University of Miami), Elizabeth Wayland Barber (Occidental College), Helena Barba Meinecke (Subdirección de Arqueologia Subacuática, INAH), Nic Barth (University of California Riverside), Sara Becker (University of California Riverside), Vania Carrillo Bosch, Belem Ceballos Casanova, Marina Elliot (University of Witwatersrand), Francisco Estrada-Belli (Boston University), Juan Fernandez-Diaz (NCALM, University of Houston), Charles Graninger (University of California Riverside), Scott Hutson (University of Kentucky), Takeshi Inomata (University of Arizona), Donald Johanson (Arizona State University), Peter Leach (Geophysical/University of Connecticut), Mark Lehner (Giza Plateau Mapping Project), Eric Lo (University of California San Diego), Leonardo López Luján (Templo Mayor, INAH), Aline Magnoni (USAID), Blanca Maldonado (Colegio de Michoacán), Dominque Meyer (University of California San Diego), Eylene Parrish (Earth Search), Tony Roche (National Monuments Service, Ireland), Julie Russ (Arizona State University), Piper Severance (Los Angeles Museum of Art), Payson Sheets (University of Colorado, Boulder), Donald Slater (Phillips Academy), Sabrina Simon, Sabrina Ta'ala (Defense POW/MIA Accounting Agency), Karl Taube (University of California Riverside), Marla Taylor (Robert S. Peabody Museum of Archaeology), Wilma Wetterstrom (Harvard University), Phil Wilke (University of California Riverside), Jill Yakubik (Earth Search).

Introduction

In the grand scheme of things archaeology is a relatively recent profession, only stretching back into the nineteenth century as a widely accepted scientific endeavor. Yet the foundations on which archaeology rests, a fascination with humanity's past, reach back well before recorded history. There are many reasons for our interest in the past. At a basic level, however, is the fact that the present in which we live and experience the world could not exist without the collective accumulation of all that passed before us. And we, as human beings, realize this. In the words of the nineteenth-century French philosopher Henri Bergson (cited in Marquardt 1994, 203), "the present drains the past to irrigate the future."

Whether the remains of that past are spectacular monuments such as the pyramids of Giza (Egypt) or more mundane forms of evidence such as the discarded trash of the people who labored to erect these monuments, the material fragments of past

FIGURE 1.1 Archaeologists strive to study not only the leaders of past societies, but all groups of people. The Ancient Egypt Research Association (AERA), directed by Mark Lehner, has gone to great lengths to study the archaeology of the Giza Plateau of Egypt, where some of the world's most famous monuments are located. The work by AERA has uncovered an entire community of workers who labored to build the monuments found there today; the Great Pyramid of Khufu is the only one of the seven wonders of the ancient world which still stands today. Although this and the other monuments are a testament of the elites of Pharaonic Egyptian society, AERA has shed light on how other classes of society lived by uncovering spaces such as the areas where brewing for the workers occurred.

© WitR/Shutterstock.com

Bottom image: Copyright 2018 Ancient Egypt Research Associates. Photo by Mark Lehner. AERA_Pedestal_bldg_pedestals.tif

human activities represent a tangible "window into the past". With these fragments, as well as oral and written histories when they exist, archaeologists create the narratives that comprise the base on which we construct the social order sustaining modern-day societies throughout the world. We could not literally be who we are today without the complex histories of social and environmental change, which led to the complicated world we currently live in, just as our actions now will mold the world in unimaginable ways for the generations to come when we, and the material remains of our accomplishments, become the broken fragments of the past in their world. In many ways the "past" is an intrinsic part of our identity, and in some sense is not only the key to understanding who we are as individuals and groups, but ultimately addresses the existential question of who we are as humans. In this light, the past is powerful.

Yet the past is a social construction, open to negotiation, open to contestation. The past only exists as part of our social world today. In this world, one individual's narrative of what happened in the past may differ greatly from another's. And, these differences may have great consequences in our contemporary societies. How many times have we heard the phrase "history is written by the victors"? Although this quote is often attributed to Winston Churchill, the fact is that people have long known our "histories," or perhaps more aptly stated our "contemporary narratives of the past," are colored by particular viewpoints, and that these viewpoints often reflect some vested interest in the modern world. Who won a war matters, but also how it was won and what the conflict was about in the first place. Who settled an area first matters, but also the complex history of migration and interaction that followed initial settlement over the course of thousands and even millions of years of human existence in particular regions of the world. Claims to power, land, and other resources, and particular ways of doing things (e.g., language, social organization, and economic structures) are often based on narratives of the past which in many ways legitimize them, and these narratives are variable. The "past" is tremendously important to our contemporary world. It can set the standard for how things should be done. And, these standards are highly political and in many cases contentious.

Establishing the importance of the past to contemporary society is one thing. Investigating it in a clear and seemingly "unbiased" way is quite another. Archaeology is the scientific study of humanity's past through the analysis of material remains. With this said, the task set before archaeologists is more difficult than it might seem. Unlike most areas of academic research, archaeology is faced with a largely incomplete data set. Archaeologists study the material remains of past societies. What generally remains of the material culture of past peoples, however, is usually a fraction of one percent of what once existed. It is like reconstructing a 1,000-piece puzzle with only two and a half of the pieces; and those pieces are not always in very good shape. Further complicating the matter, many behaviors of past peoples that archaeologists want to understand did not leave any material trace, ever. So, to be an archaeologist is to accept the realization that the study of the human past will always be incomplete. This is not to say that archaeologists cannot make important steps toward understanding past societies, but that we will never know the full picture of the complex tapestry of human existence in the past no matter how much research is performed.

As a science, archaeology is complicated not only with a fragmentary set of data, but also with the fact that archaeologists live in cultural contexts that influence their way of thinking about the data that *have* survived. Although all scientific studies may have some sort of human bias based on cultural context, archaeology is not a science like physics where variables can be placed into an equation and a relatively clear answer is calculated. Even though many archaeological data are quantifiable, there are no equations which give you the answer to questions concerning topics like the rise of civilizations or the origins of agriculture. There is usually some degree of subjectivity in archaeological research. When something happened may be a difficult question, but *why* it may have happened is degrees harder to answer in most cases. This lack of more straightforward answers does not lessen archaeology's place as a science, but does make more room for cultural biases to enter the interpretive process. An archaeologist who sees the first pollen of domesticated plants appear at the same time that the first temples were built in an ancient society may reach the conclusion that agriculture allowed for the construction of monumental architecture; agriculture providing a surplus in most societies freeing up some people to perform other nonsubsistence tasks such as building monuments. Although the archaeologist may be right, they may also overlook other explanations that do not follow their cultural logic, closing the door to other modes of potentially valuable ways of interpreting the data. To be an archaeologist is to constantly evaluate potential biases in your own research and to be aware that **equifinality**, or the potential for more than one valid interpretation, is likely.

We begin this book with these caveats not to turn the reader off to archaeology, but to build awareness from the beginning of the difficulties of archaeological research. Archaeology is a tremendously exciting field that little by little, fragment by fragment, helps humanity not only "rediscover" its past, but create narratives that inform us of who we are. Some of archaeology is highly sensational. Most of it will never make the pages of *National Geographic*. Yet, all of it changes our views of the past in profound ways. To perform archaeology well, however, we must be sensitive to the issues just mentioned and accept them as part and parcel of archaeology as a science. Archaeology is highly important, but not easy.

This book is written as an introductory text on archaeology as a profession. Although we use numerous examples of archaeological research throughout the world to illustrate our points, this is not a book about past societies. Instead, this book provides readers with the significance of the archaeological discipline in our society. In so doing, we discuss a basic knowledge of how and why archaeology is performed. In this chapter, we will review some of the basic background of archaeology and the concept of the past. In the following chapters, we will discuss the history of archaeological research including ethics and theory and then move into topics of methodological concern. We begin by situating archaeology within anthropology.

Archaeology as Anthropology

Although universities in some European and Asian countries include archaeology as part of history, most universities in the United States teach archaeology as part of anthropology. In no uncertain terms anthropology is the study of human beings, which gives it a very broad range of inquiry. Definitions of **anthropology** vary, but coalesce around certain core ideas. In this book, we define anthropology as the scientific study of the origin, behavior, physical variation, and cultural development of human beings. Although many professions in one way or another study some facet of human existence, anthropology concerns itself with all aspects of humanity. Thus, anthropology is holistic, asking questions about human existence from multiple research angles. Given this wide breadth of research potential, it is not unsurprising to learn that anthropology is divided up into various subfields, which in turn are further divided into a complex web of research foci that crosscut each other in sometimes surprising ways.

At a basic level, anthropology is traditionally divided into four broad subfields; archaeology, biological anthropology, cultural anthropology, and linguistic anthropology. The latter three subfields are not the focus of this volume, but all four are united by the concept of **culture** and a knack for questioning virtually everything, regardless of how dear we hold it. There are many definitions of culture and, although it is considered the unifying concept of anthropology, it is also considered to one of the more contentious terms. Monaghan and Just (2000, 34) state that despite the lack of consensus in the field as to how the term should be defined, culture "has to do with those aspects of human cognition and activity that are derived from what we learn as members of society." Taken in a very simple form, this is what culture is. How the concept of culture is approached, however, serves as the basis for dividing the subfields.

Cultural anthropology (also broadly known as social anthropology or sociocultural anthropology, although there are specific differences in the usage of these terms in certain scientific circles) is generally the study of contemporary cultural variation, including changing hierarchies, heterarchies, ideologies, and contested meanings, practices, and identities. Cultural anthropologists rely primarily on **ethnography**, the scientific description and study of individual contemporary cultures and **ethnology**, the comparative analysis of various living societies, to perform their research. As we will discuss later in this book, there are important overlaps between archaeology and cultural anthropology. Living societies can inform us much about past cultures. Yet, it is the past/present boundary as well as a focus on materiality which *generally* divides the research questions; cultural anthropologists may have some time depth to their research, but usually in the scale of decades rather than the deeper time of most archaeological studies.

Biological anthropology (also known as physical anthropology) is the study of both behavioral and biological facets of humans, hominins (ancestral species), and nonhuman primates. Researchers in this subfield work with very old remains stretching back to the "dawn" of humanity in evolutionary time millions of years ago, but also work with contemporary populations of humans (often focusing on the interplay between the body and culture) and nonhuman primates. There is substantial overlap between biological anthropology and both cultural anthropology and archaeology. Particularly relevant for archaeology is the focus of many biological anthropologists on past human and hominin remains. In some cases, archaeologists work in conjunction with biological anthropologists trained in the recovery and analysis of these remains. In other cases, researchers trained as archaeologists are

FIGURE 1.2 Some bioanthropologists study human evolution, in particular hominins. Hominins include our own species (*Homo sapiens sapiens*) and close ancestors of the genera, *Ardipithecus, Australopithecus, Paranthropus, and Homo*; not to be confused with hominids, which also include the Great Apes. This image recreates a scene of a hominin, in this case a Neanderthal, blowing pigment on a cave wall to create a negative image of a hand.

© Nicolas Primola/Shutterstock.com

FIGURE 1.3 Bioarchaeologists working alongside archaeologists to excavate a Maya burial (ca. AD 700 in a rockshelter at the Maya site of Yaxuná, Mexico.

© Sabrina Simon

specially trained in these techniques. They are known as **bioarchaeologists**.

Linguistic anthropology is the study of how languages, an integral part of culture, shape social life. Differing from **linguistics**, which is the study of language and its structure, linguistic anthropology has a strong focus on present cultures, although there are researchers who focus on topics with considerable time depth in some areas of the world. Thus, there is some overlap with archaeology, but there are more substantial overlaps with cultural anthropology, specifically with a focus on ethnographic methods.

The focus of this book, **archaeology**, concerns humanity's past through the study of its material remains. Although archaeologists often use **oral** and **written history** when they exist to complement their research, archaeology differs from history in that it uses principally material data sets. Material data are more widely available than historic texts, which are often limited to certain topics (e.g., religious texts) or segments of society (e.g., the elites) when they are present for a past society. Further, archaeologists are often wary of historic data as they reflect the viewpoints of particular people in the past and questions concerning their validity are sometimes raised.

Archaeology and its focus on the past, however, are not always situated in anthropology. Beyond the question of history as a separate pro-

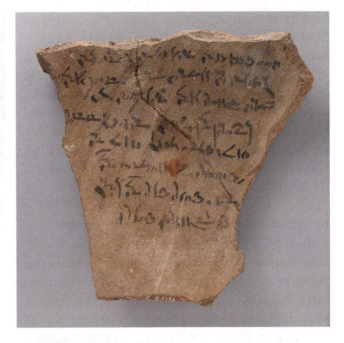

FIGURE 1.4 An ostracon with a demotic inscription from Ptolemaic period (ca. 650–630 BC) Egypt. Ostracons are potsherds (broken pieces of pottery) with inscriptions; found with some frequency in the eastern Mediterranean. The material remains of such inscriptions are found by archaeologists, but can be subjected to analysis by historical linguists and epigraphers.

Ostracon with Demotic Inscription Egypt, early Demotic Period - Ptolemaic Period (650–30 BCE). Terracotta 5 1/2 × 5 1/2 in. (14 × 14 cm). Los Angeles County Museum of Art, Gift of Jerome F. Snyder (M.80.202.200)
Photo © Museum Associates/LACMA

fession investigating the human past, archaeology as a subdiscipline of anthropology developed in a uniquely North American tradition separate from its emergence in the classics and in relation to geology and antiquarianism in Europe. European archaeology developed out of three very different interests in the past. The first was a realization of deep time and history through the relatively rapid development of geology as a profession, spurred on by the increased need for knowledge of the earth and its resources with the advent of the Industrial Revolution in Europe in the eighteenth century. Increased digging into the Earth revealed very old geological formations, fossils, and ancient cultural material dating up to hundreds of thousands of years old. These discoveries led to an interest to explain them as they did not fit into established narratives of the past in Europe at the time. Thus, a desire to explain hominin fossils and very old cultural remains developed in some ways in tandem with geology. **Paleoanthropology**, or the study of early humans and their cultural remains, still retains close ties to geology today.

The second interest in the past that led to the development of a nonanthropological archaeology in Europe came out of history. Europe is a land with a deep and rich historic record. In particular, an interest in the historic sites across the Mediterranean world (e.g., ancient Egypt, Roman Civilization, and Classical Greece) spurred some scholars with a knowledge of their history to actually conduct excavations at sites believed to be identified in the texts. Thus, a second version of archaeology developed out of history in Europe, today known as **classical archaeology**. Classical archaeologists tend to focus on contexts that have relation to existing historic texts or have the potential for revealing new ones in societies classified as classical civilizations; primarily limited to the highly hierarchical and literate societies of the Mediterranean and southwest Asia prior to the middle ages. Since classical archaeologists tend to focus on historic questions and elite contexts that are relevant to historic texts, there are cases of anthropological archaeologists working on the same society, but from a very different point of view. Unfortunately, in many cases there is very little communication between these two groups of archaeologists who see their research questions as being, in many cases, highly distinct.

The development of a third branch of archaeology in Europe revolved around an interest in more recent archaeological sites (those not stretching back to the Paleolithic) that do not have the rich history of those studied by classical archaeologists. Labeled **prehistoric archaeology**, this tradition developed early on among Scandinavian archaeologists interested in the transitions among the Stone, Bronze, and Iron ages in particular. Although the links to geology and history were not as strong as the other two European traditions, prehistoric archaeology did not emerge from an anthropological academic context.

FIGURE 1.5 The Coliseum in Rome is one of many well-known structures from Classical societies. Since vast numbers of texts are known from Roman society, Roman archaeology has gravitated toward understanding the material record in light of historically known events.

© Andrey Yurlov/Shutterstock.com

FIGURE 1.6 A drawing of King Frederik VII of Denmark visiting the excavations of Jens Worsaae, an early professional archaeologist, at the site of Jelling in 1861.

Source: Drawing by J. Korncrup, 1861

So how did an anthropological archaeology develop and why is it so prominent throughout many parts of the world? The answers to these questions lie in an understanding of the process of European colonization of the United States in particular (see more in Chapters 3 and 4). As stated earlier in this chapter, the remains of the past are particularly important for creating, maintaining, and negotiating identities and ties to the land. In general, as Europeans began to take control of vast tracts of land, the existing monuments and symbols of the past of Native Americans were marginalized and subjected to a process of "forgetting" in the new narratives that Europeans created. These remains often stood as impediments to the claims of new populations moving into the region. As time went on, subsequent generations of primarily settlers of European origin, who formed their own ties to the land and built their own monuments to solidify their new identity as Americans, began to wonder what some of the surviving monuments, obviously dating prior to the arrival of Europeans, actually were. A whole series of speculations, called the mound-builder myths, were offered as explanations for the existence of these edifices that were encountered by European colonists as they pushed further west to settle new land. These included explanations ranging from the monuments having been constructed by a lost tribe of Israelites to people from the sunken continent of Atlantis. Yet, none of these "theories" ever pointed back to the ancestors of contemporary Native Americans, a fact that we take for granted today.

As the land that would eventually constitute the continental United States was further settled, primarily by people of European descent, the US government became interested in documenting Native American groups that were still living in what was considered a traditional lifestyle. By the late nineteenth century, it was believed that these lifestyles were in danger of "extinction" and the **Bureau of American Ethnology** (BAE) was created in 1879 (first called the Bureau of Ethnology, the name change occurred in 1897). Under the directorship of **John Wesley Powell** the BAE promoted anthropological research particularly in western states such as New Mexico and California where Native Americans had been less impacted by European settlements. Although work published during the 1890s by **Cyrus Thomas**, building off of the early mapping work of Native American sites by **Squier** and **Davis** (1848), systematically dismantled the mound-builder arguments and rightfully identified the ancestors of Native Americans as their source. Ethnologist such as **Frank Cushing** working with contemporary Native American groups in the western United States began to see links between the people with whom they worked and the ruined architecture and ancient material culture scattered across the landscape, thus linking modern Native American populations with those of the past. Their work, and the inclusion of archaeologists within the BAE, set the foundation for a four-field anthropology that counted archaeologists among its ranks.

As we shall see in greater detail in Chapter 4, as North American archaeology developed it eventually drew more and more off of the social approaches inspired by an anthropological approach. It also

FIGURE 1.7 Major John Wesley Powell (1834–1902), director of the Bureau of American Ethnology (BAE).

Major John Wesley Powell (1834–1902), explorer of the American West, c. 1880/PVDE/Bridgeman Images

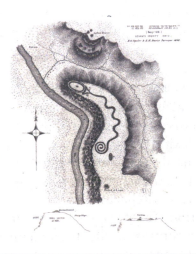

FIGURE 1.8 Map by of Squier and Davis (1848) of Serpent Mound, located in Ohio.

From Ancient Monuments of The Mississippi Valley by Ephraim G. Squier and Edwin H. Davis. Copyright © 1998 by the Smithsonian Institution. Reprinted by permission.

FIGURE 1.9 Drawing of pueblo architecture in ruins by Cushing (1881).

Source: Frank Cushing, 1881

benefited from the holism of anthropology. Today, anthropological archaeology is found throughout the world, not only approaching the evidence from the past from very diverse perspectives, but also asking the difficult social questions whose answers broaden our understanding of what it means to be human.

Archaeology as Science

Yet beyond the question of where archaeology is situated as a profession, we can clearly state that archaeology today is a science. And, as any scientific discipline, research in archaeology follows the scientific method. This method consists of first formulating a **hypothesis** based on a question. It is the question that drives research. Apart from archaeological data which are salvaged from eminent destruction (unfortunately, something that is performed with increasing frequency in our world today), all archaeological fieldwork that disturbs material data in one way or another is performed with the purpose of answering well-formulated questions. Archaeologists do not just "dig to find out what is beneath the surface." They carefully calculate how and where to perform research to answer particular questions. Once the question is known and the hypothesis formulated the archaeologist will then go about collecting data to test the hypothesis. If the hypothesis is refuted, the archaeologist may start the process over and reevaluate the question. They may, however, formulate a new hypothesis concerning that same question and begin collecting further data. If the hypothesis is supported they may continue to collect more data to test the hypothesis or move on to a new question. The idea of the scientific method is to continue to test hypotheses until they have been supported a sufficient number of times to convert them into theories.

The idea of a theory, however, is a bit of a slippery concept. In science we have theories, such as the theory of gravity or the theory of evolution, that have been tested innumerous times and are virtually universally accepted in academia. These are theories. In archaeology, however, beyond evolution (which is a cross-disciplinary concept), we are hard pressed to see many, if any, hypotheses that have been tested successfully so many times that they might be considered theories in this sense. There are many strongly supported hypotheses that in some cases most, if not all, archaeologists would agree with. Yet, in a strict sense they have not been subjected to the rigorous level of testing as have the theories mentioned earlier. May archaeologists one day have theories in this strict sense of the scientific method? Given the fragmentary nature of the data such a feat might be difficult, if not impossible, to achieve. This does not lessen archaeology's place as a science, but again, stresses the importance of reflecting on the limits of archaeological data.

However, this has not stopped some researchers from using the term "theory" in archaeology. In fact, you can see this term used with relative frequency within the field. In one sense, the term theory is used to mean the conceptual frameworks with which archaeologists use to interpret their data. A body of theory (e.g., gender theory, phenomenological theory, and complexity theory) in this sense does not refer to the process of testing hypotheses, but the approach that is used to analyze and interpret data. The same data set can be looked at from different interpretational lenses, each of which can be just as informative as another. This is a correct use of the term theory. There are archaeologists, however, that use the term "theory" as a way to discuss their particular interpretation of a set of data. It is not uncommon to hear an archaeologist say something along the lines of "In contrast to the interpretations of Professor X, my theory about the disappearance of red ceramics in the second millennium B.C. is . . .". It is both obvious and logical that if there are competing "theories" about a question, then there is no academic consensus and thus no "theory" really being discussed. What "theory" means in this context is really "hypothesis." This practice of substituting theory for hypothesis is not limited to archaeology. It is found to some degree or another across the sciences (think of the Big Bang theory, which is one of several competing scientific ideas about the origin of the universe). Yet, the practice is quite common in archaeology and readers should be aware of its usage in the field. The use of the term theory appears to bring some greater sense of validity to an idea being proposed, stressing the need for evaluating archaeological research with a critical eye at all times.

This use of the term "theory" brings up the idea of the "truth." The idea that an ultimate "truth" is "out there" waiting to be discovered underlies much scientific research. As we shall discuss further in Chapter 4, archaeologists have increasingly treated this idea with caution since the advent of postprocessual archaeology in the early 1980s. The "truth" of an event is often just as much related to one's point of view in virtually any situation in life as it is to the facts that one can assess concerning the event. Ten people can witness the same event, use the same facts, and come up with 10 different versions of what happened. The question is, which one, if any, is the "truth"? The same thing can happen to 10 archaeologists. Therefore, the application of critical thinking, assessing multiple possibilities for interpreting data, and in many cases stating something along the lines of "I'm 90 percent sure it happened this way, but these other two possibilities are also somewhat plausible" are essentials for an ethical archaeology in today's world. A modern archaeology is open to multiple points of view, ever so important in a field that works with fragmentary data. This is not to say that archaeologists cannot build consensus around the answers to particular research questions. It just means that there can be multiple points of view and "theories" that should be evaluated with a critical eye.

FIGURE 1.10 Reconstruction of a room with the modeled heads of cattle decorating the walls at the site of Çatalhöyük, Turkey. Çatalhöyük was a large Neolithic site that is considered to be one of the first (ca. 7500–5700 BC) large aggregations of people in the world (possibly up to 10,000 people at its height). Ian Hodder has directed archaeological research at the site since 1993 using a reflexive methodology and healthy skepticism of an ultimate interpretive truth. For Hodder (1998), a singular truth does not exist and multiple viewpoints are valid.

© Firdes Sayilan/Shutterstock.com

FIGURE 1.11 Originally built in the late fourth millennium century BC, the site of Newgrange, Ireland, is a large monument with a chambered passage thought to be a tomb for the dead. Associated with the monument are a series of carved designs including these spirals. Given the great antiquity of the site and, thus, the lack of ethnohistoric data which could shed light on their meanings, as well as the abstract nature of the art, deciphering the meaning of the images has been challenging. This situation has led to a number of competing interpretations that are difficult to evaluate given the ambiguity of the data. Such situations are not uncommon in archaeology, further demonstrating that the idea of an interpretive "truth" can be quite problematic.

© Eireann/Shutterstock.com
© UnaPhoto/Shutterstock.com

The Time Frame of Archaeology

So, now that we have situated archaeology as a science we can now ask: how far back in time do archaeologists focus their research? Contrary to the belief of many people, archaeologists do not study dinosaurs; that is the domain of **paleontology**. Archaeologists only focus on humans and hominin ancestors. Other organisms, including fossil species of mammals such as mastodons, may also be included in archaeological research, but only if the analysis of their remains pertains to a greater understanding of humanity (e.g., animals or plants that were utilized by ancient peoples). The question of how far back in time archaeologists may perform research then has everything to do with how we define our human ancestors. Anthropology is the study of humanity, so archaeologists can only work so far back into the past as we define hominin ancestors; and this definition has shifted over the years.

Over a hundred years ago, researchers investigating human evolution generally believed that the defining characteristic that makes us human is our higher cognitive capacity. Our intelligence sets us apart from other organisms on this planet. In a basic sense, our cognition enables us to *be* human. So, it was thought that the first human "ancestors" (hominins) would demonstrate an increase in the size of the brain early on in evolution, but would basically still look very "ape-like." In a very real sense, our evolutionary ancestors go back billions of years and went through radical transformations that we do not consider human. So, the use of brain size (as a proxy for intelligence) was an arbitrary characteristic that was utilized to say that once this appears we can now talk about something we feel more comfortable calling human.

Yet, another characteristic that called researchers' attentions as a basic human trait at the time was **bipedalism**, habitually walking on two feet. It was thought that this trait must have come later in the evolutionary sequence, although the only hominins that were known at the time were Neanderthals (in Europe) and *Homo erectus* (in Asia), both that we now know are relatively late species with larger brains and bipedal locomotion. In 1924, however, **Raymond Dart**, an Australian researcher working in South Africa, reported on the first hominin remains in Africa, a roughly three million-year-old species he dubbed *Australopithecus africanus*. The acceptance of the fossil specimen as an ancestral species of humans initially met with fierce resistance from the academic community as it demonstrated a relatively small brain

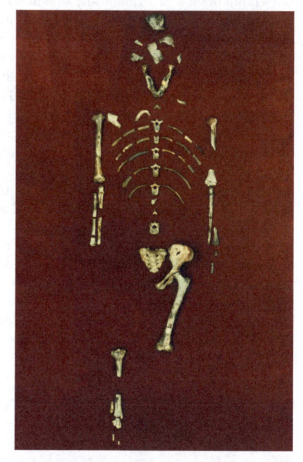

FIGURE 1.12 The fossil specimen dubbed "Lucy" was the most complete early example of a hominin when it was discovered by Donald Johanson in 1974. This fossil specimen of an *Australopithecus afarensis* was one of the key elements used by researchers at this time to push bipedalism in hominins past the three-million year mark. Although older evidence of bipedalism has since been found, Lucy still remains one of the most well-known hominin ancestors in the world.

Image courtesy Institute of Human Origins, Arizona State University.

size on a creature that walked upright; the very opposite of what was believed to be the case for early human ancestors. Yet, eventually the African data won out and the first hominins were defined by bipedalism, meaning that archaeologists only work as far back in time as bipedal hominin ancestors can be dated, which is currently around five to seven million years ago.

So, if we can set the oldest limits of archaeology based on what it means to be human, what criteria do we use to set the youngest limits? In other words, how far up to the present can archaeology be conducted? That coffee you bought this morning is technically in the past, but it would seem odd if an archaeologist was digging in your trash later today to recover it. Yet there are archaeologists who work in contemporary contexts, and who in fact even retrieve people's trash as they put it out for collection. Most of this modern work is aimed at gathering data in a living context to inform us about older data (ethnoarchaeology, see Chapter 10), but there are a considerable number of projects focused on data recovery on contexts that are not old by any stretch of the imagination. For example, some archaeologists work on the excavation of human remains from war sites (e.g., recovering Missing In Action [MIA] remains from recent warzones) and contexts where genocide has occurred (e.g., the Balkan conflict and Guatemalan civil war dating back to the 1990s). So, while most archaeology is conducted on contexts that we would consider "ancient," archaeology works up into the present.

FIGURE 1.13A The recovery of the remains of World War II Missing In Action (MIA) personnel off the coast of Koror, Palau, in the western Pacific Ocean. Archaeologists are increasingly involved in such operations.

Source: U.S. Navy photo by Mass Communication Specialist 2nd Class Tyler Thompson.

The Past in the Present

It is not just the fact that archaeological research is conducted up into the present that keeps archaeologists' minds on the contemporary world, though. However strange this phrase might seem at first, as we stated at the beginning of this chapter, the idea of the past only exists in the present, a fact noted by British philosopher/archaeologist Robin G. Collingwood in 1939. The past itself is no longer. But what of the remains of the past, such as artifacts and monuments? Since the 1970s, archaeologists have focused on what is termed the **formation processes** of archaeological contexts (see Chapter 7).

FIGURE 1.13B This image of the terracotta warriors that guarded the tomb of the first emperor of China shows a group of figures that were altered by formation processes.

© SEMENOV1980/Shutterstock.com

Formation processes are those that shape archaeological contexts after material culture has been deposited. Many different things can happen to archaeological contexts over time. Even in very well-preserved contexts material can decay, be moved around by plants and animals, change its chemical composition, and weather due to numerous erosional processes. After a time, those materials are not the same as when they were originally deposited. These differences underline one of the reasons archaeologists hold to the idea that the past is in the present. What we see in material remains of the past is how they look *today*, not necessarily how they looked in the past.

Yet, adding another layer to this idea that the past exists in the present brings us back to something mentioned earlier in this chapter; our interpretations of the past exist in a modern context and are colored by the social world in which we live. At the end of the day, the past is really the narrative we create to explain the fragmentary data which are the result, in large part, of past human activities. That narrative, and thus the past, is a social construction, which is constantly changing through a process of negotiations among people in a society. Although some parts of these narratives may be more resistant to change, the past, that narrative, is never static. Archaeologists must recognize this fact and embrace it to situate their research in the proper context.

An example that well illustrates how cultural contexts can influence interpretations comes from the work of **John Myres**, a British archaeologist who worked in the Mediterranean in the early twentieth century. In his book *Dawn of History*, Myres (1911) argued that hierarchical societies all emerged out of pastoral groups who, in the words of Trigger (2006, 241), "were forced by drought to leave their homelands and to conquer and rule politically less innovative peasant societies . . . [an idea] based on the widespread belief that pastoralists, who were equated with the medieval European aristocracy, were natural rulers, while farmers, like medieval peasants, were by nature submissive and predisposed to be ruled by others." Although this example comes from over a century ago when an acknowledgement of the influence one's own cultural context on interpretations was not widely recognized by archaeologists, scholars today must remain acutely aware of how who we are impacts how we interpret.

Change over Time

The past may only exist in the present, but that does not mean that the contemporary narratives archaeologists create do not have validity. Archaeological work is like a forensic team looking at an old crime scene, a very old crime scene. Events *can* be reconstructed with careful work. Yet, archaeologists are not just interested in the singular events, small slices of time we research through **synchronic analysis**. They are interested in understanding social changes over periods of time using **diachronic** analysis. Things rarely, if ever, remain static and one of the main goals of archaeology is to explain those changes. Given the large time range available, diachronic analysis is especially suited for archaeology, meaning that one of the field's most pertinent contributions to the sciences is to specifically address questions of how and why human behavior changes.

To use one of the great questions in archaeology as an example of diachronic analysis, we can take the "rise of civilizations." Over 20,000 years ago, all of our ancestors on this planet lived in small-scale, nonhierarchical societies. These societies were generally mobile and characterized by low population densities, although they were not all the same and show considerable diversity

FIGURE 1.13C This diachronic reconstruction of the site of Dos Pilas, Guatemala, shows the site as it was at its height during the Classic period (above) and what it looked like during the Classic Maya collapse (early ninth-century AD). During the collapse period, the site was reoccupied by people who dismantled the temples and other building in the ceremonial center to build houses in the central plaza as well as fortification walls to protect themselves from the increased regional violence that occurred during this turbulent time. Without a diachronic view of their data, archaeologists would not be able to see such changes in the past.

Maya settlement of Dos Pilas in two views before and after 761 AD, 1993 (colour litho), Schlecht, Richard (b. 1936)/National Geographic Creative/Bridgeman Images

across time and space. After 7,000,000–5,000,000 years of human evolution including over 100,000 years with modern looking *Homo sapiens sapiens* skeletons present, something began to change around 16,000 BP (BP = before present, meaning before AD 1950, around the time that radiocarbon dating was invented, see Chapter 8), first in the area known today as the Middle East. Within a relatively short amount of time (in comparison to the time scale of human evolution), many people began to develop more hierarchical forms of life in different parts of the world. Archaeologists have been fascinated with this question, wondering what the causes of these changes were and why they occurred relatively late in human history. Early archaeologists, such as **V. Gordon Childe** (1950, an Australian researcher who is famous for studying early urbanism and state formation), identified certain tendencies among these "civilizations" what he called the "urban revolution" as he saw them

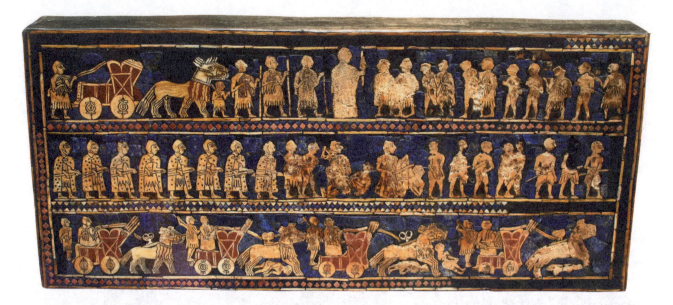

FIGURE 1.14 Throughout the last 10,000 years of human history, many societies experienced social changes that involved increased inequality and the development of urban centers. The Standard of Ur is a hollow box found in the tomb of Ur-Pabilsag, a king of the Mesopotamian City of Ur who died during the twenty-sixth-century BC and depicts a story of violence and captive taking that often accompanied the formation of state-level societies throughout the world.

© Kamira/Shutterstock.com

related to the development of urban forms of life. According to Childe, these tendencies broadly included the following:

1. Cities that were more extensive and had more people than earlier settlements.
2. Urban populations that included people that performed different kinds of activities such as full-time craftworkers, merchants, officials, and religious specialists. Surplus was provided by rural peasants living in the hinterland of cities.
3. A tax or tribute system.
4. Monumental architecture.
5. Extreme inequality that included ruling class that consumed much of the tax or tribute.
6. Writing and numeral notation.
7. Predictive sciences such as arithmetic, geometry, and astronomy.
8. Sophisticated stylistic expression.
9. Frequent long-distance trade.
10. A state organization based on residential location rather than kinship.

Regardless of the usefulness of the items on Childe's list, each case throughout the world has been found to be in some ways unique and the development to more ranked societies appears to have taken different paths at different times and in separate parts of the world. Yet, getting back to the point, if archaeologists only focused on one slice of synchronic time, they would not see these changes at all. It is by taking a diachronic approach across time that we can identify these changes and ask questions of them. Why did urban life develop in the ancient world? This question can only be addressed if we look at the cultural contexts of various moments in a society's trajectory. And, this is really what archaeology is about. Explaining changes over time. Regardless of whether those explanations have to do with peoples' adaptations to changing environmental conditions or the changing way people perceived their world, all archaeologists strive to explain changes.

Working in Archaeology

So, let us say that your interest in archaeology has now been piqued. You are now considering majoring in this field. Where can you find employment? Jobs for archaeologists are generally limited to a small number of areas, but yes, there is work. The majority of archaeologists find employment in the world of **contract** or **salvage archaeology**. These archaeologists are tasked with the recovery and documentation of archaeological data that would be destroyed, primarily by the development of the modern world, if no intervention was taken. Many countries have formal laws protecting cultural heritage in one way or another and in some countries like the United States there are many archaeologists who labor in this area. Others find employment in the academic community, teaching institutions such as universities and colleges or museums. There are even some research institutes dedicated specifically to archaeological investigation. Some archaeologists get a bit more creative and enter the cultural tourism market (quite large in certain areas of the world), organizing and leading professional tours of the archaeological sites in particular world regions.

Given the voluminous amount of knowledge already accrued for archaeological regions throughout the world (exponentially increasing as the years pass by, although it is only a tiny fraction of the material data still to be researched) and the technical knowledge needed for specific kinds of research, archaeologists are forced to specialize. And, there are many ways in which they form their specific research identities, all of which will be important when they are on the job market looking for employment. Most archaeologists initially divide themselves up by world region. Both of the authors of this book are Mesoamerican archaeologists with a concentration specifically in the Maya region. Other archaeologists may identify themselves with their world region. Archaeologists may also classify themselves temporally, by the periods of time they work with. For example, one archaeologist working in Greece may focus on the Hellenistic period, whereas another may focus on the Roman period; a third may even focus on the period of the initial

FIGURE 1.15 In some areas of the world archaeologists working on very different questions may actually be performing research in the same place. This picture of Mouseion Hill in Athens, Greece shows the new line of the city's fortification wall built and modified in early Hellenistic period (late fourth to third century BC). In the center of the image is the funerary monument of Philopappos, Roman consul and Athenian citizen, who was granted the exceptional honor of burial within the city (ca. AD 114–116). While not visible in the image there is also a Macedonian fortress that housed a garrison (third century BC). Athens' shifting fortunes in these centuries can often be traced in the monumental record and demonstrates the temporal complexity of some sites.

© Denver Graninger

colonization of Europe by modern humans, tens of thousands of years before the other two periods. This is particularly common in areas with deep cultural sequences. Paleolithic archaeology (early hominin) and historic archaeology (recent societies with written documents) are both particular subfields based on temporal periods.

Archaeologists may also specialize in particular field or laboratory techniques. Some may specialize in the analysis of particular types of artifacts (bone, ceramics, and lithics), whereas others in specialized techniques such as chemical analyses or remote sensing. Another way for archaeologists to divide themselves is by the theoretical frameworks they develop. So, for example, an archaeologist can focus on residue analyses of ceramics in ancient Mesopotamia and frame their research using gender theory. Adding another layer they may work specifically in caves or in underwater contexts (**underwater archaeology** is a specific subfield that requires particular methodological training including diving and aquatic data recovery). And, when a job opens up they argue their case for the position using these strengths to convince their potential employer that this is the kind of archaeologist they want. So, when a student selects archaeology as a profession they little by little have to make these decisions about where their particular foci will lie.

FIGURE 1.16 Underwater archaeologists documenting the RMS Tweed, which sunk 1849 after running into a reef off the coast of Mexico (courtesy of Helena Barba Meinecke, SAS-INAH).

© Helena Barba Meinecke, SAS-INAH

Bibliography

Binford, Lewis R. *Constructing Frames of Reference: An Analytical Method for Archaeological Theory Building Using Hunter-Gatherer and Environmental Data Sets.* Berkeley: University of California Press, 2001.

Childe, V. Gordon. "The Urban Revolution." *The Town Planning Review* (1950) 21: 3–17.

Collingwood, Robin G. *An Autobiography.* Oxford: Oxford University Press, 1939.

Cushing, Frank H. "A Study of Pueblo Pottery as Illustrative of Zuni Culture-Growth." In *Second Annual Report of the Bureau of Ethnology to the Secretary of the Smithsonian Institution, 1880-81*, edited by J. W. Powell, 467–522. Washington, DC: Government Printing Office, 1881.

Davis, Hester. "Heritage Resource Management in the United States." In *Cultural Heritage Management: A Global Perspective*, edited by P. M. Messenger and P. A. Shackel, 188–198. Gainesville, FL: University of Florida Press, 2010.

Greene, Kevin. *Archaeology, an Introduction: The History, Principles, and Methods of Modern Archaeology.* London: B.T. Batsford Ltd, 1983.

Hamblin, William J. *Warfare in the Ancient Near East to 1600 BC: Holy Warriors at the Dawn of History*. New York: Routledge, 2006.

Hodder, Ian. "The Past as Passion and Play: Çatalhöyük as a Site of Conflict in the Construction of Multiple Pasts." In *Archaeology Under Fire: Nationalism, Politics, and Heritage in the Eastern Mediterranean and Middle East*, edited by L. Meskell, 124–139. London: Routledge, 1998.

———"Ethics and Archaeology: The Attempt at Çatalhöyük." *Near Eastern Archaeology* 65 (2002): 174–182.

———"Archaeological Reflexivity and the 'Local' Voice." *Anthropological Quarterly* 76, no. 1 (2003): 55–69.

———"Multivocality and Social Archaeology." In *Evaluating Multiple Narratives: Beyond Nationalist, Colonialist, Imperialist Archaeologies*, edited by J. Habu, C. Fawcett, and J. Matsunaga, 196–200. New York: Springer Publishing, 2008.

———"Is A Shared Past Possible? The Ethics and Practice of Archaeology in the 21st Century." In *New Perspectives in Global Public Archaeology*, edited by K. Okamura and A. Matsuda, 19–28. New York: Springer Publishing, 2011.

Larsen, Clark S. *Bioarchaeology: Interpreting Behavior from the Human Skeleton*. 2nd ed. Cambridge: Cambridge University Press, 2015.

Marquardt, William H. "The Role of Archaeology in Raising Environmental Consciousness: An Example from Southwest Florida." In *Historical Ecology: Cultural Knowledge and Changing Landscapes*, edited by C. L. Crumley, 203–221. Santa Fe, NM: School of American Research Press, 1994.

Meltzer, David J. "North American Archaeology and Archaeologists: 1879–1934." *American Antiquity* 50, no. 2 (1985): 249–260.

Monaghan, John, and Peter Just. *Social and Cultural Anthropology: A Very Short Introduction*. Oxford: Oxford University Press, 2000.

Myres, John L. *The Dawn of History*. New York: Henry Holt and Company, 1911.

Squier, Ephraim G., and Edwin H. Davis. *Ancient Monuments of the Mississippi Valley*, edited by David J. Meltzer. Washington, DC: Smithsonian Books, 1998[1848].

Trigger, Bruce G. *A History of Archaeological Thought*. 2nd ed. Cambridge: Cambridge University Press, 2006.

Goals, Responsibilities, and Ethics in Archaeology

Although the general idea behind archaeology concerns understanding human behavior in the past, there are many goals which archaeologists strive to achieve. With these goals come many responsibilities, and the ethics for performing archaeology as a profession can be complex. In this chapter, we review some of the major goals archaeologists set for their research and discuss what it means to conduct an ethical archaeology.

Major Goals in the Field

If you ask a number of archaeologists what the primary goal of their work is, you may be surprised that the answers can vary. Although scholars focused on research questions may have a tendency to respond with a "greater understanding of the past" answer to this question, archaeologists working in the world of contract archaeology may more often come back with a "documenting cultural heritage" response. It is not that one of these goals is more important than the other. They are both essential parts of performing archaeology and all archaeologists recognize the importance of each. Yet, individuals may see their work contributing to one area more than another, emphasizing the importance of reviewing the major goals of the field.

As just stated, one of the most fundamental goals of the field is to **preserve cultural heritage**. Important material culture representing the remains of past human activity is constantly in danger. The reasons for the destruction of monuments, artifacts, and archaeological contexts are manifold. All sort of processes of weathering and decay impact innumerous archaeological sites without any involvement of modern human activity. Yet, humans are often the agents of this destruction through processes

FIGURE 2.1 The adobe construction of the Huaca del Sol at the site of Cerro Blanco, Peru, has been exposed to weathering processes for well over a thousand years. Not only has rain, including violent El Niño storms, damaged the structure, but the Spanish diverted the nearby river into the structure to search for gold.

© Christian Vinces/Shutterstock.com

as diverse as the expansion of infrastructure (such as roads), looting, and the intentional erasure of the past in attempts to make social and political statements. Even archaeological excavations themselves are destructive; once a context is excavated it is no longer there for future scholars to directly observe, underscoring the importance of meticulous documentation.

The most sensational cases of intentional destruction of archaeological sites have occurred recently in the Middle East. For example, in 2001 two monumental statues of Buddha dating to the sixth-century AD were obliterated with explosives by the Taliban in Bamiyan, Afghanistan causing an outcry from numerous parts of the world. It was not the first time the statues had been effaced in some manner; earlier damage from cannon fire, for example, can be traced to around a century ago. Yet, the destruction in 2001 was by far the worst recorded for the statues. Intentional destruction of archaeological sites to erase history is nothing new. It can be gleaned in medieval documents in various parts of the world and has likely been a practice dating back to millennia into the past. For instance, King Edward I of England ordered the Roman ruins of Caerleon destroyed in the thirteenth century given their local association with Arthurian legend and use as a symbol of Welsh resistance to the crown. Unfortunately, this kind of destruction is still prevalent in our contemporary world and in many cases it is extremely difficult for archaeologists to stop.

FIGURE 2.2 A Buddha of Bamiyan after the destruction wrought on the monument.

© Torsten Pursche/Shutterstock.com

FIGURE 2.3 The Roman ruins at Caerleon in Wales have been associated with Arthurian legend for quite some time. In particular, the amphitheater (shown in this photo and nineteenth-century engraving) has inspired stories concerning the round table of King Arthur and his knights.

© Morphart Creation/Shutterstock.com
© Michael Neil Thomas/Shutterstock.com

Most of the intentional destruction of archaeological sites is less sensational, although nonetheless just as damaging. The large mound (calculated at originally 25 m tall, the second largest prehistoric mound in the United States after Monks Mound at Cahokia, Illinois) at the site of Troyville, Louisiana, mined and used as construction fill for a bridge project in 1931, is a cogent example of the indifference shown to archaeological remains by some developers. This kind of destruction is all too common throughout the world and underlines the importance of contract archaeology (known as **Cultural Resource Management** or **CRM**) in the recovery and documentation of data in danger of destruction in the name of development and progress. Roads will be built, cities expanded. Archaeological sites will be impacted and in many cases destroyed. Within the context of our modern world, archaeologists are tasked with saving and documenting as much data as possible. And some sites, deemed to be exceptionally important, *are* saved in the face of development. In a very public case, a diverse group of activists which included archaeologists were able to stop the construction of a luxury condominium in downtown Miami in the wake of the discovery of a circle of basins and post-molds cut into the bedrock at the site. These exceptional prehistoric remains, known as the Miami Circle and dating to around 2,000 years ago, represent a critical part of Florida's history; specifically argued to belong to the Tequesta tribe. Yet, cases such as the Miami Circle are rare and such sites are often saved only after long and costly legal battles.

Another one of the most destructive activities that impact archaeological sites is looting. Fueled primarily by a black market centered on antiquities, looting has caused tremendous damage to archaeological sites in the search of particular artifacts that have some value for potential buyers. Innumerous sites have been impacted with important contexts altered or completely obliterated. Artifacts and human remains deemed not valuable are often strewn and broken across the surface.

FIGURE 2.4 The site of Troyville (located in Jonesville, Louisiana) was victim of development projects in the early portion of the twentieth century. Recent salvage work by the Cultural Resource Management (CRM) firm Earth Search has uncovered *in situ* deposits, including this fragmented ceramic vessel, where the substantial site center was once located.

Copyright © Earth Search, Inc.

FIGURE 2.5 Photo of the Miami Circle, left open ⊘ public viewing. Cases where such development is halted tend to be rare.

© Felix Mizioznikov/Shutterstock.com

There are sites, such as ancient cemeteries on the coast of Peru, which look like the surface of the moon given the extent of the looting. Some of this looting is well organized and targeted with sophisticated organizations behind them. Yet, much of the looting in the world is rather disorganized and haphazard, often driven by poor economic conditions where local people sell looted material culture to intermediaries who fetch much higher prices in other markets. Looting, however, is not limited to artifacts that are illegally sold on the black market. The collection of artifacts at archaeological sites by aficionados and so-called amateur archaeologists constitutes looting as well. Collections of artifacts, such as "arrowheads," which some people amass are artifacts taken out of archaeological contexts by nonprofessionals with little to no documentation. Regardless of whether they are eventually sold, these artifacts are also looted, mitigating the ability of archaeologists to understand these objects and the contexts they come from.

Regardless of the reason that material culture may be in danger, archaeologists are charged with the preservation of the cultural heritage related to the past as a core element of the discipline. Helping to preserve cultural heritage may include active participation in the passing and enforcement of legislation that protects archaeological sites, educating diverse publics about the importance of preservation, and performing conservation work on archaeological materials and sites. Probably, the most fundamental part of preserving cultural heritage is the **documentation** of

FIGURE 2.6 Photo of the looted landscape of the Cerro de la Orca Cemetery, located on the central coast of Peru. The looting in areas where archaeological pieces can be sold for profit can lead to extensive destruction of archaeological contexts.

Source: Travis Stanton

archaeological materials and contexts. Although archaeologists will not be able to stop the majority of processes destroying archaeological data (again, even our own work can be destructive), they can document these data before they are gone forever. Meticulous documentation of archaeological data is an essential part of archaeological work toward the goal of preserving cultural heritage.

A second goal, one that resonates broadly across the field, concerns an **understanding of how and why did things happened in the past**, specifically, as mentioned in Chapter 1, explaining changes from a diachronic perspective. On the one hand, archaeologists are very much interested in understanding the **culture-history** of past societies; in other terms, broadly reconstructing the events that occurred in a society over time. On the other hand, archaeologists are interested in not just understanding the

sequence of events, but explaining why those events occurred. Archaeology as anthropology is about *understanding* human behavior and since the 1960s, the field has moved beyond a more simplistic historicity of human societies.

Since the 1980s, there has also been a movement toward trying to understand how people in the

FIGURE 2.7 Studying the experiences of people in the past is challenging, but is a critical part of modern archaeological research. Although some individuals in the past are more recognizable than others (e.g., elites who may be represented in iconography or may have written texts showing their side of history versus commoners who mostly likely lack these kinds of data), archaeologists must also confront the issue that different people may experience the world in very different ways regardless of whether they lived in the same place and at the same time. Archaeology increasingly acknowledges different kinds of identities (gender, class, ethnicity, and age) in the past to account for the diversity of human experience and perception. For example, Nefertari, an Egyptian ruler represented in the sculpture here (ca. thirteenth-century BC), may have shared similar experiences with other royalty based on her social class, but may have seen the world differently from her husband, Ramses II, based on her gender.

© Andrea Izzotti/Shutterstock.com

past **perceived and experienced the worlds they lived in**. These more cognitive approaches to archaeological interpretation touch on the importance of humanizing the past and understanding the complexities of *being human* in contexts where we cannot actually talk to people about their feelings, experiences, and beliefs. Thus, a goal beyond how and why things happened in the past is what those things meant to people who lived in those contexts.

Many archaeologists also identify with another goal of **applying knowledge gained through archaeological research to practical problems in the present**. George Santayana, a late nineteenth- and early twentieth-century Spanish philosopher, once remarked that "those who cannot remember the past are condemned to repeat it." In a twist on this famous statement, many archaeologists hope that by reconstructing the past we can learn from the actions and decisions of past peoples. For example, some archaeological work in the Maya region supports the idea that the extensive destruction of the rainforest during the eighth and ninth centuries AD was a contributing factor in the Classic Maya Collapse when many of the political and religious institutions of this society failed and many Maya cities were largely abandoned. Some archaeologists working in this region hope that their continued work to understand this past process will help to guide policy regarding the current process of deforestation in the same region.

Yet, not all of this type of work is in the vein of providing cautionary tales for critical reflection on our contemporary world. For example, in Bolivia, archaeological research on raised fields in the high Andes has resulted in experimental work to see if this ancient form of agricultural technology might actually perform better than modern industrial techniques. Other projects have recreated ancient recipes for foods as diverse as chocolate and beer, demonstrating a different kind of "applied" archaeology for modern societies.

FIGURE 2.8 This engraving by Frederick Catherwood shows the monuments of Maya royalty from the site of Copán, Honduras, as he found them when visiting the site in the early part of the nineteenth century. Maya society experienced great social upheaval during the ninth-century AD, resulting in the abandonment of many of the cities that dotted the tropical landscape of the Yucatán Peninsula at this time. Archaeologists working in this region of the world have been keen to understand this "Classic Maya Collapse" and the implications findings might have for climate change and widespread intentional deforestation occurring today.

Broken Maya idol at Copan, Guatemala (engraving), Catherwood, Frederick (1799–1854) (after)/Private Collection/Bridgeman Images

FIGURE 2.9 Experimental raised fields to the side of the Kalasasaya complex at Tiwanaku, Bolivia, the result of a program to test the productivity of the ancient raised fields that supported the subsistence economy of this pre-Inka highland Andean center.

© Sara K. Becker

One last important goal that archaeologists strive to achieve that we would like to stress here is to **disseminate knowledge**; both within the discipline and to the public. Dissemination can take numerous forms; academic publications, accessible technical reports, popular magazine articles, website and public talks, among others. Regardless of what form it takes, the essential idea is that knowledge should not be restricted and should be made accessible. Yet, the work that archaeologists perform is complex and detailed and must be presented in the appropriate format for the intended audience. We can organize dissemination efforts into three categories; technical reports, academic publications, and public engagement (including engagement with descendent communities). Technical reports present the full raw data and sweet of analyses performed on those data must be stored in an accessible place such as a university, museum, or government archive. These archives may be digital or physical. All of the meticulous documentation of archaeological data will go for naught if they are not fully accessible to future researchers; and publications do not usually include the level of detail used in the field to document archaeological data. Thus, archaeologists are ethically compelled to disseminate knowledge in this fashion. Limits on the accessibility of some of these data, however, may be important. Archaeological reports can contain sensitive data such as the location of sites that may be of interest to looters. Therefore, some screening of who can access these data often occurs to prevent further destruction of archaeological contexts.

The data contained in technical reports, however, can often be overwhelming and archaeologists usually publish their work in more distilled forms for academic venues. There is a famous phrase in academia, "publish or perish," and publications are "part of the job." Yet, it is not this necessity of academic jobs that drives most publications, but both the desire and ethics to communicate one's research to the rest of the field. The "thrill" of archaeology is often portrayed as the process of "finding" some data which transform our interpretations about the past; the tomb of a "lost" ruler or a "missing link" in the evolutionary sequence. Although fieldwork can be a greatly rewarding experience (it can also be filled by logistical hardships and long days of meticulous and slow work), publications can also be highly satisfying; the publication process is how interpretations are articulated. This is where archaeologists get to work through all the ideas generated by looking at the data. Publications can be highly academic and include peer-reviewed books, book chapters, and journal articles, but can also include pieces of work that are not just for the other members of the field, but for the general public as well. Again, an ethical archaeology means including diverse publics in the process of accessing archaeological data and interpretations. Although the academic publications are important, archaeologists should attempt to reach various audiences through their written work as well as public presentations.

Heritage, Preservation, and "Control of the Past"

As we have discussed, heritage and its preservation are extremely important. When archaeological contexts are altered and/or destroyed, the ability to understand what happened in the past and why is forever lessened. Given the importance of archaeology-based narratives in the construction of identities and claims to resources and power in our contemporary world, preserving heritage is of paramount importance. But, when we *are* successful at preserving heritage, who actually controls the material remains of the past? Who controls the narratives based on those remains?

Control of the Past

Narratives of the past can often be contentious given their importance in the modern world. Although there are usually diverse narratives of how to interpret the past, attempts to "control" those narratives happens in different ways. Some attempts are subtle, whereas others are overt. Some are thought out with well-defined objectives, whereas others are rather unintentional. For example, the destruction of the Temple of Bel at the ancient Roman period city of Palmyra, Syria, in 2015 is an example of a blatant and spectacular attempt to reenvision a particular past by erasing its material remains. Yet, funding agencies' guidelines concerning what type of archaeological research to support (area of the world, particular spectrum of research questions, or theoretical frameworks) can also greatly impact the kinds of narratives that are generated by the archaeological community in a not so overt and spectacular manner. Archaeologists must always remember that research is conducted in particular sociocultural contexts and that we must reflect on how these impact interpretations. For example, the heavy funding of research at sites deemed to be emblematic of a nation, such as Stonehenge (Great Britain), Tiwanaku (Bolivia), or Tenochtitlan (Mexico) can function to marginalize other spectrums of the cultural diversity that once existed in these areas of the world.

FIGURE 2.10 The Temple of Bel, located at the Roman ruins of Palmyra, Syria, was obliterated by members of the Islamic State in 2015. Given that this temple was consecrated to the Mesopotamian god Bel, it represented a past at odds with that of the Islamic State and was thus targeted for a process of erasure.

© Monik-a/Shutterstock.com
Syria: The destruction of the Temple of Bel, or Baal, by the Islamic State in Iraq and the Levant, Palmyra, August 2015 (photo)/Pictures from History/Bridgeman Images

FIGURE 2.11 Although all countries have innumerable archaeological remains, some sites are often selected to promote national identities. Tiwanaku, Bolivia, often interpreted as the large capital of a pre-Inka state or empire, has become emblematic of Bolivia as a nation state and substantial resources have been spent on investigations of its history. The Gateway of the Sun shown here is one of the most iconic monuments at the site and its iconography (prominently showing the enigmatic Staff God) has become a symbol of Bolivian national identity.

© Adwo/Shutterstock.com

There are other vested interests in the creation of narratives of the past that go beyond politics and identity construction that can also influence narratives. A case in point is the tourist industry, which often uses and in many cases manipulates archaeological work to promote cultural tourism, a big industry in many parts of the world. There are many instances of ancient societies being "exoticized" to make them more sensational, and thus desirable, places to visit; a practice which has the tendency to impact local people who often become exoticized as well. Media outlets such as documentary television and the movie industry have also played large roles in the construction of narratives of the past. In many cases, the use and portrayal of the past (both in fiction and nonfiction) is accepted by both public and academic audiences. In some extreme cases, however, criticism of the portrayal of past societies is leveled at the media. Such was the case of the 2006 film *Apocalypto*, which generated a vehemently negative response from indigenous civil rights groups and professional archaeologists for its overly bloody portrayal of the ancient Maya, among other grave inconsistences with actual archaeological data.

FIGURE 2.12 Archaeological tourism is big business in some parts of the world. The Riviera Maya of the Mexican Caribbean is one of these areas, attracting numerous tourists to its spectacular beaches each year. Many of these tourists visit nearby sites, like Chichén Itzá, a large Maya city in the central portion of Yucatán (ca. ninth to eleventh centuries AD). Pictured in this image is El Castillo, a massive pyramid at the site that draws particularly large crowds during the Spring Equinox, at which time a solar alignment casts the undulating shadow of a serpent (left side) down the balustrade of one of the four staircases to the stone head of the Feathered Serpent deity at the bottom. Although this kind of tourism brings money into such areas, tourism can also have its drawbacks. For example, El Castillo is now closed to people climbing the staircases as the building was being worn down by the passage of such large numbers of people.

© Borna_Mirahmadian/Shutterstock.com

The type of response that *Apocalypto* generated among professional archaeologists begs the question of whether there should be any control of the narratives of the past. As trained professionals, should archaeologists get involved in "policing" narratives based on archaeological data? As might be expected, the answer to this question is also complicated. Beginning in the 1980s, a movement to acknowledge and engage with alternate narratives of interpretation of the past was promoted, specifically in regard to the inclusion of local, in many cases indigenous, narratives of the past. The idea was that if archaeologists could create legitimate narratives of the past using the scientific method, local peoples whose ancestors were responsible for the material culture researched by archaeologists could also have legitimate alternative narratives. For example, in many local communities across the state of Yucatan, Mexico, local Yucatec Maya people will often tell you that the massive ruins that dot the landscape were created by a separate race of Maya who were giants. Our own archaeological research does not support this local narrative and indicates that the ancient Maya was neither of larger stature nor from a different genetic line, but an "inclusive" archaeology considers the local narrative to be a legitimate way to construct an alternate narrative.

Yet, some archaeologists have criticized the idea that all alternative narratives should be considered legitimate and have argued that the field should act as a filter in some way, particularly if those narratives disenfranchise or in some way harm people. Thus, the film *Apocalypto*, deemed an inaccurate and damaging portrayal of the ancient Maya by many in the field, caused numerous archaeologists to speak out against it. The airing of **pseudoarchaeology**, nonscientific-based speculations of archaeological data, on national television is a glaring issue for archaeologists in this respect.

Pseudoarchaeology is as old as archaeology. People have speculated on the meaning of archaeological data, with little to no support for their conjectures, for millennia if not longer; think of the mound-builder arguments mentioned in Chapter 1. This did not change with the rise of archaeology as a scientific discipline. Rather, pseudoarchaeology emerged as a parallel to archaeology precisely because such speculations could now be falsely presented to a public in the guise of science with the insidious intent to scam the public into believing a whole host of outlandish, and in many cases disenfranchising, stories. The Internet today is rife with such stories, often originating from dubious print books. One book about giants in the past, who are argued to have built and occupied mound centers in the Ohio Valley and sites in Great Britain such as Stonehenge, has spawned a whole host of intentionally altered images of skeletal remains from actual archaeological research that increase the perception of their size; distributed on the Internet to convince the public that stories about giants from biblical sources can be proven through archaeological remains.

Such attempts to manipulate "archaeological-based" narratives of this sort can be traced much farther into the past. The case of the Cardiff Giant is particularly relevant to the topic of giants. In 1869, an approximately 3-m tall stone giant, argued to be a fossil, was encountered on a farm in the small town of Cardiff in upstate New York. In similar fashion to the case above, this find was argued to prove the biblical stories of giants and it was opened to the public, for a fee of

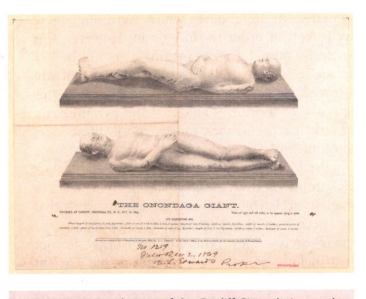

FIGURE 2.13 Renderings of the Cardiff Giant dating to the nineteenth century.

Source: Library of Congress

course, for several months. Although scientists from places like New York City suspected it was a hoax, it was not until George Hull, a professed atheist, confessed to having created the object with the intent of pulling one over on his more pious neighbors that the Cardiff Giant was proved to be a fake; but not before Hull sold his share in the giant for nearly nine times what it cost him to manufacture it.

Although the Cardiff Giant is one of several infamous forgeries known to have been created to play with public and scientific opinion of archaeological narratives over the past two centuries (the altered giant imagery on the Internet today are also considered hoaxes), we can see rampant speculations concerning archaeological data and biblical narratives going back much farther into the past, although not only in the form of hoaxes. One such story, still around today, interprets the great pyramids of Giza, Egypt, as granaries built by the biblical figure Joseph. This interpretation is famously memorialized on a mosaic dating to AD 1204 at St. Mark's Cathedral, Venice, Italy, that supposedly was copied from an image in the Cotton Genesis, a fourth- or fifth-century Greek manuscript of the book of Genesis heavily damaged in a fire in AD 1731. Regardless of the fact that archaeological investigation of the pyramids indicate that they were not granaries under no uncertain terms, this long-standing idea was even questioned centuries ago by church cleric Bernhard von Breydenbach in his work *Peregrinatio in terram sanctam* (*Journey to the Holy Land*) in AD 1468. "Beyond the Nile we beheld many pyramids, which in ages past the kings of Egypt caused to be built over their tombs, of which the vulgar say that these are the granaries or storehouses which were built there by Joseph in order to store grain. However, this is clearly false, for these pyramids are not hollow inside" (Colavito 2015). Despite the fact that von Breydenbach noted the obvious problem with this speculation centuries ago, that the pyramids are in large part solid rock constructions, these ideas continue today.

Pseudoarchaeology today is an eclectic group of diverse speculations that seek to explain archaeological data in a framework that has been sometimes referred to as fringe or fantastic archaeology. These frameworks do not just include modern religious ideas, but ancient aliens, lost continents, and even ancient curses. In no case are these claims supported by systematic analysis of archaeological data and in some cases they include invented "data" (hoaxes). Detailed analysis of the ocean floors and tectonic activity disprove lost continent arguments. "Evidence" of extraterrestrials is proved time and time again to fit well into the cultural contexts of the past. Yet, such speculation persists and has a negative impact well beyond misinforming the public about ancient societies.

A case in point is the idea of ancient aliens. Popularized by **Erich von Däniken** in his 1968 book *Chariot of the Gods*, the idea that ancient societies were somehow influenced by extraterrestrials is quite widespread today. In one particularly famous argument, von Däniken discusses

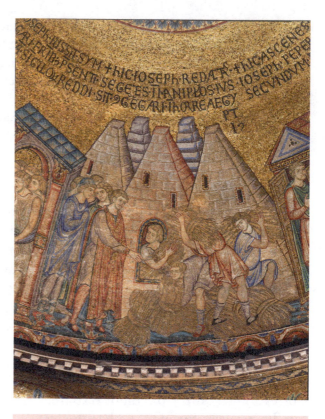

FIGURE 2.14 Among the thirteenth-century mosaics from St. Mark's Cathedral in Venice, Italy, is this one which has been interpreted to depict Joseph collecting wheat before the famine with the Great Pyramids of Egypt rendered as grain silos in the background.

St. Joseph collecting wheat before the Famine (mosaic)/San Marco, Venice, Italy/Cameraphoto Arte Venezia/Bridgeman Images

FIGURE 2.15 Archaeological features like the colossal stone heads (*moai*, which do have buried bodies, ca. twelfth to seventeenth centuries AD) on Rapa Nui have been the targets of fringe archaeology for decades, often attributed in one way or another to extraterrestrials.

© Anthony Booker/Shutterstock.com

the imagery on the sarcophagus lid of K'inich Janaab Pakal I, an eighth-century Maya ruler of the city of Palenque, Mexico. He identifies the image of the king as an ancient astronaut manipulating the controls of his spaceship. Although the imagery on the sarcophagus is quite complex, helping to advance his argument among readers not familiar with Classic period Maya iconography, all of the imagery fits well into the cannons of Maya ideas of death and the afterlife for Maya rulers. What is portrayed is the king falling across the world tree (the deity known as the Principle Bird Deity perched on its top) into the jaws of the underworld. Intentional mischaracterizations of this sort are too numerous to mention here, but also include ideas such as the inability of ancient peoples to create monuments with large stone architecture such as Stonehenge and Saksaywamán (an Inka fortress outside of Cuzco, Peru) without the aid of alien technology and identifying the function of geoglyphs such as the Nazca lines (Peru) as landing sites for spaceships. These pseudoarchaeological ideas often presupposed that ancient people were unable to create such material culture on their own. How could they have laid out stones in an arrangement that could only be fully appreciated from the air? How could they have carved and moved stones of such great size without the aid of modern technology? Yet, it only takes a fairly simple knowledge of basic mechanics and engineering (and often, but not always, a substantial amount of labor) to move such stones. And the fact that the Nazca geoglyphs can only be fully appreciated from the air neither means that they were meant to be viewed from the air nor that they could not be created without access to a bird's-eye view (a simple understanding of how to translate drawings from

FIGURE 2.16 The sarcophagus lid of K'inich Janaab Pakal I of Palenque, Mexico (ca. seventh-century AD). The iconography depicts the king falling across the cross-shaped world tree into the maws of the underworld. The complexity of the design helps the cause of pseudoarchaeologists as the iconographic elements can be difficult to pick out. However, all of the symbolism is firmly attributed to Classic period Maya beliefs concerning the cosmos.

© Belem Ceballos Casanova

different scales is enough to accomplish this feat from the ground). Although we are sure that some archaeologists would actually relish the opportunity prove the existence of aliens (what a career that would make!), no archaeological evidence recovered to date implicates extraterrestrial activity in the human past. Pseudoarchaeology continues to be big business, though, as print and television media continue to promote it and there is a substantial market for such ideas.

FIGURE 2.17 Archaeological sites in Peru have been the target for pseudoarchaeological interpretations for quite some time. The massive well-fitted stones of the Inka fortress of Sacsaywamán (right) have been a source of discussion considering the difficulty in moving stones of this size; which can be done with simple technologies and large amounts of human labor (not requiring antigravity devices). The geoglyphs of the Nazca region (left) have also generated much debate, some pointing out that they can only been fully appreciated from the air. That fact, however, does not mean they were meant to be seen from the air and ignores the symbolic importance of the imagery, which can be easily produced with basic understandings of scale and survey methods; the lines are composed of the vacant areas where stones were removed to the side, creating a thin path in the desert.

© John Kershner/Shutterstock.com
© Byelikova Oksana/Shutterstock.com

But, what is the harm in pseudoarchaeology? It is all just entertainment, right? Did we not just discuss the importance of alternate narratives in an inclusive archaeology? Well, to start with, it is not just entertainment; many people actually believe such claims. Yet, more importantly these ideas paint the ancestors of particular modern peoples as incapable of having reached such achievements. These unsubstantiated claims disenfranchise people from their past. For example, saying that aliens built the pyramid at Palenque is really stating that the ancestors of the Maya who live around the ruins today were incapable of creating such monuments; to put it another way, stating that their ancestors were "savages" or "uncivilized." Keeping in mind the importance of identity in the past, this is quite an insult. Considering that *most* such arguments are made by the western media and concern nonwestern archaeological remains, pseudoarchaeology has been characterized as both racist and an extension of colonial injustices. In any event, pseudoarchaeology has a distinctly negative impact, leading archaeologists to be wary of the idea that all interpretations of the past have equal validity in modern society.

These examples, however, in some ways pale in comparison to the negative impacts of some questionable archaeological interpretations and their use by politicians over the years. A tremendous example of the misuse of archaeological interpretation (not pseudoarchaeology, but nonethical archaeology) comes from Nazi period Germany. Heinrich Himmler, Adolph Hitler's chief of the SS, oversaw the Nazi regime's Ancestral Heritage program, which was designed in many ways to prove the antiquity and extent of ancestral "Aryan nation." Using dubious archaeological interpretations made by **Gustaf Kossinna**, an influential scholar who argued cultural ideas were passed from more "advanced" societies to their neighbors and that ethnic groups could be identified by material culture, the Ancestral Heritage program identified archaeological sites in other countries as evidence of the previous extent of Germanic control. These sites were used as part of the justification for the invasion of some of Germany's neighbors during the 1930s under the rhetoric of "uniting" the ancestral Germanic fatherland. Thus, while archaeologists

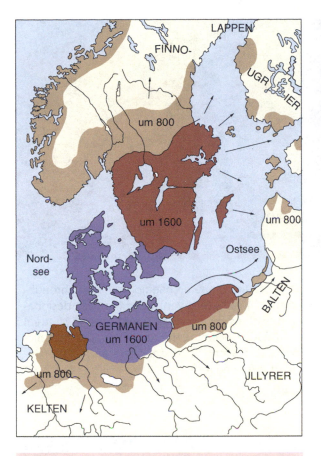

FIGURE 2.18 Maps, such as this one created and published by Hans Reinerth in 1940, show how some Germans in the early part of the twentieth century invented a geography of an ancestral fatherland. As Bettina Arnold points out, these maps have their origin in the work of Gustaf Kossinna, which uses strong nationalistic language. "The dedication of the 1921 edition of Gustav Kossinna's seminal German prehistory: a preeminently national discipline reads: 'To the German people, as a building block in the reconstruction of the externally as well as internally disintegrated fatherland' (1921: Dedication)." (Arnold 1990, 465)

have advocated for the inclusion of alternative non-scientific narratives, the issue is complex and most archaeologists will state that not every narrative should be included in public and academic discussion. Who has the right, and how, to filter narratives of the past, however, is unclear. As the Ancestral Heritage program example demonstrates, interpretation of archaeological data comes with great ethical responsibility given the importance of the "past" to contemporary societies as discussed in Chapter 1.

Yet, beyond questions of the attempts to control or influence archaeological narratives, who actually controls the material remains of the past? Who can legally have archaeological materials in their possession or control access to archaeological sites themselves? The answer to this question is complicated by the fact that countries have differing legislation pertaining to archaeological materials. In Mexico, where both the authors of this book work, the law stipulates that all archaeological sites and material culture are part of the national patrimony and, hence, belong to the federal government. In the United States, this is not the case. As professionals, archaeologists are expected to understand the laws in the context in which they work and follow them accordingly.

This is not to say, however, that by strictly following the laws in the context which they work, archaeologists can easily navigate issues of control of the past. In many cases, archaeologists find themselves in the midst of social and political tensions over who actually has the right to control the remains of the past and existing legislation on these matters is sometimes contentious. In some cases, federal legislation is at odds with local ideas of heritage preservation and management. For example, federal laws may stipulate that archaeological material may be removed from local communities, but the local communities (who may have direct ties to the people who lived and died at the archaeological site) may view this as an act of disenfranchising them from their cultural heritage. Tension may even exist between national and international interests when sites are named world heritage by **UNESCO** (United Nations Educational, Scientific, and Cultural Organization). Thus, the politics and ethics over the control of the remains of the past are complicated and should be clearly understood and navigated by researchers in each specific context.

Control of, or increased access to, archaeological materials and sites by descendant populations has gained momentum in some countries over the past few decades. For example, a greater appreciation of the importance of sacred places and landscapes has been acknowledged by numerous countries at this point. Important sacred places such as the sites of Tikal, Guatemala, Stonehenge, Great Britain, and Tiwanaku, Bolivia are now made accessible to indigenous groups to perform rituals at key moments of the year like the summer solstice. In a critical piece of legislation in the United States, Native American groups were given legal control over the actual physical remains of their ancestors. The **Native American Graves and Repatriation Act** (NAGPRA) stipulates that the human remains of Native Americans that are in private and public collections (such as museum and university collections) must be returned to descendant populations for proper reburial. It also provides legislation for the excavation and analysis of Native American remains, which can only be conducted in consultation with Native Americans, who decide if and how archaeological research can proceed. NAGPRA has been an important piece of legislation that has begun to attend a series of basic rights denied Native Americans concerning their ancestors for years

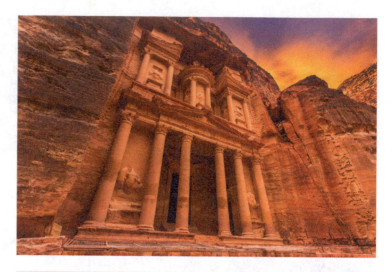

FIGURE 2.20 There are many archaeological sites throughout the world that have been given world heritage designations by United Nations Educational, Scientific, and Cultural Organization (UNESCO) including the site of Petra, Jordan (pictured here); a city with a long history and famous for its architecture cut out of the living rock.

© Kanuman/Shutterstock.com

FIGURE 2.21 Inti Raymi was a festival for the Sun God that was celebrated by the Inka on the winter solstice and is still celebrated today. This image shows a recent celebration of Inti Raymi at the Saksaywamán fortress on the outskirts of Cuzco, Peru.

© SL-Photography/Shutterstock.com

stretching back to the days (and beyond) when it was legal to display real "Indian" remains in cigar stores.

Despite protective legislation such as NAGPRA in some countries, though, some archaeological sites are in danger from forces within the established social and political systems. As stated above, for example, archaeological tourism is a tremendously lucrative industry in some parts of the world. Some key archaeological sites in countries fomenting this type of tourism are developed to accommodate the market. Yet, due to the vested interests of the private sector, these sites may be subjected to processes which lead to their increasing deterioration. The Upper Paleolithic cave of Altamira, Spain, with its incredible rock art, was closed to the public in the 1960s and 1970s due to the damage incurred by the changes in humidity of the cave due to peoples' breath; an unintentional

FIGURE 2.22 The stunning cave art of the Paleolithic site of Altamira, Spain, dates as far back as 35,000 BP and is considered an important part of the world's cultural heritage. Due to the negative impact of the carbon dioxide generated by tourists, the cave has very limited access and there is a wait list that can take years to actually enter the cave. Thus, detailed replicas of the cave art, shown here, are accessible to tourists who are not on the wait list.

© EQRoy/Shutterstock.com

impact of allowing visitors to view the original art. Visits are now extremely limited and there a three-year wait list to see the paintings. Examples of damage due to increased visitation are too numerous to mention, but are in many cases difficult to manage given the money at stake.

Another very important and relevant issue is the distribution of ancient material culture outside of its country of origin. How ancient material culture found its ways into others areas of the world are varied. In some cases, ancient trade and exchange were the culprits. Material culture from medieval period Mediterranean societies has been found in archaeological contexts as far afield as Scandinavia. In these cases, no questions of ownership have been raised. In other cases, material culture is constantly being looted from archaeological sites for sale on the black market. These items are often smuggled into other countries where the wind up in private collections and, in some cases, museum exhibits. When such pieces are identified, a request for the return of these objects is often filed and a legal process to repatriate the object ensues. As we shall see, there are some international laws which protect against such illicit transactions, although much more could be done along these lines.

The very famous case of the Elgin Marbles, however, illustrates the complexities of ownership of international material culture and the legacy of colonial imperialism. In 1801, Thomas Bruce, the seventh Earl of Elgin, supposedly obtained a permit from the Ottoman Empire (which ruled this Aegean nation at the time) to remove a large number of sculptures from the Parthenon of Athens and transport them to Great Britain. They are now an important display at the British Museum after the government purchased the monuments in 1816. The modern nation state of Greece has petitioned for their return, but the plea for their repatriation has met resistance from Great Britain, which among other reasons is concerned with the potential repatriation of most of its pieces, as this process would effectively empty it, as well as other museums throughout the world.

FIGURE 2.23 The Elgin Marbles, now in the British Museum, were taken off the Parthenon in Athens, Greece. You can still see the cuts where they were removed from the building.

© Tony Baggett/Shutterstock.com
© Anastasios71/Shutterstock.com

FIGURE 2.24 This image (right) is an engraving of the Obelisk of Axum, Ethiopia, from the 1800s demonstrating how they looked in situ to travelers in the nineteenth century. The obelisk has now been repatriated to its original place (left) after the period of time it spent in Italy.

© Dmitry Chulov/Shutterstock.com
© Morphart Creation/Shutterstock.com

Although the Elgin Marbles are perhaps the most famous case, there is a tremendous amount of archaeological material outside of its country of origin. Some of this material has been returned. In the case of the Obelisk of Axum, taken by Italian troops back to Rome in 1937 during Italy's military campaign in Ethiopia as part of the spoils of war, the monument was finally repatriated in 2002 long after a United Nations' (UN) agreement to return it was signed in 1947. Given the costs of repatriation, Emperor Haile Sellassie of Ethiopia reportedly gifted the monument to the city of Rome after the UN agreement. This act of "gifting" was challenged by the following military regime which overthrew the emperor in 1974 and renewed calls for the return of the Obelisk of Axum were initiated. Eventually, a subsequent government negotiated the successful return of the monument in 1997, although it only returned to Ethiopian soil after a series of hurdles pertaining to the technical difficulties and cost of transportation, including the lengthening of the runway at the Axum airport, was resolved.

In a rather unusual case, the Egyptian government gifted the Temple of Debod to Spain in 1968; one of four monuments gifted to foreign countries during this decade (Italy, the United States, and the Netherlands are the other three). Originally constructed as a small chapel dedicated to the god Amun, king of the gods, by the Adikhalamani (a Kushite king of Meroë) in the second-century BC, this building was expanded and rededicated to the goddess Isis (deity of health, marriage, and wisdom) by several members of the later Plotemaic dynasty. This temple originally stood near Aswan, where during the 1960s a very large dam construction projected sparked the relocation of several important monuments including the famous Abu Simbel monuments commissioned by Ramesses II in the thirteenth-century BC. The Temple of Debod was gifted to Spain as a symbol of Egypt's appreciation of Spanish assistance with the UNESCO sponsored salvage project to save examples of Egypt's World Heritage from the imminent negative impacts of the Aswan dam project. This heritage has remained in Spain uncontested since that time. These cases demonstrate that the politics of "heritage abroad" are complicated, but clearly important to reflect on.

FIGURE 2.25 The Temple of Debod (left), now located in Spain, was originally part of the Aswan region of Egypt, which was flooded by a dam project in the 1960s. Its origin was as a temple dedicated to the god Amun by Adikhalamani, a Kushite king of Meroë, Sudan (center). However, the temple continued to be modified and rededicated during Ptolemaic and Roman times. The Aswan dam project resulted in the flooding of an area rich in archaeological remains including the temple of Abu Simbel (right), a monument built by Ramses II in the thirteenth-century BC. Although the Abu Simbel complex (note the missing head, removed by Giovannie Battista Belzoni and now in the British Museum, see Chapter 3) was relocated to a nearby area, the Temple of Debod was gifted to Spain for its help with the dam project, showing very different treatments of cultural heritage in this context.

© LucVi/Shutterstock.com
© Martchan/Shutterstock.com
© Nestor Noci/Shutterstock.com

International Legislation to Protect Cultural Heritage

So, what kinds of legislation have been enacted to protect cultural heritage? Some protection efforts can be traced several centuries into the past, indicating that the awareness of the importance of cultural heritage is not necessarily new. For example, the first monuments act was enacted in Sweden in 1666. Peter the Great in Russia fomented research and protection of cultural heritage in the early eighteenth century; including the establishment of the Kunstkammer, the first museum in Russia, in 1718. In Peru, fines for the unauthorized excavation of archaeological buildings, called *huacas*, was in place by 1822. Today, there are several bodies of important international legislation that have relevance to this issue. Building off earlier agreements prior to the establishment of the UN, specifically the conventions of The Hague in 1899 and 1907 and the Washington Pact of 1935, UNESCO ratified the **Convention for the Protection of Cultural Property in the Event of Armed Conflict** in 1954 (a second protocol was ratified in 1999). Responding to the extensive looting that occurred during World War II, this convention included protections for archaeological sites among other examples of cultural heritage of "great importance."

Another important agreement is the UNESCO **Convention on the Means of Prohibiting and Preventing the Illicit Import, Export, and Transfer of Ownership of Cultural Property**, passed in 1970. This legislation was designed to prevent the acquisition of cultural property, including items classified as cultural heritage, and refers specifically to archaeological materials. The convention, however, did not provide a real mechanism for the return illegally exported materials and stipulated that "innocent" buyers be compensated during any repatriation process. In 1972, the UNESCO **Convention Concerning the Protection of the World Cultural and Natural Heritage** followed up by defining tangible "cultural heritage" (instead of cultural property, a phrase that reflects western ideas of property) as including "monuments, groups of buildings, and sites of outstanding universal value from the historical, aesthetic, ethnological, or anthropological point of view" (Messenger and Smith 2010, 1–2); reflecting the direction of UNESCO's heritage conservation efforts in the following decades. These important conventions have been followed up by others, such as the **Convention on the Protection of the Underwater Cultural Heritage** (2001) and the **Convention for the Safeguarding of the Intangible Cultural Heritage** (2003). According to the latter convention, intangible cultural heritage is related to "practices, representations, expressions, knowledge, skills—as well as the instruments, objects, artefacts, and cultural spaces associated therewith—that communities, groups and, in some cases, individuals recognize as part of their cultural heritage" (UNESCO 2003); these include oral traditions, performing arts, social practices, festivals, rituals, knowledge and practices regarding cosmology, and traditional crafts, some of which may leave material marks, but are not necessarily material.

It is important to note that not all countries have adopted these conventions, and their application is uneven. Also, while laws and conventions are critical components to efforts to safeguard and protect cultural heritage, their enforcement is equally important, and is variable from context to context. Further complicating the matter of preservation, the material modification of cultural heritage is occasionally acceptable in certain cultural contexts. For instance, Buddhists in Thailand perform restorations of pagodas (known as *stupas*), many of which are quite old, as part of a cultural tradition which views the past as a state of becoming; thus, the past can become something new. This example starkly contrasts with the case of a farmer in Zhangguying, a rural village in China, who was jailed in 2003 for repairing an archaeological wall in danger of collapse in the courtyard of his home. He was jailed after being denied available funds from the government to offset the substantial costs to pay for specialists to repair this feature of his home, protected by Chinese law in 2001.

UNESCO is not the only organization to ratify international agreements concerning the protection of cultural heritage. Another major international convention pertaining to the protection of cultural heritage is the **UNIDROIT** (International Institute for the Unification of Private Law) **Convention on Stolen or Illegally Exported Cultural Objects** ratified in 1995. Although this legislation privileges pieces stolen from individuals rather than nations, there is a provision that contemplates the return of the object in question. In this case, the provision favors a compensation to be paid to the individual or institution, which currently has the object in its possession regardless of knowing whether the object was stolen or not. Thus, we can see that while international legislation exists, much work still needs to be done to protect cultural heritage on a global scale. Other notable conventions include the **Convention on the Protection of the Archaeological, Historic, and Artistic Heritage of the American Nations** ratified in 1976 by the member states of the Organization of American States to address looting in the Americas (in particular in Latin America) and the **Convention on Cultural Property Implementation Act**, ratified in 1997. This latter convention was a bilateral agreement between the United States and Canada that protected archaeological and ethnological materials through import/export restrictions and provisions for repatriation. This convention lapsed in 2002, however, and has not been renewed.

Legislation in the United States to Protect Cultural Heritage

Although legislation at the national level varies by country, the United States has been relatively active in passing laws to protect cultural heritage. Concerted efforts can be traced back to the **Antiquities Act**, passed in 1906. This legislation was the first to provide protection of sites on federal land by levying penalties for their unauthorized disturbance. Although other laws have been enacted over the years, there are three major pieces of more modern legislation that bear discussion for the United States. The first is the **National Historic Preservation Act** (NHPA) passed in 1966; followed up by the **National Environmental Policy Act** (NEPA) in 1969. This legislation stipulates that federally assisted agencies need to take into account the effects of their projects on historic properties and give the **Advisory Council on Historic Preservation** the opportunity to comment on them. When it was passed, this legislation also established the **State Historic Preservation Office** (SHPO) and constituted the first affirmative management programs for the preservation of historic sites.

The second piece of critical legislation is the **Archaeological and Historic Preservation Act** (AHPA) passed in 1974. This act requires federal agencies to document historic and archaeological properties that may be impacted by land management activities. The already mentioned **Native American Graves Protection and Repatriation Act** (NAGPRA), passed in 1990, is the last piece of important legislation currently on the books and is focused on giving Native Americans control over the physical remains of their ancestors. Other legislation, such as **American Indian Religious Freedom Act** (1979, which recognized sites of important for Native American ritual practices) and the **Abandoned Shipwreck Act** (1987, which stipulated federal control over historic shipwrecks in the territorial waters of the United States), is also important to note.

Concluding Comments: Ethics and Interpretation

Clearly, cultural heritage is important and warrants extensive efforts to preserve it. Yet, the material remains of the past and the narratives that surround them are often contentious and politicized. Archaeologists are not peripheral to these matters. Ethics in archaeology includes a commitment to the protection and documentation of the remains of the past. It also includes a reflexive process of how particular interpretations of those remains might be used to disenfranchise or somehow damage living peoples. As the example of Gustaf Kossinna demonstrates, archaeological interpretations can have seriously negative and far-reaching impacts. Those impacts may be unintentional on the part of the archaeologist, but efforts should be made to ensure that the interpretive work is ethical. Archaeological interpretation can have real-world consequences for us today and archaeologists should be mindful of how their work could be used.

Bibliography

Anderson, Maxwell L. *Antiquities: What Everyone Needs to Know*. New York: Oxford University Press, 2017.

Ardren, Traci.Is "Apocalypto" Pornography? *Archaeology Archive*, 2006. https://archive.archaeology.org/online/reviews/apocalypto.html

Arnold, Bettina. "The Past as Propaganda: Totalitarian Archaeology in Nazi Germany." *Antiquity* 64 (1990): 464–478.

Arnold, Dieter. *Temples of the Last Pharaohs*. Oxford: Oxford University Press, 1999.

Bradley, Richard. *The Past in Prehistoric Societies*. London: Routledge, 2002.

Byrne, Denis. "Buddhist Stupa and Thai Social Practice." *World Archaeology* 27, no. 2 (1995): 266–281.

Castañeda, Quetzil. *In the Museum of Maya Culture*. Minneapolis: University of Minnesota Press, 1996.

Colovito, Jason. "The Long, Strange History of the Pyramids as the Granaries of Joseph. Blog," November 6, 2015. http://www.jasoncolavito.com/blog/the-long-strange-history-of-the-pyramids-as-the-granaries-of-joseph

Davis, Hester. "Heritage Resource Management in the United States." In *Cultural Heritage Management: A Global Perspective*, edited by P. M. Messenger and P. A. Shackel, 188–198. Gainesville, FL: University of Florida Press, 2010.

de Lama de la Cruz, Víctor. *Relatos de viajes por Egipto en la época de los Reyes Católicos*. Miraguano, SA: Ediciones, Madrid, 2013.

Endere, María L. "The Challenge of Protecting Archaeological Heritage in Argentina." In *Cultural Heritage Management: A Global Perspective*, edited by P. M. Messenger and P. A. Shackel, 8–20. Gainesville, FL: University of Florida Press, 2010.

Feder, Kenneth L. *Frauds, Myths, and Mysteries: Science and Pseudoscience in Archaeology*. Mountain View, CA: Mayfield Publishing Company, 1990.

Greenfield, Jeanette. *The Return of Cultural Treasures*. 3rd ed. Cambridge: Cambridge University Press, 2007.

Hayden, H. H. *The Geology of Northern Afghanistan*. Calcutta: Geological Survey of India Memoirs, XXIX.

Hitchens, Christopher, 1911*Imperial Spoils: The Curious Case of the Elgin Marbles*. London: Chatto and Windus, 1987.

Howell, Raymond. "The Demolition of the Tetrapylon in Caerleon: An Erasure of Memory?" *Oxford Journal of Archaeology* 19 (2000): 387–395.

Hunt, Terry L., and Carl P. Lipo. "Late Colonization of Easter Island." *Science* 311 (2006): 1603–1606.

Iwaniszewski, Stanisław. "The Stone Circles at Odry, Poland." In *Heritage Sites of Astronomy and Archaeoastronomy in the Context of the UNESCO World Heritage Convention. IAU-ICOMOS Joint Thematic Study*, edited by C. Ruggles and M. Cotte, 41–44. Bognor Regis: Ocarinabooks, 2011.

Jambrina Martín, Carlos. "El viaje del templo de Debod a España." *Historia* 16, no. 286 (2000): 42–53.

Kaizer, Ted. *The Religious Life of Palmyra: A Study of the Social Patterns of Worship in the Roman Period*. Stuttgart: Franz Steiner Verlag, 2002.

King, Thomas F. *Cultural Resource Laws & Practice: An Introductory Guide*. 2nd ed. Walnut Creek: AltaMira Press, 2004.

Kossinna, Gustav. *Die Deutsche Ostmark: Eiri Heimatboden der Germanen*. Berlin: Publisher, 1919.

———*Die Deutsche Vorgeschichte: Eine Hervorragend Nationale Wissenschaft*. Berlin: Kabitzsch, 1921.

Lertcharnrit, Thanik. "Archaeological Resource Management in Thailand." In *Cultural Heritage Management: A Global Perspective*, edited by P. M. Messenger and P. A. Shackel, 176–187. Gainesville, FL: University of Florida Press, 2010.

Martini, Guido, and Salvatore Paolini. "The History of the Buddhas of Bamiyan." In *After the Destruction of Giant Buddha Statues in Bamiyan (Afghanistan) in 2001*, edited by C. Margottini, 15–60. Natural Science in Archaeology. New York: Springer, 2014.

McKey, Doyle, and Stéphen Rostain. "Farming Technology in Amazonia." In *Encyclopaedia of the History of Science, Technology, and Medicine in Non-Western Cultures*, edited by H. Selin, Dordrecht: Springer Publishing, 2015.

Messenger, Phyllis M., and George S. Smith. "Introduction." In *Cultural Heritage Management: A Global Perspective*, edited by P. M. Messenger and P. A. Shackel, 1–7. Gainesville, FL: University of Florida Press, 2010.

Morales Fajardo, María Esther, Marcos Mejía López, and Araceli Galeana Estrada. "Terrorismo y Patrimonio Cultural: Destrucción y Recuperación de los Budas de Bamiyán y del Sitio de Palmira." *Contexto* 9, no. 15 (2017): 37–52.

Nelson, Stanley. "Reconstructing the Great Mound." *American Archaeology* 13, no. 4 (2009): 26–31.

Neumann, Thomas W., and Robert M. Sanford. *Practicing Archaeology: A Training Manual for Cultural Resources Archaeology*. Walnut Creek, CA: AltaMira Press, 2001.

Organization of American States. "Convention on the Protection of the Archaeological, Historic, and Artistic Heritage of the American Nations," 2018. http://www.oas.org/en/sla/dil/inter_american_treaties_C-16_Convention_Protection_Archeological_Heritage.asp

Parga Dans, Eva, and Pablo Alonso González. "The Altamira Controversy: Assessing the Economic Impact of a World Heritage Site for Planning and Tourism Management." *Journal of Cultural Heritage* 30 (2018): 180–189.

Petrov, Nick. "Cultural Heritage Management in Russia." In *Cultural Heritage Management: A Global Perspective*, edited by P. M. Messenger and P. A. Shackel, 153–161. Gainesville, FL: University of Florida Press, 2010.

Pokotylo, David, and Andrew R. Mason. "Archaeological Heritage Resource Protection in Canada: The Legislative Basis." In *Cultural Heritage Management: A Global Perspective*, edited by P. M. Messenger and P. A. Shackel, 48–69. Gainesville, FL: University of Florida Press, 2010.

Reinerth, Hans. *Vorgeschichte der Deutschen Stämme: Germanische Tat und Kultur auf Deutschem Boden*. Berlin: Bibliographisches Institut Leipzig und Herbert Stubenrauch Verlagsbuchhandlung, 1940.

Scovazzi, Tullio. "Legal Aspects of the Axum Obelisk Case." *Museum International* 61, no. 1–2 (2009): 52–60.

Shen, Chen, and Hong Chen. "Cultural Heritage Management in China: Current Practices and Problems." In *Cultural Heritage Management: A Global Perspective*, edited by P. M. Messenger and P. A. Shackel, 70–81. Gainesville, FL: University of Florida Press, 2010.

Silva, Jorge. "Heritage Resource Management in Peru." In *Cultural Heritage Management: A Global Perspective*, edited by P. M. Messenger and P. A. Shackel, 124–135. Gainesville, FL: University of Florida Press, 2010.

Squier, Ephraim G., and Edwin H. Davis. *Ancient Monuments of the Mississippi Valley*. Edited by David J. Meltzer. Washington, DC: Smithsonian Books, 1998.

Trigger, Bruce G.*A History of Archaeological Thought.* 2nd ed. Cambridge: Cambridge University Press, 2006.

UNESCO. "Convention on the Means of Prohibiting and Preventing the Illicit Import, Export and Transfer of Ownership of Cultural Property 1970," 1970. http://portal.unesco.org/en/ev.php-URL_ID=13039&URL_DO=DO_TOPIC&URL_SECTION=201.html

———"Convention Concerning the Protection of the World Cultural and Natural Heritage," 1972. https://whc.unesco.org/archive/convention-en.pdf accessed on January 15, 2018.

———"Convention for the Protection of Cultural Property in the Event of Armed Conflict with Regulations for the Execution of the Convention 1954," 1999. http://portal.unesco.org/en/ev.php-URL_ID=13637&URL_DO=DO_TOPIC&URL_SECTION=201.html

———"Convention on the Protection of the Underwater Cultural Heritag," 2001. http://unesdoc.unesco.org/images/0012/001260/126065e.pdf

———"Text of the Convention for the Safeguarding of the Intangible Cultural Heritage," 2003. https://ich.unesco.org/en/convention

———"UNIDROIT Convention on the International Return of Stolen or Illegally Exported Cultural Objects," 1995. https://www.unidroit.org/instruments/cultural-property/1995-convention

Von Däniken, Erich. *Chariot of the Gods? Unsolved Mysteries of the Past.* G.P. New York: Putnam's Sons, 1968.

Webster, David L. *Fall of the Ancient Maya: Solving the Mystery of the Maya Collapse.* New York: Thames and Hudson, 2002.

Willems, Willem J. H. "Laws, Language, and Learning: Managing Archaeological Heritage Resources in Europe." In *Cultural Heritage Management: A Global Perspective*, edited by P. M. Messenger and P. A. Shackel, 212–229. Gainesville, FL: University of Florida Press, 2010.

Zimmerman, Fritz. *The Nephilim Chronicles: Fallen Angels in the Ohio Valley.* Scotts Valley, CA: CreateSpace Independent Publishing Platform, 2010.

Zimmerman, Larry J., and Kelly M. Branam. "Collaborating with Stakeholders." In *Archaeology in Practice: A Student Guide to Archaeological Analyses*, edited by J. Balme and A. Paterson, 1–25. Oxford: Wiley Blackwell, 2014.

The Emergence of Archaeology

Archaeology as a profession developed in a particularly western context and its origins are often traced back to the Scientific Revolution in Europe in the seventeenth century. This is not to say that an interest in the past in other times and places did not lead to actual explorations of archaeological sites (e.g., the Greek term *archaiologia*, referring to the study of a remote past including their material remains, is first known to have been used in the fourth-century BC), but that the trajectory for the professionalization of a modern archaeology stretches back to this particular cultural context due to some significant developments in attitudes toward the past.

In fact, we can see explorations of archaeological sites in several important past cultural contexts throughout the world, demonstrating concerted efforts by people to understand what the remains of past societies in their worlds represented and, importantly, using them for some purpose. One of the earliest known examples of an ancient excavation comes from fifteenth-century BC Egypt when the Pharaoh Thutmose IV ordered the excavation of the Sphinx. Thought to date to the reign of the Pharaoh Khafra around the twenty-sixth-century BC, the Sphinx was already largely buried in the time of Thutmose IV, a millennium after it was constructed. Thutmose IV attributed the construction of the Sphinx to Khaf, which **epigraphers** (scholars who study inscriptions) believe must have once referred to Khafra in the now damaged text on the so-called Dream Stele Thutmose IV erected at this ancient ruin. On this stele, Thutmose IV stated that he had a dream while sleeping under the ruins of the Sphinx resting on a hunt. In the dream, the Sphinx informed the prince that if he restored the monument he would become Pharaoh; a clever way for a younger member of the royal line (he had an older brother in line for the throne) to legitimize what most scholars interpret as a grab for power by the young prince.

Another prime example of this ancient interest in the past comes from Nabonidus, the last ruler of the Neo-Babylonian Empire who reigned from 556 to 539 BC. This king commissioned

FIGURE 3.1 The Dream Stele of Thutmose IV.

© Petr Bonek/Shutterstock.com

the excavations of numerous ancient cities dating back to the Sumerian period and in fact, is said to have displayed artifacts collected by his daughter, Bel-Shalti-Nannar, in a museum. His excavations down to the foundations of ancient buildings have been interpreted as a way for Nabonidus, not a member of the royal family when he came to power, to link himself with the storied past of the region and legitimize his overthrow of the previous ruler, Labashi-Marduk.

Glimpses of such an interest in the past is seen in many other cultures throughout the world, but with no supporting textual evidence as seen in the cases of Thutmose IV and Nabonidus. For instance, at the Templo Mayor of Tenochtitlan, the capital of the Mexica (commonly known as Aztec) Empire, numerous offerings have been found that date centuries and in some cases millennia into the past. Without a writing system, these finds are difficult to interpret. Yet, excavations were clearly undertaken by the Mexica at archaeological sites to bring back ancient material culture to their capital.

FIGURE 3.2 (A) An Early Classic (AD 250–600) vessel in the style of the Central Mexican metropolis of Teotihuacan found in the much later Mexica (Aztec) city of Tenochtitlan. The Mexica deposited many relics of older Mesoamerican cultures in the Templo Mayor complex located at the heart of their capital city.

© Leonardo López Luján, INAH-Templo Mayor

Early Origins of a Professional Archaeology

Although these early examples of an active interest in the past are important, the beginning of a professional archaeology has its roots in postmedieval European societies where some early scholars were beginning to question traditional local narratives of how the universe works. The Renaissance period (fourteenth to seventeenth centuries) was a time of great change in Europe and the development of new intellectual traditions that led scholars down the path to the rapid advancement of scientific thought was a critical part of the transformation of Western societies during this period. Many of the "founding fathers" of modern scientific professions performed their work during this time, questioning the contemporary ways of explaining the world and often facing deeply rooted resistance to their findings. Galileo Galilei, Nicolaus Copernicus, and Giordano Bruno are just a few of these figures who played essential roles during the Scientific Revolution. Although there were people already investigating the past, and in fact creating narratives based on their research prior to the Renaissance in Europe (the Greek historian Herodotus is the earliest known western scholar to have done so by writing the histories of societies around the ancient Mediterranean in the fifth-century BC), scholars such as **Flavio Biondo** (who documented ancient Rome when it was still abandoned and the ruins surrounded by empty fields) and **Ciriaco De' Pizzicolli** (who recorded ancient sites and inscriptions from around the Mediterranean) began to demonstrate a more concerted interest in the past during the fifteenth century. This work was sponsored by a variety of state and religious institutions as well as by private citizens and ushered in an era marked by increased **antiquarianism**, an interest in the past, usually involving collection, where individual facts or objects are discussed without reference to their broader context.

To comprehend the antiquarian movement in Europe at this time, however, we must first contextualize it within some prevailing worldviews in Western society during the Renaissance that loomed as substantial obstacles for the success of the Scientific Revolution. The first of these views is called **stasis**, the idea that the world has remained more or less the same from the time it was created to the present. We must be mindful that the prevailing European worldview at the time was firmly entrenched in a Judeo-Christian tradition and European scholars argued that the world was practically in the same state as when it was first created by God. In the words of John Ray, an English naturalist whose work was a predecessor to taxonomic system of Carl Linnaeus, at the end of the seventeenth century: "the works created by God at first and by him conserved to this day in the same state and condition in which they were first made." Such sentiments were an impediment to several lines of developing scientific enquiry requiring that change had indeed occurred over time to explain the data that were being recovered; geologists and naturalists were especially interested in such change as we will detail further along. Although today we generally take for granted such change (e.g., mountains form and erode, species evolve), most major environmental and biological as well as many cultural changes (e.g., domestication) occur at a rather slow pace, not likely to be noticed over the course of several generations (the span of time that most orally transmitted memory fades into obscurity); the rapid cultural change we see in our modern society is a very recent development of globalized societies. Therefore, it is not necessarily surprising that stasis formed part of the general worldview of medieval Europe. Yet, when beach deposits began to be noticed in mountain ranges far above the

sea and fossil species were unearthed that little resembled, if at all, the local range of flora and fauna, it was clear that stasis as a concept needed to be questioned. The same kinds of questions about change over time were echoed over the human past as antiquarians began to unsystematically discuss archaeological evidence, which also pointed to the fact that some ancient European societies looked very different than the ones in which they lived.

The second view that required questioning had to do with the age of the Earth. Medieval European societies also held to the idea that the world was relatively young. The common way to gauge the age of the Earth during this era was to calculate the lifespans of biblical figures (some of who were supposedly centuries old when they passed), arrange them in proper chronological order, and count back to creation. There was more than one attempt to calculate the age of the Judeo-Christian creation in this way, but it was the method proposed by **James Ussher**, the Irish Archbishop of Armagh and Primate of Ireland from 1625 to 1656, which eventually reached a consensus that the world was created on the October 22, 4004 BC at around 6:00 p.m. This roughly 6,000-year period was not nearly enough to account for the changes that many Renaissance scholars had to explain in their data. So, pushing back the age of our planet and everything on it was paramount for the Scientific Revolution to continue.

FIGURE 3.3 A seventeenth-century engraving of James Ussher (1581–1656).

James Ussher, Irish Protestant clergyman (engraving), English school, (17th century)/Private Collection/ © Look and Learn/Elgar Collection/ Bridgeman Images

Antiquarians and the Speculative Period

Within this social and ideological context, an antiquarian tradition began to flourish in parts of Europe. Antiquarianism in Europe can be traced back to the Roman society and in China there was a strong inclination toward antiquarianism during the Song Dynasty (AD 960–1279; and even as early as the Eastern Zhou Dynasty, 771–221 BC) that included **historiography** (the study of historical writing) and the collection of ancient art. For example, in AD 1088, Shen Kuo precociously anticipated modern archaeologists by stating that ancient artifacts could be studied for their technology and in AD 1092, Lü Dalin created the first known artifact catalog. Yet, it was not the Chinese antiquarian tradition which was to have an impact on the trajectory of a professional archaeology in the nineteenth century, but the European tradition from which it emerged.

In the seventeenth century, the collection of "curiosities," specifically among the upper classes in countries like England and France, was becoming more common. Strange objects and organisms including rare species of animals, fossils, and ancient artifacts were collected from local contexts or, increasingly more frequent, obtained from various parts of the world through the process of European colonization. In many cases, these objects were subjected to broad ranging speculations as to their meaning. It was within this tradition that antiquarianism was situated. In a strict sense, antiquarians were those who focused their interest and collection on the "relics" of the past regardless of whether they were objects, documents, or archaeological sites themselves; and they were prone to make fanciful speculations about the past based on these relics. Yet, a broader tradition covered an interest in the "exotic" regardless of its age.

Several antiquarian societies began to form in England by the end of the sixteenth century and some of the more engaged antiquarians, such as **John Aubrey**, performed important documentary work such as mapping archaeological sites. By the seventeenth century, the impacts of the **Enlightenment** (an intellectual tradition of the late seventeenth and early eighteenth centuries that privileged observation and reason over belief and tradition) were reflected in some antiquarian work, particularly in England where the Royal Society of London was founded by King Charles II in 1660. The questions posed by such work ranged from the meaning of ancient barrows (often thought to be burial mounds, and tied to historic figures in local lore) to the significance of stone tools (commonly believed by many to be objects of the "natural" world such as the remains of lightning strikes), specifically in a local European context. In particular, the idea that stone tools could be reflective of a prehistoric ancestry for Europeans that was somehow analogous to "primitive" peoples (the terminology used at the time to refer less hierarchical societies) in the contemporary world began to gain traction among antiquarians in Britain during the seventeenth century. As early as 1656, **William Dugdale** suggested that stone tools found in the British Isles could have actually been made by people prior to knowledge of metalworking. Based on the knowledge that stone tools were made by people in the New World, a fact that surprised many Europeans, Aubrey himself "proposed that life in prehistoric England might have resembled that of the indigenous inhabitants of Virginia" (Trigger 2006, 93). Although the answers to these questions were not founded on sound research and were highly speculative, the fact that the antiquarians questioned traditional narratives and recognized a distant past unknown to modern peoples was tremendously significant.

In the mid-eighteenth century, a German antiquarian by the name of **Johann Winckelmann** undertook a substantive study of ancient Greek and Roman sculpture that anticipates the emergence of systematic methodologies that professional archaeologists would soon develop. At this time, there was a rising interest in these Classical societies, which were looked to by certain European elite as sources of cultural inspiration. Winckelmann classified ancient Greek sculpture using stylistic analysis, dividing it into four categories. Since some of the sculptures had written texts that indicated the

FIGURE 3.4 John Aubrey's (1626–1697) plan maps of places like Avebury (top right) demonstrate the kind of work that antiquarians were performing in the seventeenth century. In particular, barrow complexes, like the image of Knowth, Ireland, (bottom right), captured the attention of antiquarians in England and were often associated with a variety of local legends.

Source: Map: ca. 1675

Portrait of John Aubrey, 1666 (black lead & chalk on paper), Faithorne, William (1616–91)/Ashmolean Museum, University of Oxford, UK/ Bridgeman Images
© Pecold/Shutterstock.com

date of their manufacture, Winckelmann was able to ascertain that each of the styles belonged to a particular period of time and could thus be arranged in a chronological order. With the knowledge of the chronology of these styles, researchers could now date sculptures without associated texts, a tremendously important foundational insight for archaeological dating today. Although Winckelmann is sometimes considered to be the father of Classical archaeology, he performed his work on material with no **provenience** (knowledge of its location when it was recovered, see Chapter 7). One of the fundamental concepts of archeology is that the archaeological context, including the provenience, is critical for analysis. Thus, some archaeologists today view his contributions as more foundational to art history than to archaeology while acknowledging that his ideas had a great impact on the field.

Echoing this upward turn of interest in the past, **Charles of Bourbon**, king of Naples (who eventually became the king of Spain), supported the excavation of the Roman towns of Pompeii and Herculaneum in the first half of the eighteenth century after work to dig the foundations of his summer palace unearthed the first evidence of Herculaneum in 1738. Spectacularly buried when Mount

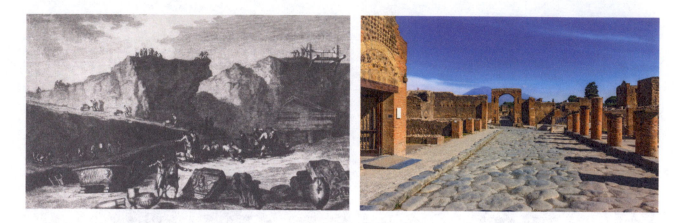

FIGURE 3.5 This eighteenth-century engraving of the work at Herculaneum documents an important period of changes in the attitudes of some Europeans toward the past. The patronage of the excavations of both Pompeii (shown here) and Herculaneum by the king of Naples resulted in the largest scale work of its time.

Source: J.-C. Saint-Non, 1781–1786

© WitR/Shutterstock.com

Vesuvius erupted in AD 79, these towns revealed a tremendously well-preserved slice of time in this area of the Roman world, one that most archaeologists dream about finding. The continued interest in the excavations by Charles after he was crowned the king of Spain demonstrates that at least some members of the ruling class of Europe were also beginning to take more notice of antiquarian issues.

Although archaeological data were neither subjected to scientific nor systematic study at this time, the growing interest in the past laid the foundations for a professional archaeology to emerge as well as the establishment of state sponsored institutions such as museums with a focus on the past. Yet, the development of a professional archaeology would hinge on the adoption of sound field and laboratory methods for collecting, documenting, and analyzing data (which the antiquarian tradition lacked) as well as taking the first steps toward embracing the scientific method in the interpretive process and leaving behind the rampant speculation that characterized this early era.

European Colonial Expansion

It was not just ancient finds in Europe that needed answers not provided by the narratives of the day. Colonial expansion by European cultures starting in the sixteenth century quickly brought numerous contemporary societies unknown to western society into view. Who the people in these faraway lands were needed explaining as did the ruins of ancient societies that caught the attention of "explorers" over the course of the following centuries in these lands. In the early years of exploration, many ships were loaded with people and goods from around the world and sent back to Europe, giving western societies an increasing sense of the great environmental and cultural diversity on this new and increasingly globalized landscape. Although many of the goods had economic value, ethnographic and archaeological objects, some of which would begin to make up future museum collections, were regularly included, piquing the interest of many Europeans. Like the antiquarian tradition, early interpretations of these materials tended to be highly speculative.

As the years went on, expeditions that looted archaeological materials became more ambitious, in many cases to fill the need for newly established museums. For example, in 1815 **Giovanni**

Battista Belzoni, an Italian circus performer, was commissioned by the British consul to Egypt to remove a seven-ton colossal bust of Ramses II from Abu Simbel back to England where it is still housed in the British Museum. One of the most well-known examples of such looting comes from Napoleon's campaign in North Africa, which was accused of amassing large amounts of ancient Egyptian material culture in Cairo by the British, who took possession of a large percentage of this material after the French were defeated by joint British and Ottoman forces. One piece collected by Napoleon's military in particular was critical for the eventual decipherment of ancient Egyptian writing. In 1799, the **Rosetta Stone** was discovered by French troops strengthening a fortified position. Now in the British Museum, this stone contained an extensive inscription written in three

FIGURE 3.6 This early nineteenth-century lithograph shows the removal of Young Memnon's head from the Abu Simbel complex in Egypt by Giovannie Battista Belzoni. The head now resides at the British Museum.

Mode in which the Young Memnon's head was removed, from Plates illustrative of the Researches in Egypt and Nubia, Giovannie Battista Belzoni, Pub. 1822 (colour lithograph), Aglio, Agostino (1777–1857)/Private Collection/The Stapleton Collection/Bridgeman Images

different texts, Greek, Demotic, and ancient Egyptian, meaning that epigraphers could start with a relatively known system (Greek) and work into the unknown (ancient Egyptian). It was in 1822 that **Jean-François Champollion** was able to decipher the Egyptian text using the others.

FIGURE 3.7 Jean-François Champollion and the Rosetta Stone.

Rosetta stone (Egypt) studied by Jean Francois Champollion, Egyptologist, in 1799. It's a decree by Ptolemee written in 3 languages: hieroglyphs, demotic and greek. With this stone Champollion could decipher hieroglyphs. It's at the British Museum/Bridgeman Images.

Across the Atlantic, interest in an indigenous past was also becoming more apparent in the late eighteenth century. **Thomas Jefferson** is the earliest known case of someone purposefully excavating a mound site. Rightly attributing the mound and associated village near his home in Monticello, Virginia, to Native Americans, Jefferson tested various hypotheses dealing with the function of the mound as a mortuary monument. He has been considered by some to be the father of American archaeology.

Soon after Jefferson's time, however, the realization that such constructions were the work of Native American ancestors gave way to a series of popularized mound-builder myths. As mentioned in Chapter 1, over the course of the colonial period and moving into the post-Revolutionary War era there was a process of forgetting Native American monuments and history. This process gave way to rampant speculation of what the mounds across the landscape signified and who built them. With no actual field research such as those conducted by Jefferson to go on, people speculated on a bewildering array of "theories" as to who built the mounds, including a lost tribe of Israel, Mesoamericans, Vikings, Africans, Welsh, and inhabitants of lost continents such as Atlantis. In fact, it appears that some evidence was even fabricated to prove such farfetched ideas. For example, a stone tablet with incised symbols, dubbed the **Bat Creek Stone**, collected at a site in Tennessee in 1889 by a project directed by Cyrus Thomas, had been argued as recently as 1970 to contain a script in Paleo-Hebrew proving a connection to the Old World as far back as the first centuries AD. The symbols have been demonstrated to have similarities to an inscription in a Freemason book and the tablet was proved to be a hoax that was pulled over the respected Thomas. In any event, the myths of the mound-builders had become well entrenched in American thought. As discussed in Chapter 1, this situation began to change with the publication of Squier and Davis' *Ancient Monuments of the Mississippi Valley* in 1848 leading to general consensus in scientific circles of the Native American origins of mound sites by the late 1800s with Cyrus Thomas' work.

Antiquarian interests in the Americas were not restricted to just the United States during this period though. In a part of New Spain that would soon become Mexico, for example, **Don Ramón de Ordoñez y Aguilar** visited the now famous Maya site of Palenque in 1773 and during the 1780s a surveyor and architect by the name of **Antonio Bernasconi** was sent to examine the site further under the guard of a small military force commanded by **Colonel Antonio del Río**. This work was eventually published in 1822 in a press located in London which set the stage for a series of subsequent visits to the site by early explorers including **John Lloyd Stephens** and **Frederick Catherwood** who published books on their travels through the Maya region, capturing the public's imagination of lost cities in the jungle, in the following decades.

FIGURE 3.8 An early nineteenth-century lithograph of the main temple at the site of Tulúm, Mexico, by Catherwood (1844). Catherwood's collaboration in documenting Maya archaeological sites with Stephens (1969) resulted in the first real dissemination of knowledge of past Maya society in places like the United States and Europe and led to the development of popular ideas surrounding lost cities in the jungle.

Temple and pyramid, Tulum, Yucatan, Mexico, 1844 (coloured litho), Catherwood, Frederick (1799–1854) (after)/Private Collection/ Jean-Pierre Courau/Bridgeman Images

The Impact of Geology

At the time this interest in the human past was growing, work in the field of geology was beginning to tackle some of the lingering contentious questions regarding stasis and the age of the Earth. Geology, however, had a much different trajectory toward the development of a scientific profession than did archaeology. One of the principle reasons for this difference was the early demand for geologists in the emerging European economy of the Industrial Revolution (late eighteenth and early nineteenth centuries). In particular, the high demand for material resources like coal and metals to feed the industrial machine required the service of geologists to find those resources. Thus, with the economic outlook for this field looking so bright there was a rapid development of the profession; and with that development a knack for questioning how geological deposits were formed. With holes being dug into the Earth at a pace never before seen in human history, geologists were at no loss for things to question.

One of the founding fathers of geology was **James Hutton**, a Scottish scholar who lived during the eighteenth century. Hutton formulated one of the basic principles of the field, changing how geologists understood the earth. He called this principle **uniformitarianism**, the idea that the processes which form geological deposits today are the same as those that formed deposits in the past. It may seem logical for us today that rivers eroding the landscape can create canyons and that slow-moving water deposits fine instead of coarse particles; and that when we see such fine particles or evidence of canyons that this is how they were formed in the past. However, this was not the case during Hutton's time. In fact, one of the popular ideas was that all rock formations had precipitated out of a single flood in the past. Uniformitarianism was eventually accepted by the field and provided the key for geologists to understand how landscapes had changed. If a geologist could find clues as to how those deposits formed, then the sequence of changes could be reconstructed. Importantly, Hutton was well aware that the processes that formed many of the deposits he examined were exceedingly slow. The 6,000-year sequence since

FIGURE 3.9 James Hutton is often considered to be one of the founding fathers of geology. His idea of uniformitarianism was groundbreaking and explained how features such as canyons (such as the Grand Canyon, picture here) could form over long periods of time through the erosion of the bedrock by rivers and streams. The deep time needed for these processes to work challenged the idea of a young Earth.

creation could not possibly count for the gradual (as opposed to catastrophic) processes that formed and eroded mountains. Thus, the idea of **deep time** began to take root in geological circles, a theme that would be central for reaching a working framework for a modern geology.

Numerous other geologists who labored in the years following Hutton's work contributed to the development of these ideas. In the end, many of the conceptual tools created in geology, such as uniformitarianism and deep time, were adopted by archaeologists, and as mentioned in Chapter 1, Paleolithic archaeology actually developed with a close relation to geology itself. Other concepts, like **stratigraphy** (study of the layers or **strata** of deposits), developed by a turn of the nineteenth-century Englishman by the name of **William Smith**, were essential to the impending professionalization of archaeology. It was **Charles Lyell**, however, who synthesized and furthered many of these ideas with the publication of *Principles of Geology* in 1830–1833. This Scottish geologist is considered to be the foremost scholar in the field during the nineteenth century and was a close friend and colleague of **Charles Darwin**. Additionally, he visited archaeological excavations such as those directed by William Pengelly at Brixham Cave, where the Royal and Geological Societies of London sponsored research on the Paleolithic. Lyell was also instrumental by pushing the limits of deep time back to three hundred million years and was an avid proponent of evolution; although his conviction in **natural selection**, the mechanism proposed by Darwin to explain evolution, was a bit reserved. Yet, the acceptance of evolutionary concepts by geologists, who were finding fossil remains at a relatively high rate, marked the convergence of earth scientists with naturalists leading to the publication of Darwin's momentous *On the Origins of Species* in 1859.

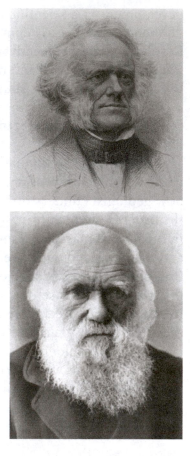

FIGURE 3.10 Charles Lyell (top) and Charles Darwin (bottom) were familiar with each other's work, each contributing to the idea of deep time in different ways.

© Everett Historical/Shutterstock.com

The Contribution of Naturalists

Geologists were not the only scholars collecting and contemplating the meaning of fossils during the seventeenth and eighteenth centuries. Naturalists, the forerunners to modern-day biologists, were not only studying and classifying living species, but some of them were also questioning the meaning of fossils that were increasingly found from the onset of the Industrial Revolution. The study of fossil species would lead naturalists to originate the idea of **evolution**, which simply means biological change in heritable traits in a population over time. Although the mechanisms to explain such changes were varied and debated for years prior to the publication of Darwin's now accepted idea of natural selection, it was painfully obvious to many early naturalists that both the commonly held ideas of stasis and a young world could not be correct to account for the biological changes seen in the fossil data; thus, naturalists also contributed to changing the intellectual climate in Europe in ways that provided a firm footing for archaeology to be established as a profession.

An eighteenth-century Frenchman, **Georges-Louis Leclerc** (later known as Comte de Buffon), was one of the most influential figures among the early naturalists. In *Histoire naturelle, générale et particulière* (published from 1749 to 1788 in thirty-six volumes), Buffon moved away from a biblical account of the Earth. In particular, he tackled questions of modern-day plant and animal diversity by explaining that as organisms moved away from a single center of creation that they improved or degenerated; in no uncertain terms outlining the concept of biological change. Critically, he identified climate change as a cause for this change. Such ideas caused him to be condemned by the Faculty of Theology at the Sorbonne, but he continued his work and in *Les époques de la nature*, published in 1778, he argued that the world (first created along with the other planets by a comet crashing into the sun) was 74,832 years old.

Around the turn of the nineteenth century another Frenchman, **Georges Cuvier**, made a significant impact on the field by proving that extinctions had occurred. Interestingly, Cuvier opposed the idea of evolution and preferred to view the changes in the fossil record as a series of creations, each followed by a catastrophe that caused the species living in each era to become extinct. It was Cuvier, however, who first proposed an era dominated by reptiles and is considered to be the father of modern paleontology by some.

Numerous other naturalists contributed their ideas to the debates concerning evolution and how to classify species during this period. None of them, though, had the impact **Jean-Baptiste Lamark** wrought on the field at the turn of the nineteenth century. A staunch proponent of evolution, this French naturalist contended that biological change must have occurred do to some sort of natural laws. Lamark argued that evolution happened at the level of the individual, not populations, and individuals could change themselves physically through necessity. For example, if an animal needed to reach the higher leaves on a tree in order to survive, its neck would become increasing longer during its lifetime; hence the evolution of giraffes. Importantly, these changes acquired through the lifetime of individuals were hereditary. Lamark's ideas were controversial, but widely influential and are considered to constitute the first cohesive "theory" of evolution. It is in this context, that the stage was set for Darwin's work on natural selection.

FIGURE 3.11 Georges-Louis Leclerc (left) and Georges Cuvier (right) were naturalists whose work challenged the idea of stasis by positing change in biological diversity over time.

Georges-Louis Leclerc/National History Museum, London, UK/Bridgeman Images
© Georgios Kollidas/Shutterstock.com

Darwin and Natural Selection

As we have outlined, Charles Darwin was not the first to discuss evolution. His major contribution was providing a viable mechanism to explain evolution, one that he termed **natural selection**. In many respects, natural selection was the culmination of the work of countless scholars combined with Darwin's fieldwork and comprehensive manner of providing logical and astute interpretations of the data. Darwin was widely read and understood the importance of uniformitarianism and deep time, among other essential concepts including **Thomas Malthus'** work on population demographics, which held that population levels were determined by the amount of food available, increasing to carrying capacity when there is a surplus. In this sense, Darwin is yet another towering figure in the transformation of western thought toward a world characterized by change and deep time. Yet, the publication of his work led to more widespread and serious consideration of the idea of evolution, a central idea in anthropology that would greatly influence the emergence of archaeology as a profession in the latter part of the nineteenth century.

In a nutshell, Darwin's natural selection was composed of several core ideas:

1. Individuals in populations physically vary.
2. These variations are hereditary.
3. Populations produce more offspring than can survive.
4. Individuals with more favorable variation are more prone to survive.
5. The survival of these individuals leads to the population slowly changing.

At this time, there was no knowledge of genetics; **Gregor Mendel's** mid-nineteenth-century work on the inheritance of physical traits remained in obscurity until turn of the twentieth century and the existence of genes was unknown during the 1800s. Although this other essential part of understanding evolution (concerning genetics) was still lacking, Darwin's ideas reverberated throughout scientific and public circles immediately after the publication of his work. Although Darwin did not mention the possibility of human evolution in *On the Origins of Species*, others began to discuss the idea of natural selection in these terms. Coincidently, the first hominin finds, Neanderthal remains from Germany, were also brought to light to the scientific community in the mid-nineteenth century, fueling the debates over human origins.

With the surge in discussions concerning evolution, however, another important impact on anthropology was rendered on the field by Darwin's work; the application of evolutionary ideas to culture. Despite the fact that their term evolution was being used in a strictly biological sense in the mid-nineteenth century, **Edward Tylor**, an English cultural anthropologist, proposed that societies passed through stages of development over time in his book *Primitive Culture*

FIGURE 3.12 Unilineal models of social evolution depict societies changing from small-scale mobile societies to large-scale states and empires. Social change, however, takes many paths and does not always go from the small scale to the large scale.

© Belem Ceballos Casanova

in 1871. Heavily influenced by another English anthropologist and biologist by the name of **Herbert Spencer**, who coined the phrase "survival of the fittest" in 1864, Tylor's work had a tremendous impact on the field. These evolutionary sentiments were soon echoed across the Atlantic by an American cultural anthropologist, **Henry Morgan Lewis**, who in his book *Ancient Society* (1877) adopted a three-stage system in which societies pass; savagery, barbarism, and civilization. Morgan's system was not only **ethnocentric** (evaluating other cultures based on preconceived notions originating in one's own culture) with its characterization of "non-civilized" societies as savages and barbarians, but it also assumed that all societies evolve through a set linear series of stages with civilization being the optimum end product. Such views had a great impact on the further development of anthropology and archaeology into the twentieth century. In the mid-twentieth century, for example, two cultural anthropologists, **Elman Service** and **Morton Fried**, proposed new terminology to such evolutionary schemes to avoid ethnocentric bias. Yet, the assumption that societies necessarily pass through these stages and that there was an ever present evolutionary pressure to reach a better form of "civilized" life remained central to many models of cultural change in archaeology. We know today that societies transform in many different ways and that there is neither one path that they take nor a value that can be placed on people's lifestyles (that one way of living [e.g., urbanism] is better than another [e.g., mobile hunting and foraging]). Yet, the legacy of these evolutionary ideas remains present to some degree in modern archaeological thought.

Elman Service	Morton Fried
Bands	Egalitarian
Tribes	Rank
Chiefdoms	Stratified
States	State

FIGURE 3.13 Henry Morgan Lewis was an influential American social theorist whose work pushed the idea of unilineal social evolution.

Morgan Lewis, litho by Endicott, 1844 (litho), D'Avignon, Francis (c.1813–71) (after)/Free Library of Philadelphia/Print and Picture Collection - Jackson Collection of American Lithographs/Bridgeman Images

Nationalism and the Emergence of Professional Archaeology

So as the Renaissance and Industrial Revolution continued, the stage was being set for the first professional archaeologists to appear out of the antiquarian tradition. There are several people who are sometimes referred to as the "first archaeologist." It was a man by the name of **C.J. Thomsen** who combined systemic excavations, a system of control and recording of archaeological contexts, and interpretations based on field data who most aptly typifies the shift from the antiquarians to professional archaeologists. Working in Denmark during the early half of the nineteenth century and associating artifacts with their stratigraphic contexts, Thomsen demonstrated that there were significant technological changes in artifacts over time in Scandinavia; explained by migration and diffusion.

He proposed a three-age system (Stone, Bronze, and Iron) still utilized by archaeologists today. With the realization of the utility of associating artifacts with their contexts, the professionalization of archaeology began to take hold in the latter half of the nineteenth century. It was a volunteer working with Thomsen, **Jens Worsaae**, who became the first formally trained professional prehistoric archaeologist. In 1847, Worsaae would become Denmark's Inspector for the Conservation of Ancient Monuments and became the first professor of archaeology at the University of Copenhagen in 1855. Worsaae's work in Britain and Ireland was instrumental in demonstrating how the chronology worked out originally by Thomsen was applicable over a larger regional area.

Yet, during this transition from antiquarianism to professional archaeology the political situation in Europe began to take a rather nationalistic turn. Some strong nation states were taking measures to promote national identities, and ancient cultural heritage was brought directly into play in many cases. One of the key strategies for promoting unified cultural identities (one that still exists in many parts of the world today) was to flatten cultural variability within the

FIGURE 3.14 C.J. Thomsen, depicted here at the Museum of Northern Antiquities, is often considered by many to be the first professional archaeologist.

Source: Contemporary drawing, 1848

borders of the state territory. For example, France implemented policies to reduce the linguistic variability of the country by promoting a Parisian dialect during the nineteenth century. Thus, to be French meant to speak the language in a particular way. The past, as a powerful anchor for individual and group identity, was also utilized to rally citizens around a unified identity. A shared past, that also flattened the cultural variability of centuries and millennia of history, was a key symbol to create national identities that wide-ranging populations could buy into. Continuing with the French example, we see the intentional promotion of a Celtic identity by the government. In fact, Napoleon founded the *Academie Celtique* in 1804 with the intention of promoting studies of a Celtic French past and Napoleon III supported major excavations at Celtic sites in the 1860s.

The Celts were one of many "archaeological cultures" that were in some ways "imagined" by Western societies around this time. Often known for shared artistic styles, the "Celts" were first identified through the distribution of Roman period oppida, fortifications in areas where Roman historians identified "barbarian tribes." Thus, where these oppida were found, so would be the Celts. Using the distribution of particular types of material culture, be they architectural forms, ceramics

FIGURE 3.15 Roman period oppida, like this one at Alésia, France, have often been associated with Celtic societies and have served an important role in nationalist discourse. Alésia in particular was commemorated by Napoleon III to mark the fall of Vercingetorix, a Gallic chief defeated by the Romans at this site. The defeat has been used to serve as a reminder to the French people of the role of colonialism in the creation of a common French identity; a reminder that has helped the state to legitimize the internal rule of France by way of hearkening to a united prehistoric Gaul.

© JLJUSSEAU/Shutterstock.com

styles, or ancient artwork, to identify ancient societies would become the staple of **culture historical** archaeology for the years to come. This method makes some sense in that it was virtually impossible for archaeologists to identify actual ethnic groups in the past at this time in the absence of written documents or oral history that could give clues as to how the ancient peoples actually identified themselves. Yet, we know that groups who consider themselves very different ethnically and who even speak different languages may use similar types of material culture in many contexts throughout the world. Therefore, the identification of ancient societies based on this method uses a huge assumption that styles equal identity, resulting in the invention of archaeological cultures. In the context of nineteenth century, nationalistic movements looking to flatten cultural variability to rally people with distinct backgrounds and pasts around unified national European identities, this method worked very well.

These nationalistic efforts created some of the first professional jobs in archaeology through the creation of museums and institutes which in large part served the interest of the state. By the 1880s, there was a notable increase on the jobs available for archaeologists in countries such as England and the United States. Throughout the nineteenth century, museums, universities, and research institutions were being founded and by the end of the 1800s professional archaeology was firmly entrenched on both sides of the Atlantic; the Bureau of Ethnology was founded in the United States in 1879. From this moment would begin the era of culture history in archaeology, to which we turn in the following chapter.

Bibliography

Bryan, Betsy M. *The Reign of Thutmose IV*. Baltimore, MD: The Johns Hopkins University Press, 1991.

Catherwood, Frederick. *Views of Ancient Monuments in Central America, Chiapas, and Yucatan*. London: F. Catherwood, 1844.

Clayton, Peter A. *Chronicle of the Pharaohs: The Reign-By-Reign Record of the Rulers and Dynasties of Ancient Egypt*. 2nd ed. New York: Thames and Hudson, 1994.

Darwin, Charles. *On the Origin of Species by Means of Natural Selection, or the Preservation of Favoured Races in the Struggle for Life*. London: John Murray, 1859.

Dean, Dennis R. *James Hutton and the History of Geology*. Ithaca, NY: Cornell University Press, 1992.

Dietler, Michael. "A Tale of Three Sites: The Monumentalization of Celtic Oppida and the Politics of Collective Memory and Identity." *World Archaeology* 30 (1998): 72–89.

Feder, Kenneth L. *Frauds, Myths, and Mysteries: Science and Pseudoscience in Archaeology*. Mountain View, CA: Mayfield Publishing Company, 1990.

Greene, Kevin. *Archaeology, an Introduction: The History, Principles, and Methods of Modern Archaeology*. London: B.T. Batsford Ltd, 1983.

Harris, Marvin. *The Rise of Anthropological Theory*. New York: Harper Collins, 1968.

López Luján, Leonardo. *La recuperación mexica del pasado teotihuacano*. Mexico, DF: Instituto Nacional de Antropología e Historia, 1989.

Mainfort, Robert C., Jr., and Mary L. Kwas. "The Bat Creek Fraud: A Final Statement." *Tennessee Anthropologist* 18 (1993): 87–93.

Mayr, Ernst. *The Growth of Biological Thought*. Cambridge: Harvard University Press, 1981.

Ray, J. D. *The Rosetta Stone and the Rebirth of Ancient Egypt*. Cambridge: Harvard University Press, 2007.

Scott, James C. *Seeing Like a State: How Certain Schemes to Improve the Human Condition Have Failed*. New Haven, CT: Yale University Press, 1998.

Squier, Ephraim G., and Edwin H. Davis. *Ancient Monuments of the Mississippi Valley*. Edited by David J. Meltzer. Washington, DC: Smithsonian Books, 1998.

Stephens, John L. *Incidents of Travel in Central America, Chiapas, and Yucatan*. New York: Dover Publications, 1969.

———*Incidents of Travel in Yucatan*. Mexico: Panorama Editorial, 1988.

Taylor, Walter W. "A Study of Archaeology." *American Anthropologist* 50, no. 3 (Part 2, 1948): 69 Memoirs of the American Anthropological Association.

Trigger, Bruce G. *A History of Archaeological Thought*. 2nd ed. Cambridge: Cambridge University Press, 2006.

Willey, Gordon R. *Prehistoric Settlement Patterns in the Viru Valley, Peru*. Bulletin 155. Washington, DC: Bureau of American Ethnology, 1953.

The Rise of Modern Archaeology

As we discussed briefly in the previous chapter, the coalescence of a professional archaeology happened with the development of **culture-history**. As the professionalization of the field gained traction in the second half of the eighteenth century, early archaeologists had to begin with the basics; piecing together the general changes in material culture over time and its variation in space. Today, archaeologists working all over the world draw on the basic knowledge of material culture change accumulated by generations of archaeologists. Although some areas of the world have better known material sequences than others, we now have a rough idea of what we are liable to find in any given area of the world; like how ceramic styles, burial practices, or lithic technology changed over time. There is still a tremendous amount to learn, but much of the basic "inventory" of material cultural is known, freeing up modern archaeologists to fill in important details and turn to asking important social questions of the data. This was not the case for early archaeologists. The first archaeologists to work in a region were faced with understanding basic stratigraphy and material culture change, trying to place some sort of spatial and chronological order on the data. Common questions during this period revolved around how material culture changed and who the people were whose remains they studied. This situation led to an intense focus on **culture historical archaeology**, assigning ethnicity to archaeological cultures through the use of material culture.

The Era of Culture History

This early period of professional archaeology was characterized by description. As evidence for little known societies of the past were recovered, archaeologists documented this material. From the time of C. J. Thomsen, researchers understood that material culture needed to be documented in time and space in order to recognize patterns in its variability. Thus, the first major goal of archaeological research coalesced within the field; basic documentation. Although the quality of the documentation was generally below the accepted standards of archaeological research today, early archaeologists nonetheless recognized its central importance to understanding the past and labored to publish their descriptions. New methods for documenting archaeological contexts were developed at this time that laid the groundwork for increasingly better descriptions. **W. M. F. Petrie**, working in Egypt in the 1880s, created more detailed plan drawings of his excavations where major finds were noted, increasing the detail of documented archaeological data in horizontal space. Also working in Egypt and Sudan around the turn to the twentieth century, **George Reisner** was the first to standardize the use of profile and section drawings of excavations to extend this higher level documentation across vertical space so that stratigraphy could be more systematically recorded. And, little by little, field recording methods and documentation of basic contexts began to improve.

As more was known about particular regions of the world, archaeologists began to see patterns in their data. For example, certain artifacts appeared in some regions earlier than others. To recognize these patterns, archaeologists created **typologies** (systems of categorization), manifested specifically in the categorization of material culture (a topic we will return to in Chapter 10). It was painfully obvious at this time that a wide array of material culture, such as projectile points, ceramic vessels, architectural forms, and grave goods, patterned based on similarities in specific attributes (e.g., their form or decoration was similar). By grouping material culture into types, archaeologists could more easily manage their data and see how the characteristics they used to create the categories patterned over time and space. So, instead of treating hundreds of thousands of artifacts as individual pieces of data, archaeologists could more easily see material patterning by comparing a much smaller number of types. Importantly, many of the patterns they saw in the data could be linked to stylistic variation. Heavily influenced by the diffusionist ideas of **Oscar Montelius**, a Swedish archaeologist who traced cultural ideas in Europe to the Near East, the idea of culture history first developed in the latter half of the nineteenth century in Germany through the

FIGURE 4.1 W. M. F. Petrie's plan drawing of the Palace of Apries, Egypt. This kind of spatial documentation was pioneering at the end of the nineteenth century.

Source: Petrie (1909)

work of **Rudolf Virchow** and others such as Gustaf Kossinna, who we mentioned in Chapter 2. Culture historical archaeology soon spread and became the base of archaeological interpretation by the turn of the twentieth century replacing evolutionary models (a la Lewis Henry Morgan) with **diffusionism**, the idea that cultural traits are created in one place and then spread to others.

For example, researchers had recognized that similar styles in beaker-shaped pottery over a large portion of western Europe during the Late Neolithic (roughly 2800–1800 BC for this phenomenon) could be broken into two major types, All Over Ornamented and Maritime, which were further classified into subtypes such as All Over Corded. Thus, based primarily on the decorative styles of the vessels, early professional archaeologists working on the Late Neolithic in western Europe were able to plot the spatial distribution and timing of the appearance of a relatively durable cultural expression that was found over a large area. Since there was no record of the people who made such pottery, researchers used the stylistic similarities to create an ethnic designation for the phenomenon, which was termed Bell-Beaker culture during the early years of the twentieth century.

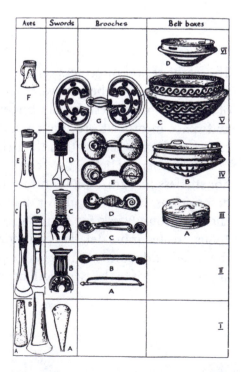

FIGURE 4.2 Oscar Montelius' typologies in northern Europe not only set standards for early archaeological artifact analyses, but paved the way for diffusionist ideas based on the categories that archaeologists created.

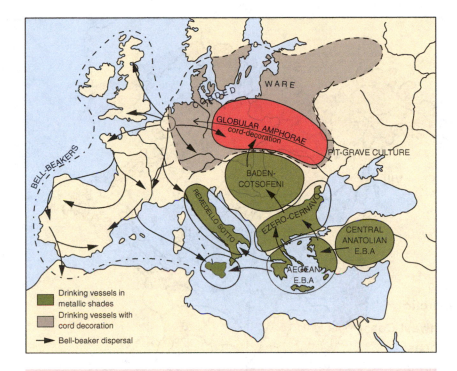

FIGURE 4.3 An archaeological reconstruction of the spread of Bell-Beaker pottery across Europe (after Sherratt 1987). These kinds of temporal models for the spread of pottery have been used to postulate potential migrations of people from the Late Neolithic to Early Bronze (ca. 2900–1800 BC).

© Kendall Hunt Publishing Company

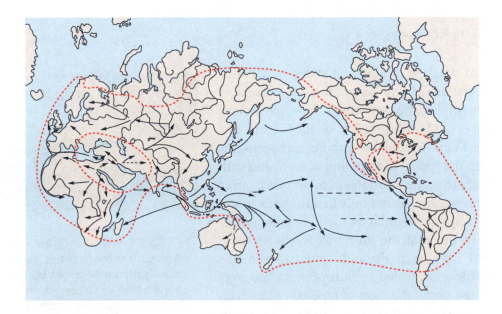

FIGURE 4.4 Hyper-diffusionist model by Smith (1930). Smith argued that certain characteristics of "civilization" originated in Egypt and then spread to other areas of the world.

© Kendall Hunt Publishing Company

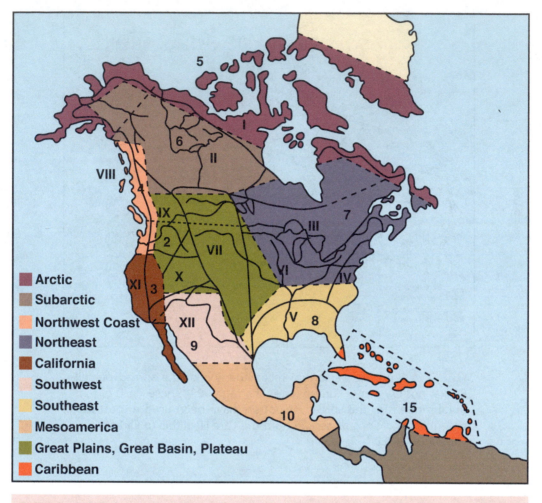

Arctic
Subarctic
Northwest Coast
Northeast
California
Southwest
Southeast
Mesoamerica
Great Plains, Great Basin, Plateau
Caribbean

FIGURE 4.5 Wissler's culture areas (after Kroeber 1939: Map 10).

The common practice of equating styles with ethnic groups through the use of typology at this time fueled an intense interest mapping the movement of people around ancient landscapes and the diffusion of ideas from one place to another. With Bell-Beaker culture, archaeologists attempted to map the spatial distribution of early sites with this type of pottery to argue for routes of migration to areas with later evidence; assuming not only that the pottery was reflective of peoples who would have identified themselves with one another, but that the only way for those styles to spread would have been through actual movements of people, both ideas contested in European archaeology today. Through the popularization of typology in archaeology, diffusionism became a common method to reconstruct the culture histories of many areas throughout the globe, even leading to some arguments termed **hyperdiffusionism**, which assumed that some far-flung cultural

FIGURE 4.6 V. Gordon Childe, who excavated places such as the Neolithic site of Skara Brae (ca. early third-millennium BC, pictured here) on the island of Orkney, Scotland, explored social questions to a much greater degree than the majority of his contemporaries in the early part of the twentieth century.

traits indicative of "civilizations" had to originate from a single source. In 1929, an Egyptologist by the name of **Grafton Elliot Smith** (1933) argued that many of the large monuments found in places as far as Europe, Mesoamerica, and the Andes could only be explained as poor copies of Egyptian pyramids, the idea of which had diffused from this original source. Although the argument by Smith (1933) was an extreme and controversial view at the time, his logic was indicative of the popularization of diffusionist arguments and migrations during the early decades of the twentieth century.

It was also during this early period that **culture areas** were created for ancient landscapes. The idea of culture areas was first developed in cultural anthropology where it was used as a tool to define a geographic region that was quite similar in terms of its environment and cultural expressions. Two American cultural anthropologists who also focused some research in archaeology, **Clark Wissler** and **Alfred Kroeber** (1939), were the first to apply this idea to the past, opening up the way for typology to be used as a method of defining areas of cultural similarity. This work was followed by increasing reliance on diffusionist arguments in the New World.

Although diffusionism was taking hold of archaeology in the first part of the twentieth century, hints of broader conceptual discussions are found in the work of V. Gordon Childe. Influenced heavily by Marxist thought, Childe remained somewhat wary of equating material culture with ancient ethnic groups; while at the same time applying diffusionist ideas in his work. Childe's contributions included a desire to get more ethnographic reconstructions of ancient people and how they lived and he asked more socially oriented questions regarding the economies, ideologies, and social and political organizations of ancient societies.

It was around this time that western-style archaeology began to spread to other areas of the world. In Japan, for example, an American zoologist by the name of **Edward Morse** with experience excavating shell mounds in the eastern United States performed excavations at a shell mound in Omori in 1877. Although Morse was an evolutionist, prominent Japanese archaeologists of the late nineteenth century (often trained in Europe and in fields other than archaeology) tended to follow the culture historical school. The Anthropological Society of Tokyo was founded by **Tsuboi Shogoro** (whose research focused on Mesolithic Jomon culture and its relationship to modern Japanese people) and several of his students in 1884 and the culture historical tradition remained central to the understanding of the Japanese past through the mid-twentieth century.

In China, where an interest in the past (primarily focused on historiography) has deep roots, field archaeology developed during the first decades of the twentieth century. As part of a rather broad attempt to integrate scientific knowledge from western societies during the turbulent New Culture Movement (also known as the May 4th Movement, an anti-imperialist movement tied to an increase in nationalist sentiments from 1915 to 1921), the first major archaeological field projects were undertaken by foreign nationals such as **J. G. Anderson**, a Swedish geologist who worked on the Neolithic Yangshao culture, and **Davidson Black**, a Canadian anatomist who performed the first research at the famous Paleolithic cave site of Zhoukoudian. **Li Ji**, who earned his doctoral degree from Harvard University, became the first head of the Department of Archaeology in the National

FIGURE 4.7 A conjunctive approach using both textual and material data was pioneered in China early in the twentieth century. Divination texts on "oracles bones" such as this Shang Dynasty turtle plastron, allows archaeologists to compare texts to other data in contexts as early as the late second-millennium BC.

Pictogram on turtle plastron with divination text (turtle plastron), Chinese School, Shang Dynasty (1766–1050 BC)/ Musee Guimet, Paris, France/De Agostini Picture Library/Bridgeman Images

Research Institute of History and Philology of Academia Sinica in 1928 and excavated at the late Shang Dynasty site of Yinxu. This research was revolutionary in China as it combined the analysis of the many inscriptions found at the site (the study of written texts having a deep history in China) with material data.

Professional archaeology in many other parts of the world, such as India and the Middle East, developed in colonial contexts, but each has complex ties to western traditions. In some cases, more recent periods are more closely scrutinized than earlier periods. For example, in Nigeria the use of local ethnographic data is promoted and in sub-Saharan Africa in general there is a tendency to focus on the historical relationships among the ancestors of modern ethnic groups. In any event, professional archaeology has now reached practically every corner of the globe that has material remains of the human past. Most archaeological sites remain understudied or unexplored, but work has now begun in each region.

Glimmers of a Scientific Archaeology

Returning back to a distinctly western tradition, the shift from an evolutionary to a diffusionist focus in archaeology was in many ways influenced by several nineteenth-century German ethnologists. In particular **Franz Boas**, who immigrated to the United States to take a position as a curator at the Smithsonian Museum in 1887 (later to become an influential professor of anthropology at Colombia University in 1899), had a tremendous impact on tenor of archaeology, particularly in the Americas. It is Boas who introduced the idea of a four-field anthropology and many of his students were highly successful and founded anthropology programs in the United States and Latin America.

Boas is known for many contributions to the field including his opposition to the idea of race as a biological concept. He was an opponent to the evolutionary ideas of the day and promoted the idea of **cultural relativism**, that cultures are unique and to be understood on their own terms; there is no universal standard to assess the degree of development of a culture, thus, no culture is "better" than another. Boas also believed that cultures changed through the interactions of people and the diffusion of ideas, an idea that would resonate with archaeologists in the first half of the twentieth century. Today this idea is called **historical particularism**, that each culture is the end product of a unique historical sequence where diffusion was a major agent of change. Finally, holding a doctorate in physics, Boas was a proponent of the scientific method. Although "science in archaeology" did not emerge at this time, the influence of Boasian anthropology and Boas' commitment to the scientific method are notable to understand the eventual concerted debates over the role of science during the 1960s.

FIGURE 4.8 Franz Boas is one of the most important figures in early American anthropology.

Franz Boas, 1920 (b/w photo)/© SZ Photo/ Scherl/Bridgeman Images

In the context of a Boasian anthropology at the beginning of the twentieth century and responding to criticisms that American archaeology lacked chronological control, archaeologists working in the Americas began to gravitate toward the creation of typologies that could be analyzed in tandem with stratigraphic excavations. In particular, the work of **Nels Nelson** and **Alfred Kidder** in the American Southwest demonstrated how a focus on typology and stratigraphy could illustrate how artifacts changed over time. Kidder (1924) termed each period of time in his chronology a "culture" in his landmark culture historical synthesis of this region (*An Introduction to the Study of Southwest Civilization*), the first of its kind attempted in the Americas and published one year before V. Gordon Childe's *The Dawn of European Civilization*. During the first Pecos Conference (1927) archaeologists working in the Southwest adopted a standardized chronology, creating a language for understanding chronology across the region. Although criticized and refined over the years, this chronology represented a watershed event for archaeology in the Americas and a wholesale adoption of culture historical archaeology parallel to what was happening in Europe. Diffusionist interpretations did not take long to appear in the North American literature. In 1941, **James Ford** and **Gordon R. Willey** (1953) published a synthesis of the culture history of eastern North America, replacing the Near East as the source of cultural innovations (as found in the European work of Montelius and Childe) with Mesoamerica. Rather than adopting culture history from their European colleagues, however, archaeologists in the Americas had reinvented this method; a major difference being that nationalistic discourse did not color interpretations as it did in Europe.

FIGURE 4.9 Pecos Pueblo is an archaeological site in the American Southwest where Pecos conference took form. Alfred Kidder was engaged in fieldwork at the time and the conference was an open-air event, one that still continues today.

© Ricardo Reitmeyer/Shutterstock.com

As this descriptive period of culture history took hold of American archaeology, critics voicing their discontent began to be heard, specifically from the ranks of cultural anthropologists. An ethnologist by the name of **Julian Steward** was quite vocal in his criticisms. In a coauthored article with archaeologist F. M. Setzler, published in 1938, Steward expressed his frustration with culture history and its heavy emphasis on description and typology. Steward believed that cultural anthropology could benefit from a diachronic view of culture, but was foiled from asking questions concerning demography, settlement patterns, and subsistence economies (particular themes that interested him) over long time scales by the way archaeological data were being treated by his colleagues actually working on the past. Steward recognized that the archaeology of the time was not being performed as anthropology. Importantly, Steward's interest in settlement patterns and the ways that human behavior is impacted by the environment would have a tremendous influence on changes soon to be experienced in archaeological theory. His interest in **nomothetic** (the study of scientific laws) anthropological research and a commitment to the study of general laws of human behavior would also impact the direction of future archaeological research.

However, discontent with the culture historical framework was not only being expressed in the United States. Across the Atlantic, these sentiments were echoed by philosopher/archaeologist **Robin Collingwood**, who in 1939 stated that archaeologists should attempt to understand the "intentions, goals, and knowledge that motivated the people being studied" (Trigger 2006, 305).

Alternative theoretical currents that did influence archeologists at the time, and on both side of the Atlantic, came from cultural anthropology. These currents would serve as the base for what would soon to be called the **New Archaeology**, a term in use by the late 1950s.

Cultural anthropology during the 1920s and 1940s was heavily influenced by the Functionalist School, created in British anthropology by scholars such as **Bronislaw Malinowski** and **E. R. Radcliffe-Brown**. In general terms, **functionalism** in anthropology concerns the understanding of how cultural traits or phenomenon fit into a systemic whole. Analogous to all of the parts of the body functioning to make up a person, functionalism conceives of societies composed of many parts which are functionally interdependent. In its original applications, functionalism was applied to

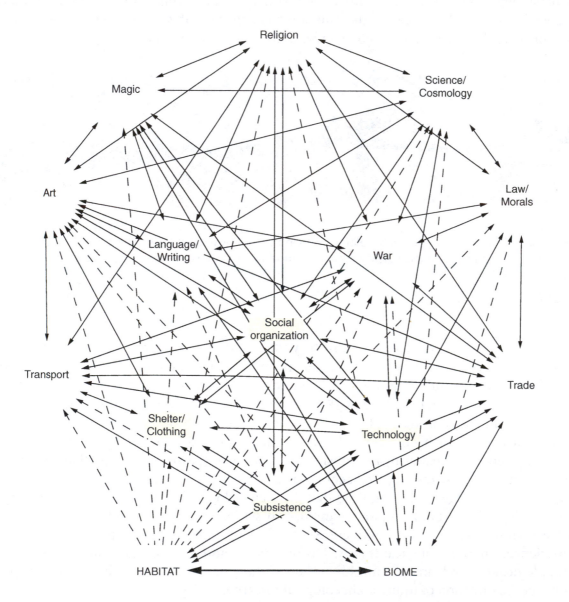

FIGURE 4.10 Early conceptualization of systems theory in archaeology by Clark (1953) included numerous interrelated cultural factors that were linked to the environment.

synchronic slices of time. **Processualism** takes functionalist systemic frameworks and applies them across time to evaluate how and why systems change. Although functionalist disinterest in historical analysis did not appeal to archaeologists, the idea of conceiving societies as systems, specifically in regard to their relationships to the environment began to call the attention of some archaeologists working in the culture historical tradition. For example, Marxists archaeologists such as V. Gordon Childe and numerous researchers working in the Soviet Union examined social, economic, and political variables in a framework that considered changes to cultural and social systems in terms of their own internal dynamics rather than from outside influences as the culture historical framework was operating. **Grahame Clark**, an influential British archaeologist, was the first to link cultural and environmental factors in a single system in 1953. This work demonstrated a heavy influence from functionalist thought with its emphasis on systems and laid the groundwork for the arrival of the New Archaeology, heralded as the arrival of scientific approaches to the past. The scientific approach in anthropology advocated by influential ethnologists of the time such **Clyde Kluckhohn**, however, was one that was defined as a search of generalizations of human behavior; in other words, a search for laws.

In this scholarly climate, a young archaeologist by the name of **Walter Taylor** (1948) published a sharp critique of archaeology in 1948 entitled *A Study of Archaeology*. Ruffling the feathers of the established archaeological community, Taylor (1948) demonstrated that the goal of archaeology up to this point had been to reconstruct prehistory. What archaeology had failed to accomplish, or in fact even attempt, was to explain what had happened in the past or reconstruct past ways of life. Taylor (1948) disparagingly called archaeology "mere chronicle." Yet, not only was Taylor (1948) critical about the lack of interest in explanation of the past, he called archaeologists out for not collecting and/or analyzing all of the potential data. He demonstrated that certain data (such as those not used in creating and refining cultural chronologies, e.g., floral and faunal remains) were not given preference and that to move forward with an archaeological agenda that includes the reconstruction of past human lifeways that all data must be adequately collected and analyzed. Although Taylor's (1948) critique did not adequately consider the contemporary changes on both sides of the Atlantic toward a more functionalist/processual archaeology, instead focusing heavy criticism on culture historical archaeologists, his work is considered an important precursor to the processualist agenda of the 1960s and the vocal movement way from culture historical framework. In addition to the development of settlement pattern research (the spatial analysis of archaeological sites across the landscape, see Chapter 12) by **Gordon Willey** in the 1950s (see Chapter 11), Taylor's work set the tone for the momentous changes in American archaeology during the 1960s.

The New Archaeology

During the early 1960s, American archaeology was thrown into a more than lively debate concerning how the field should approach the past. An influential group of primarily younger archaeologists, using systemic ideas drawn out of functionalism, undertook a vociferous attack on culture historical frameworks. Led by **Lewis Binford**, this movement, called the New Archaeology or **processual archaeology**, was evolutionist, behavioralist (concerned with the outward behavioral aspects of thought, not the inward experiential aspects), ecological, and above all, positivist. **Positivism** is the belief that positive or authentic knowledge can only come from observations of natural phenomena and interpreted through reason and logic; thus the only "true" knowledge derives from the scientific method. Taking the call for a scientific anthropology/archaeology from the likes of Julian Steward and Clyde Kluckhohn, processualist archaeologists embraced an **epistemology** (theory of knowledge) based on a "science of people" that had as its goal the development of laws of human behavior and culture change. In this sense, this new program in archaeology was an explanatory one. With the New Archaeology, there was a sense the field had finally moved beyond "mere chronicle."

The focus on a "scientific" archaeology led to much discussion on the use the scientific method and how to create logical arguments. Granted, there was a lack of use of the scientific method prior to processualism and its explicit implementation beginning at this time was a welcome change. But, it must be remembered that what was offered by the New Archaeology was a particular brand of science. The idea of the scientific method is traced back to **Francis Bacon**, an English philosopher who died in 1626. Substantially influencing core ideas concerning reasoning during the Enlightenment, Bacon argued that scientific knowledge should be based on **inductive reasoning** (the premises give strong evidence for the conclusion) and careful observations of phenomena in nature whereby a skeptical and methodical approach is employed. These ideas have served as the base of an empirical scientific method for centuries. Yet, as relativists point out, the scientific method is embedded in society and can include all kinds of cultural biases. This realization means that "how" the scientific method is employed can be variable; stressing the importance of understanding how processualists framed their work at this time.

The New Archaeology was inherently evolutionary and, in particular, Steward's focus on understanding culture change in regard to ecological adaptations was highly influential, as was the work of another prominent cultural anthropologist by the name of **Leslie White**. Thus, to a great degree, environments determined cultures and culture change. The line of reasoning that environments determined cultures and culture change would be a cornerstone of Binford's work until the end of his career and lead him and other processual archaeologists to embrace cross-cultural comparisons with a heavy emphasis on environmental factors. For Binford culture was an "extra-somatic means of adaptation." In other words, culture is how humans adapt to the environment by nonbiological means.

However, archaeological interest in the environment was not new at this time. Archaeologists were thinking about the impact of the environment and attempting paleoenvironmental reconstructions as early as the mid-nineteenth century. Yet, the level of environment determinism in processual studies about the past was unparalleled in this history of the field. In a very functionalist fashion, processualists conceived the environment as an essential variable in systemic models of culture change. Changes in cultural systems were due to adaptive responses to population pressure, competition with adjacent cultural systems, and, above all, the environment. As would be a cornerstone of the future critique of processual archaeology, the beliefs that people held were unimportant to archaeological study. In the words of **Kent Flannery** (1967, 105), an important figure of the early processualist movement who would take the interest in **General Systems Theory** beyond ecology, "[t]he process theorist is not ultimately concerned with the 'Indian behind the artifact' but rather with the system behind both the Indian and the artifact." Processual archaeologists believed that ancient peoples would have made rational decisions (using a modern Western logic) based on how to adapt to environmental conditions and, thus, that these decisions would be predictable and reflected materially in readily accessible archaeological data such as floral and faunal data for the study of settlement patterns and subsistence systems (Chapter 12).

The New Archaeology movement was highly influential in the Americas during the 1960s and many archaeologists began to perform research under this framework in a relatively short amount of time. This is not to say, however, that the processual movement was uniform. Divisions within the New Archaeology began to appear during its early years and by the 1970s several relatively distinct schools began to coalesce.

Evolutionary Ecology

One school to emerge from the processual tradition was **evolutionary ecology**. Given the emphasis on human adaptations to the environment in processual frameworks, this school fit well within the cannons of the New Archaeology. Evolutionary ecology has been defined as "the application of natural selection theory to the study of adaptation and biological design in an ecological setting" (Winterhalder and Smith 1992, 5). In particular, many studies using this interpretive framework have focused on the social organization and resource availability among small-scale/mobile societies often known as hunting-gathering societies. **Optimal foraging theory**, which presupposes that people in such societies make decisions concerning their subsistence based on rational decisions aimed at optimizing their food resources, is a common element of this type of research.

Behavioral Archaeology

Another early focus in processual archaeology came to be known as **behavioral archaeology**, which at its core is a science of material culture, specifically focused on human-artifact relationships. Keeping in line with processual goals, behavioral archaeologists work toward a goal of a "science of material culture" whereby regularized material patterning can be used to create interpretive generalizations that can explain human behavior and the current state of material culture which archaeologists recover.

Within the first decade of the publication of Binford's 1962 manifesto for an "archaeology as anthropology," there was a growing realization that the living contexts that produced the "archaeological record" were not at all the same as what archaeologists recovered in their investigations. Contemporary material patterns in the archaeological record were in fact distortions of what had actually occurred in the past. In order to eliminate these distortions, archaeologists needed to understand the **formation processes** that created the material contexts which archaeologists encountered in a modern-day context (see more about formation processes in Chapter 7). In other words, there was recognition that understanding how archaeological contexts were created and transformed was essential to archaeological interpretation. The study of formation processes was spearheaded by **Michael Schiffer**, but Binford quickly recognized the importance of Schiffer's ideas and made formation processes an essential part of what Binford called **middle range theory**, which sought to "establish the spatial, temporal, and formal correlates of specific forms of human behavior and their material expressions in the ethnographic record and to identify similar residues in archaeological contexts" (Trigger 2006, 414). Both Schiffer's and Binford's work were predicated on the use of analogy and led to an explosion of work in **ethnoarchaeology** and **experimental archaeology** (see Chapter 10).

Selectionist Archaeology

Although, in general, processual archaeology has strong roots in evolutionist thought, one group of scholars began to draw on more biologically oriented evolutionary theory as the New Archaeology became more established. One of the main proponents of the interpretive framework known as **selectionist archaeology** (also known as **evolutionary archaeology** and **Darwinian archaeology**) was **Robert Dunnell** (1980). Dunnell and his colleagues argued that cultural change could be understood by using ideas from biological evolutionary theory and that there must be a cultural equivalent to natural selection. In other terms, there is a vast world of opportunities in which human behavior and material culture can manifest and those opportunities can compete somehow based on Darwinian notions of natural selection. To use one crude example of how selectionist interpretive frameworks can be applied, we can consider clothing styles. The clothes we wear, as members of a market-driven economy, change each year, with the styles currently being produced competing for consumers to buy them. Successful clothing styles that result in fads are those best adapted to the current social and economic environment and thus "survive" and are "reproduced" in greater numbers. Although this is a rather simplistic example, all sorts of models and ideas from biological evolutionary theory have now been applied to cultural contexts in which archaeologists work. The challenge for selectionist archaeology has been in its attempt to reconcile the mechanisms by which traits are transmitted in biological and cultural systems. Yet, despite these challenges, explorations of the applicability of Darwinian evolution remain an area of research in the field.

Contemporary Processualism

Although, as we will see, the New Archaeology was roundly critiqued by the postprocessualist movement beginning in the early 1980s, processualist types of interpretive frameworks are still a prominent part of the field. They have not disappeared by any stretch of the imagination. Behavioral archaeology, selectionism, and evolutionary ecology are still part of archaeologists' "method and theory toolkit" and these interpretive frameworks are constantly being reconfigured and explored. Newer frameworks, such as **cognitive archaeology** (also known **cognitive-processual archaeology**), created by **Colin Renfrew**, a prominent British processualist archaeologist who in the 1980s (around the time that the postprocessual movement in Britain was critiquing the New Archaeologists for ignoring cognitive aspects of human life) began to call for a "scientific" archaeology of the mind, have appeared. Processual archaeology is alive and well. In very general terms, the use of systems theory and the focus on human adaptations to the environment are still very well entrenched among archaeologists working under the frameworks of **complexity theory** and **resilience theory**. This work has advanced thinking on how functionalist and positivist work can contribute to a contemporary archaeology and adds to the increased diversity of interpretive frameworks available to archaeologists today, a diversity that really began to augment with the critiques by the first postprocessualists.

Postprocessualism

For nearly two decades, processualists influenced the practice of the archaeological interpretation with no real viable alternative. During the 1970s in Great Britain, however, new theoretical influences from cultural anthropology began to take hold and by the 1980s manifested in a new way of approaching archaeological data that was dubbed **postprocessual archaeology**. Understanding postprocessual archaeology is a bit complicated as it is sometimes used as an umbrella-like term that encompasses all sorts of interpretive frameworks in archaeology that challenged processualist epistemologies such as feminist archaeology, Marxist archaeology, and structuralism. Others view postprocessual archaeology, sometimes referred as **interpretive archaeology**, as separate from some of these other interpretive traditions and use the term more restrictively, emphasizing the use of subjective interpretations as a hallmark. In this section, we will discuss the initial history of the postprocessual movement and situate nonprocessual interpretive frameworks that appeared from the 1970s onward, some of which may be considered strictly postprocessual, in the context of a more contemporary archaeology.

Marxism, Structuralism, and the Critique of Processualism

The movement in Britain to find alternatives to processual archaeology began with a stinging critique of the New Archaeology and an initial movement to engage Marxist–structuralist literature in sociocultural anthropology by archaeologists at Cambridge University led by **Ian Hodder**. In 1982, in the first of a series of influential volumes edited by Hodder, he blasted the positivist archaeology espoused Binford and others, claiming that the New Archaeology's use of functionalist thought was naïve and outdated. In particular, Hodder criticized the environmental determinism of processualist research and pointed out that the systemic frameworks used in this research left no room for consideration of individuals, the real people of the past who were just as complex and in many ways unpredictable as people today. For Hodder and others, processual archaeology did not explain the great cultural diversity seen in the past and ignored instances of uniqueness in favor of homogenizing human behavior in the search for general laws. This critique would signal a movement that would take the postprocessualists down a path to bring "people" into the past, a change in theoretical focus toward a humanistic archaeology. In this line of reasoning, British archaeologist **Ruth Tringham** argued that archaeology's goal was to replace the "faceless blobs" of a systemic processual archaeology, where individuals did not matter, with narratives of actual people; people, who through their own decision-making (not just responding to predictable, law-like causal factors such as the environment), shaped the past.

The postprocessual critique continued, citing the New Archaeology's lack of focus on symbolic behavior and ideology, among other factors. Needless to say processual archaeologists did not take kindly to the criticism and fired back that the postprocessualists were moving the field back to a "non-scientific" archaeology that would result in speculative interpretations of the sort that, processualists argued, characterized the era of culture history. Further, processualists charged that the postprocessualist critique was just that; more critique than a proposal of an adequate alternative. In the beginning of the postprocessual movement, archaeologists were trying to find bodies of theory that fit their vision of how to approach the past and there was ample theoretical experimentation. Often, published works were heavy on the theoretical discussion and rather light on the application of theoretical frameworks to hard data; opening up room for criticism that postprocessualists could not demonstrate the scientific applicability of their ideas. Although the original theoretical frameworks explored by early postprocessual work tended to gravitate toward a combination of Marxism and structuralism, with the passing of the years postprocessualist frameworks began to crystalize around several areas and the question of lack of data was addressed. Yet, during the development of early postprocessualist thought it was increasingly apparent that a scientific archaeology involved subjective elements and that archaeological interpretation was impacted by the cultural contexts in which archaeologists live and worked. Objectivity, a cornerstone of Binford's work, was called into question.

FIGURE 4.11 Humanizing the people of the past has become an important goal of contemporary archaeological work, but can also be quite challenging (shown: relief of Assyrian warriors at Persepolis, Iran, ca. second half of the first-millennium BC).

© Anna Fevraleva/Shutterstock.com

Feminist Archaeology

Around the same time as Hodder began his critique of the New Archaeology, feminism and gender studies entered archaeological discourse. In North America, the first research under a feminist archaeology was focused on gender bias in the practice of American archaeology and interpretation of archaeological data. In particular, the "Man the Hunter" models of early human prehistory that presupposed that males undertook hunting activities, whereas females gathered and were responsible for childcare were found to have an **androcentric** (male-oriented) bias. Further studies demonstrated the inequalities between men and women in the field in terms of employment and access to research funding. These critiques quickly turned into a concerted search for women in the past, and then to nuanced considerations of gender in the past. In 1992, American archaeologist **Elizabeth Brumfiel** called for the study of gender, class, and factional affiliation in the past, emphasizing the point that archaeologists need to pay more attention to social diversity and identity to move beyond the "faceless blob" research of positivist systems theory. As the work of Brumfiel demonstrates, the impact of a feminist archaeology has spread beyond analyses of females/males in the past and has inspired work in many aspects of human diversity including studies of childhood, the body, and **queer theory**, which examines how interpretations of the past are shaped by heteronormative assumptions of those who practice archaeology.

Agency Theory

The concern for human behavioral diversity began to take more form under a body of theory termed **agency theory**, a framework which began to gain momentum in archaeology during the 1990s. Although there is ample debate as to what the term "agency" means, this framework generally conceptualizes humans having a complex knowledge of the context in which they live. Social rules exist and are understood, but can be manipulated. Importantly, people are conceptualized as not always being rational (regardless of whether this rationality is that of the archaeologist or of any person of the past being studied) and can act in unpredictable manners. Further, the actions taken by people may have consequences not intended by them. Yet, people do not live in a vacuum and can be influenced by the world

they live in. Agency theory accounts for this fact by conceptualizing human action as able to change the social structures and natural environments in which people live. In turn, these structures and environments influence human decision-making and action. In sum, this framework places the unit of analysis on peoples' decision-making and action. Rather than people only reacting to their environment like automatons, their actions are framed in the context of the social and natural context in which they lived.

Phenomenology

Another manifestation of postprocessual archaeology is **phenomenology**. A very humanistic form of archaeology, the application of phenomenology concerns the study of human experience in the past. In some sense, most if not all archaeologists have employed phenomenology. It is hard to resist the temptation to imagine what it would have been like to have actually lived in ancient times, inserted into the contexts researched by archaeologists. Phenomenology, however, takes this idea and makes it a central part of its research agenda. Past human experiences are explored to be able to learn about the attitudes, ideologies, and feelings that motivated the actions of ancient people.

Choosing Theoretical Frameworks

The landscape of interpretive frameworks in archaeology is quite complex today. There are lots of options to choose from and we could say that a modern archaeology is a pluralistic archaeology, with no one right way to perform research. Much like modern politics, there are some very clearly delineated theoretical camps with which certain researchers self-identify in publications and at conferences. Some people make no bones about being interpretive, cognitive, behavioral, or Darwinian archaeologists. Yet, also like modern politics, there are a lot of "independent voters" who pick and choose elements from particular theoretical frameworks and mix them together to, continuing with the analogy, construct their "platform" and explore the past. How do you know which framework or elements of frameworks is best for you? The only way to do this is to explore the different options and convince yourself that by moving forward with certain ideas that you can contribute in a meaningful way to a greater understanding of the past.

Bibliography

Barnard, Alan J. *History and Theory in Anthropology*. Cambridge: Cambridge University Press, 2000.

Barrett, John C., and I. Ko. "A Phenomenology of Landscape: A Crisis in British Field Archaeology?" *Journal of Social Archaeology* 9, no. 3 (2009): 275–294.

Binford, Lewis R. "Archaeology as Anthropology." *American Antiquity* 28 (1962): 217–225.

———"A Consideration of Archaeological Research Design." *American Antiquity* 29 (1964): 425–441.

———"Archaeological Systematics and the Study of Culture Process." *American Antiquity* 31 (1965): 203–210.

———"Smudge Pits and Hide Smoking: The Use of Analogy in Archaeological Reasoning." *American Antiquity* 32 (1967): 1–12.

———"Archaeological Perspectives." In *New Perspectives in Archaeology*, edited by S. R. Binford and L. R. Binford, 5–32. Chicago, IL: Aldine, 1968a.

———"Some Comments on Historical Versus Processual Archaeology." *Southwestern Journal of Anthropology* 24 (1968b): 267–275.

———*An Archaeological Perspective.* New York: Seminar Press, 1972.

———"In Pursuit of the Future." In *American Archaeology: Past and Future,* edited by D. J. Meltzer, J. A. Sabloff, and D. Fowler, 459–479. Washington, DC: Smithsonian Institution Press, 1986.

Blackmore, Chelsea. "How to Queer the Past without Sex: Queer Theory, Feminisms, and the Archaeology of Identity." *Archaeologies: Journal of the World Archaeological Congress* 7, no. 1 (2011): 75–96.

Broughton, Jack M., and James F. O'Connell. "On Evolutionary Ecology, Selectionist Archaeology, and Behavioral Archaeology." *American Antiquity* 64, no. 1 (1999): 153–165.

Brumfiel, Elizabeth M. "Distinguished Lecture in Anthropology: Breaking and Entering the Ecosystem—Gender, Class, and Faction Steal the Show." *American Anthropologist* 94 (1992): 551–567.

Childe, V. Gordon. *The Dawn of European Civilization.* London: Kegan Paul, 1925.

———*Skara Brae: A Pictish Village in Orkney.* London: Kegan Paul, 1931.

Clark, J. Grahame D. "The Economic Approach to Prehistory: Albert Reckitt Archaeological Lecture, 1953." *Proceedings of the British Academy* 39 (1953): 215–238.

Collingwood, Robin G. *An Autobiography.* Oxford: Oxford University Press, 1939.

Conkey, Margaret W., and J. Gero. "Programme to Practice: Gender and Feminism in Archaeology." *Annual Reviews of Anthropology* 26 (1997): 411–437.

Conkey, Margaret W., and Janet Spector. "Archaeology and the Study of Gender." In *Advances in Archaeological Method and Theory,* Vol. 7, edited by M. B. Schiffer, 1–38. New York: Academic Press, 1984.

Copi, Irving, Carl Cohen, and Daniel Flage. *Essentials of Logic.* 2nd ed. New York: Routledge, 2006.

Desroches, Dennis. *Francis Bacon and the Limits of Scientific Knowledge.* London: Continuum, 2006.

Dunnell, Robert C. "Evolutionary Theory in Archaeology." In *Advances in Archaeological Method and Theory,* Vol. 3, edited by M. B. Schiffer, 35–99. New York: Academic Press, 1980.

Earle, Timothy K., and Robert W. Preucel. "Processual Archaeology and the Radical Critique." *Current Anthropology* 28 (1987): 501–538.

Flannery, Kent V. "Culture History v. Cultural Process: A Debate in American Archaeology." In *Contemporary Archaeology,* edited by M. P. Leone, 102–107. Carbondale, IL: Southern Illinois University Press, 1967.

———"Archaeological Systems Theory and Early Mesoamerica." In *Anthropological Archaeology in the Americas,* edited by B. J. Meggers, 67–87. Washington, DC: Anthropological Society of Washington, 1968.

———"The Cultural Evolution of Civilizations." *Annual Review of Ecology and Systematics* 3 (1972): 399–426.

Ford, James A., and Gordon R. Willey. "An Interpretation of the Prehistory of the Eastern United States." *American Anthropologist* 43 (1941): 325–363.

Johnson, C. David, Timothy A. Kohler, and Jason Cowan. "Modeling Historical Ecology, Thinking about Contemporary Systems." *American Anthropologist* 107 (2005): 96–107.

Harris, Marvin. *The Rise of Anthropological Theory.* New York: Harper Collins, 1968.

Hodder, Ian. *The Present Past: An Introduction to Anthropology for Archaeologists.* London: B.T. Batsford, 1982a.

————"Theoretical Archaeology: A Reactionary View." In *Symbolic and Structural Archaeology*, edited by I. Hodder, 1–16. Cambridge: Cambridge University Press, 1982b.

————"Interpretive Archaeology and Its Role." *American Antiquity* 56 (1991): 7–18.

Hodder, Ian, and Scott R. Hutson. *Reading the Past: Current Approaches to Interpretation in Archaeology*. 3rd ed. Cambridge: Cambridge University Press, 2003.

Hodder, Ian, Michael Shanks, A. Alexandri, V. Buchli, John Carman, J. Last, and G. Lucas. *Interpreting Archaeology: Finding Meaning in the Past*. London: Routledge, 1995.

Kidder, Alfred V. *An Introduction to the Study of Southwestern Archaeology*. Papers of the Southwestern Expedition, No. 1. New Haven, CT: Philips Academy, 1924.

Kohler, Timothy A., and Sander van der Leeuw, eds. *Model-Based Archaeology of Socionatural Systems*. Santa Fe: SAR Press, 2007.

Kroeber, Alfred L. "Cultural and Natural Areas of Native North America." *UCPAAE* 38 (1939): 1–12, 1–242.

LaMotta, V. M., and Michael B. Schiffer. "Behavioral Archaeology: Toward a New Synthesis." In *Archaeological Theory Today*, edited by I. Hodder, 14–64. Cambridge: Polity Press, 2001.

Lyman, R. Lee, and Michael, J. O'Brien. "The Goals of Evolutionary Archaeology: History and Explanation." *Current Anthropology* 39 (1998): 515–562.

Meltzer, David J. "Paradigms and the Nature of Change in American Archaeology." *American Antiquity* 44 (1979): 644–57.

O'Brien, Michael J., R. Lee Lyman, and Michael B. Schiffer. *Archaeology as a Process: Processualism and Its Progeny*. Salt Lake City, UT: University of Utah Press, 2005.

Patterson, Thomas C. "History and the Post-Processual Archaeologies." *Man* 24 (1989): 555–566.

Patterson, Thomas C. *A Social History of Anthropology in the United States*. Berg Publishers Oxford, NY, 2001.

Petrie, W. M. Flinders. *The Palace of Apries (Memphis II)*. London: School of Archaeology in Egypt, 1909.

Plog, Fred T. "Systems Theory in Archaeological Research." *Annual Review of Anthropology* 4 (1975): 207–224.

Preucel, Robert W. "The Post-Processual Condition." *Journal of Archaeological Research* 28 (1995): 147–175.

Redman, Charles L. "Resilience Theory in Archaeology." *American Anthropologist* 107, no. 1 (2005): 70–77.

Renfrew, Colin. "Towards a Cognitive Archaeology." In *The Ancient Mind: Elements of a Cognitive Archaeology*, edited by C. Renfrew, 3–12. Cambridge: Cambridge University Press, 1994.

Salmon, Merilee. "What Can Systems Theory do for Archaeology?" *American Antiquity* 43, no. 2 (1978): 173–184.

Schiffer, Michael B. "Archaeological Context and Systemic Context." *American Antiquity* 37, no. 2 (1972): 156–165.

————*Behavioral Archaeology*. New York: Academic Press, 1976.

————*Formation Processes of the Archaeological Record*. New Mexico, NM: University of New Mexico Press, 1987.

————*Behavioral Archaeology: First Principles*. Salt Lake City, UT: University of Utah Press, 1995.

Shanks, Michael, and Christopher Tilley. *Social Theory and Archaeology*. Albuquerque, NM: University of New Mexico Press, 1987.

————*Re-Constructing Archaeology*. London: Routledge, 1987.

Sherratt, Andrew. "Cups that Cheered." In *Bell Beakers of the Western Mediterranean: Definition, Interpretation, Theory, and New Site Data: The Oxford International Conference 1986, Part I*, edited by W. H. Waldren and R. C. Kennard, 81–114. BAR Intrernational Series 331(i). Oxford: British Archaeological Reports, 1987.

Smith, G. Elliot. *The Diffusion of Culture*. London: Watts & Co, 1933.

Steward, Julian H. "Cultural Causality and Law: A Trial Formulation of the Development of Early Civilizations." *American Anthropologist* 51 (1, 1949.): 1–27.

Steward, Julian H., and Frank M. Setzler. "Function and Configuration in Archaeology." *American Antiquity* 4 (1938): 4–10.

Taylor, Walter W. "A Study of Archaeology." *American Anthropologist* 50, no. 3 (Part 2, 1948): 69 Memoirs of the American Anthropological Association.

Thompson, Raymond. "The Subjective Element in Archaeological Inference." *Southwestern Journal of Anthropology* 12 (1956): 322–327.

Tilley, Christopher. *A Phenomenology of Landscape: Places, Paths, and Monuments*. Oxford: Berg, 1994.

————*Interpretative Archaeology*. Oxford: Berg, 1993.

Trigger, Bruce G. *A History of Archaeological Thought*. 2nd ed. Cambridge: Cambridge University Press, 2006.

Watson, Patty J., Stephen LeBlanc, and Charles L. Redman. *Explanation in Archaeology: An Explicitly Scientific Approach*, 3–57. New York: Columbia University Press, 1971.

White, Leslie A. *The Evolution of Culture: The Development of Civilization to the Fall of Rome*. New York: McGraw-Hill, 1959.

Willey, Gordon R. *Prehistoric Settlement Patterns in the Viru Valley, Peru*. Washington, DC: Bulletin 155, Bureau of American Ethnology, 1953.

Winterhalder, Bruce. "Optimal Foraging Strategies and Hunter-Gatherer Research in Anthropology: Theory and Methods." In *Hunter-Gatherer Foraging Strategies*, edited by B. Winterhalder and E. A. Smith, 13–35. Chicago: University of Chicago Press, 1981.

Winterhalder, Bruce, and Eric A. Smith. "Evolutionary Ecology and the Social Sciences." In *Evolutionary Ecology and Human Behavior*, edited by E. A. Smith and B. Winterhalder, 3–23. New York: Aldine de Gruyter, 1992.

Starting a Project

So now you are ready to get your project together. You have chosen archaeology as a profession and it is time to get to work. Where do you start? What sort of plans do you have to draw up to get into the field or laboratory and perform research? As we discussed in Chapter 1, with any solid scientific research, the beginning always starts with a question. Archaeologists performing research today do not just go out and "dig" to see what they will find. They collect information based on how they think those data may help them to answer specific questions. These questions guide the research. In this chapter, we explain how archaeologists design their research strategy prior to conducting any work in the field and laboratory, how they get from the question to actually attempting to find answers. The details of archaeologists' strategies may vary greatly from project to project, but the overall structure remains fairly consistent. To be a professional archaeologist, you must employ such a structure to be successful.

Research Design

Research design is the means that directly lead archaeologists to gather and examine specific data in order to resolve their questions. But returning to the above discussion, why is it so important to start out with questions? Imagine, for example, that you are tasked to draw a map of your classroom for ten minutes. If you do not have a question that addresses what you want to know about the classroom, you might have trouble creating a map that helps you know something specific about the space in the future. Having a question in mind from the beginning helps guide the drawing process that will help to answer a question about the classroom when you are no longer there. For instance, if your question addresses the maximum capacity of accommodating students in the classroom, you might draw chairs on a map or pay close attention to the dimensions of the space. If you want to know something concerning the technological capacity of the classroom, you might focus on computer devices, lighting system, and projectors rather than chairs and dimensions. Yet, in these cases you might ignore graffiti on tables attached to student chairs because of limited resources (in this case time to draw). Such scribbles, however, would provide insight to a question focused on students' attitudes in the classroom. The questions help guide the data collection process (and analysis) to ensure that you will collect the data that are really pertinent to what interests you. In archaeology, this targeting of useful data is important for several reasons. First, archaeological research is expensive and time-consuming. To maximize resources and time in a productive way, data pertinent to questions should be gathered. Second, archaeological research is often destructive. Collecting data is simply not ethical if the resulting destruction does little to push further our understanding of that culture.

Research designs may vary given the nature of the project and destruction may even be inevitable. For instance, cultural resource management (CRM) projects are often designed to assess the importance of archaeological data with the intent to preserve and/or recover those data under threat of disturbance or destruction from development (see also Chapter 2). In contrast, academic research usually focuses on long-standing questions such as people's engagement in the building of monumental architecture, the processes behind the shift from a mobile to a sedentary lifestyle, and the origins of social inequality, among others. It is to answer questions such as these that archaeologists need to collect and systematically analyze relevant data. The analysis of data allows archaeologists to interpret the phenomenon they observed, and therefore informs their question. We call this process **problem-oriented research**, which can be divided into nine steps: (a) previous research; (b) formulation and sampling; (c) permission and funding; (d) building an archaeological team; (e) logistics, camp, and provisions; (f) data collection; (g) data processing and analysis; (h) interpretation; and (i) dissemination. In this chapter, we focus on steps a to e and you will find the other four steps in the following chapters.

Previous Research

So once you have your question, where do you start? To make a long-standing question testable, archaeologists conduct background research. It is prudent to learn as much about the area of research as possible to be able to frame your study well. In some cases, the question that is of interest may have already been adequately addressed by previous research and there is no need to repeat the study. You *need* to know this before embarking on research. Although archaeology is a relatively recent profession,

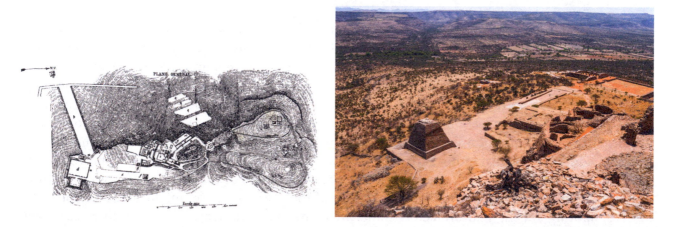

FIGURE 5.1 Archaeologists should always review the previous research in the area where they are working, which in some cases can stretch back several centuries. Here, we see map of La Quemada, Mexico, by Batres (1903) juxtaposed with a modern photo of the site that shows the results of restoration work performed by more recent projects. Future work at this site in northern Mexico will have to contemplate the impacts and interpretations of these previous projects.

Source: Batres Plan image circa 1903.

archaeologists have carried out scientific research around the world over the last century and it is likely that there is at least a regional base of work from which to draw; from basic studies of material chronologies to more sophisticated research along your lines of interest. In cases where this previous work has addressed the question you are interested in, it is often the case that you can reformulate the question to go even further than earlier studies. In fact, the more problem-oriented research that is conducted, the more questions arise; contrary to the belief of some, in many ways archaeologists have barely scratched the surface of the past and new questions are constantly being generated as research advances. If the results of previous archaeological work are published, they are accessible through libraries, bookstores, online journals, or Internet sources. Recently, scholars tend to upload their publications to sites such as *academia.edu* or other social networking websites. However, not all results are accessible to the public and not all information on the Internet is reliable. Some results, including those from CRM, are only accessible through contacting local archaeological institutes or museums where special permissions are necessary.

FIGURE 5.2 Archaeologists and students converting old maps to digital form at the Eastern Information Center of the University of California Riverside, one of several data repositories in the state. Such centers make large quantities of data available to researchers.

Source: Travis Stanton

Yet, it is not only previous archaeological work that should be included in a review of the literature. Archaeologists should review other areas of research that may pertain to their question including geography, geology, history, ethnohistory, environmental science, and biology, as well as theoretical frameworks and methodologies that will help them guide their research designs. Archaeology is inherently multidisciplinary and the research undertaken in many different fields proves essential for answering questions. Archaeologists must command this literature to perform innovative and informed research.

For example, historical documents are direct resources that narrate the local past in the area. They are one of the most powerful resources we can have access to perspectives of ancient people and can even inform us of periods prior to the existence of writing. We do, however, have to be careful with historic documents as they inform us of only certain literate perspectives on the past. A vast majority of people in the area might not have had the ability or opportunity to write about their perspectives, and in many cases socially, politically, and economically powerful people were the only ones who could write and preserve their vision of the world. Moreover, writing systems are a relatively recent invention that does not go back beyond 6,000 years ago in even the earliest contexts. And, some peoples around the world did not use writing until quite recently.

Historical documents can also be important for understanding the formation process of archaeological sites, even when the stories they tell come from much later contexts. Knowing that an archaeological site was exposed to mechanized agriculture in the early twentieth century or was the site of nineteenth-century battle might help to better understand the spatial distribution and preservation of artifacts and features dating to much earlier times. Even understanding previous archaeological work can help to clarify patterns in the data you collect. For example, researchers in Guatemala found high levels of iron in soil tests at the ancient city of Ceibal. This discovery led the team to think about what ancient activities could have produced this pattern before realizing that the iron was due to the small shavings from the sharpening of machetes used by their own crew to clear the buildings of brush in previous field seasons. Thus, knowing land use in more recent years can be important even when you are working on periods hundreds or even thousands of years prior to the existence of written history in an area. Archaeological sites are not static and not all of the material patterns you might identify date to the period of time being researched.

A curious thing about written histories is that their existence often divides archaeologists into groups, even though archaeologists focus on the material record for their research. Some who work in contexts with absolutely no writing systems clearly identify themselves as prehistoric archaeologists while others who work more towards the modern age, especially in the last few centuries in contexts where writing systems were more extensive, explicitly identify themselves as historic archaeologists. Many researchers, however, fall into a gray area between prehistory and history. For example, some ancient writing systems, such as ancient Zapotec (Mexico) and the Linear A script of Minoan civilization, are for the most part not yet deciphered and archaeologists focused on these societies are essentially working contexts without a known history. In other contexts, such as Classic Maya and ancient Egyptian societies, where writing systems existed and are in large part legible to scholars today, writing was not utilized with the same frequency by different communities or has not preserved well enough at all sites to shed light on historical data evenly. Although epigraphers can read Classic Mayan or Egyptian hieroglyphs, archaeologists working in rural areas and even some large cities do not recover such data and are working in contexts without local histories. In the end, though, when evidence of writing is recovered at archaeological sites, it provides a valuable source of material data that can help to interpret human behavior in the past.

FIGURE 5.3 A Minoan Linear A clay tablet (ca. second-millennium BC) (left) and a Classic period hieroglyphic text from the site of El Palmar, Mexico (right) (AD 820).

Source: Kenichiro Tsukamoto

Clay tablets with Linear A writing/De Agostini Picture Library/G. Nimatallah/Bridgeman Images

Oral histories are also important resources for archaeologists. Oral histories transmit the past events, beliefs, legends, myths, values, norms, and morals of a social group from generation to generation through the narration of stories. One successful example of the integration of oral histories in archaeological research is the San Pedro Ethnohistory Project, directed by Colwell-Chanthaphonh and Ferguson. These researchers have collaborated with official representatives of four tribal governments in Arizona, comparing and contrasting the archaeological record to tribal oral histories. The results have enriched the reconstruction of San Pedro history, which embraced scientific results with indigenous perspectives.

Ethnohistory, the study of indigenous people through historical records and ethnographic data, is another related area that should be researched at the beginning of a project. A critical difference between history and ethnohistory is that the latter approach focuses on people who have historically been ignored. One of the aims for archaeological research is to retrieve voices of social actors who were marginalized in a community. For this reason, archaeologists often use documents written during colonial periods, although ethnohistorical resources are not limited to these contexts.

Moving beyond historical sources, background research into local **geography** is an essential part of archaeological work as it reveals the surface conditions in which the past people explored available resources and how they adapted, modified, managed, and interacted with natural environment. Local geography does not determine human activities, but often guides and constrains them. Similar to the local geography, the study of **geology** provides information on the evolutionary history of the area and local sources, especially the formation of rocks (igneous, sedimentary, and metamorphic) and sediments. Over the course of millions of years of human existence, people relied on the exploration of geological formations as principal natural sources, especially for lithic (stone) tools, ceramic vessels (clays and inclusions or tempers), ores for metals, and architectural materials such as the rocks used to build the pyramids of Egypt and the sediments used to make adobe bricks in the American Southwest. The formation processes of sediments also impacted agricultural practices as well as craft production in the past. For example, the distribution of archaeological sites for the Bell-Beaker culture mentioned in Chapter 4 tends to correlate with the distribution of loess soils (windblown silts good for agriculture) and near water in valley floors and plains leading archaeologists to postulate

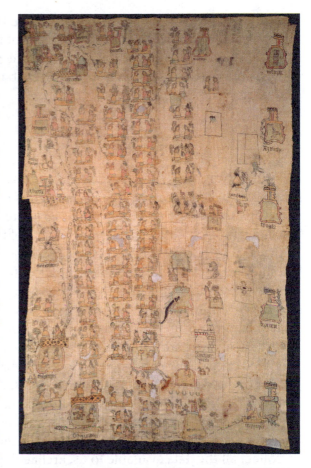

FIGURE 5.4 Ethnohistoric documents such as the sixteenth-century AD Lienzo of Ihuitlan (shown here), an indigenous pictographic document from central Mexico, can provide important information about the past. In particular, documents like this *lienzo* provide indigenous perspectives on periods of time often dominated by imperialistic and colonial histories. Researching nondominant or nonimperial views of history is important when such data exist.

Lienzo of Ihuitlan (ink on cotton), Mexican School/Brooklyn Museum of Art, New York, USA/Carll H. de Silver Fund/Bridgeman Images

that the Bell-Beaker phenomenon was related to the introduction of an agricultural lifestyle at this time. Geological processes are also important for understanding the formation processes of archaeological sites and the landscapes people in the past inhabited. Geological studies can inform archaeologists of questions such as how sites were buried and how and why material culture is distributed and preserved.

Formulation and Sampling

Once the background investigation is done, the initial idea for the research needs to be formulated into a testable question or a research problem. In so doing, the theoretical frameworks you have chosen will help you to generate a specific hypothesis (or prediction) and guide the research strategy. As we have seen in Chapters 3 and 4, there are a wide variety of theoretical frameworks that can be employed to explain both social and natural phenomenon. Background research narrows your initial idea down to a concrete question within specific temporal and spatial frameworks. Theoretical frameworks, in turn, help to give you a prediction, formulating a hypothesis or hypotheses from your specific question in a logical manner. The hypothesis may change and new hypotheses may emerge as the research is actually carried out in the field or laboratory; and that is just fine. At that moment, the research strategy will also need to be refined. Well-designed research, however, retains the course of the overall research, even if the field strategy is modified once the work has begun. So then, what is the next step in formulating the research strategy?

A good place to start is to think about a **sampling strategy**, choosing to collect and analyze a set of the potential data available to you. Returning to the example of classroom mapping mentioned earlier, we explained that archaeologists are not able to gather all the data at an archaeological site because the universe of potential data is immense. Yet, even if we had enough time and resources to collect all the data available to us, archaeological research is often destructive and we should preserve undisturbed areas for future generations of researchers who might be able to revisit primary data in the field with new methods, technologies, and questions. If we destroy all archaeological contexts with our research, those opportunities will not be available to future archaeologists.

The entire set of potential data available for archaeologists to collect and analyze is termed a **population** (also called a data universe). The population may be something like all of the lithic tools from a single site or all of the settlements from across a region. Based on the questions archaeologists have and the research strategies they employ to find the answers, populations of potential data are defined. To take a look at a subset of those data, archaeologists use a research strategy called sampling. **Sampling** is a way of extracting a subset of elements from the population in order to make inferences about the entire population. The idea behind sampling is that you pick a part of something to make inferences about the whole, assuming that the smaller subset is reflective of the whole. For example, if you have a forest of a million trees and you only have time to classify a thousand in the field, you should employ a sampling strategy that you believe will give you a **representative sample** of the trees in the forest; thus the numbers of elms you count in the sample of a thousand should hopefully represent the percentage of elms in the entire forest.

Sampling Strategies

Sampling strategy is a crucial step to formulate your research in a realistic way. As previous research avoids repeating the same questions archaeologists have already tested many times, sampling strategy helps you avoid spending your time and money for unnecessary data gathering. The goal of the sampling strategy is to maximize the collection of archaeological data for the minimum cost.

Further, to address research questions, we need to measure variables. A variable is a characteristic that varies with a population. For example, people vary in height, weight, running speed, and so on. Ceramic vessels vary in color, form, and size, among other attributes. Settlements can vary from small hamlets to large cities. So, before understanding different sampling strategies, archaeologists need to understand the different types of variables that exist in the world and how they pertain to their data. Data can be organized in the following manners.

a. **Nominal**: Descriptive categories (e.g., cat, dog, ceramic types), which cannot be ordered (e.g., we cannot say that cat is ordered before dog).
b. **Ordinal**: Ranked data, which tell us the order in which they occurred (e.g., small, medium, large), although these data do not indicate the differences between values (e.g., a small vessel is three times bigger than a medium vessel).
c. **Interval**: Continuous data without true zero (calendar dates: 300 BC or AD 200, Celsius temperature, elevation). Data at this level can be useful for statistical analyses.
d. **Ratio**: Continuous data with true zero (weight: 20, 40, 0.5, 3, etc., Kelvin temperature). These are essential data for quantitative analyses.

Keeping different kinds of data in mind, we can return to the point that the choice of sampling strategies depends on your research questions. In archaeology, the first step in sampling is to define your research area within a spatial and temporal framework. The spatial scale of the research area (e.g., a single trash deposit, room, site, or region) as well as the temporal frame (e.g., 10, 100, 1,000 years, the range of time the data pertain to) will help define the population. Sampling, however, happens in the present; a single time frame. Regardless of whether data date to 100 or 1,000 years ago, your collection of those data will happen in a small slice of modern time. Thus, sampling has more of a spatial component in fieldwork settings and we divide study areas into spatial **units** to organize the collection of data in the field.

There are two ways of dividing the spatial units: nonarbitrary or arbitrary. **Nonarbitrary** units are a division of natural or cultural boundaries. Natural boundaries are features like rivers, lakes, escarpments, mountains, and other environmental zones. Cultural boundaries include data like rooms, walls, houses, sites, polities, or states. **Arbitrary** units are artificial boundaries that archaeologists determine based on a specific criterion. A common arbitrary unit in the field is a **grid system** that divides the study area into equal-size squares (also called quadrats). We call each square a sampling unit. The size of each quadrat depends on the size of the target area. If the study area is a structure, a 1.0 m × 1.0 m or 2.0 m × 2.0 m square is often used as a unit of study. If the study area is a site, we might project a 100 m × 100 m or bigger grid on a map. If the goal of research is to find sites in a large region, a 500 m × 500 m would be a realistic size. **Geographical coordinates** (a cross point of coordinates) and **transects** (parallel corridor of certain width) are also used as arbitrary units. For extensive study areas such as a large area between two sites, a transect is preferable to a grid system because it is easier to walk in a corridor than to locate a specific part of a square. On the other hand, a grid system is useful for plotting artifact densities by using relative coordinates beginning from the southwest corner of each square. In the laboratory, we convert these relative coordinates into Universal Transverse Mercator (UTM), which is a two-dimensional Cartesian coordinate system, dividing the surface of the earth into sixty zones. In practice, archaeologists often situate transects in a grid system, covering long distances, but recording the provenience (location) of material data in squares or in reference to UTM coordinates with elevation data (masl, meters above sea level). For systematic ground surveys and excavations, arbitrary units are often employed, whereas nonarbitrary units are useful for reconnaissance. A great advantage of arbitrary units is its comparability. All data gathered from sample units are comparable because the units are divided equally in size and shape.

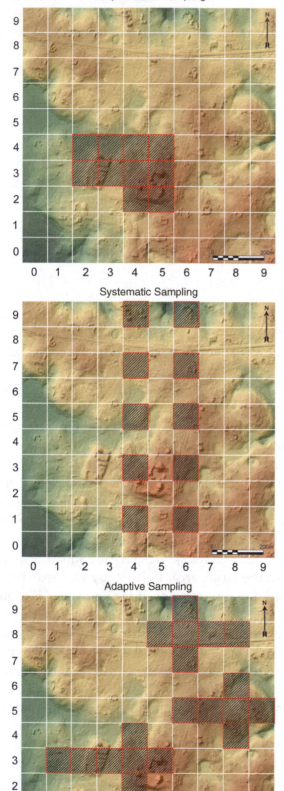

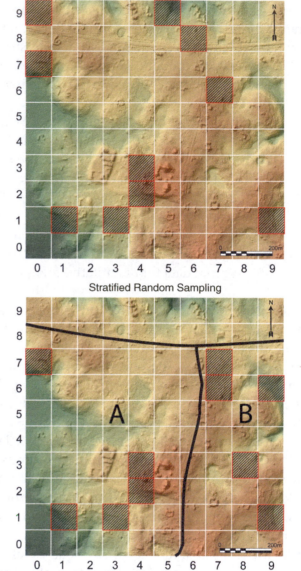

FIGURE 5.5 Five different sampling methods shown over a LiDAR image of El Palmar, Mexico. Note that the locations of simple random sampling are determined by the random number table (Table 5.1) and it covers ten percent of the total survey area.

Source: Kenichiro Tsukamoto

Although sampling is often used by archaeologists to collect data in the field through survey, surface collection, and excavation, it is also employed in the analysis of data after fieldwork has ended. For example, a project may have found millions of fragments of pottery in excavations. Although all of these data may be subjected to basic macroscopic analysis, more expensive and/or time consuming specialized studies such as chemical composition analyses may have to be run on a smaller sample of the total data collected. So, the archaeologist may sample only one hundred pieces of pottery to perform this analysis. It is important to note that large sampling fractions do not always reflect the entire population. A good example is national censuses, which make inferences about the sociopolitical opinions of the entire population through a sample of less than 1 percent of people who live in the country. Because researchers can carefully focus on a smaller sample, the result is often more reliable and precision than that of studying millions of millions of opinions that individually cannot be treated with greater care. Although the spatial units used in the collection of these data may figure into the sampling method, they do not necessarily have to be taken into consideration and the nonspatial elements, such as the presence or absence of particular decorative elements, may take precedence.

Regardless of the use of spatial data in sampling, one question that archaeologists face is how to obtain a sample that accurately represents the entire population and how we can identify the range of errors our sample may reflect. In order to confront these issues, archaeologists employ sampling strategies from statistics. We can broadly divide these strategies into two approaches: nonprobabilistic and probabilistic sampling techniques.

Nonprobabilistic sampling uses prior information such as local informants, maps, previous archaeological research, and aerial and satellite images to guide the collection and analysis of data. The idea here is that you may already have some information as to where to sample in order to answer your questions. If previous archaeological research indicates that sites are often located near bodies of water, then you might want to focus your survey near lakes and rivers. If you are interested in how decorative symbols on pottery transmitted certain messages to a population, you would want to focus analysis on decorated pottery and leave the plain pottery out of the more intensive analyses. If you have an aerial photo that clearly shows the location of archaeological sites or a local informant who knows where sites are, you may want to let that information guide your research. Archaeologists often use their own judgement regarding this kind of information, including their own experiences, to guide the sampling process (**judgmental sampling**), which accelerates data gathering. Nevertheless, the selection of data for collection and analysis through the judgmental sampling is intentionally biased and therefore the results are detached from the population, meaning that there is no way of defining whether or not our sample represents the population. Although nonprobabilistic sampling is useful for a new research area where archaeologists had never investigated, probabilistic sampling or the combination of both sampling methods are often more useful for problem-oriented research.

Probabilistic sampling is based on statistical criteria that enable archaeologists to evaluate how close a sample represents the population; the total number of units selected for research is called the **sample size**. Probabilistic sampling was introduced into archaeological practice on a full scale in the 1960s through the advent of New Archaeology (Chapter 4). Archaeologists need to identify an ideal sample size according to the population they seek, so that we can make inferences about the population. A key sampling method is employed to maximize the chance that it accurately represents the population under study. **Random sampling** is an effective way to maximize the chance of accuracy because it eliminates any selection bias and the results of randomization can be expected to have normal distribution. Random sampling is based on a rigorous method in which each unit has an equal chance for selection. There are five probabilistic sampling methods that archaeologists usually employ: simple random, systematic random, stratified random, cluster, and adaptive. We will use the example of a spatial grid to illustrate our points concerning sampling, although it must be remembered that these sampling methods can be applied in nonspatial ways to data (e.g., the ceramic example used previously).

Simple random sampling is the most basic way of defining sample units based on a table of random numbers (Table 5.1) or a computer program. The sampling units in the population are numbered in sequence. For example, you set a grid over your research area such as a site or a region, and then number the row and column in each grid square, specifying a starting point in a corner of the whole grid. In this case, you have two numbers (one from the row and the other from the column). When using the random number table, you should close your eyes and touch the table with your index finger. Then you open your eyes and look at what number your finger touches. The number your finger points is used for a starting point and then follow the consecutive numbers reading in either direction of column or row of the table. If your finger points the number 43, which is located at the eighth column from left to right and the fourth row from top to bottom in the table, for example, you select a grid square located in the fourth column from left to right and the sixth row from bottom to top (remember, horizontal coordinates are usually measured from southwest to northeast corner of the grid). Then, you can continue from left to right, which is 68, 42, 68, 59, and so on, in the table, or from top to bottom, which is 09, 30, 28, 73, and so on. If you find the number that you do not have in your grid square, you can ignore that number. Each time you use the table for different sampling areas, you must use a different starting point and should never use the same sequence of random numbers twice. In this method, each sample unit in your data can have an equal chance of selection, and therefore the result provides you with your best chance of obtaining a sample that accurately represents the population.

TABLE 5.1 Random number table.

16	41	58	17	48	58	52	52	12	26
47	74	34	66	56	05	29	54	04	23
31	57	00	41	21	27	49	34	04	34
62	51	14	17	34	07	69	43	68	42
68	59	31	19	31	07	11	09	76	17
19	58	73	05	22	78	48	30	35	03
16	40	51	69	66	63	05	28	04	09
27	13	75	52	76	12	35	73	72	43
44	15	31	70	75	60	07	09	01	14
74	79	59	24	74	16	77	20	56	47
03	72	71	02	59	02	28	14	40	42
79	48	57	14	22	49	54	11	50	70
34	55	55	41	19	44	76	78	67	65
76	57	67	33	29	32	51	30	79	05
41	41	60	04	68	41	26	33	05	69

A simple random is a reliable sampling strategy, but the application in archaeological research is often problematic. When documenting sites based on a grid system over an extensive region during fieldwork, some of the sample units selected from a random table are, in many cases, not accessible because of several reasons. The sample units may be on private lands that you may not have obtained permission from the landowners to enter, areas that modern construction projects have completely destroyed, or located in accessible places such as cliff. When one of the sample units is avoided, this violates the fundamental principle of the simple random sampling. We may exclude these problematic units from the beginning of sampling units, but this alters the population.

Systematic sampling is an application of a simple random sampling. You select the first unit based on a random number table and then choose subsequent units following equal intervals from the first one (e.g., every other unit, every fifth unit, and so on). This sampling strategy facilitates data collection from units in a certain spatial or other distance (e.g., every fifth artifact taken out of a bag). In some cases, systematic sampling is combining with transects. For example, mapping of a large city may focus on transects of a particular width emanating from a central point off, often in cardinal directions. Transects may also be parallel such as rows of transects 500 m wide spaced 4 km apart. What unites these sampling methods is that they are operationalized in a systematic manner. This systemization ensures some degree of even coverage of the population. One problem, however, is if some data (let's say granaries) are distributed in equal intervals, you may hit them in every one of your units or not find them at all, if they are, using the example above, spaced every 4 km. For instance, in Classic Maya society stone benches are often located in rooms. If the site you are working at has benches located in an interval of every other room, your systematic sampling in the interval of every other room could hit all the benches or none of them. Of course, your interpretation about structures and the use of benches will be quite different depending on which room you started with. Theoretically, the systematic sampling has a sample size of only one because only the first unit in the sample is randomly selected. Therefore, it is impossible to estimate representativeness of the sample in the population (a confidence of interval) in the sample.

Stratified random sampling is applicable when the population has the range of variation that appears to be important for our research. We divide the variation into subgroups as if each subgroup was an independent population and select a separate sample of elements from each of the subgroups. Once subgroups are defined, a random sampling is applied. All samples from the subgroups are later combined to make inferences about the original population. How can we apply for stratified random sampling in archaeological research? A common example is a regional survey. Let us say that you have a project in a desert area with a river running through it, like the Nile Valley in Egypt. You know from previous research that the majority of the sites will be located within just a couple of kilometers of the river's edge and you want to concentrate your efforts there. You also know, however, that some sites, such as stone quarries, mines, and cemeteries, are often located farther out into the desert environment. You also do not want to omit the possibility of finding these sites, but do not want to commit too many resources in an area where you have less of a chance of coming across a site. Thus, you might employ stratified random sampling. In this scenario, you might divide the study region into river and desert areas and randomly place 80 percent of your units in the river area of greater interest and only 20 percent of your units in the desert area. This way you can prioritize some areas of the population and also ensure that each area will receive some degree of coverage; in a simple random sample it could be possible for all of the units to be randomly selected in just one of the two areas of interest.

Cluster sampling is a method sometimes employed by archaeologists to confront certain logistical challenges caused by the organization of material data once it has been collected. In many cases, sampling in archaeological research is spatially based sampling. For example, you may have recovered 100,000 ceramic sherds from 200 grid squares (or excavation units) at a site. If you use a simple random sampling for ceramic analysis, you have to number all the sherds one by one from different excavation units. In practical terms, performing this work is time consuming because you have to open all the boxes or bags, which are separated by excavation units and then line all the sherds up. The cluster sampling is a way of saving your time and money, increasing the number of sherds you can analyze. In the cluster sampling, you select randomly excavated units and then analyze sherds using a simple random sampling in each unit. Of course, we cannot cover all the excavated units and this method results in greater sampling errors than simple random sampling, but in many cases such practical concerns are important for archaeological research.

Adaptive sampling is the procedure to modify sampling designs through values obtained in the sample. The best way to understand this sampling method is to use it with an example. First, you use a simple random sampling in your study area divided by a grid system. The result shows that you found archaeological features in six of a hundred grid-based units. Then, you select these six units as starting points and select every adjacent unit, left, right, above, and below of each unit, as subsequent sampling units. If some of these units detect a feature or features, then you continue expanding the sample units until you do not find features in a subsequent unit. A cluster of units that contain features is called a **network** and adjacent units of the cluster that do not have features define the network size. This sampling strategy greatly improves the precision of estimates.

Permission and Funding

Usually, at the stage that the archaeologist has finished elaborating the research design and can begin to discuss in detail what questions are of interest and how those questions can be answered, a concerted effort to raise funding for the project and obtain permissions for work must be made. Archaeological work is usually quite costly, although the amount of funding required can vary considerably. An archaeologist working a couple of kilometers from their home, and using a few student volunteers, may not have need a large amount of funding to conduct survey and excavations, especially if the scale of this work is rather modest. Yet, some projects require international travel, lodging, food, and staff salary, as well as a host of costs related to conservation and analysis. And, the scale of some of these projects in terms of the number people working for them and their duration in the field and laboratory each year can necessitate very large budgets. Since most archaeologists do not pay for this research out of their own pockets, where will you find the funding?

In the case of CRM and government contracts, each agency issuing the contract has its own mission and they provide the necessary funding for the research. In many of problem-oriented investigations, however, the principal investigators (PIs) of the project are responsible for obtaining funds themselves. The sources of funds can be divided into public and private sector categories. Public funds usually include competitive, peer-reviewed programs, whereby the PIs submit a proposal that specifies research objectives and goals, previous research, theoretical and methodological approaches, significance of the proposed project, broader impacts, and itemized budgets. The proposals are reviewed by a group of archaeologists familiar with the type of research proposed and a committee decides which proposals are funded based in large part on the comments by the committees. In the United States, public funding agencies that support archaeological research include the **National Science Foundation** (NSF) and **the National Endowment for the Humanities** (NEH).

Archaeologists often receive funds from the private sector as well. In many cases, these funding agencies are foundations that have similar competitive, peer-reviewed proposal processes as public funding sources. Examples of such foundations include the Wenner-Gren Foundation and the National Geographic Society. The level of competition and the amount of detail expected in the proposals for such grants can vary. It is also important to consider the type of research that these foundations fund, which may have restrictions to particular types of research questions or geographic areas. Funding from private donors is also not uncommon in archaeology. Some people have a great appreciation for archaeological research and are willing support research. Finding such donors, however, can be a challenge, although the benefits can be enormous if a donor commits to support long-term investigation.

Other than funding, the archaeologist must also ensure that any permits required are in place before starting fieldwork. In general, government agencies and/or landowners hold authority, but the situation varies from country to country and archaeologists must be aware of the laws that regulate archaeological work in each specific context. At one level, archaeological work requires permits from governmental agencies, which in many cases require similar proposals for fieldwork as those submitted to granting agencies. In the United States, archaeological work is regulated through federal laws and state statutes in all the states. In some other countries, such as Mexico and Guatemala, archaeologists must obtain permits from governmental institutes before the start of any fieldwork, regardless of whether the research area is owned by the government or a private landowner. In some other countries, no permits are required from the government if the research area is not on state-owned property. Additionally, few countries allow the removal of artifacts outside the country, sometimes necessary for specialized analyses, without special permits issued by government. Yet, just because an archaeologist has the proper governmental permits does not ensure that fieldwork will take place. If the research area is, even in part, on private or communally held lands, permission for work must be obtained from landowners. Some landowners are very excited about archaeological research on their lands and others are steadfast against it, for many different reasons. Working with landowners and communities can be both rewarding and challenging, but, as discussed in Chapter 2, an effort to engage local stakeholders in research should be made and permissions for fieldwork on their lands must always be granted prior to starting work.

Building an Archaeological Team

Archaeological research is a collaborative work and you will need to assemble a team before heading into the field. Today, few archaeologists work alone in the field. An archaeological project often involves different specialists, and project directors are responsible for assembling a team suitable to achieve their research goals. Archaeological projects can vary greatly in size, and who you need will depend on the scale and type of research. For example, if the project aims to solve a regional problem, conducting fieldwork at several sites, the project will need a number of field directors to cover each site; a situation that may not be the case if research is conducted in a small area. This does not imply, however, that the archaeologist directing a small project is less knowledgeable. When a project has fewer participants with modest funding, each individual has to cover a variety of tasks simultaneously. Therefore, building an archaeological team depends on the research goal and funding availability of each project. A typical archaeological project consists of (a) project directors, (b) field directors (crew chiefs), (c) field archaeologists, (d) technical experts, (e) students, (f) workers, (g) volunteers, and (h) other specialists such as cooks and medics. Members of archaeological projects are responsible for their areas of specialization and are expected to have a command of certain knowledge and techniques. However, each member should be flexible and ready to adapt to changing circumstances. Archaeological work can be challenging and full of surprises and team members need to work well in collaboration and be ready to help out in areas outside of their specialization. Keeping the flexibility of archaeological projects in mind, the following descriptions characterize the stereotypical roles certain members play in the project.

The **project director** (sometimes codirectors) manages the entire archaeological project from field and laboratory work to report writing and dissemination to the administration and logistics of the project. She or he is often called a **Principle Investigator (PI)**, although several PIs can participate in an archaeological project that is directed by a single project director; for example, one project director may hold a permit under his or her name, whereas several PIs have a grant to conduct the research together. When archaeological research operates in a foreign country, the project tends to be codirected by both national and international archaeologists, although this is not always the case. Codirected projects of this nature often lead to both smoother operations (e.g., obtaining permissions) and rich cultural exchanges and different perspectives. International projects operate similar to codirected projects.

Field directors (sometimes referred to as **crew chiefs**) run operations in the field when the project director cannot be present all the time; the reasons for which may vary. The field director serves as a proxy for the project director and must be knowledgeable and well experienced in the field, providing flexibility for any unforeseen incidents that happen during fieldwork. Archaeological work is full of surprises. Although you may have an idea of what you might find when you begin work, you never really know what you will find until the work is underway; clutch decisions regarding excavation strategies and conservation often need to be made in a short amount of time in the field. And, keeping project logistics going can keep a director on his or her toes. What happens when the water purification system breaks or someone gets injured in a remote area of the world? Although every project is different in terms of its field situations, these are the types of issues that directors have to be ready to resolve. Further, she or he must make sure that project guidelines for data collection are followed to ensure comparability of data.

Field archaeologists are in charge of specific areas of fieldwork on a project. Some projects are very large and spread over wide regions and the project and/or field director needs trustworthy archaeologists with experience in the field to supervise work; in these cases the project/field director often make the rounds to different work areas to check on the work, but cannot supervise any one operation. Field archaeologists should be trained in archaeological work, but often rely on the guidance of project/field directors when they encounter issues that they cannot resolve.

Technical experts help archaeologists collect, analyze, and preserve specific data through their special knowledge and training. There is far too much technical knowledge in archaeology for anyone to master all of it. Although the project director, field director, and field archaeologists may have specialized training in some areas, there are often other areas that the

FIGURE 5.6 Archaeological projects can be composed of researchers who have very different specialties and roles. For example, at the site of El Palmar, Mexico, there are researchers such as bioarchaeologists, ceramic specialists, and epigraphers, all of whom contribute to the greater goals of the project.

Source: Kenichiro Tsukamoto

project must rely on an outside specialist to perform certain work. Physical anthropologists, environmental scientists, geologists, paleobotanists, paleozoologists, remote sensing specialists, and geochemists, for example, are all specializations that many projects do not have represented among their staff. Project directors tend to invite specialists during fieldwork when certain data need to be collected or preserved. For example, an expert in ground penetrating radar might be invited at the beginning of excavations to guide the excavation process or a conservator invited to preserve and curate unexpected organic artifacts found in a waterlogged context. In other cases, specialists do not join the project in the field, but collaborate from their home institutions, often performing laboratory analyses (e.g., radiocarbon dating, use-wear analysis). These specialists may be paid for their services and/or invited to collaborate in the analysis and publication of the research. In particular, **conservators** prevent the loss or deterioration of features and objects. They work in both the field and laboratory, including preservation, conservation, and restoration of architectural elements and monuments in the field, as well as perishable objects such as textiles and wood sculpture in the laboratory. Their work is not limited to perishable objects and they often deal with more durable objects including stone sculpture. Conservation work needs special skills, chemical knowledge, and practical experiences of handling a variety of problems in different environmental conditions.

Students and **volunteers** are often important elements of archaeological projects. Although we learn about archaeology in the classroom, learning in field contexts is also essential for being a professional. It is one thing to engage with archaeology in the classroom and quite another to engage with it in the field. Every project director started out on their first project as a student. Certain archaeological knowledge is transmitted better in a fieldwork context. It is important to remember to closely follow project guidelines and constantly ask questions during the first field experiences as archaeological work can be destructive and working with real data is a great responsibility.

Local workers are also often critical members of archaeological projects. Although some projects do not employ local workers, others hire large numbers of people. Archaeological projects tend to employ local persons who live near the study area because they know local history and environment much better than anyone else and such local knowledge is always helpful for archaeologists to adapt research strategies under local circumstances. In some cases where archaeological work has been ongoing for decades, the knowledge and experience of some local workers can surpass less-experienced field archaeologists or students.

Other than people mentioned earlier, there are often other members of projects who do not work in the field or laboratory, but who are nonetheless important for the project. For example, in remote areas it may be critical to have a medic on the project, or on large projects, a full-time cook.

Logistics, Camp, and Provisions

Before going into the field, the project director needs to plan the logistics, often one of the more challenging aspects of fieldwork. Where will the project members live? What will they eat and drink? What equipment will they need and how will they access it? Who do they need to contact or hire? How will they deal with transportation? Although each project has its own set of logistical issues, these are the kind of questions that need to be worked out prior to the start of research. Some projects pitch tents out in the desert and have to transport all their food and water at the beginning of the field season as it is too difficult to make various trips, whereas others build permanent or semipermanent field camps out in the remote tropical forests and install water purifiers. Some projects hike up to mountain tops each morning, whereas others fly in to their field sites. In many tropical areas of the world, archaeologists often wait to perform field during the dry season so avoid difficult roads and swarms of mosquitos. In colder climates like Alaska, archaeologists often have to work in the summers when the swarms of mosquitos are at their peak. It is the project/field director's duty to think about these issues and have a suitable work plan in place prior to the start of field research. It often takes years of working in the field to get a good sense of best logistical practices from the area of the world in which you conduct research and it is important that you not only learn about performing archaeological fieldwork during your first field seasons, but that you pay attention to how projects logistics are run so you have a base of knowledge about what to do, or not to do, when you have the opportunity to direct your own research.

Final Comments

Once the research design is in place, the project funded, all necessary permits obtained, the team put together, and an adequate logistical plan developed, you are ready to start work and complete the final stages of the research design; data collection (Chapters 6–7), data processing, and analysis (Chapters 8–13). In the following chapters, we will discuss many of the methods regarding data collection, from survey to excavation.

Bibliography

Batres, Leopoldo. *Visita a los monumentos arqueológicos de "La Quemada", Zacatecas.* Mexico, DF: Imprenta de la Fda. De Francisco Díaz de León, 1903.

Colwell-Chanthaphonh, Chip, and T. J. Ferguson. "Virtue Ethics and the Practice of History: Native Americans and Archaeologists along the San Pedro Valley of Arizona." *Journal of Social Archaeology* 4, no. 1 (2004): 5–27.

Drennan, Robert D. *Statistics for Archaeologists: A Commonsense Approach.* 2nd ed. Interdisciplinary Contributions to Archaeology. New York: Springer Publishing, 2009.

Harrison, Richard J. *The Beaker Folk.* New York: Thames & Hudson, 1980.

Hole, Bonnie L. "Sampling in Archaeology: A Critique." *Annual Review of Anthropology* 9 (1980): 217–234.

Moshenska, Gabriel, and Sarah Dhanjal, eds. *Community Archaeology: Themes, Methods, and Practices.* Oxford: Oxbow Books, 2012.

Mueller, James W. *The Use of Sampling in Archaeological Surveys.* Washington, DC: Memoirs of the Society for American Archaeology, No. 28. Society for American Archaeology, 1974.

Neumann, Thomas W., and Robert M. Sanford. *Practicing Archaeology: A Training Manual for Cultural Resources Archaeology.* Walnut Creek, CA: AltaMira Press, 2001.

Orton, Clive. *Sampling in Archaeology.* Cambridge: Cambridge University Press, 2000.

Packard, David W. *Minoan Linear A.* Berkley: University of California Press, 1974.

Stoltman, James B., Zhanwei Yue, Zhichun Jing, Jigen Tang, James H. Burton, and Mati Raudsepp. New Insights into the Composition and Microstructure of Ceramic Artifacts Associated with the Production of Chinese Bronzes at Yinxu, the Last Capital of the Shang Dynasty. *Archaeological Research in Asia* (in press).

Terry, Richard E., Fabian G. Fernández, J. Jacob Parnell, and Takeshi Inomata. "The Story in the Floors: Chemical Signatures of Ancient and Modern Maya Activities at Aguateca, Guatemala." *Journal of Archaeological Science* 31, no. 9 (2004): 1237–1250.

Survey and Mapping

Archaeological fieldwork begins on the surface. The first order of business when performing fieldwork is actually finding sites, in some cases a much more difficult prospect than in others; the Great Wall of China is hard to miss, while deeply buried sites such as Joya de Cerén are completely invisible on the surface. Although a great number of archaeological sites are already known to us today, the majority of sites actually still await identification and many places where humans once lived and worked have left precious little evidence, if any, of their existence. Thus, finding sites is often an essential part of research designs.

Once sites have been located the next step, sometimes the principle goal of fieldwork, is to document surface data. Except in some cases where interventions through excavations are precipitated by unusual circumstances such as ongoing site destruction, noninvasive surface documentation to understand the spatial layout and types of archaeological data visible on the surface is performed. In this chapter, we outline field methods that focus on site location, surface survey, and mapping. Although a popular belief is that archaeology is excavation, work on the surface is an indispensable step of archaeological research.

FIGURE 6.1 Some archaeological features, such as the Great Wall of China, are very easy to locate, whereas others, such as the site of Joya de Cerén, El Salvador (a site deeply covered by a volcanic eruption around the seventh-century AD), are impossible to locate without a chance find or the use of remote sensing techniques.

© Daniel Indiana/Shutterstock.com
© Yuri Yavnik/Shutterstock.com

Archaeological Survey

Archaeological **survey** generally refers to the field methods archaeologists employ to collect data without excavation. Through survey, archaeologists detect and record archaeological evidence on the ground surface, although some more sophisticated methods of **remote sensing** (the collection of data without physically touching them) also allow archaeologists to detect data beneath the ground surface without disturbing them. Archaeological survey begins with attempts to locate sites, known as **reconnaissance**, but also includes the documentation of surface data including the physical collection of surface data and mapping. During reconnaissance, archaeologists document the surface characteristics and geographic coordinates of sites and other archaeological features. Documenting the absence of archaeological sites in certain areas during reconnaissance is equally important as actually locating sites since the lack of these data helps researchers understand why certain areas might have been avoided. How detailed archaeologists document sites depends on different factors including the size and accessibility of the research area, density and complexity of each site, time and available funds, and the research design. Above all, much of how research is conducted hinges on the scale of analysis.

Defining Research Scale

Before discussing the methods associated with remote sensing, survey, and mapping, it is important to introduce the concept of scale. Archaeologists collect and analyze data at different scales. Sometimes the focus is on the very small scale, such as an individual artifact or feature. In other

FIGURE 6.2 Offering 4 from the site of La Venta, Mexico (upper image), is a spectacular example of Olmec figurines that has been studied at the small scale; interpreted as a gathering of important people around a series of stelae represented by greenstone celts. However, widening the scale of analysis to include other areas of Mesoamerica, archaeologists are able to see how the style of carving of such images was widespread across the region (such as the image to the right), raising questions of what the sharing of such an art style might mean for the interregional dynamics of early sedentary societies.

Ceremony of offerings, figures and stele in jade from La Venta, Mexico/De Agostini Picture Library/G. Dagli Orti/Bridgeman Images
Crouching Male Transformation Figurine. Mexico, Olmec, 900 - 300 BCE. Serpentine with traces of cinnabar.
Height: 4 1/4 in. (10.8 cm). Los Angeles County Museum of Art, Gift of Constance McCormick Fearing (M.86.311.6).
Photo © Museum Associates/LACMA.

instances, the scale of analysis can be very grand, covering large regions. The choice of the scale of analysis is often dependent on the research question, and archaeologists can shift the scale they employ to ask different questions of archaeological data. For example, the analysis of one particular set of figurines at a small scale might, such as the famous cache of figurines from the Olmec site of La Venta (Offering 4), shed light on a particular historical context; in this case, the ritual burial of figurines commemorating a gathering of people. Broadening the scale analysis to include contemporary figurines across Mesoamerica (large scale), however, could shed light on other types of questions including the nature and intensity of cultural interaction among far-flung groups living in early hierarchical societies, demonstrating that the style of representing humans in Mesoamerica at this time was widely shared. When thinking about performing survey, scale is an essential element to consider. Reconnaissance, remote sensing, and mapping can be performed at widely ranging spatial scales.

Although the scale of archaeological research is continuous, for convenience we divide it into three different categories: small, medium, and large. To illustrate some points about scale in this book we use **small scale** to refer to specific things, from individual artifacts and ecofacts to features such as hearths (places where people made fires), storage facilities, and structures such as temples and palaces. **Artifacts** refer to portable objects that have been modified or made by humans. Examples of artifacts include stone projectile points, metal axes, and ceramic vessels. Although humans (and some other animal species) use raw materials to perform tasks, unless the material has been physically modified in some way, it is not considered to be an artifact. So, if a farmer throws a stone to chase away some animals eating the crops, the stone is not an artifact. If the farmer breaks the stone to make it smaller before throwing it, we can now consider it an artifact as it has been morphologically modified by human action. **Ecofacts** are, in contrast, unmodified remains of biological materials in archaeological contexts. Ecofacts include, for instance, wild animal bones and plant remains (e.g., pollen, wood, and phytoliths). The presence of ecofacts in archaeological contexts can be the result of natural processes such as wind, water flow, and animal activity, or even cultural processes that do not result in the modification of the remains. Yet, there is a rather gray zone between artifacts and ecofacts. For instance, the domestication of animals often results in the modification or changes of the bone structure of particular species over many generations. Although most archaeologists would classify otherwise unmodified (e.g., not worked into tools) domestic horse bones as ecofacts, there is a way to argue for intentional modification. Regardless of these kinds of questions, the careful examination of ecofacts in concert with other archaeological remains offers a greater understanding of past human behavior in a given environment. Finally, **features** are nonportable facilities that were created by humans. Examples of archaeological features are hearths, burials, storage pits, roads, and other architectural elements; "things" that cannot be moved without disturbing the spatial relationship of their parts. Composite features such as houses, temples, and palaces are separately treated in archaeological research,

FIGURE 6.3 A sectioned pit feature from the site of Troyville, Louisiana (located in the town of Jonesville). Although artifacts and ecofacts might be recovered from it, the feature itself cannot be removed without altering it.

© Jill Yakubik, ESI

although we consider many of them to occupy relatively small spaces on the landscape and can be studied at a small scale. Some features, such as parts of the Great Wall of China or Inka roads, stretch for long distances and can be considered at larger scales of research.

FIGURE 6.4 Complex architectural features can be quite large, such as the Vittala Temple complex (left) in Hampi, India (dedicated to Lord Vishnu in the fifteenth-century AD), or even bigger yet, Hadrian's Wall (right) in Great Britain (built by the Roman emperor Hadrian in the second-century AD as a defense against the Britons of the north). These kinds of features are composite, with many individual parts.

© Pikoso.kz/Shutterstock.com
© Phillip Maguire/Shutterstock.com

In this book, we use the **medium scale** of archaeological research to refer to analyses that go beyond small-scale foci on individual "things" such as artifacts and houses, but are still somewhat constrained spatially and do not reach the scale of larger regions. Archaeological sites often fall into this category. **Sites** refer to spatial clusters of artifacts, ecofacts, features, and/or structures. In this sense, sites can be defined as a geographic locality where human activities are identified through material remains. A site can be as small as a surface scatter of a few artifacts or as large as a city; thus some sites might be considered at small-scale research, whereas others might be considered as medium scale. The presence of more than three artifacts in a place is often used as a benchmark to define a site in the United States, whereas other countries have different criteria. In some places in the world, it is difficult to find a spatial cluster of three artifacts together for certain periods of time. Open air Paleolithic sites in Europe, for example, are notoriously difficult to locate due to the dearth of material remains; finding three artifacts together might be considered a substantial find. Yet, for other periods of time, a cluster of three artifacts might go relatively unnoticed among a wealth of other data across a region, for instance, in Roman period Italy. The ancient city of Rome is so large in fact that it can even be divided up into an analysis of neighborhoods, each of which could also be considered at the medium scale of analysis.

FIGURE 6.5 Sites like Rome are so large that they can be divided up into numerous areas. The Forum, a central public space, is depicted in this image.

© Viacheslav Lopatin/Shutterstock.com

Defining the spatial limits of archaeological sites is, in many cases, also problematic. We often think of the spatial structure of settlements to be clearly defined. Towns and cities have limits that are often clearly marked. In other cultural contexts in the past, however, these conceptions of bounded space might not have existed, or if they did exist were not marked in ways we can "read" them, or if they were marked and we can identify those symbols, were contested by some of the people who lived in that cultural context. There are many sites around the world that have clearly defined features such as walls and moats that enclose areas that we might assume to be the bounded area of a site. Yet, in the vast majority of cases there is other evidence of human occupation outside of these bounded areas. In the Maya area, for example, there is evidence for continuous occupation between some large sites. The settlement between the large monumental centers with stelae (upright stone monuments) naming distinct dynasties might be rather sparse in the intermediate areas that separate them, but structures are there nonetheless. Because the site boundaries blur together, archaeologists sometimes assign arbitrary limits as an analytical unit based on the distance between the two concentrations on monumental architecture, a decline in frequency of archaeological remains, or the kinds of artifacts or features found. This means archaeologists often have different criteria to define site boundaries. Problem-oriented research defines sites in accordance with a research question an archaeologist addresses. The important point is that criteria to define sites should be consistent among researchers working together on an archaeological project or within the same region since not all archaeologists define sites in the same way. It is also important to keep in mind that not all archaeological sites are the result of people living somewhere. There are bewildering arrays of sites, some of which may have been formed within the course of a few hours, whereas others were occupied for millennia. Sites can include caves or rock shelters, battlefields, mountaintop shrines, series of raised fields for agriculture, offerings deposited at the bottom of a lake, quarries, and seasonal sites for hunting, gathering, and fishing.

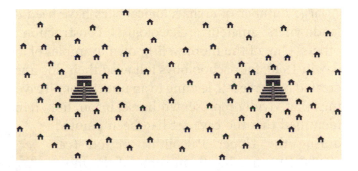

FIGURE 6.6 There are many cases where the boundaries of archaeological sites are not particularly obvious. In this schematic, where you draw the boundary between the sites centered on the pyramidal structures is rather arbitrary. The house structures in between them grade into each other across the region.

Source: Travis Stanton

For our purposes here, we consider the **large scale** of archaeological research **regions** that are beyond the limit of a single site. A region can be defined by both natural and cultural boundaries, although the scale of analysis can vary greatly with some researchers looking at local regions such as individual valleys or a small stretch of coastline and others looking and broad regions such as the Mediterranean or the Andes. Natural boundaries include mountains, valleys, rivers, and seas and archaeologists consider cultural boundaries of regions through shared cultural traits and sociopolitical divisions (see Chapter 4), which can sometimes be problematic as they tend to fluctuate over time; for example, the area occupied by Maya-speaking peoples in ancient times does not appear to be the exact same area occupied by Maya-speaking peoples today.

Why is the regional scale of archaeological research important? Traditionally, many archaeologists focused on a single site, dismissing inter-site areas as vacant spaces even if scatters of archaeological remains existed between sites. A regional approach is a way of integrating these data into archaeological research without arbitrary division, which provides a broader picture of human interactions sharing a single cultural or natural landscape. An American archaeologist, Gordon Willey was a pioneer of archaeological research in a regional level. He started conducting archaeological research at the Virú Valley of Peru in 1946, forming an interdisciplinary team of archaeologists, ethnologists, and geographers. His results demonstrated how a regional approach sheds light on the way people disposed themselves over the landscape where they lived, a line of research that is known today as **settlement archaeology** (Chapter 12).

Site Location

One of the most essential tasks in archaeological research is to locate and document sites and archaeological features. Some sites such as the Parthenon in Greece and Roman Colosseum are well known throughout the human history, but most are less obvious and are lost to human memory. There are two general ways that archaeologists discover sites, accidental and project-oriented.

Accidental Discoveries

A large number of archaeological sites have been discovered accidentally. These sites were found by landowners, amateur archaeologists, construction workers, real estate agents, and children, among others. One of the more well-known examples of a chance discovery is Lascaux Cave in France. One day in 1940, four schoolboys followed their dog after it fell through a cavity in the ground, which was created by a tree fall, leading to an underground cavern. Inside the cavern, they discovered mural paintings that vividly represented horse, bison, lion, reindeer, rhinoceros, and others. Archaeologists later identified that the cave art had been painted during the Upper Paleolithic period (ca. 17,000 BP), making them some of the most important examples of early art in the world. Another sensational example of an accidental discovery comes from China where the terracotta army, which was dedicated to the very first emperor, was discovered in 1974 when local farmers were digging for a well. This army is only part of the tomb complex of Qin Shi Huang, a polemical figure in modern-day China who represents the ills of dynastic rule as well as the founder of a regional Chinese identity through his empire building.

FIGURE 6.7 The Paleolithic cave site of Lascaux, France (ca. 17,000 BP) (top), and the tomb of the first emperor of China (bottom) where a terracotta army forms part of a nearly 100 km² necropolis (ca. third-century BC) were found by accident.

© thipjang/Shutterstock.com
© Bule Sky Studio/Shutterstock.com

These kinds of accidental discoveries are becoming more frequent around the world with increasing development and come to the attention of archaeologists on a regular basis. For example, in 1978, when electrical workers were excavating in the summer heat of downtown Mexico City, they discovered a large round monolith of over 3 m in diameter. The carved stone represents a figure of a dismembered woman, which was later determined to the Aztec moon goddess Coyolxauhqui who, according to myth, had been killed by her brother, the war deity Huitzilopochtli. Although these accidental discoveries have contributed to further archaeological research, if work is not stopped immediately and professional archaeologists brought in, crucial information can be lost forever. Unfortunately, some building contractors destroy archaeological sites intentionally; to not fall behind on construction projects, to use the materials for construction fill, and even to loot the site, among other reasons.

FIGURE 6.8 The Coyolxauhqui monument, found in the Templo Mayor complex at the heart of the Mexica (Aztec) capital of Tenochtitlan, represents a Moon goddess who was dismembered by her brother, Huitzilopochtli, a god of war. Coyolxauhqui had attacked their mother with her 400 brothers when she learned she was unexpectedly pregnant with Huitzilopochtli. When he was born, Huitzilopochtli killed his siblings and raised them into the sky as the moon and stars.

© Leonardo López Luján, INAH-Templo Mayor

Project-Oriented Discoveries

Despite the fact that many sites are discovered by accident, it is actually archaeologists who record sites, features, and nonsite features such as artifact scatters through systematic archaeological surveys. In many countries, laws obligate urban developers to contract archaeologists who conduct a surface survey before the construction is carried out. In the United States, cultural resource management (CRM) deals with archaeological surveys in the area of development. When a site is located as part of such a survey, CRM archaeologists record and evaluate the site as part of the development. Academic research projects also conduct surveys at ground level and through aerial images. To find archaeological sites in a given landscape, archaeologists employ several methods that include textual sources, aerial survey, ground reconnaissance, and surface and subsurface surveys. In this section, we review these different methodologies for finding sites.

Textual Sources

All around the world the physical location of countless places used by people in the past have been lost to human memory. In some cultural contexts, however, clues concerning their whereabouts may lie in written texts for archaeologists and ethnohistorians to explore. For example, mining towns of the far western United States dating to the 1800s and early 1900s are often mentioned in old documents. One of the most famous examples of using texts to find "lost" archaeological sites concerns the ancient city of Troy. An early German explorer/archaeologist named **Heinrich Schliemann** (1820–1890) became

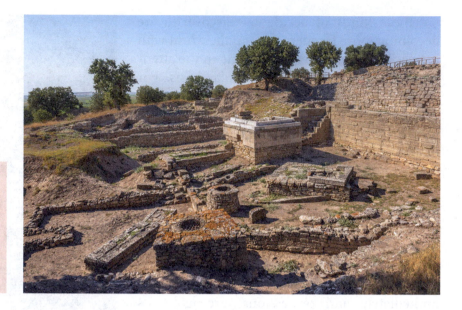

FIGURE 6.9 Heinrich Schliemann believed that the site of Hissarlik, Turkey, home to an impressive series of ruins including a much later Roman period occupation, was the fabled city of Troy.

© isa_ozdere/Shutterstock.com

enamored with Homer's narrative poem, *The Iliad*, concerning the Trojan Wars. Learning over a dozen foreign languages, he became a successful international merchant, accumulating enough funds to look for the legendary city he believed to exist in ruins. Through readings of the original Greek text of the Iliad, he and his collaborator Frank Calvert believed that the site of Hissarlik, Turkey, home to an impressive series of ruins, was the ancient city they sought. During his excavations from the 1870s to 1880s, Schliemann identified a series of overlapping settlements, the second earliest of these he called Troy. Later excavations, however, identified that this occupation was much earlier than the city of Troy from Homer's narrative, which, in fact, corresponded to the seventh occupation from the bottom. Despite his stratigraphic misidentification of the level for Homeric Troy, Schliemann's pioneering research demonstrated how textual resources were useful for the site discovery, leaving an impact on the study of the origins of Greek society. Other historic texts such as ancient maps, diaries, novels, poems, and religious texts are equally important to find ancient sites.

Aerial Survey and Remote Sensing

The development of aerial technologies has provided substantial advancements in archaeological survey. During World War I, airplanes began to be regularly used to spy on enemy positions behind the front lines. It was soon realized that the kind of aerial photography used during the war had other applications and the first remote sensing techniques in archaeology were born with pilots such as Charles Lindbergh contributing to locating archaeological sites. **Remote sensing** is the collection of data without physically touching them and there are various techniques that can be used to detect both surface and subsurface archaeological remains. This section focuses on aerial techniques of remote sensing that are used to identify mainly surface features.

Before the advent of Google Earth or Bing Maps (satellite photography that archaeologists sometimes use, although the images are not high resolution), the most common approach to aerial remote sensing had been the use of aerial photographic prints pioneered soon after World War I. Still utilized by archaeologists, aerial photos consist of vertical and oblique images, each of which has advantages and disadvantages. In oblique aerial imagery, taken at an angle, it is easier to recognize archaeological sites because topographic reliefs make terrains light and dark, often highlighting cultural features

FIGURE 6.12 A vertical photograph of the Roman settlement Aquis Querquennis in Galicia, Spain.

on the landscape. However, it is difficult to measure the accurate location and dimension of sites because of the distortions generated by its diagonal perspective.

Vertical imagery provides more accurate measurements because the straight down view has fewer spatial distortions. This means that the vertical aerial image is useful for the verification of a terrestrial anomaly on the ground by converting it into either geographic coordinates (latitude and longitude) or the **UTM** (Universal Transverse Mercator coordinate system, a two-dimensional system often used to spatially reference place on the Earth's surface) coordinates; associating spatial data such as maps and photographs to such coordinate systems is known as **georeferencing**. Georeferencing can be accomplished by using three points (e.g., a corner of modern road, building, or other visible feature) that are identifiable in aerial images and/or maps, relating them to the measured distance of the topographic map in the aerial photograph. The orientations of sites can also be determined by the same method. Then, we save the point of the site with the coordinates in a handheld **global positioning system** (GPS), with which archaeologists go to the field to verify whether the anomaly in the photographic image is an archaeological site or not. Today, the same method is commonly used for car navigation, in which a destination's reference point is located through the geographic coordinate system. The disadvantage of vertical aerial images is that plan views make it difficult to identify archaeological features because these images do not illuminate subtle topographic variation. To resolve this problem, archaeologists using vertical aerial photography have traditionally made three-dimensional (3D) views by using overlapping pairs of aerial vertical photographs (**stereoscopy**). Looking at two vertical photographs with a 40 to 60 percent overlap in the area, each photo looked at by a different eye, gives the human brain the perception of depth, thus bringing some archaeological features into relief. More recently, archaeologists use online images such as Google Earth or Bing Maps for the first stage of a project. Nevertheless, print aerial images are still helpful because aerial images taken several decades ago are usually available, revealing vanished evidence that has been gone due to modern human activities or natural transformations. Furthermore, print images taken in the same area, but during different days, seasons, and years provide different lighting effects whose light and shadow make archaeological features visible under different environmental conditions. These aerial photographs are especially useful for vegetation areas where buried archaeological features generate different vegetation growth, leaving **crop marks** on the surface that are difficult to appreciate on the ground, but can be more easily visible from the air. Some plants grow shorter and thinner over buried structures, but they grow taller and thicker when planted over pits and ditches.

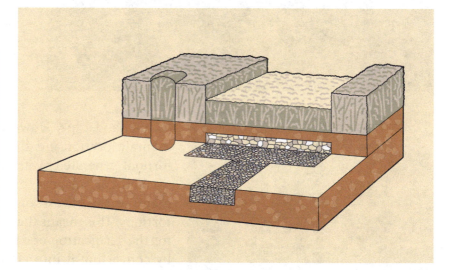

FIGURE 6.13 Crop marks show up in aerial images because the plants respond to the underlying soil context. For example, where stone foundations occur near the surface the crops do not do as well and tend to be lower. In contrast, ditches and other deeper features filled with a soil matrix usually result in crops growing taller.

© Belem Ceballos Casanova.

Aerial photography has traditionally been conducted by airplanes, although archaeologists have employed helicopters, kites, and weather balloons over the years as well. Most recently, portable aircraft known as a **drones** (or **unmanned aerial vehicles** [UAVs]) have dramatically improved aerial surveys for archaeological research. Some drones are relatively small quadcopters fitted with cameras. These have a limited range and a short battery life. Fixed-wing drones are much larger and can cover greater distances. It is relatively easy to take aerial photographs, being remotely controlled by a human operator through a laptop, tablet, or smart phone or by automated computer programs that take the drone through a preplanned flight path. The control of a drone requires some skill, but the automated programs have improved dramatically. Some computer software links to drone preset

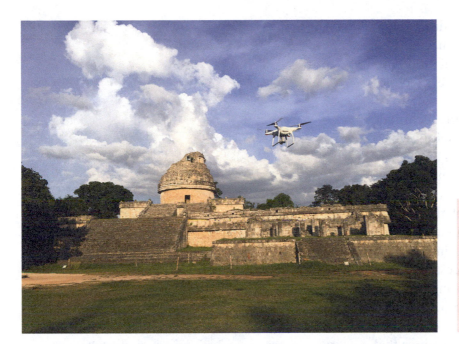

FIGURE 6.14 Some drones, like this quadcopter being used for photogrammetry at the Caracol complex at Chichén Itzá, Mexico, are relatively small and inexpensive, but have limited flight time.

Source: Travis Stanton

FIGURE 6.15 Fixed wing drones, like these models created by the Cultural Heritage Engineering Initiative at the University of California, San Diego, have the potential to fly much farther than the smaller quadcopters.

© Eric Lo

flight paths, continuously taking a series of vertical photos with a specific interval and archaeologists can remotely control the horizontal and vertical angles of the mounted camera, creating different vertical and oblique aerial photographs. Many drones are now equipped with automated landing systems and anti-crashing technologies, which have saved more than a few of them from trees and other obstacles. Since a drone is generally equipped with GPS, its camera registers each aerial picture with the geographic coordinates. However, the coordinates of these aerial images often contain horizontal and vertical errors, which should be rectified (matching spatial points in two separate images to project them into the same spatial plane) and georeferenced, which many archaeologists do now through **geographic information system** (GIS) programs that will be described below. Further, many drones can capture an aerial video, allowing archaeologists to look at continuous aerial surveys. These digital images are particularly useful for archaeological research if a size of the digital image created by a drone camera surpasses 10 megapixels for photo and 4,000 pixels for video. Although commercial drones are still limited to the duration of flight and the quality of aerial images, their portability and accessibility will undoubtedly continue to improve with new technological advances.

Another aerial remote sensing technique concerns laser-based aerial mapping, which has become increasingly popular in archaeological research since the first applications of **LiDAR** (Light Detection and Ranging) in the field around the turn of the millennium. Among different techniques, LiDAR has had revolutionary impact in archaeological research in tropical forests, as well as in other environments throughout the world. Airborne LiDAR, also known as ALS (airborne laser scanning), uses an aircraft equipped with GPS and a laser scanner that pulses a series of beams to the Earth. As with the case of the recent improvement of drones, the laser pulse rates of LiDAR have continuously improved from several thousand times per second to hundreds of thousands times per second. Return signals of laser create a three-dimensional **point cloud**, which consists of the coordinates of unequally spaced points captured by the sensor that records multiple stops or full return signals per laser pulse as it passes vegetation and hits the ground surface. In the laboratory, the original point cloud is processed to classify the returns as vegetation, artificial structures, or the ground surface for archaeological research. Some classified points, in turn, allow researchers to produce an accurate **digital surface model** (DSM) and **digital elevation model** (DEM); we will explain DEMs in more detail below. In other words, LiDAR penetrates forest canopies, exposing both the ground surface and vegetation shapes. Software processing the point cloud can also remove shadows and change the angle of the sun, visualizing features under the desired lighting conditions, among other types of data processing and manipulation. Some of the most successful results have been reported in "invisible" areas covered with dense vegetation, which include

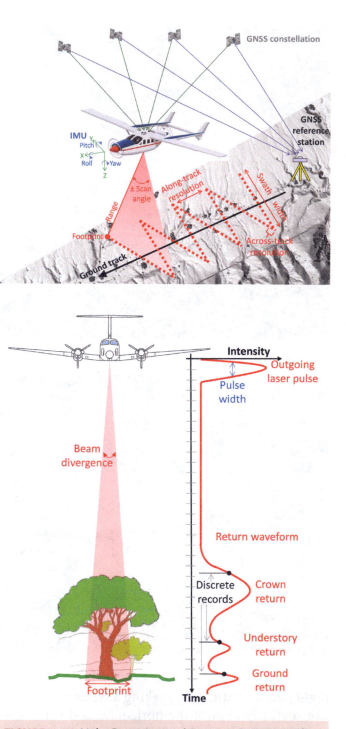

FIGURE 6.16 Light Detection and Ranging (LiDAR) is often mounted on a fixed-wing aircraft and flown across a region. It works particularly well in forested areas where aerial photography can be difficult, as some of the laser shots pass between the leaves and give the distance from the LiDAR to the ground, allowing researchers the ability to create topographic images of the ground surface. Since the LiDAR is georeferenced with GPS connections to satellites, the images can be precisely located in space.

© Juan Fernández

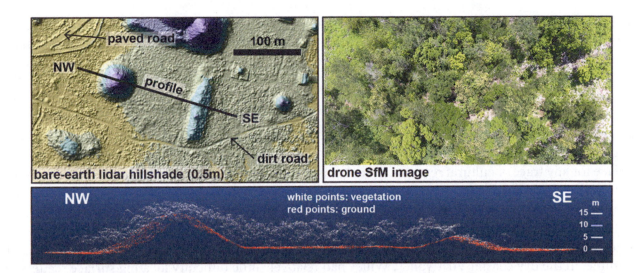

FIGURE 6.17 This hillshade/digital elevation model (DEM) image created from Light Detection and Ranging (LiDAR) data shows an architectural complex at the site of Yaxuná, Mexico, that would be greatly obscured by the forest otherwise (both top images show the area of the complex). LiDAR can also be used to create profiles whereby the ground surface can be classified separately from the above vegetation (the bottom image is a profile of the same complex).

© Nic Barth

Central America and Southeast Asia. LiDAR has huge potential for archaeological research, but it is an expensive method and is not accessible to the public. There are some environmental conditions that limit the data recovery through LiDAR. Among different situations, secondary vegetation, resulting from agricultural activities such as slash-and-burn agriculture and the leaves of certain plants such as banana trees, prevents LiDAR beams from penetrating to the ground as effectively. The result often produces more amorphous areas in DEM imagery. In these areas, archaeologists have few other options but to conduct pedestrian survey on the ground.

Other aerial remote sensing comes from satellite imagery, which NASA (National Aeronautics and Space Administration) provides to the public. One of the most commonly used by archaeologists is the **Landsat** series. The images are taken by scanners that record multispectral waves, measuring the intensity of reflected light and the infrared radiation of the electromagnetic spectrum from the ground surface. Since the resolution is relatively coarse (2.85 m resolution), the images are used to trace large features. Google Earth uses Landsat images. As we use it in everyday life, Google Earth and Microsoft's Bing Maps now enable archaeologists to detect archaeological sites in the world. More expensive images that archaeologists can purchase are infrared and thermal imagery. Infrared images represent invisible radio frequency radiation that enhances ground marks created by construction and agricultural activities. Thermal photographs detect the differences in heat flow through materials, representing thermal properties in different colors on both surface and subsurface remains. The resolution of images varies by geographic area and the software used. Nevertheless, it is important to note that the

FIGURE 6.18 A Landsat image of the Nile River.

© Voran/Shutterstock.com

detection of archaeological sites in aerial photographs require trained eyes, especially those in dense vegetation such as tropical forests. Moreover, archaeological sites detected through aerial reconnaissance always need to be verified through ground surveys.

Ground Reconnaissance

Ground reconnaissance is the most basic method that archaeologists have used for locating archaeological sites; recording past cultural resources by walking in the research area, studying the ground surface for any trace of cultural remains. Since the pioneering research conducted by Willey in the Virú Valley of Peru, archaeologists have been concerned with the adaptation to and use of landscapes surrounding sites, encouraging them to extend their research area from particular sites to broader regions. Walking the landscape has provided a reliable method for finding cultural materials. Environmental conditions, however, vary considerably, impacting how ground reconnaissance is conducted. For example, in the dry coastal Virú Valley, Willey had relatively little difficulty locating surface scatters of artifacts (sometimes a sign of deeper deposits or even buried structures) as most of the ground surface is visible. In tropical forest environments, this visibility can be very much reduced, especially if there is a thick, low canopy. Such environments obscure horizontal visibility and even large buildings only 10 m from a survey team might be invisible. Forest litter such as leaves and other detritus can also cover the ground surface, making many artifact scatters invisible. Therefore, the sampling strategies employed in ground reconnaissance might differ depending on the environmental conditions. For instance, a survey team working in coastal Peru might walk in parallel lines 40 or 50 m apart from each other, whereas in the dense tropical forests of northern Yucatán they might walk only 10 or 20 m apart. Hilly or watery terrain might also complicate ground reconnaissance strategies with obstacles impeding systematic movement on the ground. Yet, as a compliment to remote sensing techniques (e.g., **ground-truthing** or checking anomalies on aerial photography) or a methodology used on its own, ground reconnaissance is an essential part of archaeological survey.

Archaeologists can conduct reconnaissance survey with relatively economically priced equipment, which includes portable GPS units, maps, compasses, and tapes. Modern ground reconnaissance attempts not only to detect and document archaeological remains, but also to investigate natural resources such as rocks, sediments, sources of water, and vegetation. In so doing, archaeologists should study local geography and geology before reconnaissance survey or integrate experts such as geologists and environmental scientists in their team (Chapter 5).

A critical part of ground reconnaissance, as well as any other type of fieldwork, is documentation. As we emphasized in Chapter 2, documentation of archaeological remains is a major goal of the field. Before starting ground reconnaissance, a work flow to document cultural remains

FIGURE 6.19 Field reconnaissance is an essential part of archaeological work. Although remote sensing techniques can show where many archaeological features are located, in some environments, such as the tropical forests of the Maya area shown here, it is difficult to get high resolution of smaller features and surface contexts much be inspected firsthand.

Source: Travis Stanton

should have been developed during the planning of the research. This work flow takes into account the sampling strategy as well as the kinds of data that will be gathered and how they will be collected. In some cases, often due to time and funding restraints, ground reconnaissance is a quick and dirty affair where some GPS points, photographs, and quick notes and/or sketches are taken before moving on. In other cases, survey teams have more time and may collect much more kinds of data and often at a better quality. Field notes that record the observations of the survey team are an essential part of ground reconnaissance. Other common kinds of data that can be collected during ground reconnaissance include photographs, GPS points, drawings, maps (using a variety of methods that have different results in terms of quality; see below), soil samples, and artifacts obtained through surface collections or minimally invasive excavations (see below).

Surface Survey

As we have stated before, archaeologists need to contemplate the scale, extent, and type of sampling strategy before conducting survey. Surface survey employs either a nonprobabilistic or a probabilistic sampling method (Chapter 5). A nonprobabilistic sampling survey (also known as unsystematic survey) is to walk across the research area, locating and documenting features and artifacts on the surface without systematic paths using a grid system or transect. This survey method generally leads researchers to focus on the area with obvious archaeological remains, leaving other areas less subjected to scrutiny. The results provide rich archaeological data, but the distribution of features and artifact is often biased as we explained in the previous chapter and therefore the data are not as reliable for subsequent spatial analyses and statistical studies. At the same time, unsystematic survey often brings successful results with limited time and money.

Probabilistic sampling methods usually rely on systematic surveys through a grid system or transects, examining the study area independent of natural and cultural environments. Researchers examine each grid square or transect. If the study area is set by a large grid such as 500 × 500 m, archaeologists often set a smaller space for each walker, subdividing the grid into equally spaced units dependent on visibility. The great advantage of systematic survey is that the collected data are useful for statistical analyses and researchers can locate themselves relatively easily on a map.

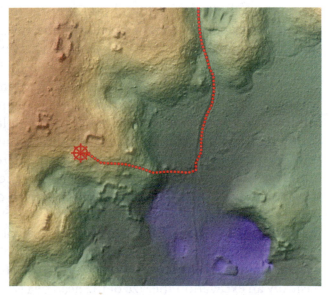

FIGURE 6.20 Verifying LiDAR data using a tablet and RTK-GNSS device. The right image represents a LiDAR map with trace tracking.

Source: Kenichiro Tsukamoto

They can also more easily plot features and artifacts as vector data on a GIS-based map. Nevertheless, systematic survey usually requires a number of archaeologists to cover a large area. If the field crews have diverse skills and experiences to detect artifacts, ecofacts, features, and sites in the field, it would alter the accuracy of documentation. Therefore, previous training is important and archaeologists standardize criteria about the documentation of features and artifacts by sharing the standardized recording format.

Subsurface Survey

Ground survey is always limited because many artifacts and features are buried beneath the surface. The spatial distribution of a site can often be difficult to calculate with surface data, and complete site chronologies might not be well represented by the material culture visible on the surface. A way of mitigating these problems in lieu of extensive excavation is called subsurface survey. There are four principal techniques of invasive testing, which can be considered minimal excavations in a sense. The least invasive, but those that can reach the greatest depths are core and auger surveys. **Cores** are hollow tubes that are driven into the ground, whereas an **auger** is a large drill run by human or machine power. The most common equipment used by archaeologists is a metal corkscrew auger with a T-shape handle. The holes made by cores and augers may be quite small (e.g., 10 cm in diameter), but as attachments can be connected, they can sometimes reach relatively extensive depths, sometimes showing areas where cultural materials are buried, as well as giving a good sense of the stratigraphy. For example, a systematic core survey across a 10-m spaced grid around where a surface artifact scatter was located might show that the subsurface artifacts extend to some length in areas where they are not found on the surface. Additionally, such a survey could give a good idea of the variability in the

FIGURE 6.21 Soil matrix being cleaned from an auger sample.

© Robin Nieuwenkamp/Shutterstock.com

site stratigraphy prior to more extensive excavations and could help guide future research. Yet, although cores and augers do provide very useful information, it must be remembered that they are also destructive. An archaeologist might core right into a human burial or other important feature without realizing it until the context has been damaged. Further, cores and augers do not work well in certain environments, for example, those with lots of stones or really hard-packed clay. Although coring tests recover strata of the study area without any intermittent process (the core is inserted only once), auger tests have a risk of mixing different deposits because the auger needs to be pulled out every time a small sample is taken. Pulling the head of an auger from the excavated hole causes the possibility that part of strata collapse and fall down to the bottom of the hole. Finally, given the narrow diameter of these excavations, few artifacts can be recovered mitigating the possibility that archaeologists can well understand a site's chronology.

One way of getting around the kind of blind subsurface testing provided by cores and augers is to use shovel tests. **Shovel testing** refers to the use of shovel to make a small round hole on the ground, basically an excavation the size of the head of a shovel. Shovel tests are standard in CRM archaeology in North America and are used to various degrees throughout the world. As they open up a larger area, they have the advantages of helping to see possible deposits as they are encountered and collecting a large sample of cultural material due to the increased excavation diameter. Yet, they usually cannot go very deep, restricted in extreme cases to the length of the shovel itself in loose, easily excavated deposits; they can also be extremely difficult to excavate in stony or hard-packed deposits.

Test pits are the most time-consuming subsurface method, but can yield greater results given their larger size (see also Chapter 7). More like larger excavations in terms of the methodology used to dig and record (e.g., straight walls, use of a more formal datum), test pits straddle the line between subsurface tests and more horizontal exposures, but are often employed to get a relatively quick look at the materials and stratigraphy beneath the surface of an area. Unlike the shovel

FIGURE 6.22 A shovel test pit from the Coptic Church site, Florida.

© Traci Ardren

test pit, which rarely reaches bedrock, test pits can examine deeper deposits at the site as archaeologists can actually enter the excavation; although the depth of the pit may be limited due to dangers regarding the stability of the pit walls and may not reach the end of cultural deposits in certain situations. The horizontal dimensions of test pits are usually 1 m², but can range in some cases up to 2 m². Because of their larger size, test pits enable archaeologists to observe its profiles clearly. When excavating a series of test pits in different parts of the site, archaeologists attempt to correlate different events to reconstruct the site history. Due to the limitation of horizontal dimension of each test pit, this reconstruction is not always successful, but it is important to compare different test pits to understand the distribution of data. They are also suited to a simple random sampling or stratified random sampling. But, as always, we should keep in mind that these subsurface methods are destructive and thus careful planning with a specific goal is needed.

Subsurface Remote Sensing

More recently, archaeologists have employed a series of nondestructive techniques that can, to variable extents, locate archaeological data beneath the surface without disturbing buried artifacts and features. There are two types of ground-based remote sensing devices: active and passive techniques. **Active** geophysical sensing techniques are similar to LiDAR, in the sense that they measure the response of energy or echoes that are penetrated into subsurface contexts, detecting different conductivity and resistivity created by the presence of artifacts, features, and cavities. In contrast, **passive** devices measure physical characteristics without sending energy into the subsurface. These techniques measure the intensity of the field, especially magnetic intensities and gravity as physical properties. Subsurface remote sensing is generally applied to areas already known to contain archaeological data, but that are not very visible on the surface.

For subsurface survey, there are several active remote sensing techniques that archaeologists have frequently used. **Earth conductivity survey**, also known as electromagnetic (EM) survey, is one of the most utilized techniques. This technique functions by running an electrical current through the ground. The conductivity of the electrical current is measured by placing two stationary (or remote) probes in the Earth and then taking readings with two mobile probes at varying intervals across a site. Although this subsurface technique is useful to detect anomalies relatively near the ground surface, it does work well in matrices where soil contrasts are weak and is essentially two-dimensional detection that does not discriminate the depth of anomalies well. Further, as with all subsurface remote sensing techniques, Earth Conductivity Survey only shows where anomalies are found below the ground surface, essentially where significant changes in the subsurface composition are located. What these anomalies are might be difficult to assess. In some cases, the regularity of the anomalies might suggest human activity, but it might be difficult if not impossible to differentiate a naturally buried boulder from some other cultural feature. Experts trained at reading the imagery have learned to distinguish certain types of features in the data depending on experience in particular cultural contexts and environments, but it is important to stress that this technique, and the others, only demonstrate anomalies that may be of interest.

A second active ground-based remote sensing technique similar to Earth Conductivity Survey is **Resistivity Survey** (also known as Earth Resistance Survey or Resistance Survey). Resistivity Survey is an active technique that measures the resistance (instead of the conductivity) of the matrix to the passage of an electrical current through electromagnetic energy injected into the soil.

Magnetic Susceptibility (also known as **low-field magnetic susceptibility** due to its application to weak magnetic fields) is another active technique that provides a measure of the ability of a material to be magnetized when a magnetic field is applied. This technique is a bit more time-consuming than many of the others, but is widely applicable to different kinds of buried contexts and can provide very useful information concerning formation processes (e.g., magnetite or maghemite often forms in surface soil layers) and features such as hearths.

The fourth active technique is **ground penetrating radar** (GPR), which has become increasingly popular in archaeological research. GPR devices use emitters to send radio pulses into the ground. The echoes of these pulses that bounce back can be interpreted to reveal subsurface changes in sediment and voids or solid materials. Unlike other ground-based remote sensing devices, GPR can reveal the depth through measuring the travel time of the pulses. This means that GPR is capable of creating 3D maps of buried archaeological remains in form of slice-maps. The combination of numerous individual reflections can develop two-dimensional vertical or horizontal time slices that represent different buried features located in specific intervals of the depth.

Active remote sensing can also be employed in underwater contexts, popular for finding old shipwrecks and other submerged features in archaeology. **Bathymetric surveys** are the equivalent of topographic surveys on land and there are several methods that can provide digital terrain models of the bottom of bodies of water where features of interest to archaeologists might be identified. For example, LiDAR is a commonly used method. Another well-known active sensing technique in bathymetric surveys is multibeam sonar. As with LiDAR, sonar data can be used to create 3D imagery of features.

In contrast to active subsurface remote sensing techniques, there are relatively a few passive techniques used by archaeologists. A **magnetometer** is a common example of an instrument used in a passive technique. The magnetometer measures variation in the magnetic intensity of the field; a compass that measures the direction of the Earth's magnetic field is an example of a magnetometer, although there are a variety of more sophisticated pieces of equipment that can be employed. Magnetometry is particularly useful for detecting features that have been exposed to heat 700° C or higher such as hearths (which realign particles), as well as pits, ditches, and iron objects. Although the unbaked clay represents randomly oriented magnetism, the magnetism of the baked clay lines up, becoming a weak permanent magnet, creating a distortion in the magnetic field. Other passive techniques might also be employed by archaeologists including thermometers that could measure the temperature differences between different kinds of subsurface materials in particular contexts.

Mapping

Once data begin to be collected, whether through remote sensing or surface survey, maps are created to document and help visualize those data. Maps are essential for any archaeological research. They contain important data and help communicate them to different audiences. Some maps created at a large scale that might show the location of numerous sites across region. Others are created at much smaller scales to document small features and artifact scatters. Yet, they all do the same thing; situate data in space. What kinds of data are represented on maps is usually driven by the research questions that archaeologists are interested in and what they are trying to get across to potential audiences. Natural features such as lakes and rivers, entire sites, structures, artifact densities, hearths, topography, or individual artifacts, among other data, might be depicted on maps. Some mapping seeks chronological or vertical data, whereas other mapping techniques are designed for the representation of horizontal dimension or landscape, which allows us to examine available resources in local environment. In addition to selecting the kinds of data to be placed on a map, archaeologists must make decisions concerning how to visualize those data. Different visualization conventions are available and might serve different purposes. For example, some maps are purely topographic, whereas others are plan drawings that depict data in certain styles. Archaeologists usually make planimetric or topographic maps, or the combination of these. Yet, we should keep in mind that one of the critical values of a map is to situate data in space. Therefore, it is important to always include the orientation (usually marked by a magnetic or true north arrow), the scale to which it is drawn, and relevant data on the location of the map so that it can be interpreted correctly.

Maps are often created during survey, reconnaissance, and remote sensing work. As we have already seen, there are many different techniques that archaeologists can use to find and document archaeological data. These techniques, along with environmental conditions and constraints on time and funding, have an impact on how maps are created. For example, a survey team covering a large area might not have the time or resources to create detailed maps of surface sites they come across. In some cases, a few GPS points might be taken along with some photographs and notes, and the team might be forced to move on. The GPS points could be plotted on a map using a GIS program giving archaeologists a very general idea of the surface data located in this area.

In other cases, the team might have a bit more time to create more detailed, but still rough maps of sites. Often, such maps are usually planimetric and are made through **pace and compass** or **tape and compass** methods. In the absence of useful remote sensing data such as LiDAR and aerial photography where visible archaeological data might be plotted out ahead of ground survey, rough distances and orientations are calculated on the ground to create maps. Many archaeologists know the distance of their paces or steps for this very purpose, although measuring tapes are also often employed. These are relatively fast, but less accurate techniques. Archaeologists commonly use these during the initial stage of the project with limited funds.

In contrast to planimetric maps, topographic maps represent elevation differences through contour lines. Although topographic maps can be created by tape and compass through measuring vertical angle, archaeologists commonly use more sophisticated instruments such as a level, transit, theodolite, total station, or high-precision GPS or **Global Navigation Satellite Systems** (GNSS) unit. The use of a total station or high-precision GPS unit, the preferred equipment for archaeologists today, is often the final stage of surface survey right before excavation. Although cheaper GPS units can be employed in certain contexts where accuracy is not as important for the research plan, high-precision GPS/GNSS units and total stations are fairly expensive, but provide much better accuracy. A total station combines an electronic theodolite with an **electronic distance measuring** (EDM) device. The theodolite records

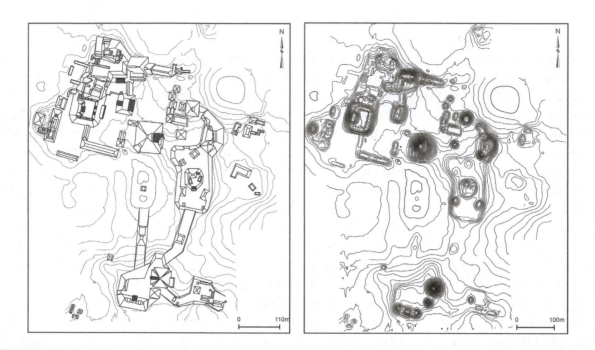

FIGURE 6.23 Planimetric and topographic maps of the site of El Palmar, Mexico.

Source: Kenichiro Tsukamoto

FIGURE 6.24 Mapping with a total station on the Giza Plateau of Egypt.

© 2018 Ancient Egypt Research Associates. Photo by Mark Lehner. AERA_team_2000.tif

FIGURE 6.25 GNSS-RTK (Global Navigation Satellite System-Real Time Kinematic) positioning technique. A pair of antennas, each serves as a base station and rover), allow archaeologists to locate a position with accuracy up to seven millimeters.

Source: Kenichiro Tsukamoto

the vertical and horizontal angles, whereas the EDM measures the distance using a modified infrared carrier signal that is shot from the theodolite to a prism on a stadia rod. In clear environments, shots can cover several kilometers, but it is common to have to move the theodolite frequently when obstacles are found on the landscape. When the total station is set up correctly it is very accurate. Usually, two-person teams work a total station; one person at the theodolite and the other person at the stadia rod. However, there are robotic total stations that can be worked by one person at the stadia rod. Total station and GPS mapping does not just record topographic points as LiDAR does. Since people are on the ground they can classify points as they take them, identifying them as cultural or natural features such as corners of buildings, artifacts scatters, and cave entrances. Thus, the final product is a DEM with culturally relevant data important to the research questions; these data are often classified by the person working the stadia rod and communications between the two-person teams is critical during fieldwork. It is important to remember, though, that while the quality of data gathered through this kind of mapping is much better than techniques such as pace and compass, it is also much slower and more expensive in terms of the price of equipment and person-hours in the field. Archaeologists should choose the most appropriate mapping strategies based on the particular research situation.

Finally, when archaeological features are visible on available remote sensing data, maps can also be created using these data. For example, planimetric maps can be drawn using aerial photography and topographic maps can be created from LiDAR data without having visited the actual sites. However, it is important to stress that many features visible on the surface do not show up in remote sensing data and it is even possible to misidentify natural features as having human origin in some environments. Thus, ground-truthing, or ground survey, and more detailed ground mapping are important complements to mapmaking using remote sensing data. With the advent of new technologies such as LiDAR and photogrammetry (see below) more and more mapping efforts combine remote sensing with ground mapping. For example, DEMs can be loaded on to a tablet connected to a GPS/GNSS and archaeologists can see themselves walk around the DEM as they check features and map. Data recorded on the tablet, such as photographs, can also be stamped with spatial coordinates and added directly to a GIS database facilitating the data collection process.

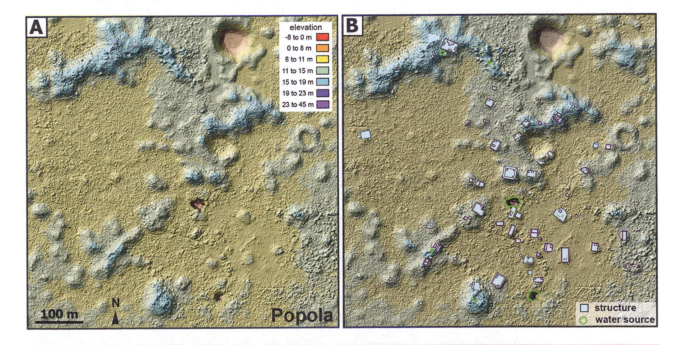

FIGURE 6.26 Light Detection and Ranging (LiDAR) images of the small Maya site of Popolá, Mexico, with and without the map of the site superimposed. Many of the structures are the site are clearly not visible in the LiDAR data given their small size, the uneven topography, and dense forest cover that covers the site underscoring the need for checking data on the ground.

© Nic Barth

3D Modeling

3D modeling based on topographic or remote sensing data has become increasingly important in archaeological research, but goes beyond efforts to map the landscape. Such modeling is applied to pretty much any kind of material data in archaeology and there are several techniques used to generated 3D data. Similar to LiDAR, there are ground-based scanning devices that shoot a large number of laser points that create relief images of features or individual artifacts. **Photogrammetry** is another technique that makes measurements from photographs. Advances in the computer processing of digital photographs have revolutionized photogrammetry in recent years and it is a quick, accurate, and detailed way of created 3D images of landscapes, fea-

FIGURE 6.27 Using a ground-based Light Detection and Ranging (LiDAR) system at Chichén Itzá, Mexico.

Source: Travis Stanton

tures, and objects. For example, using aerial photographs taken by a drone and ten to twelve ground points (or also called control points) taken by a total station, programs such as Agisoft PhotoScan calculate the accurate location of each picture and can generate a georeferenced point cloud that can be used in turn to create a DEM and thus, 3D models. Such data can be applied to visibility and watershed analyses across landscapes. These programs can also identify points of overlap among the photos and stitch them together without designating control points and some cameras even have attached GPS units that georeference the photographs when they are taken, streamlining the process. Among different software for rendering 3D models of archaeological sites preferred in the field are Autodesk AutoCAD (Computer-Aided Design), Golden Software Surfer, and ESRI ArcMap, which contain an option of automate contour creation based on ground point data. They also have important map representations such as shaded and color relief, 3D wireframe, 3D surface, which allow archaeologists to analyze the landscape surrounding sites. The same technology can be applied to features and individual objects. Archaeologists can now make 3D models of their excavations and artifacts, representing a tremendous increase in the quality of documentation. Importantly, 3D photography and other modelling can be published digitally in standard formats such as Adobe PDF files so that readers can rotate images while reading a text. Finally, advances in 3D printing have made the reproduction of 3D models accessible for a wide variety of purposes that include education and dissemination.

Surface Collections

Another common aspect of survey concerns the collection of sample artifacts and/or ecofacts located on the ground surface. Not all survey projects include surface collections, but it is employed with great frequency and entails gathering material data in an area to provide a basis for functional and temporal interpretations. Artifacts on the surface can be a good indicator of the chronology of archaeological sites and features, but can also provide useful information concerning the kinds of activities that took place at a location, such as a fishing or habitation site.

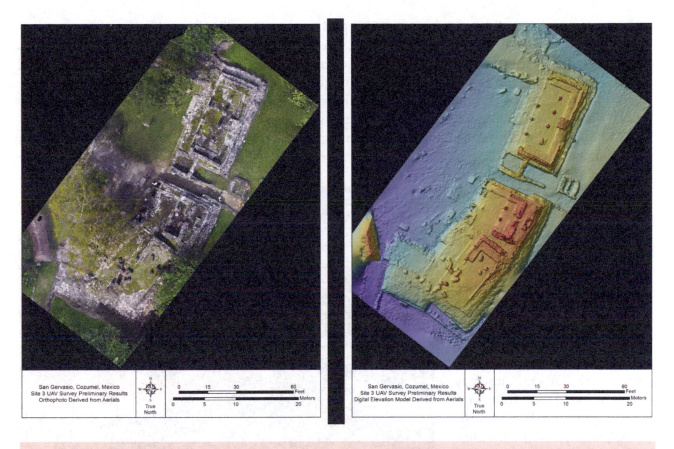

FIGURE 6.28 An aerial photo and digital elevation model (DEM) created through photogrammetry of an architectural complex of the Late Postclassic (AD 1250–1521) Maya site of San Gervasio, Cozumel, Mexico. The three-dimensional (3D) model created by stitching the photos together can be converted into a point cloud much like those generated by Light Detection and Ranging (LiDAR) data. Unlike LiDAR, however, photogrammetry does not work well in areas with dense vegetation as lines of sight are essential to create the 3D models.

© Peter Leach

There are two general methods to collect artifacts on the surface: nonsystematic and systematic techniques. Nonsystematic methods are usually employed to collect artifacts when archaeologists conduct ground reconnaissance, walking in a study area. They document and record the location of artifacts, sometimes using a portable GPS. However, the goal of nonsystematic surface collection is not to examine questions such as the density of artifacts (which can be an indicator of the intensity or longevity of human activities in an area), but provide relatively quick data on function and chronology, usually over larger areas. Systematic survey, in contrast, divides a study area into a grid system and collects artifacts strategically based on either total data gathering or sample data gathering, usually over a smaller area. Each grid square determines provenience of artifacts. **Total coverage surface collection** includes all the units as subjects of investigation in the study area. This method functions to collect material over the entire area of study and it is time-consuming, often with a great number of artifacts collected. A more realistic way of collecting artifacts on the surface is a **sample coverage surface collection**. As we have discussed in Chapter 5, archaeologists employ probabilistic sampling such as a simple random sampling, stratified random sampling, cluster sampling, and adaptive sampling. For surface collections, archaeologists collect artifacts based on targeted grid squares. Sampling strategies may also target specific kinds or artifacts or materials regardless of whether total or sample coverage surface collections are employed. For example, ceramics might be collected, but other materials such as lithics and shell might be left behind. Or, certain types of forms might be targeted, such as lithic tools, whereas other lithics such as production debitage might be left in place. In many cases, archaeologists collect what are termed **diagnostic artifacts** that help them better answer the questions their research is focused on.

A famous case study of using ground reconnaissance and surface collections is the Teotihuacan Mapping Project that started in the 1960s. Teotihuacan was one of the largest cities in the New World prior to AD 1500 and it is located about 50 km northeast of modern-day Mexico City. According to over a century of continuous research, Teotihuacan became an urban center during the period 150 BC to AD 1 and flourished as the capital of the Valley of Mexico with over 100,000 inhabitants in the period AD 250–350 until it was abandoned sometime during the period AD 550–650. Using aerial photographs that cover an area of about 53 km², the team of archaeologists conducted ground reconnaissance that defined the limit of the city, some 20 km² in extension. Subsequently, they con-

FIGURE 6.29 The Pyramid of the Moon at Teotihuacan, Mexico.

© WitR/Shutterstock.com

ducted intensive surface survey and collection, recording more than 5,000 structures. With these data, an archaeologist by the name of George Cowgill carried out a cluster analysis of potsherds that were collected in different parts of the central precinct of the city. The substantial outcomes of this research include the identification of wards or *barrios* where different cultural groups coming from distant regions lived, models of the growth and decline of population over time, and the sociospatial organization of architectural compounds.

This study at Teotihuacan was tremendously successful for demonstrating that surface collections can help to well-address questions concerning the functions, chronology, and activity areas of an archaeological site. Nonetheless, many features and artifacts on the ground surface are disturbed, and it is almost impossible to detect all the historical events happened in that study area because of the process of site formation. Archaeologists around the world are particularly careful about areas where mechanized agriculture has occurred and refer to the disturbed upper levels of sites disturbed by agricultural activities as the **plow zone**. Archaeologists must be mindful that the artifacts on the surface do not always represent the full range of functions and temporal depth of a study area. In the same vein, artifact densities on the surface do not always predict subsurface deposits. Excavation is a way of examining the reliability of the survey information by exposing buried sites, features, artifacts, and ecofacts. However, it is an expensive method, time-consuming, and most importantly a destructive process.

Geographic Information Systems

The storage and analysis of geospatial data through GIS software is now essential in archaeological research. The most common use of GIS is to record the location and attributes of targeted objects; any piece of data can be georeferenced and all kinds of information concerning it such as its size, morphology, chronological placement, or photographs can be stored in the GIS database. There are two basic functions that GIS software contains: digital mapping and geospatial analyses. Digital mapping of GIS is derived from a **computer-aided design program** (CAD), which allows archaeologists to create, manage, modify, and visualize construction plans and terrain maps, storing information in a series of layers. Even today, some CAD programs such as AutoCAD and Civil 3D are more powerful than other GIS software in terms of 3D mapping. Yet, in contrast to CAD, the advantage of GIS lies in a variety of spatial analyses that use combinations of different attributes stored in separate layers.

GIS software divides attributes into two different data structures: vector and raster. **Vector data** refer to one or more coordinates used to define an object in Cartesian space (i.e., x and y dimensional coordinates), storing elevation data (z coordinate) as an attribute and converting spatial information of a discrete object into geometrical shapes such as points, lines, and polygons. In contrast to the vector data of many GIS software, CAD systems use the vector format composed of 3D coordinates (i.e., x, y, z coordinates). The vector format is useful for some spatial analyses including Kernel density estimates and network analyses. Kernel density estimates measure a two-dimensional probability density (the "kernel"), which visually clusters the distribution of artifacts, features, or sites. Network analysis works similar to social network services such as Facebook and Twitter. It connects two independent data through a node that measures local connectivity (i.e., shared cultural characteristics).

Raster data use a grid of equally sized cells or pixels to analyze and represent spatial data. This means that the study area is defined by a number of rows and columns that cover square areas called cells. Each cell has one or more attributes of the object at that location. When a cell does not have any quantitative value of the object, GIS defines it as null. The raster format simplifies object values in cells, making the geospatial data suitable for spatial analyses. A well-known example is a **Digital Elevation Model** (DEM) in which each cell has a value of elevation. The DEM is the most fundamental format used for spatial analyses such as visibility, watershed, and least cost path. Visibility analysis in GIS is based on the question of whether a target point is visible from the viewpoint. If the elevations of all cells between this pair of points are lower than these, then the two points are mutually visible (intervisible). Using this technique, an archaeologist by the name of Wheatley (1995) examined the intervisibility of

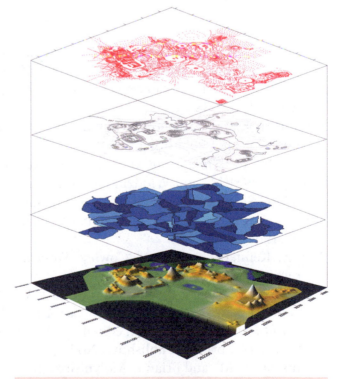

FIGURE 6.30 Different spatial data sets from the site of El Palmar, Mexico overlaid in a GIS program.

Source: Kenichiro Tsukamoto

long barrows (earthern burial mounds) in central southern England, concluding that their placement was not arbitrary, but guided by lines of sight. Similar criteria are used for the analysis of watershed (the flow of water in an area) and least cost path (easiest travelling paths). A critical point of the raster format is the cell size. If the size of the cells is small, the spatial analyses become more accurate, although the computer processing speed becomes slower and the need for more storage space significantly increases. Because of these problems, GIS software commonly combines both the vector and raster datasets. GIS software such as **Quantum GSI** (QGIS) or ESRI ArcGIS is designed for a wide range of social information that is creatable, storable, manageable, manipulative, and analyzable. Combining environmental information including soil, vegetation, elevation, slope, and streams with existing archaeological data, GIS programs can build a predicting model that delimits possible site locations in the study area. However, it is important to note that the model does not determine or reveal archaeological sites. Archaeologists always need to conduct ground verification to detect and locate sites.

Concluding Remarks

Surface survey and data collection, whether it is simply locating sites or involving detailed mapping and surface collection, can be either a prelude to excavations or the final result for fieldwork. In many cases, archaeologists never get beyond the surface, but collect important data for cultural heritage preservation and research. In other cases, destructive subsurface research follows. In the next chapter, we will discuss the methods available to archaeologists for excavation.

Bibliography

Aldenderfer, Mark, and Herbert D. G. Maschner. *Anthropology, Space, and Geographic Information Systems*. Oxford: Oxford University Press, 1996.

Ammerman, Albert J. "Surveys and Archaeological Research." *Annual Review of Anthropology* 10 (1981): 63–88.

Banning, E. B. *Archaeological Survey. Manuals in Archaeological Method, Theory, and Technique*. New York: Springer Publishing, 2002.

Barker, Philip. *Techniques of Archaeological Excavation*. 3rd ed. London: Routledge, 1993.

Bewley, Robert H., and Wlodzimierz Raczkowski. *Aerial Archaeology: Developing Future Practice*. NARO Science Series I: Life And Behavioural Sciences, Book 337. Amsterdam: IOS Press, 2002.

Binford, Lewis R. "A Consideration of Archaeological Research Design." *American Antiquity* 29 (1964): 425–441.

Brophy, Kenneth, and David Cowley. *From the Air: Understanding Aerial Photography*. Stroud: Tempus, 2005.

Chase, Arlen F., Diane Z. Chase, and John F. Weishampel. "The Use of LiDAR at the Maya Site of Caracol, Belize." In *A Primer on Space Archaeology: In Observance of the 40th Anniversary of the World Heritage Convention*, edited by D. C. Comer, 179–189. Springer Briefs in Archaeology 5. New York: Springer Publishing, 2013.

Collins, James M., and Brian L. Molyneaux. *Archaeological Survey*. Archaeologist's Toolkit 2. Walnut Creek, CA: AltaMira, 2003.

Conolly, James, and Mark Lake. 2006. *Geographical Information Systems in Archaeology*. Cambridge: Cambridge University Press, 2006.

Conyers, Lawrence B. *Ground-Penetrating Radar for Geoarchaeology*. Hoboken, NJ: John Wiley & Sons, 2016.

Crutchley, Simon P., and Peter Crow. *The Light Fantastic: Using Airborne LIDAR in Archaeological Survey*. Swindon: English Heritage, 2009.

Deuel, Leo. *Memoirs of Heinrich Schliemann: A Documentary Portrait Drawn from his Autobiographical Writings, Letters, and Excavation Reports*. New York: Harper & Row, 1977.

Fernandez-Diaz, Juan Carlos. "Lifting the Canopy Veil, Airborne LiDAR for Archeology of Forested Areas." *Imaging Notes* 26, no. 2 (2011).

Fernandez-Diaz, Juan Carlos, William E. Carter, Ramesh L. Shrestha, and Craig L. Glennie. "Now You See It… Now You Don't: Understanding Airborne Mapping LiDAR Collection and Data Product Generation for Archaeological Research in Mesoamerica." *Remote Sensing* 6 (2014): 9951–10001.

Gater, John, and Chris Gaffney. *Revealing the Buried Past: Geophysics for Archaeologists*. Stroud: Tempus, 2003.

Goodman, Dean, and Salvatore Piro. *GPR Remote Sensing in Archaeology. Geotechnologies and the Environment*, Vol. 9. New York: Springer Publishing, 2013.

Greene, Kevin. *Archaeology, an Introduction: The History, Principles, and Methods of Modern Archaeology*. London: B.T. Batsford Ltd, 1983.

Grove, David C. "Olmec: What's in a Name?" In *Regional Perspectives on the Olmec*, edited by R. J. Sharer and D. C. Grove, 8–14. Cambridge: Cambridge University Press, 1989.

Higham, Charles. *Early Mainland Southeast Asia: From First Humans to Angkor*. Bangkok, Thailand: River Books Press, 2001.

Johnson, Jay K, ed. *Remote Sensing in Archaeology: An Explicitly North American Perspective*. Tuscaloosa, AL: University of Alabama Press, 2006.

Kantner, John. "The Archaeology of Regions: From Discrete Analytical Toolkit to Ubiquitous Spatial Perspective." *Journal of Archaeological Research* 16 (2008): 37–81.

King, Thomas F. *Cultural Resource Laws & Practice: An Introductory Guide*. 2nd ed. Walnut Creek, CA: AltaMira Press, 2004.

Kintigh, Keith W. "The Effectiveness of Subsurface Testing: A Simulation Approach." *American Antiquity* 53 (1988): 686–707.

Kowalewski, Stephen A. "Merits of Full-Coverage Survey: Examples from the Valley of Oaxaca, Mexico." In *The Archaeology of Regions: The Case for Full Coverage Survey*, edited by S. Fish and S. Kowalewski, 33–83. Washington, DC: Smithsonian Institution Press, 1990.

———"Regional Settlement Pattern Studies." *Journal of Archaeological Research* 16 (2008): 225–285.

Lewis-Williams, David. *The Mind in the Cave: Consciousness and the Origins of Art*. New York: Thames and Hudson, 2004.

Lock, Gary, and Brian L. Molyneaux, eds. *Confronting Scale in Archaeology: Issues of Theory and Practice*. New York: Springer Publishing, 2006.

Magnoni, Aline, Travis W. Stanton, Nicolas Barth, Juan Carlos Fernandez Diaz, José Francisco Osorio León, Francisco Pérez Ruíz, and Jessica A. Wheeler. "Assessing Detection Thresholds of Archaeological Features in Airborne Lidar Data from Central Yucatán." *Advances in Archaeological Practice* 4, no. 3 (2016): 232–248.

Manahan, T. Kam, and Marcello A. Canuto. "Bracketing the Copan Dynasty: Late Preclassic and Early Postclassic Settlements at Copan, Honduras." *Latin American Antiquity* 20 (2009): 553–580.

Matos Moctezuma, Eduardo. *The Great Temple of the Aztecs: Treasures of Tenochtitlan*. London: Thames and Hudson, 1988.

Maxwell, G. S, ed. *The Impact of Aerial Reconnaissance on Archaeology*. London: Council for British Archaeology, 1983.

Neumann, Thomas W., and Robert M. Sanford. *Practicing Archaeology: A Training Manual for Cultural Resources Archaeology*. Walnut Creek, CA: AltaMira Press, 2001.

Oswin, John. *A Field Guide to Geophysics in Archaeology*. New York: Springer Publishing, 2009.

Portal, Jane. *The First Emperor: China's Terracotta Army*. Cambridge: Harvard University Press, 2007.

Rapp, George R. *Geoarchaeology: The Earth-Science Approach to Archaeological Interpretation*. New Haven, CT: Yale University Press, 2006.

Roskams, Steve. *Excavation*. Cambridge: Cambridge University Press, 2001.

Sanders, William T., Jeffery R. Parsons, and Robert S. Santley. *The Basin of Mexico: Ecological Processes in the Evolution of a Civilization*. New York: Academic Press, 1979.

Sullivan, Alan P., III, ed. *Surface Archaeology*. Albuquerque, NM: University of New Mexico Press, 1998.

Sullivan, Alan P., III, Philip B. Mink, and Patrick M. Uphus. "Archaeological Survey Design, Units of Observation, and Characterization of Regional Variability." *American Antiquity* 72, no. 2 (2007): 322–333.

Vincent, Matthew L., Víctor Manuel López-Menchero Bendicho, Marinos Ioannides, and Thomas E. Levy, eds. *Heritage and Archaeology in the Digital Age: Acquisition, Curation, and Dissemination of Spatial Cultural Heritage Data*. New York: Springer Publishing, 2017.

Wheatley, David. "Cumulative Viewshed Analysis: A GIS Based Method for Investigating Intervisibility and Its Archaeological Application." In *Archaeology and Geographic Information Systems: A European Perspective*, edited by G. Lock and Z. Stancic, 171–186. London: Taylor and Francis, 1995.

Willey, Gordon R. *Prehistoric Settlement Patterns in the Viru Valley, Peru*. Washington, DC: Bulletin 155. Bureau of American Ethnology, 1953.

Wiseman, James, and Farouk El-Baz, eds. *Remote Sensing in Archaeology*. New York: Springer Publishing, 2007.

Wood, Michael. *In Search of the Trojan War*. Berkeley: University of California Press, 1998.

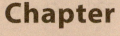

Excavation and Stratigraphy

As a data recovery method, excavation is probably the most well-known technique that archaeologists are associated with in the public eye. The romantic appeal of buried treasures revealed through digging has a long time depth in the history of the profession, propagated by sensational discoveries such as Tutankhamun's tomb by Howard Carter in 1922. Although, as we have already seen, archaeologists collect data using a wide variety of techniques, excavation is indeed a critical part of much archaeological work, in part because it reveals human activities in both specific temporal contexts (synchronic approach) and how they changed over time (diachronic approach). Excavations tend to be both costly and time-consuming, but often allow archaeologists to recover material data over temporal depths that are diffi-

FIGURE 7.1 Howard Carter with Tutankhamun's sarcophagus in 1923.

Discovery of the tomb of pharaoh Tutankhamun in the Valley of the Kings (Egypt): Howard Carter looking into the third coffin of Tutankhamun, 1923, photo by Harry Burton (p0770)/PVDE/Bridgeman Images.

cult, if not impossible in most cases, to gather through surface survey.

In this chapter, we describe basic methods of excavation. It is important to keep in mind that not all excavations are the same. In fact, there is considerable diversity in excavation strategies and methodologies. This is not just due to differences in research questions and resources, but also because sites can vary in their subsurface contexts. For example, excavation methods for a Neanderthal cave in France can be quite different from those for a Maya pyramid. A site in the Louisiana bayou is distinct from a noble's tomb in Egypt or a shell mound in Japan. In each excavation, archaeologists have to answer specific questions about how to move forward as new contexts are exposed: for instance, how to deal with water seeping into an excavation unit in a low-lying area, keeping the excavation walls from collapsing in rubble fill, or dealing with bioturbation. The list of possible situations that archaeologists confront is seemingly endless, and there is no one formula for excavation that can be applied everywhere. And yes, research questions and resources are important factors for the selection of excavation methods; such as how much to document or what tools to dig with. Thus, archaeologists should be flexible. Each excavation needs to be adapted to the condition of the site and, most importantly, to the research questions. With that said, there are some basic concepts regarding excavation that we will review in this chapter. We stress, however, that it is always important to remember that excavation is a destructive process that eliminates the archaeological context forever. Documentation methods are critical and should be thought through carefully prior to the start of work.

Preparation for Excavation

Before the actual digging starts, archaeologists must prepare the excavation area. This preparation includes taking photographs of the area as well as sometimes clearing certain surface features like vegetation. Surface features should be well documented and in many cases surface collections should be performed. Before the surface collections or excavations are undertaken, a **grid system** is set up over the area to be excavated. As we have seen in Chapter 5, archaeologists adopt a sampling strategy and set a grid square, usually adopting small-sized grid (2 × 2 m or less) for excavation; surface survey grid squares can be 10 × 10 m or more in some cases. The grid is tied to a **datum**, a point situated in three-dimensional (3D) space that all horizontal and vertical measurements are referenced to. A single datum might be required for smaller excavations like a single test pit, but for extensive excavations, **subdatums** that are situated in space by their reference to the primary datum are placed throughout the excavation to take measurements from a point closer to a specific context. In some cases, the excavation datum is also the **benchmark** for a larger map of the site. Some sites are small and the map fits within

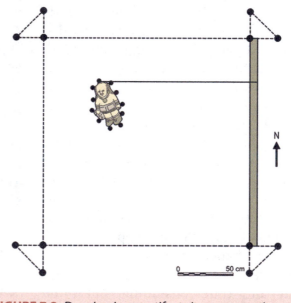

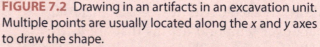

FIGURE 7.2 Drawing in an artifacts in an excavation unit. Multiple points are usually located along the *x* and *y* axes to draw the shape.

© Belem Ceballos Casanova

the excavation area. At sites that are large, such as Teotihuacan discussed in the previous chapter, different excavations may be conducted at some distance from each other. A separate datum may exist for each excavation, but they are all spatially tied into the larger grid covering the map.

There are several ways to set a grid system once a datum has been established. Many archaeologists set the base point for mapping in the southwest corner of the site or a datum for excavations southwest corner of the area to be dug, giving each square letters of the alphabet on one axis, for example, from west to east, and numbers on the other, from south to north; not all grids are oriented to the cardinal directions and some may follow cultural features. For instance, the first square of the grid at the southwest corner is A1 and the next square located east of the first square is B1, whereas the square located north of the first square is A2. Other archaeologists use Universal Transverse

Mercator (UTM) coordinates to locate a corner of each grid square. Regardless of how the grid is set up, it should be capable of expanding the excavation area in any direction as cultural contexts are exposed. Many archaeologists use each grid square as an **excavation unit**.

Types of Excavations

Broadly speaking, excavation methods selected by archaeologists depend a lot on the choice of temporal emphasis: synchronic or diachronic. Synchronic foci attempt to understand contemporaneous activities, usually over larger horizontal areas. Conversely, diachronic foci have a more vertical emphasis, gathering data that help to see changes in a specific area. In this section, we provide an overview of different kinds of excavation strategies that can have variable vertical and horizontal foci.

We have already discussed the first general category of excavation, **core/auger** and **shovel test pits** (Chapter 6). Although often employed as invasive methods of subsurface exploratory work that, because of the minimal disturbance to subsurface contexts, in some ways approximate remote sensing techniques, these methods are actually small excavations and are not technically forms of remote sensing. These kinds of minimal excavations are useful for delimiting the depth of cultural deposits and the general spatial distribution of material culture.

Another kind of excavation that we discussed as a subsurface survey method in the previous chapter is the **test pit**. This method, also called **sondage**, exposes a larger area than the shovel test pit, often reaching the sterile strata beneath cultural deposits. Its horizontal dimension is often 1 or 2 m² and allows archaeologists to enter the excavation; thus, the excavation can go deeper, and depostional layers can be more closely examined and documented. Archaeologists excavate test pits mostly to examine the occupational history of a site and recover subsurface artifacts. Therefore, test pit excavations are often implemented during the initial stage of the project when few subsurface data are available. When excavating a series of test pits in different parts of a site, archaeologists attempt to correlate events gleaned in depositional layers to reconstruct the site history. Test pit excavations can also be used as a complement

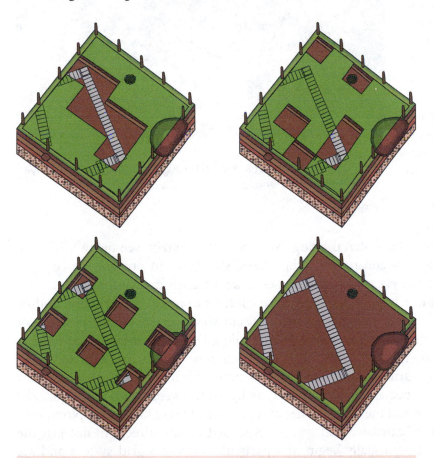

FIGURE 7.3 Different excavation strategies: adaptive sampling following a wall feature (top left); simple random sampling (top right); systematic sampling (bottom left); full horizontal coverage (bottom right)

© Kendall Hunt Publishing Company

to horizontal excavations to give a sense of depositional layers and artifact assemblage away from larger horizontal exposures.

A third technique is termed the **trench excavation**. A trench is a narrow linear excavation used as an economical way of detecting and following features in both their horizontal dimensions and vertical extents. The width of each trench is usually 1–2 m, whereas the length is variable. Oriented on the grid system, trench excavations can be conceived as a series of contiguous test pits, each one of which can be excavated along a straight line to varying depths. The trench excavation is especially useful for giving a cross section of an area. Because trenches may expose features that extend past the narrow width of the excavation, trench excavations can be adaptive and eventually expand in horizontal directions per-pendicular to their lengths. For exam-ple, a buried house structure might be encountered in the trench excavation, and due to sufficient resources, a deci-sion made to excavate perpendicular trenches or open up a larger horizontal exposure utilizing the same grid system might be taken. When the excavation hits a room wall perpendicularly, the trench excavation extends horizontally to expose the entire wall. Similar adap-tive capabilities could also be imple-mented for the previously discussed techniques (e.g., test pits).

A different application of trench excavations is termed **tunnel exca-vation**. In some archaeological con-texts, conditions permit the ability to excavate, or tunnel, horizontally into an archaeological context. This kind of excavation usually occurs in large

FIGURE 7.4 A tunnel excavated through a structure at the Maya site of Ceibal, Guatemala.

© Takeshi Inomata

architectural contexts. In some cases, the material being excavated (the **matrix**, see below), is more easily removed without much danger of collapse. In other cases, structures to prevent the collapse of the tunnel are put into place as the excavation progresses. Like a trench excavation, tunnels are excavated horizontally in a straight line but go into subsurface contexts to reveal construction and/or depositional sequences. For example, most monumental buildings in Mesoamerica are the products of a series of constructions that make these features resemble layer cakes. Due to their large size, tunnels are sometimes excavated inside of them to evaluate their construction sequences and expose buried features. Without the tunnels, deeply buried contexts might not be accessible for research. As you might imagine, tunnel excavation requires special equipment such as lights and ventilation and is usually undertaken by specialists who understand the complexities and dangers of these kinds of explorations.

Horizontal excavations are more extensive and can be expanded in any direction, not just the straight line of trench excavations. They usually begin in a particular area of a grid system and are expanded out by opening up adjacent grid squares, often following features and depositional layers. Some horizontal excavations are designed to stay near the surface, clearing deposits down to more superficial stratigraphic layers or features. In fact, such excavations are often called **clearing** or **strip-ping excavations**. The emphasis here is more on the horizontal dimension than the vertical dimension. Other horizontal excavations have strong vertical components where some or all of the grid squares are excavated down to a substantial depth. As with deeper test pits and trenches, this emphasis on the vertical dimension leads archaeologists to call these kinds of explorations **stratigraphic** or **penetrating excavations**. Although all excavations are stratigraphic, deeper excavations tend to expose more depositional layers.

Although all excavations are set up on a grid system, horizontal excavations require much more complex ways of setting up and maintaining the grid. An early kind of grid system was developed by Mortimer Wheeler who emphasized keeping areas of depositional layers intact as the excavations progressed. The **Wheeler box-grid** consists of a grid of squares divided by **balks**, which preserve profiles where the depositional layers can be seen among the excavated squares of the grid. Using this method, archaeologists can observe different layers of each grid square and correlate across the site in vertical profiles. Once the profiles are drawn, the balks are removed, recording artifacts and ecofacts inside the balks. The Wheeler box-grid method is popular in parts of Europe, and East and South Asia, where small numbers of archaeologists need to supervise a large number of workers. Nevertheless, some archaeologists have criticized the usefulness of the Wheeler box-grid because the balks that divide the excavation area prevent the identification of some spatial patterns. Other grids are marked by strings or stakes. Stratigraphic layers are recorded as each grid unit is excavated down and the matrix removed.

The tools archaeologists use to excavate and the pace at which those excavations occur can vary and depend on the research questions and the stratigraphic conditions that each project faces. For example, excavators, or backhoes are occasionally used, particularly during salvage work, to unearth topsoil of the excavation area. A skillful worker can control the machine, removing the soil with a precision of a few centimeters in many cases. Salvage excavations sometimes employ such machines because they excavate an extensive area in limited time. On the other side of the spectrum, small dental tools might be employed at a painstakingly slow pace at Paleolithic or Paleoindian sites

FIGURE 7.5 In some cases, it is appropriate to use heavy machinery in archaeology, such as this work conducted on the Giza Plateau of Egypt.

© 2018 Ancient Egypt Research Associates. Photo by Mark Lehner. AERA_Pedestal_bldg_pedestals.tif

where every piece of material data is documented *in situ* (in its original depositional location). It is important to remember that not all of these methods and tools are mutually exclusive. Quite the contrary, most projects combine different excavation methods and tools to address the research question; each has its advantages and limitations and should be selected judiciously. The crucial point here is that archaeologists have a wide array of methods and tools available to them and should remain flexible to adapt to any field situation to best document and collect data.

Key Concepts

Before moving on to the methods of collection and documentation of data used during excavations, it is important to review a few key concepts. The **matrix** refers to the material that surrounds and supports archaeological data. It usually consists of soil, sediment, gravel, and rock, but also of water and ice in other situations. **Provenience** refers to the horizontal and vertical position of archaeological data within the matrix; the 3D coordinates that locate the data in space. **Provenance** is not the same as provenience, but refers to the original location where artifacts were made. In many cases, the provenance (where it was made) of an artifact is different from its provenience (where it was deposited). As we will detail later in this book, archaeologists have various tools that can be used to assess the provenance, or source, of certain materials. **Association** is the relation of two or more artifacts, ecofacts, or features, occurring in the same matrix. The association of data can provide key information to the archaeologist. For example, a projectile point found in association with bison remains may lead to interpretive scenarios that focus on hunting, whereas a similar point found lodged into human bone might lead to interpretations along the lines of conflict.

The **context**, one of the most important concepts in archaeological research, is the final evaluation of the significance of the provenience, association, and matrix. Archaeological research is all about context. For example, the matrix may tell the archaeologist whether the context was deposited in fine alluvial sediments that might suggest flooding or with particular gravels common with glacial formations. The provenience of the data might be on the top of a mountain or at the bottom of a valley. The artifacts might be associated with a marketplace or a temple. All of these data together help tell a much richer story than any one of them in isolation. **Context is key!** Thus, archaeologists should document the context of artifacts, ecofacts, and features as carefully as possible during both survey and excavation. Once archaeological data are detached from their context, that context is almost impossible to recover. For instance, some artifacts exhibited in museums come from private collections without any context (often looted from unknown sites), meaning that their matrix, provenience, and association are lost forever. Those objects can tell us something about the past, but without their context, the potential for rich interpretations is diminished. An example is a cylinder vase of ancient Maya society, which is exhibited at Los Angeles County Museum (LACMA). It depicts moon goddess and other supernatural beings with Maya hieroglyphs. Several archaeologists, art-historians, iconographers, and epigraphers have studied this beautiful polychrome vessel, uncovering meanings of the mythological scene. Nevertheless, we do not know where it was made (provenance), and where and how it was deposited (provenience, matrix, association). With that said, there are two types of archaeological contexts that researchers commonly use: primary and secondary.

Primary contexts refer to conditions where the provenience, matrix, and association are relatively

FIGURE 7.6 A Classic period Maya vase (ca. AD 600–800) depicting a Moon goddess

Cylinder Vase with Moon Goddess and Other Celestial Beings. Mexico, Olmec, 900–300 BCE, Serpentine with traces of cinnabar, Height: 4 1/4 in. (10.8 cm). Los Angeles County Museum of Art, Gift of Constance McCormick Fearing (M.86.311.6) Photo © Museum Associates/LACMA.

undisturbed. We stress the word "relatively" because all archaeological contexts have more or less suffered from some disturbance or transformation over time. Remember, the past is in the present and, with few exceptions, time changes things. Metal objects might rust. Bones might settle as soft tissue decays. Burrowing rodents might slightly displace an artifact or two. These are relatively minor changes to the context, leading archaeologists to classify such contexts as primary, such as the famous terracotta army of the first emperor of China, where the warriors are still in their original tactical formation.

Archaeologists further break the concept of primary contexts into use-related and transposed primary contexts. **Use-related primary contexts** refer to situations where material culture was deposited in a place where people acquired, produced, or used it. Lithic tool debris at a stone quarry or ceramic vessels still located in a storage room of workshop would be examples of this kind of primary context. The idea behind this concept is that these kinds of contexts shed more light on behaviors associated directly with them. A ceramic vessel located in a burial would be classified as a primary context and archaeologists might be able to say something more about that object and its role in mortuary rituals because of context in which it was found, as opposed to, let's say, in a trash pit. Yet, broadly speaking, primary contexts tend to represent one slice of time in the history of objects and places. That same ceramic vessel may have been used to serve food before its use as a mortuary offering. The burial context may have been a storage pit prior to being the final resting place for the deceased. Although use-related primary contexts can often offer solid data for particular interpretations and are often viewed to have a privileged position in archaeological interpretation, archaeologists must not lose sight of the fact that they tend to represent particular moments in the "life-histories" of things and places. As we will detail later on in this book (Chapter 10), researchers have several tools at their disposal to look at life-history questions with data from both primary and secondary contexts.

Transposed primary contexts refer to situations where materials (e.g., artifacts, ecofacts, and even features and matrices) were deposited in a place different from activity areas where people acquired, produced, or used them. A good example of the transposed primary context is a refuse deposit, or **midden**. A broken stone figurine found in a context of domestic trash presents, in some ways, more challenges to archaeologists grappling with how to interpret the meaning of the figurine than some other kinds of contexts. Was it used in ritual activities? Was it a child's toy? Again, we will discuss some of the tools that archaeologists can employ to attempt to address life history issues later on in the book, but the fact that the figurine was found in the trash, instead of next to a religious-looking altar or in the burial of a child, changes interpretational possibilities. This is not to say that finding the figurine in a child's burial means that it *was* a toy. There might be other ways to interpret the figurine in that context. This is also not to say that finding the figurine in the midden is not meaningful. In fact, throwing the figurine in the trash was *definitely* meaningful; all material culture, even trash, has meaning. Yet, archaeologists do tend to make a distinction between depositional contexts and whether they have to do with the acquisition, production, or use of material culture associated with them.

In contrast to primary contexts, **secondary contexts** are those where the provenience, matrix, and/or association of archaeological data are disturbed, although as might be expected from the discussion of primary contexts above there are different criteria as to how much disturbance makes a context secondary. Different factors can transform archaeological contexts. Biological agents such as animals, tree roots, and insects are often responsible for altering archaeological contexts. Earthquakes, floods, tsunamis, landslides, volcanic eruptions, natural decay, and erosion can also cause disturbances of archaeological contexts. Nevertheless, the most important factor in the disturbance of archaeological data is often human agents, both in modern and ancient times. The timing of human disturbance, however, can complicate the use of the term secondary context. It is one thing if an archaeological context is disturbed by natural forces, for instance, rodents who enter a burial crypt, gnawing on the bones and moving all of the material culture around. It would be quite another if it was a human who entered the burial crypt of their ancestor 1,000 years ago and removed bones to be utilized for ancestor veneration. In one sense, the disturbance of the original context (the burial deposition) leads archaeologists to classify it as a secondary burial. The human skull found at Jericho, located in modern-day Israel, is a famous example of such behavior. The skull probably came from an earlier tomb and people covered the skull with plaster, placing white cowrie shells on the cavities of the eyes. Yet, at the same time, this disturbance

FIGURE 7.7 A human skull with cowrie shells in the eye sockets from the site of Jericho, located in the Palestinian territories of the West Bank (ca. seventh-millennium BC).

Portrait skull with cowrie shell eyes, Jericho, c. 7th millennium BC (skull, plaster, shell), Prehistoric/Ashmolean Museum, University of Oxford, UK/Bridgeman Images

created a different kind of primary context, one focused on postdepositional treatment of the dead that still informs us of ancient behavior. Depending on this slice of time that archaeologists want to draw their attention, in this case, to the original deposition of the body or to its postdepositional treatment, there may be variability concerning whether to term the context primary or secondary.

Another similar case comes from the site of Teotihuacan. Underneath the Pyramid of the Sun at the site, archaeologists located an artificial cave that led to a series of chambers underneath this immense structure. A project to explore the cave has determined that the context was entered in ancient times and looted of much of its material culture. Many archaeologists would consider this context secondary given the looting of the original deposits, which could have possibly included rich offerings accompanying the burial of an important person in the early history of the city. However, archaeologists interested in the practice of ancient looting and what it means for understanding social and political changes in the ancient Valley of Mexico might see these disturbed deposits as primary as they represent the actions of ancient peoples. Without this evidence of disturbance, certain behaviors important to understanding the history of Teotihuacan might remain invisible to researchers; the ancient looting itself it highly informative. In the end, the disturbance of the context represents a "use" of the material culture in this particular time and place. If the looting was attributed to relatively modern times, most archaeologists would term it a secondary context, but because it happened in ancient times classifying it as a primary or secondary context becomes more complicated.

Provenience Control in the Field

So now excavations have begun and you have to begin documenting the data that is being exposed. How do you go about this process? When features, artifacts, and ecofacts are exposed and evaluated *in situ*, archaeologists need to record their provenience. Traditionally, the horizontal location of artifacts and features are recorded measuring (often with a measuring tape) each data point from the southwest corner of a grid square, which, being tied into the larger site grid, can then be located in relation to all other data at a site. For example, the UTM coordinates of the south-west corner of the entire excavation grid might be 240,320 m easting and 2,050,120 m northing. If each grid square is set as 2 × 2 m and you are exca-vating the C2 grid square, the southwest corner of your unit has a location of 204,324 m easting and 2050,122 m northing. Say you find an artifact in C2 and it measures 1.3 m east and 0.5 m north of the southwest corner, the coordinates of the artifact are 204,325.3 m easting and 2050,122.5 m northing. Because the artifact is georeferenced, we can then plot it on a geographic information system (GIS) map (Chapter 6).

FIGURE 7.8 Recording the provenience of material culture in an excavation at the site of El Palmar, Mexico. Keeping track of the spatial location of archae-ological data is critical for research.

Source: Kenichiro Tsukamoto

The elevation of archaeological data is also recorded as its vertical distance from a datum or sub-datum, which is a fixed point that has either an arbitrary elevation or the absolute elevation usually expressed as **above mean sea level** (AMSL). Either optical (usually a string with a line level and a measuring tape) or electronic instruments (often a total station) may be used to measure relative elevation from the datum. Using the grid square for horizontal provenience and a datum point for vertical provenience is practical because each group of excavators in a unit can record the location of archaeological materials quickly and independently.

More recently, many archaeological projects employ total stations to record the 3D data of archae-ological materials without measuring them with a tape. A total station significantly saves time to document and record the exact location of each artifact and feature with 3D coordinates, even when there are a few crew chiefs in the field. Further, integrating a laptop with a GIS program into the work flow allows archaeologists to confirm the distribution of features and artifacts immediately in the field. Nevertheless, even if we use a total station to record provenience during excavation, the grid layout and datum are still useful for operating excavations. Excavating along a grid results in straight walls (or this is at least the hope) that are important for recording depositional layers. Another considera-tion for the importance of grid systems is that many archaeological projects do not record the exact location of every artifact, especially in contexts where there is overwhelming amounts of material data, many of which may come from secondary contexts. Moreover, as we will discuss in the next section, not all archaeological data are clearly visible in the excavation and many data are recovered after the matrix has been removed from its context. The grid system is an essential way to keep data collected together associated with a small area of provenience (e.g., a 20 cm level of a 2 × 2 m grid

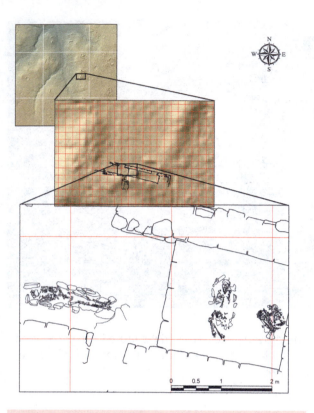

FIGURE 7.9 Multiple scales of data in GIS. The upper most image represents a LiDAR image of the entire site of El Palmar, Mexico divided into 500 m x 500 m grids. The center image represents a smaller grid of 2 m x 2 m of the area where the burials were found. The bottom image shows the location of three burials in a structure room.

Source: Kenichiro Tsukamoto

FIGURE 7.10 Screening excavated matrix at the site of El Palmar, Mexico.

Source: Kenichiro Tsukamoto

square). A further consideration is the cost of total station equipment. Many projects use such equipment, but do not have enough of them for all of the excavation areas. Thus, a total station is usually a complement to the traditional ways of recording provenience in a grid system.

Recovering Data during Excavations

To record data, however, archaeologists must first find them. Finding artifacts, ecofacts, and features is heavily dependent on excavator's ability and experience. Even some larger features might go unnoticed by the untrained eye. Adobe bricks, tamped earth floors, and even hearths may blend into the surrounding matrix and many archaeological projects have faced situations where features are seen in the profile of depositional layers after the unit was excavated. This problem stresses the importance of slow and careful work, but also the value of experience and training in the identification of archaeological data.

Another issue that archaeologists face is the size of archaeological data. Some artifacts and ecofacts are easily spotted as excavations progress. These can be documented *in situ*. Some fairly large pieces, however, might not be readily visible in the excavation. For instance, in muddy matrices that have a lot of naturally occurring inclusions such as stones, some artifacts and ecofacts might be difficult to see during the process of excavation. In other cases, archaeological data are just too small to be identified as the come out of the ground. To account for these issues, archaeologists have developed a series of methods to recover as much material data as possible.

Screening (or sieving) is a way to standardize the recovery process of hard to see items from the matrix. It involves passing the excavated matrix through a wire mesh of a particular size. Most excavations employ **dry-screening** through a wire mesh of one-quarter inch in size. The loose matrix (such as soil) falls through the screen and leaves artifacts, ecofacts, and larger pieces of the matrix (such as stones) that are larger than the holes in the mesh. Smaller screens are sometimes employed to recover tiny artifacts and ecofacts, sometimes termed **fine-screening**. Fine-screening is more time consuming and is usually employed in certain contexts (e.g., where small animal bones might be found) or on a sample of the matrix.

When matrix is sticky and cannot pass a metal mesh or obscures artifact/ecofact visibility, archaeologists sometimes employ a technique called **wet-screening**. This technique functions by immersing matrix on the screen in water allowing the matrix to dissolve, pass the screen, and make material of interest more visible. There are different methods that archaeologists can employ to perform wet-screening, such as passing water from a hose over material on a mesh or dipping a bucket with a mesh bottom full of matrix into a river. All of these methods, however, require a substantial amount of water, which might not be readily available in some areas such as deserts or some highland regions.

Flotation is similar to wet-screening in that water is used to recover materials of interest. This method func-

FIGURE 7.11 Wet-screening matrix in a Defense POW/MIA Accounting Agency (DPAA) mission to recover fallen service members from the Vietnam War in Khammouan Province, Laos. The water helps to dissolve the matrix, which can be difficult to pass through a screen in certain contexts (e.g., matrices with high clay content).

Source: U.S. Marine Corps Photo by MCIPAC Combat Camera Lance Cpl. Brook Dieters

tions, however, by separating macrobotanical or other organic remains such as insect and snail remains from mineral grains in the soil by agitating them in water, or in some cases, other liquids such as carbon tetrachloride solution. Some variations on the method are quite simple. **Wet sieving** functions by placing the matrix into a bucket of water and agitating it until the lighter material remains (called the **light fraction**), such as charcoal (wood that has been burnt) or seeds, float to the surface and can be skimmed off the surface using a net. The **heavy fraction**, consisting of the materials that sink to the bottom such as small bone and lithic fragments, is usually collected in a fine mesh at the bottom. In some cases, a series of superimposed meshes that have increasingly smaller apertures are located at the bottom of the container in order to separate materials by size. Collected fractions are then separated, dried, and then bagged for analysis. Other flotation methods are more complex than wet sieving and involve machines that agitate the samples using air or water pumps, sometimes in large containers such as oil drums. Flotation machines are especially useful for processing large numbers of samples. In some cases, flocculating agents such as detergents are used to create froth usefully for collecting certain kinds of materials. Flotation is quite time-consuming and it is nearly impossible to process all the matrices from excavations using this technique. Therefore, a sampling strategy is generally employed to sample a certain amount of the excavated matrix, which may be weighted more heavily toward specific types of contexts. Flotation is especially important for research that relies on micro-data such as research on agriculture (e.g., seeds that may be recovered in the light fraction) and activity areas (e.g., micro-artifacts that might be recovered in the heavy fraction).

Documentation

The accurate interpretation of excavation data depends upon how well archaeologists document field information. Given that excavation is destructive, documentation practices are critical and in most cases serve as the only available source of information of excavated contexts. Apart from recording provenience, there are several other basic steps in the documentation process. One of the most important of these steps is the taking of **field notes**. Even in the digital era, most archaeological projects still use paper field notes as an essential recording method of archaeological data. Creating logs of the work conducted each day, archaeologists record the progress of excavations, and can include information ranging from the weather on a particular day (which might be relevant for other archaeologists to understand decisions made in the field) to observations of depositional layers (which could provide valuable context not easily extracted from photographs and drawings). The more detailed the notes, the more likely that potentially valuable information will be recorded that can help both the archaeologist who excavated the context remember the excavations and for other archaeologists to understand that context well. The descriptions can be concise, but well enough to record objectives of the excavation unit, contexts, matrix, association, provenience, descriptions of features, artifacts, and ecofacts, and depositional layer, as well as other daily observations. A clear organization of the notes should be maintained using headings that include information such as the date the notes were taken and the context being described. In many cases, multiple excavation units will be supervised by a single archaeologist at the same time and it is critical to keep the descriptions labeled using the terminology and excavation system employed by the project (e.g., excavation operation, unit, level, or lot). If the archaeologist employs workers in the excavation unit, their names should be recorded in field notes. A log of features and/or artifact/ecofacts is also commonly employed to keep track of data.

Some projects prefer to use standardized forms in place of field notes, because they provide minimum information that any archaeologist should record in the field. Such forms are often useful for large projects involving numerous researchers with different skills. By employing such forms, project directors can standardize acquisition of the same categories of archaeological data and store these data in computer database. Therefore, the standardize forms should include the overall field recording system. Examples of standardized forms include excavation forms, burial forms, and feature forms. The disadvantage of using standardized forms, however, is its relative inflexibility. As we mentioned at the beginning of this chapter, each site may present unique challenges for excavations and archaeologists should be as flexible as possible. Thus, standardized forms are often used in conjunction with more free-form field note taking.

Drawings and photographs are also essential methods for documenting excavation data. As we discussed in Chapter 6, photography can be utilized in several ways. Drones, for example, might be employed to take vertical images or excavation areas.

FIGURE 7.12 Drone photography of an excavation at El Palmar, Mexico.

Source: Kenichiro Tsukamoto

FIGURE 7.13 Photogrammetry of an excavation at the site of Aguada Fenix, Mexico.

© Takeshi Inomata

Numerous photographs might be taken, either in the air or from the ground, to create 3D models of excavation contexts (which can also be accomplished using a laser scanner). At the very least, individual shots of the excavations should be taken at each step in the excavation process to create a good visual record of the contexts. The use of photography gives archaeologists snapshots of the beginning, middle, and end of excavations. Photographs should include a scale and orientation (often a north arrow) as well as contextual information (often on a photo board). As with all electronic data (e.g., GPS or total station points), digital photos should be downloaded on a daily basis, clearly labeled and organized, and backed up so that the data are understandable and safe. Although photography is an essential part of the documentation process, it has its limitations as photographs sometime obscure relevant data of the site by recording everything. Archaeologists usually select, visualize, and interpret particular aspects of archaeological contexts, removing irrelevant information and adding information such as numbers and comments.

In contrast to photographs, drawings are not solely visual representations of the archaeological record, but include an interpretive component. As with planimetric mapping, excavation drawings can be made using different conventions. Some archaeologists use pictorial styles similar to photographic representation, whereas others use more schematic drawing styles which employ some sort of symbolic representation or even purely interpretative drawing styles with firm lines dividing the boundaries of features and layers, but little visualization of features themselves. In many cases, archaeologists

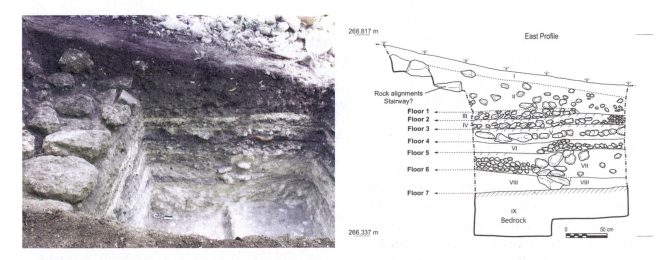

FIGURE 7.14 A photo and drawing of an excavation profile from the site of El Palmar, Mexico.

Source: Kenichiro Tsukamoto

combine these three techniques, drawing layer divisions with detailed outlines of features and artifacts. Further, archaeologists choose which data to include and which to omit. So, while drawings are very important for documentation, they should be carefully thought through in regard to the kinds of information that the archaeologist wishes to transmit. Today, field drawings are usually redrawn in an electronic format. Nevertheless, the original drawings should be scanned and stored.

With that said, drawing is a much more intensive and time-consuming process compared to photography and not everything in an excavation gets drawn. Decisions must be made in the field as to the importance of having particular features drawn in the field. Field drawings of excavation **profiles** (also called walls, sections, or cuts) have been standard in archaeology (as are plan drawings). Yet, if the depositional layer is the same in all four walls of an excavation unit, some archaeologists might choose to draw just one wall as representative of the four. In certain cases, features, such as burials, hearths, or architecture might be drawn. In other cases, every single artifact in a level might be drawn or **point-plotted** (recording the exact location). The point here is that what kinds of drawings are created in the field can be variable as are the data that are included on them. However, traditional drawing techniques by hand have slowly been replaced with digital technologies to speed up field operations. As mentioned earlier, archaeologists can now create accurate 3D models of excavation based on ground control points with x, y, and z coordinates set by a total station on the excavation unit and a series of digital pictures taking targeted features, artifacts, ecofacts, and profiles. These new technologies are particularly helpful for drawing complex features such as burials and tombs in plan view, which requires a special skill to draw by hand. Even a well-trained archaeologist or physical anthropologist takes considerable time to draw the skeleton. Software programs such as *PhotoScan* are especially powerful because they can generate the 3D contours, digital elevation models (DEMs), and ortho-image (color images such as pictures that contain geographic coordinates with accurate scale). DEM and ortho-images can be exported to ArcGIS where a georeferenced drawing can be made. In fact, with the advent of digital photographic technology, drawings can be made after fieldwork has been completed using a wide variety of different software.

Archaeologists occasionally use the same basic techniques to draw both horizontal plans and vertical sections. Regarding horizontal plans, we use the southwest corner of a grid square as a starting point, from which we measure the location of features and artifacts to draw on a millimeter paper. When complicated features or artifacts are present in the excavation unit, we tend to set a portable grid frame on the excavation unit horizontally; the ideal frame is the same size as the dimension of the excavation unit or has extendable legs. The drawing technique for vertical profiles is basically the same. We set up a series of horizontal and vertical strings on the profiles. Then, horizontal strings are usually set up with a level or a line level. A tape is laid out along the line of the string above the surface by clipping the both sides to the stakes of the excavation unit. A line is set up above the surface, using the elevation of a datum and from this line at a known point we draw features, artifacts, and layer divisions on the profile. The plans and sections should be matched each other.

FIGURE 7.15 Drawing a profile at El Palmar, Mexico.

Source: Kenichiro Tsukamoto

During the excavation process, material data such as artifacts and ecofacts will be removed for analysis in a laboratory setting. All of the recovered material should be "tagged and bagged" after being removed from the matrix. In some cases, individual objects will be bagged separately. In others, such as when the matrix from a 20 cm level of a 2 × 2 m unit is grouped as a single provenience, objects may be bagged together based on particular attributes such as material categories that include stone, ceramic, and metal. These materials may also be grouped in bags and then separated in the lab after they have been processed, which may include brushing or washing them. It is very important not to lose the provenience of these materials and bags or other material containers should be properly labeled. It is essential that they be logical, legible, and comprehensive for third persons, using acid-free paper and water-resistant inks. The bag label or tag should contain number-coded data that allow for speed in the recording process, saving of space, and easily feeding the information into the database. The example tag here contains the site name, structure name, excavation unit, layer, lot (see below), register (a person who filled out the label), and date. The structure name, excavation unit, layer, lot, type of artifact, and date can be coded as GZ1-A20-III-1-CV and 20-VI-17 (day, month, and year). CV means ceramic vessel in this case. The Roman numeral is used to write the month to prevent confusion with the Arabic numerals indicating the day. There should also be a space for comments on the tag.

Stratigraphy

Stratigraphy, a concept borrowed from geology (see Chapter 3), is the study and interpretation of **strata**, or depositional layers of natural (e.g., soils, rocks, and sediments) or cultural materials.

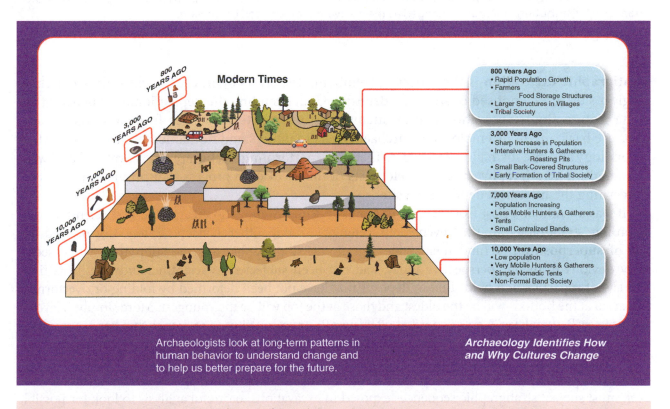

800 Years Ago
- Rapid Population Growth
- Farmers
        Food Storage Structures
- Larger Structures in Villages
- Tribal Society

3,000 Years Ago
- Sharp Increase in Population
- Intensive Hunters & Gatherers
        Roasting Pits
- Small Bark-Covered Structures
- Early Formation of Tribal Society

7,000 Years Ago
- Population Increasing
- Less Mobile Hunters & Gatherers
- Tents
- Small Centralized Bands

10,000 Years Ago
- Low population
- Very Mobile Hunters & Gatherers
- Simple Nomadic Tents
- Non-Formal Band Society

Archaeologists look at long-term patterns in human behavior to understand change and to help us better prepare for the future.

Archaeology Identifies How and Why Cultures Change

FIGURE 7.16 Archaeological sites often are formed through complex processes, which can lead to complicated stratigraphy.

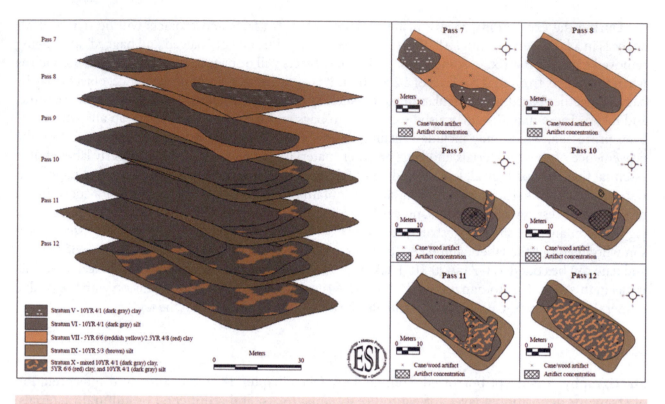

FIGURE 7.17 A series of horizontal slices from an excavation at site of Troyville, Louisiana. You can see how the horizontal distribution of features changed as the excavation progressed downward.

© Jill Yakubik - ESI

Stratigraphic excavation is the process of removing the layers of an excavation unit. All archaeological sites are composed of stratified deposits. Understanding the depositional sequence of the strata from a single excavation and/or attempting to correlate sequences from multiple excavations are basic methods employed by archaeologists to understand fundamental questions such as chronology and site formation processes. Therefore, performing stratigraphic excavations and well-documenting stratigraphy are critical elements of the excavation process that provide information concerning the historical depth of the site.

It was a Catholic priest from Denmark named **Nicolas Steno** who created the first scientific work regarding stratigraphy in the seventeenth century. Among other concepts, Steno formulated the **law of superposition**, a fundamental idea sustaining stratigraphic interpretation that, while seemingly obvious from our perspective today, had not been subjected to scientific study until his time. The law of superposition holds that in deposits that have not been deformed by folding or overturning the strata at the bottom will be the oldest and those at the top will be the youngest. More simply, if layer A covers layer B, then layer A was deposited *after* layer B; strata constitute a sequence that has accumulated in order through time. Although there are natural (e.g., geological folding or erosional patterns) and cultural (e.g., excavation of deep materials that are redeposited on the surface) reasons for strata being out of chronological order, the law of superposition generally holds for most deposits. Archaeologists, however, must subject stratigraphic sequences exposed in excavations to careful analysis to look for possible anomalies and understand the relative chronological relationships among the strata. We stress the term "relative" as stratigraphy does not resolve questions of chronology in absolute terms. With stratigraphy alone, archaeologists cannot say whether a stratum was deposited 100 or 10,000 years ago. What can be evaluated is whether one stratum is older or younger in relation to another.

When excavations cut into the surface, archaeologists can observe the **stratification** (the sequence of strata) in the sections (or vertical profiles) of the excavation unit. Prior to any excavations in an area, however, archaeologists do not know what to expect from the stratigraphy; there is no profile to guide important decisions made during the excavation process. Even in areas where previously excavated data are available (e.g., an adjacent excavation unit), each individual unit may have a relatively unique sequence and care must be taken in terms of separating materials from stratigraphic levels. Some data from remote sensing techniques such as GPR might be available, but these techniques usually do not have the resolution needed to define most stratigraphic contexts. Stated another way, archaeologists must choose to break up stratigraphic contexts as they excavate, and in many cases, this is not an easy task. Archaeologists perform stratigraphic excavations and seek to distinguish one archaeological context from the next by following natural and cultural stratigraphy. For instance, if an archaeologist is digging in a dark brown soil and a bright red soil begins to appear below it, the archaeologist stops to clear the rest of the brown soil, bag and tag all of the materials from that context, and perform any necessary documentation (e.g., photos, drawings, and measurements). The red soil beneath it is then excavated as a separate context and all of the materials found in it bagged and tagged separately so that they can be distinguished from the above materials.

Spotting changes in the stratigraphy as you excavate can be challenging, but any change in the matrix might hold some important information. If the archaeologist separated the artifacts from the brown and red soil strata, they might see that there is a difference and be able to classify those differences chronologically (the artifacts from the red soil being older). If he or she did not separate those strata and included all of the artifacts in the same bag, the potential for seeing that archaeological pattern in the data would be gone, stressing the importance of dividing strata up as excavations progress.

So, what characteristics of the strata should an archaeologist use to define stratigraphic breaks in the excavation? Well, anything really. Each stratum may differ from others based on a variety of characteristics that include color, texture (the size of soil particles), and the size, frequency, and composition of other natural and cultural inclusions. Color is one of the most common ways to identify strata. As there is variation in how people define colors, archaeologists use a standardized color system, in particular the **Munsell color chart** that illustrates different soil colors. Although the Munsell colors are standardized, it is important to keep in mind that soils and sediments change in the

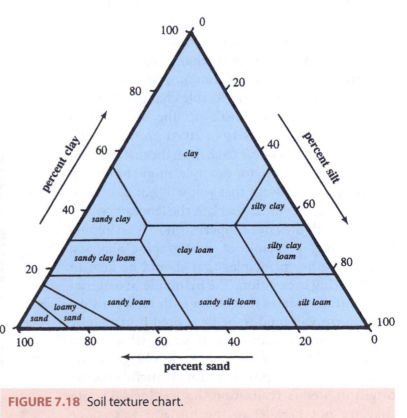

FIGURE 7.18 Soil texture chart.

© Kendall Hunt Publishing Company

darkness and intensity of their colors and projects should consistently use wet, dry, or both evaluations of color as standard practice. The evaluation of soil texture has also been standardized to some degree in archaeology. Different sized particles can be included in the matrix ranging from clay (less than 0.02 mm in size), silt (0.02–0.05 mm), and sand (0.05–2.0 mm); larger pieces such as gravels might also be present. A standardized soil texture chart exists for classification purposes. The three smaller particles (clay, silt, and sand) are found in the three points of the triangle with various combinations of frequencies of these sizes found toward the middle (loam deposits contain particles of all three sizes). In theory, this chart functions well, although in practice archaeologists have a more difficult time calculating the exactness of particle sizes as they can color using the Munsell chart; often rubbing the soil between their fingers. It is important to note that the definition of the soil texture has nothing to do with types of minerals in the soil, but is based on the size of the particles.

Using these kinds of characteristics, archaeologists must make decisions as to whether the changes they see as more matrix is removed warrant stopping the excavation to bag, tag, and document before moving along in a new **excavation lot** or **level** (ways of separating contexts), keeping the materials separated. Maybe a few flecks of gray ash start to show up in a dark brown soil. Should you stop? Maybe it is a new stratum. Maybe it is a small feature like a hearth that needs to be exposed, documented, and removed separately from the surrounding layer. The most prudent thing to do in a case like this would be to gradually and carefully remove some more matrix to see if the flecks turn into something important and make a decision after you can explore it a bit more. Maybe it turns out to be just a couple of small flecks (that you diligently note in your field notebook and/or excavation form) and you keep excavating down. Maybe it is something that requires you to stop and change lots. Regardless, excavation is a kind of organic process that entails making these kinds of decisions on a constant basis. These kinds of characteristics, however, are not the only factor that determines whether to change lots. Depth is also an important consideration. A stratum may be very thick, with no noticeable changes. In these cases, archaeologists break up the strata using arbitrary levels, such as 10 or 20 cm. Although the matrix might not appear to change, the material you collect in the screens, for example, might be changing in important ways that you will not be able to appreciate until you are back in the laboratory.

Although the law of superposition is an important guiding principle of stratigraphic analysis, there are other principles that should be kept in mind during excavation. The **principle of original horizontality** states that strata without a consolidated form will tend to be deposited horizontally under natural circumstances; strata which were originally deposited in a slope would gradually form a horizontal position. This principle has its origin in Steno's realization that geological strata that are not parallel to the horizon were once horizontal. The **principle of lateral continuity**

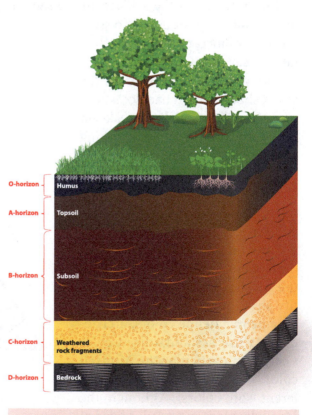

FIGURE 7.19 Soil horizons.

© Designua/Shutterstock.com

concerns the extent of a deposit. In theory, any unconsolidated deposits thin down horizontally and in a contiguous nature until they hit the edge of another deposit. If a feature divides a layer into two parts, the two parts may have been connected originally. This law helps archaeologists correlate strata that are similar in composition and depth, but may be noncontiguous because they were separated by later events such as the building of a wall or the digging of a storage pit. Finally, the **principle of stratigraphic succession** indicates that any unit of archaeological stratification is located in the stratigraphic sequence from its position between the undermost of all the units above it and the uppermost of the units below it.

Another factor to consider when discussing stratigraphy concerns **soil horizons**. Soil horizons are layers of soil that differ from each other due to weathering patterns. Although geologists and soil scientists often use a complex system that includes an O Horizon (the humic or organic layer) and R Horizon (bedrock), archaeologists tend to utilize the A, B, and C horizon layers. The **A Horizon** is the topsoil and predominantly contains minerals with rich organic materials. The lower **C Horizon** is composed of soils weathering off the parent material and generally includes large unbroken rocks. The **B Horizon** is the soil condition between the A and C horizons, a subsoil usually rich in minerals that are leached from above.

Harris Matrix

Some stratified deposits are relatively straightforward and easy to interpret, while others are very complex and much more difficult; those difficulties are compounded when stratigraphic profiles from different areas of a site are compared. An archaeologist by the name of Edward Harris confronted the

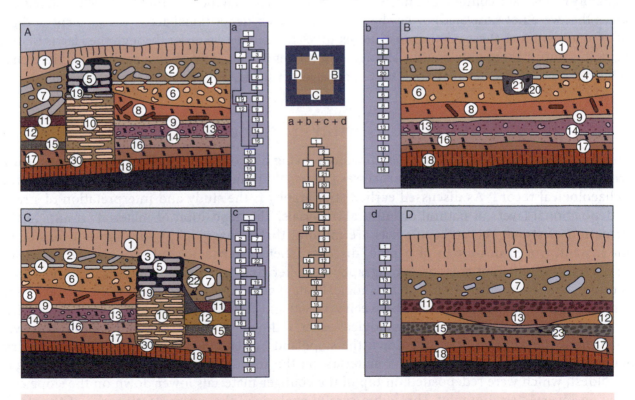

FIGURE 7.20 The Harris Matrix analysis of the four profiles of an excavation (from Harris 1989).

problem of stratigraphic interpretation while working through the data from the Lower Brook Street site in Winchester, England, which had a complex sequence of buildings from the Roman period to the late medieval period. In 1974, he developed a method of understanding depositional contexts representing them in a simple manner. His book, *Principle of Archaeological Stratigraphy*, introduced the basic outline of this recording technique, which is called the **Harris Matrix**. The heart of the Harris Matrix is to visualize the logical analysis and interpretation of sequentially layered archaeological deposits with a diagram. Plan and profile drawings can help to understand depositional sequences, but they represent the stratification of specific areas of excavation individually. In contrast, the Harris Matrix illustrates archaeologists' views of stratification, which may include broad areas with different excavation units of a site, into a master diagram of the intra-site sequence. It uses a flow diagram in the form of boxes with vertical and horizontal lines that represent stratigraphic relationships. The diagram visually explains which layers are deposited on top of the others, which layers are contemporaneous, and those which have no relationship. The Harris Matrix converts layers, deposits, and **interfaces** (contact surfaces between layers which may have important cultural meanings such as cuts to dig a pit) into Arabic numbers, writing each of the numbers into a rectangular box and join boxes by vertical or horizontal lines. Thus, the Harris Matrix is a way of reconstructing associations, contexts, and sequences in a logical manner.

The basic principles of the Harris Matrix are quite simple. There exist only three possible relationships between two given units of stratification: (1) no direct stratigraphic relationship (or physical contact), (2) superpositional relationship, and (3) correlated relationship. The first relationship indicates that two strata developed independently. They may or may not be contemporaneous. The second relationship is one layer was deposited on the other. The third relationship pertains to strata that were originally formed as a contiguous unit, but the continuity between them cannot be directly established (areas that were not excavated) or has been broken by later depositional activity (e.g., a cut to dig a pit). Once identified, these relationships are set in relative sequential order through the Harris Matrix form. It is important to note that the stratigraphic sequence should be constructed without reference to the results of artifactual analyses found in the layers (Chapter 10) or dating (Chapter 8).

Formation Processes

One last topic that needs to be discussed before moving on from stratigraphy concerns **formation processes**, the natural and cultural processes that result in the formation and development of the archaeological record. As discussed earlier, stratigraphy is the study and interpretation of strata, or depositional layers of natural or cultural materials. The deposition of materials results in the formation of strata. Yet, archaeologists are mindful that archaeological sites are not formed in one instant, frozen in time until people "discover" them. Archaeological sites change over time for a variety of different reasons. Stratigraphy can offer clues to these changes, which are critical to understand when interpreting archaeological data. For instance, a trash deposit may have been deposited on a slope over a period between AD 300 and AD 600. At AD 600, the strata making up the deposit were in correct chronological order, following the law of superposition. Yet, over time, the material began to erode down the slope and be redeposited at a lower level. The first materials to erode were the youngest materials on the surface. The last materials to erode were the oldest, which were redeposited on top of the younger materials lower down on the slope creating an inverted stratigraphy. Through a careful analysis of the entire stratigraphy of the slope, archaeologists might be able to identify this inversion, which may have important implications for interpretations of the materials.

Many different processes cause archaeological deposits to form and change. Floods, wind erosion, animal, and human activity, and a host of other factors are involved. Archaeologists tend to divide these processes into **n-transforms** (natural or noncultural processes such as organic decay, wind, water, volcanic eruptions, tsunamis, earthquakes, and bioturbation such as animal and plant activities) and **c-transforms** (cultural processes, provoked by human agents who disturb archaeological deposits intentionally or unintentionally through activities that include plowing, building, and looting) based on the work on formation processes by Schiffer, a behavioral archaeologist (see Chapter 4). When excavating, archaeologists should consider all evidence concerning the formation and transformation of strata at an archaeological site.

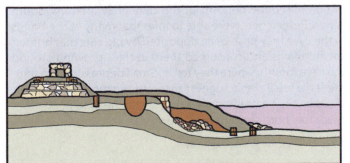

FIGURE 7.21 Archaeological sites are formed by both cultural and natural processes. In this image a site is transformed by both processes, starting with a small living structure with a midden off the drop-off to the right (top). In the second image from the top the first structure is razed and a new structure is built to the left, leaving some rubble and postholes to mark the first occupation. New agricultural terraces cover the original midden deposit. Next, this new structure is expanded and a storage pit dug. The terraces are abandoned and refuse is deposited on them. A new structure is built to their right. Finally, the site is abandoned and a flood deposit covered the lower area. An altar is erected by nearby peoples as a monument to the ruins.

Source: Belem Ceballos Casanova

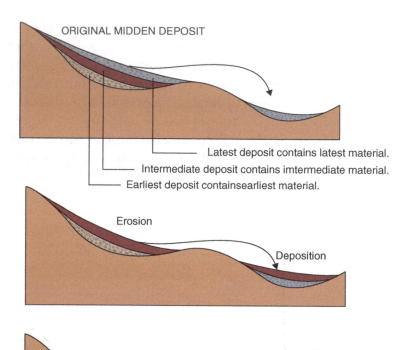

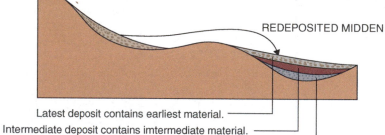

FIGURE 7.22 An example of how stratigraphy can become inverted due to erosion on a slope. As the water washes down the slope it erodes the trash midden, taking the youngest layers first and redepositing them in inverse order at the bottom of the slope.

© Kendall Hunt Publishing Company, modified from Ashmore and Sharer (2014).

FIGURE 7.23 A reconstruction of the formation processes of hominin bone deposits at the cave of Swartkrans, South Africa. Researchers were able to infer that many of the bones in the cave may have been deposited by big cats that hunted the hominins and consumed them in trees growing around the cave mouth, where they fell in. Small depressions on fragments of fossil crania suggest that, just like modern leopards, these ancient cats lifted their prey by the head to keep other predators from stealing their meal.

© Kendall Hunt Publishing Company

FIGURE 7.24 The acropolis of the Maya site of Copán, Honduras, where it has been eroded by the Copán River.

Source: Morley 1920

Bibliography

Ashmore, Wendy, and Robert J. Sharer. *Discovering Our Past: A Brief Introduction to Archaeology*. 6th ed. New York: McGraw-Hill, 2014.

Balme, Jane, and Alistair Paterson. "Stratigraphy." In *Archaeology in Practice: A Student Guide to Archaeological Analyses*, edited by J. Balme and A. Paterson, 26–46. Oxford: Wiley Blackwell, 2014.

Barker, Philip. *Techniques of Archaeological Excavation*. 3rd ed. London: Routledge, 1993.

Brain, C. K. The Hunters or the Hunted? An Introduction to African Cave Taphonomy. Chicago: University of Chicago Press, 1981.

Carmichael, David L., Robert H. Lafferty, and Brian L. Molyeaux. *Excavation*. Archaeologist's Toolkit 3. Walnut Creek, CA: AltaMira, 2003.

Collis, John. *Digging up the Past: An Introduction to Archaeological Excavation*. Stroud: Sutton, 2004.

Harris, Edward C. *Principles of Archaeological Stratigraphy*. 2nd ed. New York: Academic Press, 1989.

Harris, Edward C., Marley R. Brown, III, and Gregory J. Brown, eds. *Practices of Archaeological Stratigraphy*. New York: Academic Press, 1993.

Kipfer, Barbara A. *Encyclopedic Dictionary of Archaeology*. New York: Kluwer Academic/Plenum Publishers, 2000.

Neumann, Thomas W., and Robert M. Sanford. *Practicing Archaeology: A Training Manual for Cultural Resources Archaeology*. Walnut Creek, CA: AltaMira Press, 2001.

Purdy, Barbara A, ed. *Wet Site Archaeology*. Boca Raton, FL: CRC Press, 1988.

Roskams, Steve. *Excavation*. Cambridge: Cambridge University Press, 2001.

———Interpreting Stratigraphy: Papers Presented to the Interpreting Stratigraphy Conferences 1993–1997. Oxford: BAR International Series 910. BAR, 2000.

Schiffer, Michael B. *Formation Processes of the Archaeological Record*. Albuquerque, NM: University of New Mexico Press, 1987.

Struever, Stuart. "Flotation Techniques for the Recovery of Small-Scale Archaeological Remains." *American Archaeology* 33, no. 3 (1968): 353–362.

Winstone, Harry V. F. *Howard Carter and the Discovery of the Tomb of Tutankhamun*. Manchester: Barzan Publishing, 2006.

Dating

Controlling for time is a critical component of archaeology. Without a temporal framework, archaeologists cannot order material data for the purpose of understanding one of the fundamental goals of the field; assessing change over time (see Chapters 1 and 2). Therefore, archaeologists have gone to great lengths to use and develop methods for dating. Without archaeological dating, diachronic analysis would simply be impossible. Despite its importance, the substantial development of dating methods in archaeology as a discipline is relatively recent. We have seen in the previous chapter that the legacy of eighteenth- and nineteenth-century geology introduced the concept of stratigraphy to archaeologists, now an essential research method that has implications for dating. However, the first chronometric method that allows archaeologists to situate archaeological remains into calendrical years (more often ranges of years) did not develop until the mid-twentieth century. Since the 1950s, archaeologists have invented and adapted a wide variety of dating techniques. Yet, there is no single method that can date all archaeological remains, as each method has its strengths and limitations. Therefore, archaeologists need to choose an appropriate dating method or the combination of different methods in accordance with local circumstances. There is a variety of dating methods in science and this chapter introduces common physical or chemical methods archaeologists and their collaborators use. It is also important to note that archaeologists cannot always obtain direct dating of artifacts, ecofacts, and features. In many cases, archaeologists need to use an indirect dating method that dates materials associated with archaeological data for which there is a need to determine a temporal framework, that is, the matrix, association, and context of material remains are always the key to reconstruct chronology (see Chapter 7).

Dating techniques are divided into two general types: relative and absolute. **Relative dating** methods order things in sequences, meaning that they help to temporally distinguish data by ordering them in relative older or younger categories from each other. Setting events in order is crucial for an understanding of social processes. For example, did the brain enlargement of early hominins occur before bipedalism? Did the origins of agriculture come before sedentism? Did social inequality provoke the building of monumental architecture or vice versa? If the chronological sequence of any of these events changes, our understanding of the world would drastically change. **Absolute dating** methods assign an age in calendrical time, usually expressed as a range in years. So, for instance, instead of knowing that bipedalism came before brain enlargement using relative dating techniques, employing absolute dating techniques can determine more or less when in time (in this case millions of years of difference) these changes occurred.

Relative Dating

As we have seen in Chapter 7, the study of stratigraphy in excavations provides archaeologists with a relative chronological sequence. However, stratigraphic analysis is not the only method that archaeologists have at their disposal in terms of relative dating. In this section, we will begin with a short review of stratigraphy and then discuss other methods of relative dating.

Stratigraphy

As discussed in Chapter 7, stratigraphic analysis rests on principles developed in geology, such as the law of superposition, which help researchers reconstruct the relative order of deposition, which at archaeological sites is determined by both cultural and natural formation processes. By analyzing stratigraphy, archaeologists can determine the relative order of the deposition of artifacts, ecofacts, and features. In some cases, stratigraphic analysis can be relatively straightforward. In other cases, especially when there has been a lot of postdepositional disturbance and/or that multiple noncontiguous (spatially distinct) excavations are compared, stratigraphic analysis can be quite challenging. In the case where the stratigraphic profiles of noncontiguous excavations are compared, archaeologists use a cross-dating technique to compare consistencies in stratigraphic deposits between different parts of a site or between sites in a region. Dates are relatively determined through comparison of layers and associated cultural materials. In so doing, characteristics of the matrix are often more helpful than materials deposited in layers for comparison because the same material could have been reused, discarded, and redeposited over time.

Although stratigraphic sequences provide only relative dating, archaeologists often combine stratigraphic analysis with absolute dating methods to establish more precise understandings of time. With this combination of techniques in mind, there are two important concepts expressed by Latin phrases which are important to review; *terminus ante quem* (limit before which) and *terminus post quem* (limit after which). *Terminus ante quem* signifies a date for which the deposition of a layer cannot be more recent than the manufacture of artifacts or features deposited in it. For example, let's say that we have a stratigraphic profile from an excavation in which several coins were recovered.

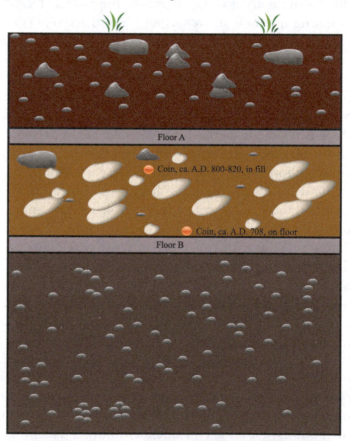

Floor A

Coin, ca. A.D. 800-820, in fill

Coin, ca. A.D. 708, on floor

Floor B

FIGURE 8.1 A stratigraphic profile illustrating the example of *terminus ante quem* and *terminus post quem* from the text.

Source: Travis Stanton

In this profile, Floor B is completely sealed by Floor A without any postdepositional disturbances such as intrusions. In the construction fill of Floor A (not on the floor), archaeologists recover a coin that has an image of a particular ruler. From historical documents, we have dates for the reign of this ruler at AD 800–820, during which time we know the coin was manufactured. Applying the concept of *terminus ante quem*, Floor A cannot have been laid before AD 800; otherwise the coin could not have been deposited in this context as it would not have existed. Let's also say that the archaeologists find another coin with an actual date of AD 708 stamped on it on Floor B. This finding would signify that Floor B would have been laid in AD 708 or after according to *terminus post quem*. Thus, Floor B could have been therefore laid between AD 708 and AD 820. Although these concepts are useful, one or two artifacts are usually not enough to determine a layer's date. Archaeologists should always look at multiple lines of evidence to date stratigraphic layers.

Architecture

The concept of stratigraphy also pertains to architectural constructions, and in many cases the remains of architecture are seen in stratigraphic profiles; Edward Harris' pioneering example of stratigraphic analysis (where he developed the Harris Matrix, see Chapter 7) is an excellent example of architecture forming part of the stratigraphy of a site. In many societies, the construction process is not just a onetime event. People built and rebuilt houses or other architecture repeatedly in the same place and, in most cases, they did not remove previous buildings completely. These past buildings often became the foundation for subsequent construction. Through stratigraphic excavations, archaeologists can observe and order the sequence of buildings. However, in a similar fashion, people sometimes extend their architecture

FIGURE 8.2 A series of ancient Greek coins. Through their styles and sometimes epigraphic dates such artifacts can help researchers date the contexts they explore.

© Glevalex/Shutterstock.com

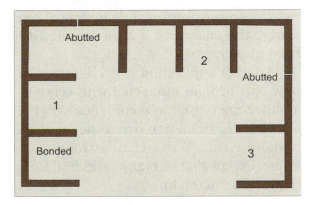

FIGURE 8.3 A simple drawing of abutting and bonded adobe walls.

Source: Kenichiro Tsukamoto

FIGURE 8.4 The site of Pueblo Bonito, located in Chaco Canyon, New Mexico, has many bonded and abutted walls that have helped researchers piece together the construction sequence of the large architectural complex.

© Underawesternsky/Shutterstock.com

horizontally, whereby the temporal relationship of construction can be identified by observing the joint lines of two walls. **Abutted walls** are those that are built up against existing construction and are temporally later. **Bonded walls** are those that were built at the same time. A good example of abutted and bonded walls comes from the site of Pueblo Bonito, located in Chaco Canyon in northwestern New Mexico. Roughly dating to the ninth to twelfth centuries AD, Pueblo Bonito is a spectacular example of Ancestral Puebloan architecture that accrued over time. Analyses of abutted and bonded walls demonstrate how this site grew over time. Although technically the analysis of abutted and bonded walls is linked to stratigraphic analysis, because, as illustrated in the Chaco Canyon example, there is often a much stronger horizontal than vertical component to this analysis, it is often considered apart from stratigraphy.

FIGURE 8.5 The Jantar Mantars of India are good examples of celestially aligned architecture; they were built as equinoctial sundials during the early eighteenth-century AD.

© Richie Chan/Shutterstock.com

Another application of architecture to dating is related to **archaeoastronomy**; the study of how past peoples interacted with celestial bodies, primarily material alignments. Some ancient architecture is built in accordance with the specific orientation of celestial events. Since the earth changes its orientation over time, we can calculate a range of years the buildings were oriented to those events. This archaeoastronomical approach could be utilized as an absolute dating technique, except that in many cases buildings were often remodeled or partially collapsed, making the results uncertain.

Seriation

Patterns of human behavior continually change. And, as behavior changes, so does material culture. **Seriation**, the arrangement of archaeological data (such as artifacts and features) in a temporal sequence based on attributes such as material, technology, or aesthetic style is based on this premise. In other words, things change over time and we, as observant humans, often consciously or unconsciously notice those changes. The fundamentals of seriation permeate our daily lives today; changes ever more apparent given the increasing pace of technological and stylistic change we experience in the modern world. For example, since telecommunication devices were originally developed in the

FIGURE 8.6 By looking at the form of telephones, we can more or less calculate when those forms were manufactured. The same principle of changing styles and technologies can be applied to archaeological data.

© Katrevich Valeriy/Shutterstock.com

nineteenth century, they have changed frequently over time. Analog telephones were replaced with a digital telephony, which have in large part has been replaced by cellular phones in contemporary society. And even those cellular phones change at a pace of every couple of years; sometimes generating comments about who doesn't have the most up-to-date model. So, just by seeing a phone and having an understanding of when certain kinds of devices were used relative to one another, people use the idea of seriation to get at relative dating. Similar sequential changes can be observed in houses, automobiles, clothing styles, radios, and music, just to name a few. The same is true of ancient artifacts and features. Archaeologists classify these material data by their physical and stylistic attributes, situating them in a particular place in a chronological sequence, often by their place in the stratigraphy. For example, if red ceramics are found more in the bottom levels of an excavation and blue ceramics more in the upper levels, the ceramics can be seriated based on their position in the relative sequence gleaned from the stratigraphic analysis. It is important to note that the change in attributes is not always gradual, but can also be drastic in a short period of time. Yet, since these sequences are relative and not absolute, placing time frames on the changes is not possible unless some absolute dating technique is also employed in the analysis.

Sir William Flinders Petrie (1899), a nineteenth-century pioneer of Egyptian archaeology, was one of the first to use stylistic seriation. Through his work, he recovered pottery jars of diverse forms from predynastic tombs where stratigraphic sequences were absent. He systematically grouped the pottery by forms and numbered them based on their similarities. These numbers were used to order the pottery in a seriated sequence. Using this seriation, Petrie subsequently arranged the tombs in the chronological order. Later, scholars applied Petrie's stylistic seriation to other parts of the world. They developed frequency seriations that ordered the sequence of deposits by their relative frequencies. This method is based on the assumption that a new style usually starts with a small number, but it occasionally becomes more popular, increasing its frequency until the style

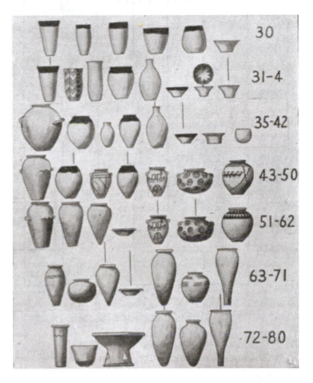

FIGURE 8.7 Ceramic drawings from Petrie's (1899) work in Egypt.

Source: Petrie, 1899

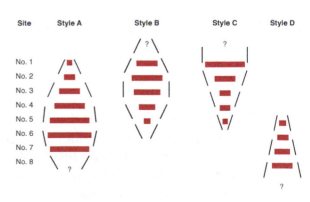

FIGURE 8.8 An example of how data are graphically represented using seriation.

From Archaeological: An Introduction, Laboratory Methods, 6/e by Mark Q. Sutton and Brooke S. Artush. © 2014 by Kendall Hunt Publishing Company. Reprinted by permission.

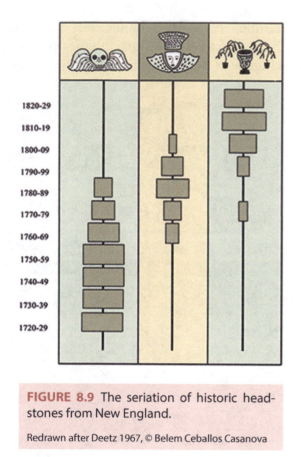

FIGURE 8.9 The seriation of historic headstones from New England.

Redrawn after Deetz 1967, © Belem Ceballos Casanova

FIGURE 8.10 Example of New England headstones with the designs recorded by Deetz.

© Donald A. Slater

fell out of fashion and faded away. The rise and fall of a style represents a battleship-like shape diagrammatically and therefore archaeologists call this pattern a **battleship-shaped curve**; early archaeologists working with such curves saw its ideal shape as like looking at a battleship from the air. A well-known example of this technique comes from a study of eighteenth- and nineteenth-century cemeteries in central Connecticut, undertaken by James Deetz and Edwin N. Dethlefsen. Relying on dates associated with the headstones, this study showed that the death's head design of tombstone was gradually replaced by cherub which in turn replaced by the urn and willow tree. The frequency of these changes indeed represents battleship-shaped curves through time. It is important to note, however, that not all archaeological data pattern into neat stereotypical battleship-shaped curves. Real data can be extremely messy and can even include styles that were created, faded away, and then came back again.

Climatostratigraphy

As we will see in Chapter 9, environmental scientists have developed a variety of methods to determine the age of climatological conditions, at micro, regional, and global scales. Likewise, geologists and other earth scientists employ various methods to date geological formations around the globe. Some archaeologists draw on these climatic and geological reconstructions to help obtain dates for archaeological data. In some cases, archaeologists themselves perform some of this work, known as **geoarchaeology**. In other cases, archaeologists draw on research directly from earth and environmental sciences. For example, the archaeological site of Quiriguá, located on an active floodplain of the Motagua River in eastern Guatemala, has been interpreted as a trading center based on the rich presence of jade, obsidian, and other products. Nevertheless, the Motagua River today is several hundred meters south of the site, thus making Quiriguá appear to have not been a strategic location for the intensive canoe trade. Geoarchaeological studies provided an answer to this discrepancy through the analysis of soils and sediments deposited areas next to the site. The stratigraphic layers of these deposits exhibit sands and gravels consistent with an extinct river channel and natural levee. This implies that the Motagua River was originally located adjacent to Quiriguá between AD 400 and AD 900. Another example comes from Alaska where more than one hundred old beach lines of Cape Krusenstern represent particular periods of occupation during the last 5,000 years. Identifying archaeological remains in association with any of these relict beaches can help to situate them in time. Although the data for this kind of environmentally based dating is diverse, including pollen records, the presence of varves (see later in the chapter), oxygen isotope records (see Chapter 9), and loess profiles (loess is windblown silt that forms during glacial periods), among others, all of these dating techniques are lumped under **climatostratigraphy**. These techniques depend on other dating methods to establish some degree of chronometric chronological control, and thus can be considered more of a series of relative dating techniques. For example, if some environmental science research has determined that the last period of glaciation (ice age) ended around 13,000 years ago, and glacial deposits, such as moraines (sediments and rocks moved by glaciers), are found in association with archaeological data now found far from glaciers, the chronological implication would be that the archaeological site dates to at least 13,000 BP. In this case, neither the archaeological data, nor the actual deposits that those data are found in, need to be dated directly. Only a good understanding of the global climate record is necessary to reach this conclusion.

Glottochronology

Despite the invention of dictionaries, formal and widespread educational systems, and mass media, our spoken and written languages change over time, even today. Resting on this fundamental fact of language, **glottochronology**, the study of related languages to calculate the length of time since they diverged, has been used by linguists and archaeologists to attempt to explain the archaeological record through the study of the relationship between two or more languages. Imagine that a social group that speaks the same language (e.g., Latin) splits into two groups for some reason (geographic isolation, migration, internal conflict, etc.). At the beginning, these two groups of people may keep using the same language. However, if there is no, or reduced interaction between them over time, one group might create its own specific vocabularies, expressions, and dialects that the other might never know or adopt. Moreover, these two groups may interact with other linguistically distinct peoples that provide new ways of speaking and writing. After hundreds and thousands years, the language of one group might be almost unintelligible to the other; nevertheless, there should still exist some words these groups share (e.g., French and Italian). Glottochronological approaches measure the similarity and difference of two or more languages, attempting to interpret how many years ago these languages split from an ancestral language. In many glottochronological reconstructions, some sort of frequency of difference is measured and a rate of language change applied to calculate the amount

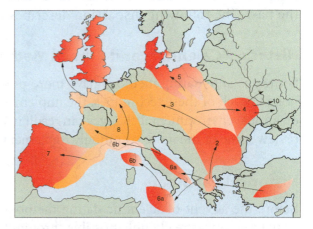

FIGURE 8.11 Map showing the proposed spread of Indo-European languages out of the Eurasian Steppes (redrawn after Renfrew 1987). Some of these kinds of reconstructions are based heavily on the timing of the appearance of Bell Beaker cultural traits (such as corded ware) across Europe.

© Kendall Hunt Publishing Company

of time that must have passed from their divergence. Although, in theory, the idea has merit, several problems exist. For example, changes in languages stem from multiple factors such as behavioral changes linked to new lifestyles (e.g., foraging vs. agriculture), the nature of exchange systems (e.g., the existence of long-distance trade), marriage patterns, and even linguistic creativity. Network analysis is a recent quantitative method that attempts to reveal linguistic relationships through the examination of structure in linguistic data. Russel Gray and Quentin Atkinson applied the network analysis to develop a phylogenetic approach that compares nodes of unknown linguistic data with historically known points of divergence for Indo-European language family; one of the most studied glottochronological sequences in the world. Although the linguistic approaches attempt to provide absolute dating, further improvement is needed. So far, many researchers are skeptical of glottochronology and consider it a rough measure of time, relegating it to relative dating.

Absolute Dating

There is no doubt that relative dating is a critical method for archaeological research. It leads archaeologists not only to reconstruct the sequence of historical events, but also to consider broader social and cultural contexts associated with artifacts, ecofacts, features, and sites. Nevertheless, archaeologists crave the ability to situate their data in actual calendar years, not satisfied to just place them in order. This is primarily because absolute dating methods facilitate the reconstruction of historical events as well as cross-cultural comparison. Absolute dating addresses the question of how many years ago an event happened. Using different dating techniques, archaeologists assign a specific calendar date to an event, such as "2,000 years ago," "300 BP," "AD 1231," or "100 BCE"; BP = before present, AD = anno Domini, BCE = before the common era. Absolute dating methods include historical calendars, tree ring (dendrochronology), and various kinds of radiometric dating. Each method has some limitations or built-in inaccuracies; in particular, the results of radiometric dating contain error ranges of years expressed with a "±" symbol (e.g., AD 544 ± 20). Despite their limitations, the absolute dating methods are powerful techniques to reconstruct the past. The following discussion describes some of the common techniques archaeologists use.

Historical Calendars and Annual Methods

Some absolute dating methods have more precise resolution than others. Although there are limitations to each of these techniques, the implementation of written dates and a variety of methods based on annual environmental changes can result in temporal resolutions of a year or less. In this section, we review some of the more commonly implemented techniques.

Historical Calendars

Before the advent of scientific dating methods, situating archaeological data in calendrical time (in actual years) was really only possible through the analysis of textual data; in particular, texts that referenced historical calendars that, first, could be read by scholars, and second, could be correlated to modern calendars. Several early complex societies such as ancient Egypt, Mesopotamia, China, Greece, and Mesoamerica recorded historical events, some of which were associated with precise calendrical systems. In cases in which the dates in those texts can be read, scholars must correlate the indigenous calendrical dates with the Gregorian calendar utilized today. Otherwise, the ancient dates cannot be understood in reference to the present; left to "float" in some indeterminable past. For example, the Classic period (AD 250–900) Maya used highly precise calendrical systems that consisted of the

Calendar Round and **Long Count**. The Calendar Round was an ever-repeating cycle of 52 years by interlocking a cycle of 260 days and a cycle of 360 days. The Maya combined the Calendar Round with an even greater cycle of the Long Count that calculated time in much larger cycles beyond the scale of human lives. Over decades, Maya archaeologists and epigraphers have attempted to correlate the Maya calendar with our Gregorian calendar and the most widely accepted correlation is 584,286 days; the days here represent the difference between the "Julian Era" calculated at January 1, 4713 BC and the August 14, 3114 BC date calculated as the beginning of the current Maya era. This correlation renders dates on ancient Maya monuments intelligible in our own calendrical system and Maya archaeologists can now talk about historical events such as battles, marriages, and ritual performances with the precision of a day (e.g., August 23, AD 734).

Although historical calendars and written texts are extremely useful for researchers, we should remember that most information associated with them is a record of dynasties and people with power. The vast majority of people lived in those periods did not have an opportunity for recording their life histories in text. Moreover, the calendar dates of historical events were often manipulated by ruling elites for their political campaigns. Thus, archaeologists should evaluate those historical events through the study of material evidence dated from other scientific techniques. Finally, as with all material data, archaeologists must pay particular attention to the contexts in which the dates are found. Just because a monument with a date is associated with a building does not mean that the building dates to that period. For instance, at the Maya site of Cobá, Mexico, people living in the Late Postclassic period (AD 1200–1521) moved many of the upright stone monuments (stelae) dating to the Late Classic period (AD 600–800) to new locations. Thus, although many of the dates on these monuments date the stelae themselves, they do not date contexts those stelae are associated with today. Further complicating matters, some of the dates on those stelae refer to events that would have been history for the Maya who carved these monuments (including the creation date in 3114 BC, long before the Maya began to write); thus, these dates neither date the monument itself or the archaeological context in which it was found.

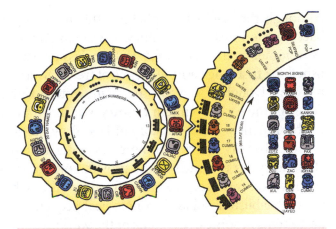

FIGURE 8.12 Peoples in Mesoamerica, including the Maya, used interlocking cycles to calculate time. The Maya in particular had interlocking cycles of 13 numbers and 20 days signs called the *tzolkin* that took 260 days to complete. These cycles then interlocked with 365-day cycle divided into 18 months; called the *haab*. It took fifty-two years for these three cycles to complete one entire circuit, which researchers call the calendar round.

© Kendall Hunt Publishing Company

Dendrochronology

Besides historical calendars, tree-ring dating (**dendrochronology**) is one of the only widespread methods available to archaeologists that has a temporal resolution of a year or less. In a nutshell, this method links the growth rings in trees to calendrical time.

FIGURE 8.13 A drawing of a tree-ring sequence.

© Peter Hermes Furian/Shutterstock.com

Although the original idea behind this method goes back to the nineteenth century, it was an American astronomer by the name of A. E. Douglass who established the first long-term sequence of tree-ring growth patterns. Douglass' work in the southwestern United States in the early twentieth century, which led to the establishment of the Laboratory of Tree-Ring Research at the University of Arizona, aimed to understand past climatic cycles recorded in the growth rings of trees. His method was accepted and refined by other scholars to establish absolute chronological sequences for past events in some dry regions of the world.

The basic principle of dendrochronology is straightforward; by counting the annual growth rings in the cross section of a modern tree one can calculate the year when the tree first sprouted. This method works because trees produce a ring of new wood every year. Although performing this exercise for a modern tree is straightforward, how does it work for archaeological dating? Dendrochronology's success as a dating method hinges on the fact that the growth rings of some trees are not of uniform thickness, but vary based on oscillating climatic conditions. Only certain species of trees can work; those whose rings are sensitive to fluctuations in climate, primarily determined by one environmental factor such as rainfall or temperature, not by multiple factors that can result in complex variation of ring thickness across a region. When there is plenty of water in a year, trees make a wider ring. When water is scarce, however, they produce a narrower ring. In temperate regions, sunlight and warm temperature also play critical roles in their annual growth, but in a general region tree rings should similarly pattern based on

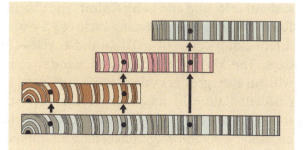

FIGURE 8.14 By matching the rings from temporally overlapping samples of wood researchers can extend tree-ring sequences farther into the past.

© Belem Ceballos Casanova

FIGURE 8.15 The American Southwest is one of the few world regions where dendrochronology has been extensively applied. This image shows the original wooden beams of a building at Aztec Ruins, New Mexico (ca. eleventh to thirteenth centuries AD).

© Rocket Photos – HQ Stock/Shutterstock.com

the overall climatic conditions. Thus, trees of the same species and located in the same region usually show the same patterns of ring growth; although researchers must be aware that the thickness of rings tends to be more narrow with the increasing age of a tree. This similar patterning means that growth rings can be matched up. For example, if you have a modern tree that is one hundred years old and one hundred-year-old tree that was cut down seventy years ago, thirty years of tree-ring patterns will overlap. In this case, you now have a tree-ring sequence going back not just 100 years, but 170 years. In dry areas of the world where there is great preservation of wood, such as the American Southwest, researchers match the tree-ring patterns of historic and prehistoric wood samples to the modern sequence to create long sequences of tree rings by matching sequences going as far back to 10,000 years in some cases; this method does not work in areas without such preservation. So, if an archaeologist finds a piece of wood that can be successfully situated into an established sequence, that wood can tell us something about dating. What it actually tells us about dating, however, is not always straightforward.

Archaeologists count the rings back to know when the archaeological sample of wood was cut down. They can calculate that "cutting date" to the exact year in an established dendrochronological sequence. However, the date when the wood was cut down may not date the archaeological context in which it was recovered by archaeologists. The problem of "old wood" is one that archaeologists in the American Southwest have faced for years. Since the preservation of wood is so good in this area, it was sometimes recycled, even centuries after the tree had been cut down. It is not uncommon for archaeologists to find that some of the wooden beams in a building have cutting dates that are decades or even centuries older than others. Archaeologists must always keep in mind that what is being dated is the cutting date of the tree. And, if the sample lacks bark, or at least part of the original outermost ring, the date of felling this timber is subjective. Because of its limitations, dendrochronology is only applied in some parts of the world outside the tropics. Nevertheless, dendrochronology is the most reliable dating method in archaeological research and provides a basis for the calibration of radioactive dating such as radiocarbon.

Varve Dating

Varve dating is much like dendrochronology. It involves counting some environmental phenomena back in time, and as will see in Chapter 9, varves can be used for environmental reconstructions. **Varves** are sediments that are deposited annually, creating laminated stratigraphy. Such deposits are more common in lakes near glacial formations; thus limiting the areas of the world in which it can be used. These lakes receive layers of sediment that are deposited annually or sometimes seasonally at their bottoms. Between spring and summer, the layers are black due to the presence of dead plankton and diatoms (a major group of microalgae), whereas during the fall and winter the presence of clay minerals make the layers white. Based on the fact that the layers are deposited annually and can vary in thickness due to environmental conditions each year, varve dating works somewhat like dendrochronology, by counting the layers of sediment (varves). There is often enough organic material preserved in the varves to perform radiocarbon dating as well, an important component to this analysis in light of the doubts concerning the method some researchers have voiced over the years.

One of the exceptional lakes where a well-preserved varve sequence is preserved is Lake Suigetsu in Japan. The Lake Suigetsu 2006 Project has refined varve counting techniques with a combination of radiocarbon dating of fossilized ancient leaves and an analysis of the varves themselves. The analysis of multiple overlapping cores from the lake has resulted in establishing a high-resolution chronology that goes back to 52,800 BP. This chronology was recognized as a global standard (IntCal 13) by the 2012 International Radiocarbon Conference. Before varve analysis was generally accepted by the field, radiocarbon calibration had relied on dendrochronology that could go back at most to 13,000 years ago. However, the results of the varve analysis from different parts of the world including that of the Lake Suigetsu extended its acceptable limit back to 52,800 BP.

Radiometric Dating

Any element in the Earth consists of protons, neutrons, and electrons. **Isotopes** are the same forms of elements; having the same number of protons, but different number of neutrons. Some isotopes are unstable and radioactive. Radioactive decay is the process of transformation from unstable radioactive isotopes into stable elements. Scientists use this principle of radioactive decay as an age-determination technique that is called **radiometric dating**. Originally, some researchers thought that the decay process of radioactive isotope was constant, independent of all environmental conditions; that by measuring the amount of decay from, let's say ^{14}C (unstable) to ^{14}N (stable), that we could easily calculate the time since the material began its decay process. Further research, however, revealed that numerous environmental factors affect the decay process of any unstable isotope and that we cannot assume a steady rate of decay, complicating radiometric determinations. Therefore, researchers use statistical probabilities to calculate a temporal length in which one half of an unstable isotope becomes a stable isotope, a process known as **half-life**. One of the most broadly used radiometric methods among archaeologists is **radiocarbon dating**, but it is not the only radiometric dating technique employed in archaeology. In this section, we will review the commonly utilized techniques in the field.

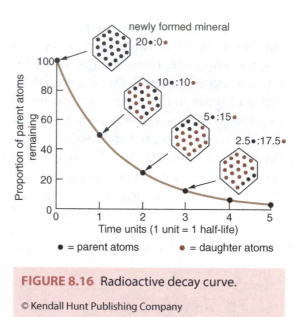

FIGURE 8.16 Radioactive decay curve.

© Kendall Hunt Publishing Company

Radiocarbon Dating

In 1949, the first radiocarbon dates from archaeological contexts were sensationally announced by the American chemist Willard Libby, who won a Nobel Prize in Chemistry for his work in 1960. By testing chronologically historically well-situated samples from the tombs of two Egyptian kings, Djoser (a third dynasty pharaoh of the Old Kingdom, ca. twenty-seventh-century BC) and Sneferu (the founder of the fourth dynasty, ca. late twenty-seventh and early twenty-sixth centuries BC), Libby was able to prove to the scientific community that his radiometric dating method could be applied successfully to archaeological contexts. Radiocarbon dating revolutionized archaeological research by providing a cross-culturally comparable dating method that could be used over the world; the materials it can date, such as wood, charcoal, or bone, are available at many archaeological sites. Since then, radiocarbon dating has been the most useful of all dating methods available to archaeological research. One of the reasons that archaeologists use this radiometric method is its accessibility; all living things on the earth are carbon based and, while the preservation of organic remains can vary from region to region, they are often found in archaeological contexts.

FIGURE 8.17 Djoser's (above) and Sneferu's (below) mortuary monuments.

© Murat Hajdarhodzic/Shutterstock.com
© Gurgen Bakhshetyan/Shutterstock.com

Radiocarbon dating works because carbon-containing organic compounds are distributed throughout the Earth's environments. This carbon is cycled by a variety of physical and chemical processes and is found in all organic material. An active part of the Earth's carbon cycle is associated with three different types of isotopes: ^{12}C, ^{13}C, and ^{14}C and their proportions in the Earth are 98.9 percent of ^{12}C, 1.1 percent of ^{13}C, and 1×10^{-12} percent of ^{14}C. Carbon isotope ^{12}C consists of six protons and six neutrons in its nucleus, ^{13}C has six protons and seven neutrons, and there are six protons and eight neutrons in the nucleus of ^{14}C (radiocarbon). This third isotope of carbon is produced constantly in the upper atmosphere by cosmic rays bombarding nitrogen (^{14}N). The excess of neutrons (eight) compared to the protons (six) in a nucleus makes ^{14}C isotope unstable; this means that after it forms it begins to decay back to a stable form of nitrogen (^{14}N). The half-life of ^{14}C decay takes about 5,700 years (5,730 years ± 40 years). Because the amount of ^{14}C in the Earth is very small as we showed above, radiocarbon dating does not work reliably beyond 50,000 years ago; there simply is not enough ^{14}C material left to obtain accurate dates in all but a few exceptional cases and the calibration curves do not extend past 50,000–60,000 BP.

Calibration

In his original work, Libby assumed that the constant decay of radiocarbon corresponds to its continuous production through cosmic radiation. Based on this assumption, Libby believed that the proportion of radiocarbon in the atmosphere should remain the same throughout time; thus, the proportion of radiocarbon in living creatures should also remain constant, whether the organism lived 1,000 or 10,000 years ago. Part of Libby's argument regarding the proportion of radiocarbon has stood the test of time; organisms living at any one period of time have the same amount of radiocarbon. This is true because carbon dioxide is absorbed by plants through photosynthesis. These plants are eaten by herbivorous animals, which in turn are eaten by carnivores. Because these consumption processes are continuous, the proportion of the three carbon isotopes in those living things should remain more or less constant. When the plant and animal dies the uptake of ^{14}C ceases, and the steady concentration of ^{14}C begins to decline in the organism's remains through the radioactive decay toward the stable nitrogen isotope (^{14}N).

Although Libby's discovery about the mechanism of radiocarbon was revolutionary, what Libby did not contemplate was that the levels of radiocarbon in the atmosphere could vary over time. The reasons for the variations of ^{14}C in the atmosphere are diverse; such as changes in the Earth's magnetic field and solar activity. Regardless of the reason, though, this temporal variation means that researchers need to systematically calibrate radiocarbon dates based on paleoenvironmental data regarding the fluctuations of radiocarbon over time. Fortunately, tree-ring dating has helped

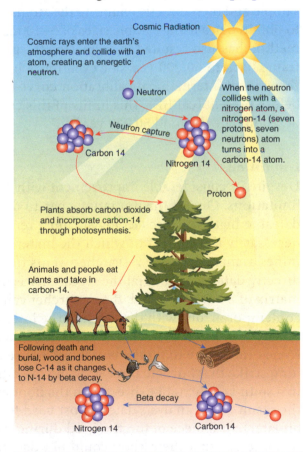

FIGURE 8.18 The diagram illustrates how ^{14}C is produced, distributed, and decayed on Earth.

© Kendall Hunt Publishing Company

tremendously with the calibration process. Tree-rings, as organic materials, provide a direct measurement of atmospheric radiocarbon. Given the chronological precision of dendrochronology, data from tree-rings produce excellent calibration curves that convert radiocarbon dates into calendar time. When a researcher gets a date back from the laboratory, it is expressed in **radiocarbon years**; meaning that the date assumes that ^{14}C and ^{12}C have remained constant over time, which we know is not the case. The range of the radiocarbon year date is calculated to one standard deviation from the mean. Calibrated dates are usually calculated to one or two standard deviations (see below).

Accelerator Mass Spectrometry

Although radiocarbon dating was one of the most powerful methods in archaeological research when it was first developed, the technique at this time required a relatively large sample of organic remains, limiting its application to certain finds. To obtain a reliable date, archaeologists had to recover 10–20 g of wood or charcoal or 100–200 g of human or animal bone (the bone itself was not dated, but the preserved collagen inside the bone). These amounts might seem small, but given many of the problems of organic preservation that most archaeologists face (see Chapter 9), recovering samples of this size can be challenging. The **accelerator mass spectrometry** (AMS) measurement technique solved this problem by separating all other isotopes and molecules in a sample and then directly counting the atoms of ^{14}C. Relying on this separation, researchers are able to obtain dates using sample sizes of 5–10 mg using AMS technology. The application of the AMS method has also resulted in increasing the precision of radiocarbon date and pushing the ^{14}C time frame back to 60,000 years or even more in some exceptional cases. However, the most recently recognized international calibration curve (IntCal13) still reaches back to 50,000 calibrated date before present (cal BP). This limits of this curve means that researchers should be careful of radiocarbon dates beyond 50,000 years.

Limitations

Despite its considerable improvement with AMS technology, radiocarbon dating does have some limitations. One of the limitations has to do with sampling. As with tree-rings and many other dateable materials, archaeologists must remember that what is being dating is the material, not necessarily the context in which the material was found. If the sample comes from some mummified remains and the researcher wants to date those remains, there is no problem. The sample directly dates the material the researcher is investigating. But, if a piece of charcoal found in the matrix of a burial is dated, the researcher cannot guarantee that the date from that sample will be contemporaneous with the death of the interred individual, or even the interment of the remains during a mortuary ritual. The carbon could have been mixed with soil that was brought from some other place to fill the burial, introduced by burrowing rodent, or been the result of a lightning strike that burned a tree growing over the burial centuries later. Even if the carbon is found in a sound context, like directly on the floor of a ritually burned temple, we do not know whether the result of ^{14}C analysis dates a post used for the original building (early), a remodeled beam (a bit later), or a piece of torches used during the ritual during its abandonment (much later). This is not to say that the carbon could not date the events just described, but that researchers must be mindful to consider the context in which the sample was found. Archaeologists should always evaluate the formation processes of the context of each radiocarbon sample before sending it to an AMS laboratory.

FIGURE 8.19 The Lewis Chessmen were found in an underground chamber on the Isle of Lewis, Scotland, in 1831. Although the pieces date to medieval times (most likely twelfth or thirteenth centuries AD), they were carved from old walrus ivory (several centuries earlier, possibly in Norway) illustrating that archaeologists must be careful of the use of old materials when dating.

Lewis Chesspieces (walrus ivory), Scandinavian school (12th century)/National Museums Scotland/Bridgeman Images

A second limitation has to do with possible contamination of the samples. Samples used for radiocarbon analysis can be contaminated in many different ways, but always occur with the introduction of older or younger carbon to the sample or the context. Contaminated samples can occur through postdepositional natural and cultural processes, as well as through the excavations themselves. For example, a tiny piece of charcoal could fall from a profile (cross section) of the excavation unit to the bottom leading to the excavators collecting it as part of the materials from the lower level. Even handling the sample with your bare hands can introduce very young carbon to the sample, stressing the need for careful excavations and handling of materials.

A third limitation associated with radiocarbon dating deals with its built-in statistical uncertainty; the range of error associated with this radiometric technique. All radiometric methods result in a date with a range of error that is usually calculated according to one (one-sigma, or σ) or two (two-sigma, or 2σ) standard deviations from the mean; respectively, that

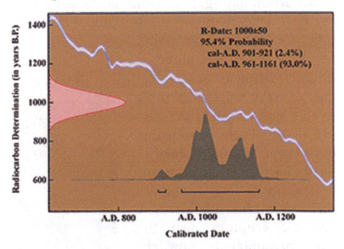

FIGURE 8.20 The radiocarbon curve for a two standard deviation date of AD 950 with an error range of fifty years. The curve has two intercepts; 2.4 percent probability from AD 901 to AD 921 and 93.0 percent probability from AD 961 to AD 1161 (generated by OxCal 4.3: http://c14.arch.ox.ac.uk/oxcal.html).

Source: Travis Stanton

there is a 68.2 percent or 95.4 percent probability that the actual date falls within the range given. A radiocarbon age expressed as 1000 ± 50 years BP (before present, calculated as AD 1950) does not mean that that organism (a plant or animal) died in the year AD 950. It implies that there is a 67 percent probability (one-sigma [σ] range) that the sample came from an organism that died between 1050 and 950 radiocarbon years BP. But of course, as we have seen, radiocarbon years need to be calibrated. A calibrated ¹⁴C date includes the combined precision of both the sample measurement and calibration data. For example, using the IntCal13 calibration curve, a radiocarbon date of 1000 ± 50 BP yields a two-sigma (2σ) range of AD 901–921 (2.4 percent) and AD 961–1161 (93.0 percent). In this example, the probabilities of the two ranges add up to 95.4 percent, but are divided into two based on where the two different modes (bimodal distribution) occur in the radiocarbon curve. Researchers need to keep these ranges and probabilities in mind as they interpret the dates. One thing that researchers can do to generate more precision is to collect several radiocarbon samples from each context and cross-check the results. In any event, there will always be some range of error in radiometric dates, like those generated from radiocarbon dating.

Potassium–Argon Dating

Potassium-argon dating is another radiometric method, one that can be used in areas with volcanic deposits. Instead of using organic remains, this technique uses 10 g of volcanic rock or volcanic ash (tuff) that contains an unstable isotope of potassium (⁴⁰K). After being expelled from a volcano, the concentration of potassium ⁴⁰K in a material begins to decline through the radioactive decay into a stable isotope of argon (⁴⁰Ar). The half-life of potassium ⁴⁰K is 1.3 billion years and researchers can date materials that are older than 100,000 BP, much older than the reach of radiocarbon dating. Potassium–argon dating has become one of the most reliable methods for the study of early hominins as many of these very old remains are found in areas with volcanic deposits. One application of this dating technique is directly dating archaeological data. A very famous example of this application is the dating of the Laetoli footprints discovered by Mary Leaky in 1976. Laetoli is an archaeological site in Tanzania where early hominins inhabited. A volcanic eruption near the site precipitated powdery volcanic ash on which three early hominins walked (commonly argued to be of the species *Australopithecus afarensis*). After a rain, the ash layer became mud and then

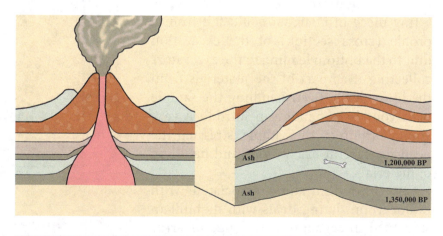

FIGURE 8.21 Potassium–argon dating works by dating the volcanic ash depositions where cultural material is found. The date of the fossil depicted here would be between 1,350,000 BP and 1,200,000 BP

© Belem Ceballos Casanova

cemented fossilizing their footprints. Using potassium–argon dating, we now know that the footprints date to 3.60–3.75 million years ago, among of the earliest evidence of bipedal locomotion (habitually walking with two feet) in the world.

Most applications of potassium–argon dating, however, are indirect. Keeping in mind what is actually being dated is when the volcanic material that was expelled from a volcano, researchers use stratigraphic analysis of volcanic deposits to place ranges of dates on cultural materials and fossils. For example, a volcano can send out a plume of ash that blankets the landscape 5,000,000 years ago. Through formation processes, other strata are laid down over the intervening 500,000 years. At 4,500,000 years ago, a hominin dies and is buried near the surface. Then, 300,000 years later, after more natural strata are deposited there is a second ash fall, effectively sandwiching the hominin fossils between the two ash layers. By dating both of those layers, researchers can situate the fossil between 5,000,000 and 4,200,000 million years ago. Although an 800,000 year range may sound like a lot, dates like these help researchers tremendously in understanding evolutionary changes in our hominin ancestors. And, in cases where volcanic activity was more frequent, the ranges are not that large; the error range for the technique itself is about 30,000 years. It is important to note that there is a gap of temporal coverage between ^{14}C dating and $^{40}K/^{40}Ar$ dating. Although ^{14}C dating covers up to 50,000 BP, $^{40}K/^{40}Ar$ dating covers periods of time over 100,000 BP. These two radioactive methods cannot cover historical events between 50,000 BP and 100,000 BP.

Uranium Series Dating

A dating method that covers this gap is **uranium series dating** (also known as uranium–thorium dating), a technique which dates calcium carbonates such as speleothems and coral. Uranium series is a radiometric method that has been used since 1970s and is based on the radioactive decay of a uranium isotope (^{234}U) into a thorium isotope (^{230}Th). Uranium is soluble in water and ^{234}U begins to decay when calcium carbonate–rich water precipitates into materials such as speleothems or travertines in caves. Over time, the ratio $^{230}Th/^{234}U$ grows, whereas the ratio of $^{234}U/^{238}U$ declines (the latter isotope becomes an isotope of protactinium ^{231}Pa). The theoretical limit of age determination by the $^{230}Th/^{234}U$ method is from 1,000 BP to 500,000 BP. with the error range of 1–5 percent; in many cases this method is used in tandem with electron spin resonance (ESR) (see below). Uranium series dating is particularly useful in cave contexts. Cave deposits, such as speleothems and flowstone, can be dated fairly accurately using uranium series dating as these deposits are formed by successive layering of materials as water drips and seeps through the caves. In some cases, archaeological materials lay on top of, or are covered by such formations. Even rock art can be covered. Dating these formations can help situate the archaeological data in time.

Fission-Track Dating

Fission-track dating also relies on an isotope of uranium, but in the case of this method it works by counting the microscopic scars (damage trails or tracks) that a radioactive ^{238}U isotope marked on rocks, minerals, and glasses as it decayed. The decay of ^{238}U, which happens at a constant rate, produces pathways (fission-tracks) etched into the crystal surfaces of a wide range of rocks and minerals that contain uranium; the method dates when the material formed. By measuring the amount of uranium in a material and then counting the number of fission tracks through an optimal microscope in the laboratory, researchers can determine the age of a given mineral deposit. This radioactive method is rarely used for independent dating, but is often used to check other dating methods where dating has been a problem. It can only be used for materials over 100,000 BP.

Other Absolute Dating Methods

There are other less common dating methods archaeologists that have used to date archaeological remains. Some of these methods have had a rocky history in the field, garnering sufficient amounts of skepticism to label them "dubious" or of "doubtful utility." Other methods once thought to have promise have been abandoned entirely, but still remain a part of the historic literature of archaeology. Further, some newer methods have not yet passed rigorous testing, but hold some promise for the future. Still, others are used when more preferential methods are not available. In this final section, we briefly review some of less commonly used methods in archaeology. Some may one day have a renaissance due to some technological breakthrough. Others will certainly remain relegated to the dust heap, but because of their historic role in past archaeological interpretations, are worth remembering how they worked, or at least were supposed to work.

FIGURE 8.22 Flowstone can accumulate on cultural materials, such as his burial from Actun Tunichil Mucnal cave, Belize, and can be dated using uranium series, giving the material a *terminus ante quem* calculation.

© Donald A. Slater

Fluorine Absorption

Fluorine absorption dating had its heyday when it was used to help prove the Piltdown bones as a hoax in 1953. Fluorine is an element found in water and can accumulate in buried bones through absorption from the groundwater. The idea here is that the more fluorine the bones contain, the older they are. Although in principle this dating technique works, the rates of fluorine absorption vary based on the amount of water the bone material is exposed to (thus variable by locality) and different materials absorb fluorine at different rates, which in the end create large error ranges not favored by archaeologists. This method is not really used anymore by the field.

Obsidian Hydration

Obsidian hydration, which dates the cumulative absorption of water by volcanic glass such as obsidian, was widely used by archaeologists, particularly in the 1970s and 1980s. Due to its sharp cutting edge, obsidian was a highly valued material for humans before the advent of metal tools and is found in a wide range of archaeological contexts throughout the world. Given that the cost of this dating method is accessible and that the technique dates the moment of production of actual artifacts, archaeologists applied this method vigorously for several decades. Nevertheless, in the 1990s several scholars began to question this method on the basis that the hydration rate can vary depending on either the composition of different obsidian sources or temperature of the matrix where obsidian was originally deposited, or both.

Obsidian (volcanic glass) absorbs water that forms a hydration rim on the exposed surface of obsidian, which archaeologists call cortex. The thickness of this layer is measured by microscope and the range of the thickness can be used to determine how long the surface has been exposed. Because past people knapped obsidian to make tools, they created new surfaces that started the hydration process anew when the artifact was made. The idea is that the age of that surface (dating the production of the artifact) can be estimated if the rate of hydration is known. However, the problem is that the hydration rate varies with the composition of obsidian and each volcanic eruption produces obsidian with different compositions. This makes it difficult to establish reliable rate of hydration. Compounding this problem, the hydration rate also changes with shifts in environmental temperature. Even if compositions of two obsidian artifacts are the same, variation in the temperatures of matrices where those artifacts were deposited can cause variations in the hydration rates, and thus the results of the dating. Because of these problems, obsidian hydration dating is thought to be less reliable than other methods and has been relegated to use as a relative dating method by some, but not all, researchers.

Patina Dating

Many types of artifacts (chert, glass, etc.) have a patina on their exteriors, resulting from different types of chemical reactions. This patina accumulates over time and its thickness can be a rough measure of time; for example, historic glass bottles have a deeper "frosted" look to them than their more modern counterparts. Like obsidian hydration, however, the accumulation of patina is not constant. This method is therefore only useful for relative dating.

FIGURE 8.23 Examples of historic glass stretching from the 19th century back to Phoenician times. Note the extensive patina on the bottles on the right.

Source: Kenichiro Tsukamoto

Cation Ratio

Much like the formation of a patina, many rocks form a varnish on their surface over time. Attempts to date this varnish forming over petroglyphs (rock art etched into the surface, thus exposing the underlying rock) were made through **cation ratio dating** in the 1980s. The idea was that the varnish contained positively charged atoms or molecules called cations (K and Ca) that changed their ratio over time. Although the method was applied to rock art from desert areas where such varnish is more stable, the ratios are dependent on environmental conditions, which are exceedingly difficult to calculate. Today, this method has been virtually abandoned.

Amino-Acid Racemization

Amino-acid racemization is a dating method that measures the change in configuration of amino acids under a polarized light. The great majority of biological tissues have amino acids that are in what is termed an "L" configuration. When the organism dies the amino acids begin to shift to a "D" configuration. Although the technique is still utilized in the field, specifically for some eggshell, bone, teeth, and mollusk shell, the rate of change in the configuration of the amino acids is dependent on temperature, which can be exceedingly difficult to estimate. This problem has minimized the use of amino-acid racemization in archaeology, although it is applied in some contexts where it can be calibrated by a second dating technique such as radiocarbon dating.

Luminescence

Thermoluminescence (TL) and **optically stimulated luminescence** (OSL) are techniques based on a measurement the light emitted from samples heated over 250° C. These methods work because electrons become trapped in the crystal structures of certain materials such as feldspar, calcite, and quartz through their exposure to natural radiation (e.g., from the sun). The idea is that the longer these materials have been around, the more electrons they will have accumulated. Thus, the materials emit more light when they are heated over 250° C for TL and stimulated by certain light conditions for OSL. Every time these materials are heated over this temperature, the radiogenic clock is reset, so what is being measured is the last time the materials were heated above 250° C. Since materials such as pottery and chert (an important lithic material that can be used if it was burnt) contain the appropriate crystals for luminescence techniques, both of these methods have been frequently been utilized. Although archaeologists, as always, need to pay attention to the contexts (e.g., that a pottery vessel was not burnt after its initial firing in the kiln), some of the issues that surround these dating techniques go beyond context. In particular, because of uncertain exposure conditions, the dates generated from these methods have fairly large error ranges (~10 percent), causing some researchers to shy away from them and even question their utility. More recently, measurements of soil matrices to measure the radiation dose has been utilized as a way to control for exposure conditions and narrow the range of error, but there are still many who doubt the applicability of TL and OSL in the field.

Electron Spin Resonance

Much like luminescence methods, **ESR** dating measures the exposure of certain materials, like tooth enamel and carbonates, to natural radiation. In this case, the amount of unpaired electrons in the crystals is measured. ESR has been used to date these materials, as well as chert and quartz temper in ceramics, among other materials, but is not widely utilized in archaeology. Only certain time ranges will work, and the amount of unpaired electrons is also dependent on temperature.

Archaeomagnetic Dating

Archaeomagnetic dating rests on the fact that there are magnetic particles in the soil (like clay) that align themselves with the position of the magnetic north pole; local magnetic variation is also important to consider. Since the Earth's poles move, the alignment of these particles also moves. However, when a material like clay is fired and hardens (thus reaching a temperature above the Curie point where particles lose their magnetic properties), these particles stop moving, frozen in the direction where the magnetic north pole was at the time the material was fired. The idea here is that if the fired clay is found in contexts where it has remained undisturbed since the time of its firing, the alignments of the particles can be measured, still pointing in the direction where the magnetic north pole was at that time. Since we have decent chronological maps of movement of the magnetic north pole over the past 10,000 years, researchers can see where the alignment of the particles intersects (potentially in multiple places within the time frame that the archaeologist believes the feature to date) and, thus, come up with a date. Since artifacts like pottery move around after they are fired, this method cannot be applied to them. But, when material has not moved, such as the clay underlying a hearth, is found, researchers can attempt to calculate plausible dates. Although this technique is used today in archaeology, it is not frequently implemented.

Rehydroxylation

Rehydroxylation (RHX) is a more recently proposed direct dating method of ceramics that has not yet been adopted by the broader field; it is still in the process of being systematically tested. The idea behind this technique is that when clay is fired it drives out all of the moisture, setting the material to a zero point and beginning the process of chemical recombination of the fired clay with environmental moisture. By measuring the mass of water that the fired clay has accumulated since it was last fired, researchers, in theory, can then calculate the amount of time that has passed since that firing episode. Recent work suggests that RHX of ceramics does not occur at a universal constant rate and has begun to focus on how to address this complication.

Genetic Dating

Another rather new dating technique is **genetic dating**. Similar in some ways to glottochronology, the premise behind genetic dating is that the time frame of the separation of populations can be calculated by their genetic divergence, in this case measured by the presence of new Y-chromosome haplotypes or mitochondrial DNA or changes in the frequencies of existing genetic material. In a study of five Upper Paleolithic genomes, researchers found a good correlation between genetic data and established radiocarbon sequences between 12,000 BP and 45,000 BP, suggesting that genetic studies of the timing of Neanderthal gene flow may be applicable to periods beyond the reach of radiocarbon analysis.

Bibliography

Aitken, Martin J., and Stephen Stokes. "Climatostratigraphy." In *Chronometric Dating in Archaeology*, Vol. 2, edited by R. E. Taylor and M. J. Aitken, 1–30. Advances in Archaeological and Museum Science. New York: Plenus Press, 1997.

Arnold, J. R., and W. F. Libby. "Age Determinations by Radiocarbon Context: Checks with Samples of Known Age." *Science* 110, no. 2869 (1949): 678–680.

Balme, Jane, and Alistair Paterson. "Stratigraphy." In *Archaeology in Practice: A Student Guide to Archaeological Analyses*, edited by J. Balme and A. Paterson, 26–46. Oxford: Wiley Blackwell, 2014.

Barrett, Gerard T. "Rehydroxylation Dating of Fired Clays: An Improved *Time-Offset* Model to Account for the Effect of Cooling on Post-Reheating Mass Gain." *Journal of Archaeological Science* 40, no. 10 (2013): 3596–3603.

Blench, Roger. *Archaeology, Language, and the African Past.* Lanham, MD: AltaMira Press, 2006.

Brainerd, George W. "The Place of Chronological Ordering in Archaeological Analysis." *American Antiquity* 16 (1951): 301–313.

Braswell, Geoffrey E. "Obsidian-Hydration Dating, the Coner Phase, and Revisionist Chronology at Copán, Honduras." *Latin American Antiquity* 3 (1992): 130–147.

Deetz, James. *Invitation to Archaeology.* Garden City, NY: The Natural History Press, 1967.

Dorn, Ronald I. "Cation-Ratio Dating: A New Rock Varnish Age-Determination Technique." *Quaternary Research* 20 (1983): 49–73.

Eerkens, Jelmer W., Kevin J. Vaughn, Tim R. Carpenter, Christina A. Conlee, Moises Linares Grados, and Katharina Schreiber. "Obsidian Hydration Dating on the South Coast of Peru." *Journal of Archaeological Science* 35 (2008): 2231–2239.

Eighmy, Jeffrey, and Robert Sternberg. *Archaeometric Dating.* Tucson: University of Arizona Press, 1990.

Giddings, J. Louis, and Douglas D. Anderson. *Beach Ridge Archaeology of Cape Krusenstern: Eskimo and Pre-Eskimo Settlements around Kotzebue Sound, Alaska.* Washington, DC: Publications in Archaeology 20. National Park Service, U.S. Department of the Interior, 1986.

Grün, R., and C. B. Stringer. "Electron Spin Resonance Dating and the Evolution of Modern Humans." *Archaeometry* 33, no. 2 (1991): 153–199.

Grün, R., P. H. Huang, W. Huang, F. McDermott, C. B. Stringer, A. Thorne, and G. Yan. "ESR and U-Series Analysis of Teeth from Paleoanthropological Site of Hexian, Anhui Province, China." *Journal of Human Evolution* 34 (1998): 555–564.

Johnson, B. J., and G. H. Miller. "Archaeological Applications of Amino Acid Racemization." *Archaeometry* 39 (1997): 265–287.

Kipfer, Barbara A. *Encyclopedic Dictionary of Archaeology.* New York: Kluwer Academic/Plenum Publishers, 2000.

Leakey, M. D., and R. L. Hay. "Pliocene Footprints in the Laetolil Beds at Laetoli, Northern Tanzania." *Nature* 278, no. 5702 (1979): 317–323.

Lekson, Stephen H, ed. *The Architecture of Chaco Canyon.* Salt Lake City, UT: The University of Utah Press, 2007.

Lengyel, Stacey. "The Pre–A.D. 585 Extension of the U.S. Southwest Archaeomagnetic Reference Curve." *Journal of Archaeological Science* 37 (2010): 3081–3090.

Lengyel, Stacey, and Rob Sternberg. "Historic Archaeomagnetic Results from the Eastern U.S., and Comparison with Secular Variation Models." In *Timescales of the Paleomagnetic Field*, edited by J. E. T. Channell, D. V. Kent, W. Lowrie, and J. G. Meert, 267–277. Geophysical Monography Series 145. Washington, DC: American Geophysical Union, 2004.

Martin, Simon and Joel Skidmore. "Exploring the 584286 Correlation between the Maya and European Calendars." *The PARI Journal* 13, no. 2 (2012): 3–16.

Moorjani, Priya, Sriram Sankararaman, Qiaomei Fu, Molly Przeworski, Nick Patterson, and David Reich. "A Genetic Method for Dating Ancient Genomes Provides a Direct Estimate of Human Generation Interval in the Last 45,000 Years." *Proceedings of the National Academy of Sciences* 113, no. 20 (2016): 5652–5657.

Nakagawa, Takeshi, Katsuya Gotanda, Tsuyoshi Haraguchi, Toru Danhara, Hitoshi Yonenobu, Achim Brauer, Yusuke Yokoyama, Ryuji Tada, Keiji Takemura, Richard A.Staff, Rebecca Payne, Christopher Bronk Ramsey, Charlotte Bryant, Fiona Brock, Gordon Schlolaut, Michael Marshall, Pavel Tarasov, and Henry Lamb. "SG06, A Fully Continuous and Varved Sediment Core from Lake Suigetsu, Japan: Stratigraphy and Potential for Improving the Radiocarbon Calibration

Model and Understanding of Late Quaternary Climate Changes." *Quaternary Science Reviews* 36 (2012): 164–176.

O'Brien, Michael J., and R. Lee Lyman. *Seriation, Stratigraphy, and Index Fossils: The Backbone of Archaeological Dating.* New York: Plenum Press, 1999.

Ortiz, J. E., T. Torres, M. R. González-Morales, J. Abad, I. Arribas, F. J. Fortea, F. García-Belenguer, and I. Gutiérrez-Zugasti. "The Aminochronology of Man-Induced Shell Middens in Caves in Northern Spain." *Archaeometry* 51 (2009): 123–139.

Petrie, W. M. Flinders. "Sequences in Prehistoric Remains." *Journal of the Anthropological Institute* 29 (1899): 295–301.

Radtke, Ulrich, Rainer Grün, and Henry P. Schwarcz. "Electron Spin Resonance Dating of the Pleistocene Coral Reef Tracts of Barbados." *Quaternary Research* 29, no. 3 (1988): 197–215.

Renfrew, Colin. *Archaeology and Language: The Puzzle of Indo-European Origins.* London: Jonathan Cape, 1987.

Rink, W. Jack. "Electron Spin Resonance (ESR) Dating and ESR Applications in Quaternary Science and Archaeometry." *Radiation Measurements* 27 (1997): 975–1025.

——— "Beyond 14C Dating." In *Earth Sciences and Archaeology*, edited by P. Goldberg, V. T. Holliday, and R. Ferring, 385–417. New York: Kluwer Academic, 2001.

Rink, W. J., and H. P. Schwarcz. "Short Contribution: ESR and Uranium Series Dating of Teeth from the Lower Paleolithic Site of Gesher Benot Ya'aqov, Israel: Confirmation of Paleomagnetic Age Indications." *Geoarchaeology* 20 (2005): 57–66.

Robinson, W. S. "A Method for Chronologically Ordering Archaeological Deposits." *American Antiquity* 16 (1951): 293–301.

Rogers, Alexander K. "Obsidian Hydration Dating: Accuracy and Resolution Limitations Imposed by Intrinsic Water Variability." *Journal of Archaeological Science* 35 (2008): 2009–2016.

Sharma, Virendra Nath. *Sawai Jai Singh and His Astronomy.* 2nd ed. Delhi, India: Motilal Banarsidass Publishers, 2016.

Taylor, R. Ervin. "Radiocarbon Dating." In *Chronometric Dating in Archaeology*, Vol. 2, edited by R. E. Taylor and M. J. Aitken, 65–96. Advances in Archaeological and Museum Science. New York: Plenus Press, 1997.

Wilson, Moira A., Margaret A. Carter, Christopher Hall, William D. Hoff, Ceren Ince, Shaun D. Savage, Bernard Mckay, and Ian M. Betts. "Dating Fired-Clay Ceramics Using Long-Term Power Law Rehydroxylation Kinetics." *Proceedings of the Royal Society A* 465, no. 2108 (2009): 2407–2415.

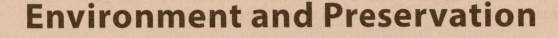

Environment and Preservation

The environment is an essential part of archaeological research. Although, as we saw in Chapter 4, the role of the environment in shaping human behavior is debated, understanding environmental conditions is critical for all archaeologists for two reasons. First, although the environment may not determine human behavior, it is an essential part of the human experience. Given that the environment today is not necessarily the same as in the past there is a need for archaeologists to reconstruct past environments, or **paleoclimates**. Our understanding of Upper Paleolithic populations living in Europe during the last "Ice Age" would not be well grounded if we did not have a good idea of the environmental conditions in which they lived. Knowing that people lived in a place that was warmer or colder, wetter or drier, or characterized by particular plants and animals helps us to better contextualize the reality of past peoples and more completely frame the decisions that they made. These decisions might have to do with the kinds of material culture that was utilized, such as clothing or shelter. Or those decisions might have to do with the kinds of social and political organizations that were present in an area. In many cases, environmental conditions heavily impacted people's **subsistence strategies**, or how they found or produced food. For example, questions concerning how processes of plant and animal domestication occurred are often linked to environmental conditions. Thus, understanding past environmental conditions is an important part of archaeological research.

Second, environmental conditions affect the preservation of archaeological data. Some environments aid in the preservation of certain types of material data and others are, for a lack of better words, absolutely terrible. Without the preservation of material data, archaeologists would have little to work with to understand past societies. So, preservation is a critical issue for archaeologists. Overall, some environments preserve certain materials better than others. But, even in regional environments that do not tend to preserve these materials well, particular microenvironmental conditions are sometimes found to have spectacular preservation. Contexts with these conditions often contain some of the most sensational archaeological materials

FIGURE 9.1 The frescos at Pompeii, Italy, have incredible preservation due to their rapid burial by volcanic materials in AD 79.

© S-F/Shutterstock.com

that capture both professional and public attention. In this chapter, we will review how archaeologists reconstruct environments and how environmental conditions impact preservation.

Reconstructing Ancient Environments

Archaeologists have quite a number of methods to reconstruct the environmental conditions of the past. Some archaeologists specialize in environmental reconstruction, whereas others collaborate with environmental scientists or draw on the extensive and growing paleoenvironmental literature in the earth and environmental sciences to further their own understanding of paleoclimatic conditions. The following review of methods is a thorough, although not exhaustive list of those available to archaeologists. These methods are the more standard and better-known methods in the field today.

Pollen Analysis

In general, it is common practice to use the remains of organisms to reconstruct environmental conditions. The remains of plants are no exception. Finding the remains of tropical palm trees indicates something different than finding the remains of alpine lichens. Although **macrobotanical remains**, larger parts of a plant such as seeds and leaves can tell you something about the environment, such remains usually do not preserve well. Some smaller, more durable parts of a plant, such as pollen for example, tend to preserve with some frequency.

Pollen analysis is sometimes referred to as **palynology**, which is more broadly the study of particles or dust. Pollen is just one of many components of dust (found in water, air, or sediments) that can be analyzed by palynologists. Archaeologists are particularly interested in pollen as it preserves well and the shape of pollen grains can tell you what species or subspecies of plant produced it, aiding archaeologists in identifying the range of plants (crops, forest cover, and grasses, among others) on the landscape during a given period of time, as well as their frequency.

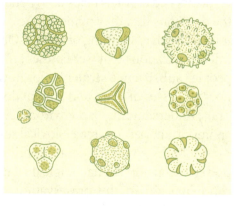

FIGURE 9.2 Examples of the variability in pollen grain forms.

© Zaytseva Darya/Shutterstock.com

Pollen is composed of microscopic grains that are released from male plants as part of the reproductive cycle of the species and then transported by insects, such as bees, as well as by the wind. It can be deposited in all kinds of archaeological contexts and by many different processes; blown in from some distance by the wind or by intentional human action such as harvesting, processing, and consuming crops. Given that pollen has a hard outer wall, called the **exospore** or **exine**, it has a higher tendency to preserve over time than many macroremains, although preservation is variable by species and is related to the environmental conditions in which it was deposited.

Grains of pollen are often collected by archaeologists in soil samples, although pollen can be found in all sorts of contexts including **coprolites** (ancient feces) and embedded on ceramic vessels and lithic tools, among many more. Given that they are invisible to the naked eye, archaeologists usually collect a small sample of soil from a context to transport to a laboratory where the grains can be separated from the sediments with a centrifuge and examined under a microscope. A sample of grains from the soil collected in the field is classified by comparing the ancient pollen to those from known plants and the frequency of pollen from particular plant species is calculated. How the soil samples are collected in the field can be variable and is related to the sampling strategy employed (see Chapter 5). During excavations, for example, archaeologists may take one or even several small soil samples from every context. In other cases, samples may be taken from only certain contexts. Yet, pollen is not just used for environmental reconstruction, but also for understanding the use of plants by peoples in the past for food and a variety of other activities (see Chapter 12); a fact that can impact sampling strategies. For example, if an archaeologist comes across a context with a number of ceramic vessels filled with soil, they may take samples from each of the vessels to see if pollen can indicate what the long-decayed contexts might have been. These pollen samples may provide useful information for paleoclimatic work, although the sampling strategy was designed to answer other types of questions.

Most pollen used for environmental reconstruction comes from anaerobic contexts such as sediments taken from core samples in places like bogs and lakebeds where pollen is trapped in the accumulating sediments at the bottom of these bodies of water, or from dry contexts such as caves where the pollen tends to preserve better. Pollen grains in these contexts are usually a good snapshot of the plants in the surrounding environment. Since the sediments are deposited incrementally, a stratigraphic analysis of the pollen found in cores can show changing frequencies of plants in the area over time. Importantly, sediments in waterlogged contexts usually have organic materials that can be dated through radiocarbon dating (see Chapter 8).

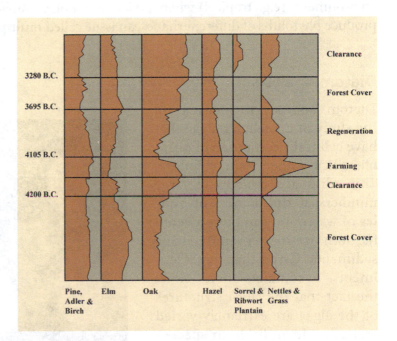

In a well-known case of pollen used for environmental reconstruction, researchers testing the bog at Fallahogy, Northern Ireland, have been able to demonstrate how tree species such as elm and oak diminished as the first farmers in the area began to clear forest for agricultural use. The dip in tree pollen correlates with an increase in open field species such as grasses that thrived in cleared areas around 4150 BC when the first major clearing took place. In fact, the pollen record of the area shows various cycles, including the regeneration of the forest and its subsequent clearance again at the hands of local peoples.

FIGURE 9.3 The pollen record from Fallahogy bog, Ireland, shows clear changes to the plant communities in the local area over time. Researchers attribute the increase in grass pollens to a period of relatively intensive farming in the mid-first-millennium BC.

© Belem Ceballos Casanova, adapted from Renfrew, Colin, and Paul Bahn. *Archaeology: Theories, Methods, and Practice.* Seventh edition. Thamks & Hudson, London, 2016.

Although pollen analysis is an excellent tool for environmental reconstruction, some care must be used in its application. For instance, there are certain situations in which the pollen recovered in specific archaeological contexts are not reflective of the surrounding environment. Pollen recovered in granaries would be heavily weighted toward the plants stored in them, rather than other plants that would have dotted the surrounding landscape. Plants transported by people from one environment to another might introduce pollen in particular contexts that do not reflect the surrounding environmental conditions (e.g., tropical lowland plants imported to temperate highland areas). Many of these types of situations can be identified through systematic research, but archaeologists should keep these issues in mind when analyzing pollen.

Phytolith Analysis

Phytolith analysis is similar in some ways to pollen analysis in that they both focus on microscopic parts of plants that can be recovered in contexts of interest to archaeologists. Phytoliths are composed of silica that vary in shape and are very durable, often remaining intact long after a plant has decayed or burned. They can be recovered in a wide variety of contexts including soil and even the dental calculus of teeth. Although the shapes of phytoliths have less variation than pollen, diminishing the ability to identify some plants by species (e.g., phytoliths from grass species look too similar to say anything more detailed about them [a problem termed **redundancy**]), phytoliths preserve much better in many environments (e.g., tropical) where pollen does not. Complicating this analysis, however, some plants produce phytoliths of different shapes, an issue called **multiplicity**.

Diatom Analysis

Diatom analysis is focused on the study of unicellular algae that have cell walls composed of durable silica rather than cellulose. This silica accumulates in large numbers at the bottom of bodies of water and can be recovered in both freshwater and marine sediments. Given that these sediments accumulate over time, the fact that the silica structures of the algae are extremely varied and often identifiable to species, and that the species of algae can reflect particular environmental conditions, diatom analysis can provide very useful data concerning past climates.

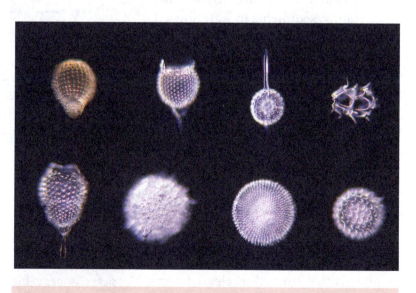

FIGURE 9.4 Examples of the variability in diatom forms.

© Dr. Norbert Lange/Shutterstock.com

DNA Analysis of Plants

Remains of the genetic code, or DNA, of plants can also be recovered from a range of archaeological contexts including lake sediments, coprolites, and on artifacts such as lithic tools used to process plants. Identifying plant species through **DNA analysis** is relatively new in archaeology, but provides researchers with data concerning the range of species present at particular times in the past.

Macrobotanical Remains

Although the macrobotanical remains of plants often do not preserve as well as many of the microbotanical remains previously discussed, they do occur in certain environmental contexts, particularly those that favor the preservation of organic remains. As we will discuss in further detail below, these contexts tend to be anaerobic, cold, or dry. In the Tehuacán Valley of Mexico, for example, archaeologists have been able to recover the remains of maize cobs in dry cave environments. These remains have been particularly important for understanding the domestication of maize as they were recovered from several levels of the cave excavations demonstrating the increase in cob size over an extended period of time. In other contexts, the macrobotanical remains themselves are not recovered, but there is some impression of the plant that proves its existence at a particular period of time. Continuing with the example of maize, excavations by Payson Sheets and his team at the site of Joya de Cerén in El Salvador detected evidence of planted maize near houses covered by a volcanic eruption of Laguna de Caldera around AD 600. The maize plants themselves had long deteriorated, but, much like the bodies at Pompeii, the spaces that the plants once occupied had voids preserving their shapes in the ash deposits, allowing the archaeologists to create casts. In any event, macrobotanical remains can provide further evidence of climatic conditions when they are recovered.

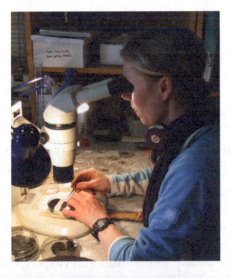

FIGURE 9.5 Charred plant remains from Egypt under a microscope. From left: lolium grains, seeds of mallow (both weeds of grain fields), and emmer wheat chaff.

© 2018 Alexandra Witsell. Photo by Alexandra Witsell. AERA _Archaeobotanist_2013
© 2018 Ancient Egypt Research Associates. Photo by Claire Malleson.

FIGURE 9.6 Early maize cobs from Tehuacán, Mexico. The size of the cobs increased over time as the domestication process continued.

© Robert S. Peabody Institute of Archaeology, Phillips Academy, Andover, Massachusetts. All Rights Reserved.

Faunal Analysis

As with the remains of plants, the remains of animals can also provide evidence of ancient environmental conditions. The Yucatán Peninsula, where the authors of this book both work, is a hot and humid tropical environment today. Yet, some archaeological contexts from around 10,000 years ago show that a very distinctly nontropical suite of animals lived on the landscape including mastodons, bears, dire wolves, and giant sloths. The existence of these species indicates that this area of the world was much colder at that time. The best data for climatic reconstruction using animal remains, however, do not often come from large animals such as Pleistocene fauna, but from small animals or **microfauna**.

FIGURE 9.7 Much like the bodies at Pompeii, Italy, many organic remains at the site of Joya de Cerén left void spaces that archaeologists have filled with dental plaster. Here, we see the molds of maize plants at the site.

© Payson Sheets

Smaller animals tend to be more susceptible to climatic change, adapting to even small changes at a quicker rate than larger animals that can often tolerate wider ranges of environmental variability. Further, the remains of smaller animals have a taphonomic tendency to preserve better and are usually found with more frequency, providing more statistically sound data on which to base interpretations.

Although **zooarchaeologists** are the specialists who study the animal bones (**faunal analysis**, see also Chapter 12), in truth, many different types of organisms ranging from mollusks to insects can provide important information regarding past environmental conditions. For example, archaeologists often find the remains of rice black bug (*Scotinophara lurida*) in ancient paddy fields of East India, South China, South Korea, and West Japan. Because rice black bugs cannot survive in wetlands over the winter, their presence indicates the development of water management systems, through which farmers drained water from paddy fields after harvests. In other words, archaeologists can infer the emergence of drainage facilities in the region based upon the analysis of rice black bug remains, even if those features have been destroyed by subsequent human activities. Nevertheless, archaeologists must be careful with such data as the remains of organisms can be found outside of their habitats; for example, the Inka emperors would have fish caught along the Pacific coast and literally run up to the mountain capital of Cuzco for their culinary pleasure. In any regard, the remains of animals provide another rich source of data on ancient environments.

On a final note, the remains of some animal species can be used to reconstruct the season of the year in which they were deposited. **Seasonality studies** are predicated on the idea that some living organisms have specific morphological characteristics at certain times of the year. For instance, many species of mammals are born in late spring in particular climates to avoid the difficult winter months when there is a scarce food supply. Likewise, certain plants generally produce pollen and seeds or fruits during particular months of the year. If excavations from an archaeological site, or even specific context, reveal data from species that indicate a human occupation during a limited span of the year, then archaeologists can attempt to reconstruct temporal occupations. Such occupations are often found to be cyclical with the same groups of people returning the same spot season after season. Seasonality studies are often employed for the study of highly mobile societies that moved around on the landscape where food sources were available. Pastoral societies that practice **transhumance**, moving herds to high-elevation pasture areas from lower valley floors during the summer, are good examples of situations where seasonality studies might be employed.

Soil Analysis

Analyses of soils can also provide information concerning past environmental conditions. Particular soils form under certain conditions and understanding soil characteristics such as mineral types, particle size, and soil chemistry can provide important information concerning paleoclimates. For example, in a study of Paharpur, Bangladesh, the site of the largest Buddhist monastery south of the Himalayas, a team of researchers discovered that the composition of clay minerals dated to the during the Pala Dynasty from AD 700 to 1100 indicate an estuary or marine environment associated with this area under cool to temperate and dry climatic conditions. In another example, researchers have identified three major

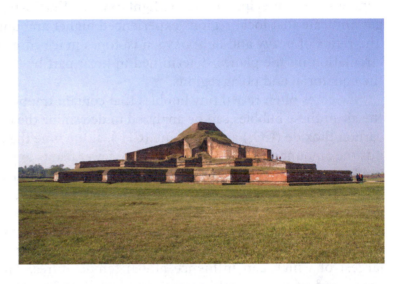

FIGURE 9.8 The Somapura Mahavira at the site of Paharpur, Bangladesh.

© mname/Shutterstock.com

soil erosion events in the Maya lowland area of southern Mesoamerica during the Preclassic (1000 BC to AD 250), Late Classic (AD 550–700), and modern periods (past several decades). Although natural climatic change could be an important factor in the formation of soil deposits associated with erosion, this research also highlights the role of humans in environmental change. Much like the pollen evidence associated with deforestation described for the bog at Fallahogy above, archaeologists suspect that intentional deforestation of the Maya jungles may have played an important role in erosional patterns in these events as well.

Ice Core Analysis

Several good indicators of climate come from **ice core analysis**. Environmental scientists are accumulating an ever growing number of cores taken from ice sheets and glaciers in many parts of the world. As these ice deposits were formed incrementally (annual growth layers), they provide stratigraphic information concerning environmentally sensitive data that was trapped in the ice when each growth layer was originally formed. One of the key elements to understanding climate in ice cores is oxygen, although hydrogen provides important information as well. During periods of colder global temperatures, the oceans have more heavy oxygen ($\delta^{18}O$) than during warmer periods, which are, in contrast, characterized by elevated amounts of light oxygen ($\delta^{16}O$). Higher ratios of heavy oxygen in the oceans mean that the light oxygen was trapped in the ice, in particular the polar ice sheets. These ratios are measurable through oxygen isotope analysis of the core samples. By calculating the ratio of heavy to light oxygen in polar regions, environmental scientists can calculate the amount of ice that covered the Earth's surface (as well as the volume of the oceans), a ratio that is related to global temperatures. In regional samples taken from glaciers, the situation is more complex as more heavy oxygen generally precipitates in these environments. Oxygen isotopes from glacial ice cores in places like the Andean or Himalayan mountains, however, can be used to measure the amount of rainfall in those regions fairly well as heavy oxygen condenses and precipitates before light oxygen. Thus, samples with elevated amounts of light oxygen indicate that local regions experienced higher amounts of rainfall during particular periods. The ratios of heavy and light oxygen isotopes in ice cores are also related to the strength of wind circulation on the planet, determined in great part by the mean temperature difference between the equatorial and polar regions.

Ice cores often reveal tiny bubbles that contain trapped ancient air. Using a mass spectrometer, the air in these bubbles can be analyzed to determine the composition of greenhouse gases, such as carbon dioxide (CO_2) and methane (CH_4), at the time the bubbles were formed. During cold periods the amount of CO_2 drops as there are fewer plants to produce it. In similar fashion, the levels of methane drop during colder periods as methane is produced primarily by microorganisms (which do better in warmer periods) found in swampy areas, although methane contributions from natural gas deposits and wild animals also have an impact.

The dust trapped in formations of ice can also provide valuable environmental data. For example, elevated levels of sulfate (SO_4^{2-}) have been used to identify volcanic eruptions, the largest of which can influence global temperatures. The levels of continental dust, which is composed of nonsea salt potassium ($nssK^+$) and nonsea salt calcium ($nssCa^{2+}$), and sea salts (sodium, Na^+) can also be indicators of wind speed and direction. Other dust particles may be used to calculate the intensity of dust storms for certain regions, which can be a product of the extent of desert regions.

Sea Core Analysis

A parallel line of research to ice core analysis is sea core analysis. As we have previously discussed, sediments accumulate in many bodies of water, such as lakes, bogs, and ponds. This is also true for the world's oceans. Sediments on the ocean floors accumulate slowly, but the deposits are laid down in stratigraphic order; absolute dates for the strata can be obtained through radiocarbon dating, uranium series dating, or paleomagnetism (see Chapter 8). Sea cores taken away from the shoreline tend to be very well stratified and can provide information on factors such as the temperature of the Earth going back several million years. For example, just as pollen gets trapped in the sedimentary layers formed at the bottom of lakes, the remains of environmentally sensitive organisms such as planktonic foraminifera (floating amoeboid protists with shells) get trapped in the sediments forming in some areas of the world's oceans. Changes in the species of foraminifera (e.g., warm vs. cold water species) can indicate changes in the environmental conditions of the Earth. Environmental scientists also study the organic molecules trapped in the sediments. Specifically, the analysis of fatty lipids can provide information regarding water temperature. Finally, oxygen isotope analysis of the shells as well as coral can provide further information concerning paleoclimates from the world's oceans. These organisms tend to incorporate great amounts of heavy oxygen in their shells as temperatures drop. Isotope analysis of other materials such as strontium and calcium in coral (datable using the uranium series method, see Chapter 8) can also reveal information concerning ocean temperatures.

Ancient Shorelines

Another indicator of ancient environmental conditions is the levels of ancient bodies of water, both marine and fresh, which can be studied using evidence of changes in their shorelines. Marine coastlines, for example, are sensitive to changes in global temperature. As we have already reviewed, as global temperatures drop, more ice is trapped in the polar regions, thus reducing the levels of the world's oceans and exposing more dry land. Conversely, rising global temperatures inundate exposed land masses, forcing coastlines to recede.

Several types of data can indicate where ancient marine shorelines were located in the past. One of the most obvious pieces of evidence is the actual geomorphological remains of those ancient shorelines. Marine coastlines tend to leave telltale material remains of their presence as the interfaces between land and sea have some quite particular and dynamic processes that shape them, such as waves that form beaches. Relict beach ridges can be located in inland areas, marking a past shoreline on the modern terrestrial landscape. Underwater ridges signaling past shorelines can also be located underwater through remote sensing techniques such as echo sounding, seismic reflection profiling, and bathymetric Light Detection and Ranging (LiDAR) (see Chapter 6 for a discussion of some of these techniques). A range of dating techniques can be applied to situate these features in time.

The shorelines of freshwater bodies such as rivers and lakes can also inform us of past environmental conditions, but in some very different ways than marine coastlines. Freshwater lakes and wetland areas often receive their water from precipitation, although contributions from glacial melt (which can be the result of very old precipitation) can also be a factor. Thus, the changes in the shoreline of a lake can often related to wet or dry conditions. For example, the ancient city of Tiwanaku, Bolivia, located near the shores of Lake Titicaca in the Andean highlands, was highly dependent on the levels of the lake to sustain its raised field agriculture. Some studies estimate that drought conditions around 1,000 years ago impacted the water levels to such a degree that the lake levels dropped 15–20 m, causing the shoreline to recede away from the centuries-old urban center. Some archaeologists believe that these changing environmental conditions contributed to a decline in the city and the collapse of the sociopolitical system it represented from AD 1000 to 1150.

The locations of archaeological sites are also indicators of changing shorelines. For example, inundated sites speak to rising sea levels. In Belize, Heather McKillop has documented an ancient Maya salt production site dating to the Late Classic period (AD 600–800) underneath a couple of meters of the Caribbean Sea. The Paynes Creek Salt Works site has produced some incredibly preserved organic remains, including a wooden dugout canoe, due to the anaerobic water-logged environment (mangrove peat sediment) caused by rising sea levels that inundated the site. In a spectacular example of the location of an archaeological site indicating changing sea levels, the Upper Paleolithic cave site of Cosquer (located on the Mediterranean coast of southern France) has produced some stunning examples of early European art dating from 27,000 BP to 19,000 BP. The mouth of the cave, however, is located 37 m below the current levels of the Mediterranean Sea indicating that when it was open to Upper Paleolithic peoples the temperatures were far much colder than they are today.

Other archaeological features and sites located on dry land may also indicate where ancient shorelines were located. For instance, midden or trash deposits, composed of the remains of shellfish are usually associated with marine environments. Finding shell middens as some distance inland can indicate that shorelines were farther inland in the past.

Global temperature is not the only factor to consider when analyzing ancient coastlines. Erosion of the coastline by the sea and new deposition expanding coastal areas (such as the delta areas of rivers) also change the configuration of shorelines. For instance, the ancient Egyptian ports of Herakleion and Canopus, are now 4–7 m below the level of the Mediterranean Sea. Archaeological work suggests that flooding, possibly historically recorded floods of the Nile in AD 741 and AD 742, may have liquefied the delta sediments on which the cities were built, in part causing the sea to envelop them.

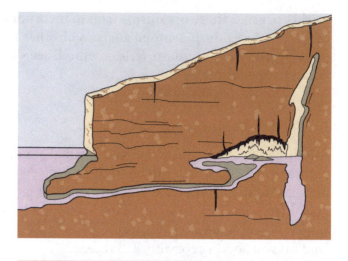

FIGURE 9.9 Today, the mouth of the cave at Cosquer, France, is located near 40 m underwater, illustrating the amount of sea level rise since the time the cave mouth was exposed during glacial episodes of the Pleistocene. The earliest cave art in the cave dates to 27,000 BP

© Belem Ceballos Casanova, drawn after Clottes and Courtin, 1996.

Other Relict Bodies of Water

Evidence of other bodies of water besides shorelines can also inform of past environmental conditions, often in the form of relict channels. For example, communities located in stretches of the Silk Road that crossed the desertic Tarim Basin of western China were abandoned as climatic conditions became much dryer during the first-millennium AD. The well-preserved city of Niya (also known as Caḍota) is one of the most spectacular examples of these once-thriving oasis communities. In more spectacular fashion, the community of Loulan was abandoned around AD 330 when floodwater from storms caused the Tarim River that provided the water for the city to change its course. This more drastic change resulted in the relocation of the military garrison at Loulan, allowing the city to fall into ruin and leaving relict channels to attest to the once available water.

FIGURE 9.10 The site of Niya, China, in 1906. The preservation at the site is spectacular and you can appreciate numerous dead trees in the background of this historic photo from an early expedition to the site.

Group portrait at the Niya site/British Library, London, UK/© British Library Board. All Rights Reserved/Bridgeman Images

Regardless for the reasons of changes in shorelines and other bodies of water, the expansion or reduction of land masses can have tremendous impacts on human populations. Rising sea levels may reduce the amount of resources (less land correlating with fewer resources). Or, falling sea levels may expose areas of land that connects previously separated land masses. These **land bridges**, such as the Bering Strait (connecting Asia to North America, known as Beringia) and English Channel (connecting Great Britain to continental Europe, known as Doggerland) can facilitate the movement of people and animals in ways impossible when the land masses were separated.

Other factors can also be responsible for land "rising" or "falling" relative to sea level. **Tectonic subsidence** (downward movement of land masses) and **uplift** can also change the environmental conditions in shoreline areas in radical ways having nothing to do with temperature change, but are the geological result of the clash of continental plates. In very different cases, the weight of glacial deposits can push land downward. As the glaciers melt, this land rises. In a famous case of moving land surfaces and weight, the principle temple of the Mexica (Aztec) city of Tenochtitlan was partially dismantled by the invading Spanish forces in the sixteenth century. New construction was placed on what remained of the temple, pushing it down into the ground. A century later, as some of this architecture began to fail and was demolished, the remains of the Templo Mayor were exposed and began to rise from the depths beneath modern-day Mexico City relative to the surrounding architecture.

Varves

Varves are sediments that are deposited annually, creating laminated stratigraphy. Such deposits are more common in lakes near glacial formations. In the spring, when temperatures are rising, water flowing from the glacial deposits increases. This "high-energy" flow leads to the deposition of coarser-grained sediments (silt and sand), usually lighter in color. When colder temperatures return in the fall, the flow of water begins to slow and finer-grained clays are normally deposited; these tend to

FIGURE 9.11 Doggerland is the area of the southern North Sea between continental Europe and Great Britain. It was exposed during the last glaciation, connecting the British Isles to the rest of the continent.

© Kendall Hunt Publishing Company adapted from Gaffney et al. 2009.

FIGURE 9.12 The Templo Mayor complex was the center of the Mexica (Aztec) capital of Tenochtitlan. Many of its buildings were partially dismantled and built over to construct colonial period Mexico City. More recently, some of these colonial buildings have been demolished, exposing the remains of Tenochtitlan. The *tzompantli* (skull rack) is pictured here.

© javarman/Shutterstock.com

be darker in color. Thus, varve deposits are an indicator of the flow of water, related to temperature conditions, on an annual basis. In this sense, varve sequences are similar to the growth of annual tree rings; with unique sequences of thick and thin deposits. Again, much like tree rings, varves have been for dating purposes (see Chapter 8), even though there has been some skepticism as to how far back in time these sequences are reliable. In any regard, they do give archaeologists important information concerning local environments in places like Scandinavia and Japan where there are relatively long sequences, as well as important fine-grained data concerning global temperatures, perhaps going back to 52,800 BP.

Speleothem Records

Caves are found with varying frequency all over the world. The formation of stalagmites, stalactites (both of these are **speleothems**), and **flowstone** (horizontal formations) in caves is related to environmental factors, specifically the deposition of minerals such as calcium carbonate that is picked up by water percolating through the geological formations above the cave. The amount of growth of these speleothems is associated with the amount of water passing through the ground and can be a good indicator of local patterns of rainfall. The time between growth intervals can also be a good indicator of climatic conditions; the layers of speleothem growth can be dated using uranium–thorium dating (see Chapter 8).

Besides the samples used for paleoclimate analysis in ice and sea cores, isotope analysis can be applied in other contexts to understand aspects of past environments, including the speleothem record. In particular, oxygen isotope analysis (heavy vs. light) can be applied to other data, many of which archaeologists might collect, that can indicate prevailing weather patterns in certain areas of the world or reveal global temperatures similar to how they are calculated from ice core data. For instance, environmental scientists have found that hurricanes have water with elevated levels of light oxygen. As this water falls, it can be incorporated into various parts of the environment. In several studies of the Maya region, often conducted through archaeological projects, it has been found that speleothems (stalagmites and stalactites) in caves incorporate the oxygen isotopes from rainfall as they incrementally grow, not only leaving the potential for hurricane signatures to appear, but to track where those hurricanes might have come from. In fact, these isotopes have even been used to differentiate if rainfall was coming generally from fresh or marine sources, an indicator of prevailing wind patterns. Although speleothem research (see more below) is one increasingly important way isotope studies can be applied outside of sea and ice core contexts, the analysis of organic remains, including those found in archaeological contexts, can provide complementary studies. Isotope data in tree rings, animal bones, and even the skeletons of ancient people themselves are beginning to prove highly informative of past climate conditions.

Another isotope that can be used in the speleothem record is carbon ($\delta^{13}C$), used to measure the presence of C3 and C4 plants. C3 plants are those that form two molecules of a three-carbon acid when they fix CO_2 in the chloroplast. These plants generally thrive in cooler environments. C4 plants convert CO_2 to a four-carbon acid and generally live in warm environments. Thus, being able to measure the amounts of C3 and C4 plants in the environment through isotope analysis can indicate temperature in the past. Although carbon isotope analysis of human skeletal material can provide essential dietary information concerning the plants that peoples in the past consumed (see also Chapter 11), carbon isotopes measured in speleothems can be an indication of the density and type surface vegetation, as well as temperature.

Other analyses, such as trace element analysis (the presence of rare elements such as phosphorus and magnesium), pollen analysis, lipid biomarkers, and speleothem fluid inclusions are other promising ways in which the speleothem record is being exploited to learn about paleoclimates. As further research in these areas continues, archaeologists may have an increasingly larger toolset from which to draw on speleothem records to understand paleoclimatic conditions. Yet, although speleothem paleoclimate records are becoming increasingly important, they must be treated with care as there are other factors besides just rainfall, including water chemistry and cave temperature, which can influence the growth of these cave formations and the levels of different isotopes. It is important to control for microenvironmental conditions inside each cave to calibrate the speleothem data. Further, it is good practice to replicate studies in a series of caves in a region rather than just rely on the study of one.

Dendroclimatology

As we have already seen (Chapter 8), trees rings provide valuable information concerning chronology. They can also contain important information concerning past climates (**dendroclimatology**). The width of annual growth rings is determined by a number of environmental factors, including the amount of soil moisture (often related to rainfall), cloud cover, wind, disease, and temperature. Not all areas of the world have trees, however, and where trees were present in the past, they do not always preserve very well. In some areas, like American Southwest, where the dry climate preserves wood samples with more frequency, tree-ring data can be an important source of paleoclimate data. In other areas where wood tends to decompose fairly rapidly, archaeologists and paleoclimatologists just do not have the samples to work with. Additionally, in some tropical areas trees grow year round and do not show clear growth rings that can be measured. Yet, since temperature and soil moisture are the major contributing factors to tree-ring width, when past wood samples are available they can contribute very useful data for understanding past environmental conditions. More recently, environmental scientists have explored x-ray microdensitometry as a technique to evaluate the wood cell size and density as a proxy for environmental conditions. Further, analysis of stable carbon isotopes ($^{13}C/^{12}C$) has been performed to understand local temperatures experienced by trees.

Preservation

As we stated at the beginning of this book, archaeology is focused on the understanding humanity's past through the study of its material remains. Without material remains then, archaeologists would not have the data necessary to perform research. Thus, the question of the preservation of material remains is paramount to the success of the field. Nevertheless, the majority of material remains from past human behaviors does not preserve, or preserve well. Further, many human activities leave little to no material trace of their existence. What does preserve then, and why?

Climate

Climatic conditions play a critical role in the preservation of materials, although it is not the only factor by any stretch of the imagination. In general, dry climates preserve materials better than wet and humid climates, and very cold environments preserve materials better than warmer ones. Thus, working in a frozen desertic context may result in conditions of preservation that far surpass working in the context of a hot and humid tropical forest.

Wet and Dry Contexts

Microorganisms like bacteria and fungi are one of the most destructive agents when considering archaeological preservation. Given that much of the material that archaeologists seek to recover is composed of organics (e.g., basketry, textiles, human and animal remains, food), preservation often hinges on the ability of microorganisms to break down such materials. Many microorganisms depend on water. Thus, in environments where water is extremely scarce preservation of organics can be quite good. Conversely, humid environments tend to provide poor conditions of preservation for many materials including organics. Environments that oscillate between wet and dry conditions can produce some of the worst conditions for preservation.

FIGURE 9.13 The Paracas culture of the Nazca Valley region of coastal Peru is well known for its incredible textile tradition (ca 200 BC to AD 200), which only survives due to the superb preservation of the dry environment. Textiles such as this one were used to wrap burials in the necropolis of Wari Kayan.

Mantle, Peru, South Coast, Paracas, 200 B.C.-A.D. 200. Camelid fiber plain weave with stem stitch and loop stitch embroidery. Textile: 57 1/4 × 98 1/8 in. (145.42 × 249.24 cm) Frame: 67 5/8 × 108 7/8 × 5 in. (171.77 × 276.54 × 12.7 cm) Strainer: 65 1/4 × 106 1/4 in. (165.74 × 269.88 cm). Los Angeles County Museum of Art, Los Angeles County Fund (67.4). Photo © Museum Associates/LACMA.

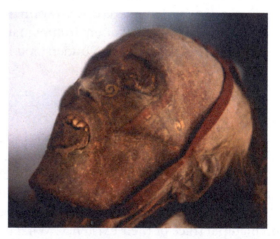

FIGURE 9.14 Mummified remains are often helped along in their preservation through human intervention, such as this Ptolemaic Period (305–30 BC) Egyptian mummy now located in the Louvre (Paris, France, left). In Egypt, bodies were heavily manipulated to aid in long-term preservation. Most mummified remains still preserved today, however, are also a product of the local environment. The soil conditions (dry with a high salt content) for the burial for this individual found in the Tarim Basin of western China (right) greatly aided in its subsequent preservation years.

© Mikhail Zahranichny/Shutterstock.com
© Elizabeth Wayland Barber

Mummified remains are probably the most famous example of good preservation from arid contexts. The mummification of human remains has occurred in several parts of the world. In many cases, the earliest examples of mummification appear to have been accidental; bodies that were deposited in very dry contexts that resulted in processes of natural mummification. Early burials in the deserts of Egypt and coastal Peru, for example, desiccated the bodies due to the lack of water in the surrounding matrix. People in these particular early societies noticed this desiccation process and took steps to improve it by preparing bodies in certain ways, such as removing organs, in order to better preserve the dead. Intentional mummification may have also occurred in other areas that are not so conducive to the preservation of organics, but archaeologists do not recover the remains in mummified form unless the conditions of preservation deter microorganisms from advancing the decay of the bodies. In some cases, other factors, such as high salt content in the soil, one of the factors that help to preserve the spectacular mummified remains around the arid Tarim Basin of China, play an essential role in the desiccation process (see below). Although deserts are common places where good preservation occurs due to the lack of water, arid caves are also known to have excellent preservation.

Cold Contexts

Just as a refrigerator helps to preserve your food, cold contexts help to preserve organics from decomposing. Cold contexts usually occur at higher latitudes and/or higher altitudes. One of the most famous examples of a well-preserved human body was discovered in the high Alps in 1991 when two mountain climbers happened across the body man emerging from the ice on the mountain. Nicknamed Ötzi, the body dates to roughly 3300 BC during the Chalcolithic period and represents the oldest known human remains with his everyday clothing and equipment that are fully preserved. Ötzi has revealed a virtual treasure trove of data that are normally not available to archaeologists. For example, researchers have hypothesized that tattoos found on the desiccated skin may be linked to therapies associated with adverse health conditions that are noted in many of these same areas of his body. The contents of Ötzi's last two meals have also been reconstructed given the state of preservation of his internal organs. Further, a study of lesions on Ötzi's body, as well as a cat scan that revealed a projectile point lodged one of his shoul-

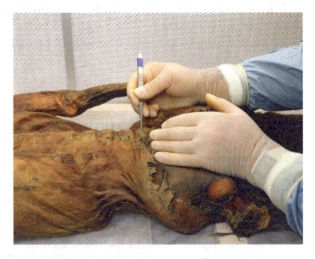

FIGURE 9.15 Ötzi was preserved in ice at an altitude of roughly 3,200 masl in the Tyrolean Alps. Note the tattooing on the back. Some scholars believe the tattoos were therapeutic, located in areas that may have caused chronic pain.

Scientist taking a sample from The Oetzi Iceman (photo) (detail)/South Tyrol Museum of Archaeology, Bolzano, Italy/ Wolfgang Neeb/Bridgeman Images

ders, has led some scholars to propose that he was intentionally killed. In some ways, the study of Ötzi's remains seem more like a forensic investigation than archaeology, but it must be remembered that what archaeologists do is very much like forensic work. Unfortunately, the preservation of the data to reconstruct what happened in the vast majority of cases does not approach the level found in a spectacular find like Ötzi.

Anaerobic Contexts

A third environment where microorganisms have trouble decomposing organic materials is composed of those with little or no free oxygen (O_2), which many microorganisms depend on to survive. Most anaerobic contexts are found in waterlogged areas such as wetlands. The bog bodies found in lowland areas of northern Europe are probably the most famous cases of preservation in wetland areas. Preserved in the anaerobic environment of the peat bogs, some of these spectacularly preserved bodies have been the subject of research regarding who they were in life and why their remains ended up in the muck at the bottom of a swamp. Many of the bodies have evidence of violent deaths including stab wounds, evidence of disembowelment, and strangulation leading archaeologists to hypothesize that the individuals may represent human sacrifices or deemed deviant members of society (e.g., criminals). Peat bogs are particularly important contexts in terms of good preservation of organic material, although they are generally acidic and can result in poor preservation of other kinds of materials such as iron and ceramics.

FIGURE 9.16 Tollund Man is one of the most well-known bog bodies. This individual was found on the Jutland Peninsula of Denmark with a rope around his neck, suggesting that he was killed and thrown into the bog (ca. fourth-century BC).

Tollund man, victim of human sacrifice by ritual strangulation/ Werner Forman Archive/Bridgeman Images

Soil Type

The chemistry of soils is also an important environmental factor in terms of conditions of preservation. As mentioned earlier, some soil chemistry conditions, such as the high salt content of the Tarim Basin, act as agents of preservation. Others, such as the generally high acidic content of forest soils, due to high levels of tannic acid from decaying leaves, can act as agents of decay for materials such as bones, teeth, and shell, which tend to fare better in alkaline conditions. Additional attributes of soils such as drainage (hydrology) and levels of dissolved organic matter can also play a role in conditions of preservation.

The Role of Animals and Plants

When animals and plants are taken into consideration of conditions of preservation, it is normally in a negative context. **Bioturbation**, the disturbance of the matrix by living organisms, often results in poor preservation. Burrowing animals such as gophers can alter and destroy archaeological contexts. Trees can rip buildings apart and intrude into buried contexts such as graves. Dogs, rodents, and other animals can sometimes dig up or find buried bone material, gnawing on the remains. The impact of bioturbation varies from ecosystem to ecosystem, but regardless of how uncommon it might be in a certain environment, archaeologists should keep an eye out for evidence of such disturbance.

A Consideration of Materials

As indicated by the previous mention of poor preservation of iron and ceramic artifacts in peat bogs, the materials themselves are also important for understanding preservation. Some inorganic materials, such as ceramics, do not preserve well in acidic soil conditions like those often encountered in bogs and temperate forests, whereas certain types of lithics such as chert or jade may preserve well. Even within material classes such as ceramics or lithics, there may be variable preservation due to composition of the materials. For example, in the Yucatán Peninsula, high-fired slate ware ceramics tempered with volcanic ash from the Terminal Classic period (AD 900–1100) preserve far better on average than lower-fired calcite-tempered ceramics from the later Postclassic period (AD 1100–1521). Similarly, Roman period glass that was manufactured with soda ash is more resistant to negative chemical reactions than later medieval glass that was made with wood ash. Thus, in addition to environment, considerations of the type of material and/or the quality of manufacture are important for understanding preservation.

FIGURE 9.17 Tree roots, such as these strangling the Mahathat temple at Ayutthaya, Thailand, can inflict tremendous damage to archaeological contexts; in particular architecture is very susceptible to this kind of bioturbation.

© Chaiwat Vuttikornvipak/Shutterstock.com

Natural Disasters

Some natural disasters completely destroyed archaeological contexts, whereas others have resulted in some of the most famous cases of archaeological preservation in the world. Although tsunamis, hurricanes, and raging floodwaters have washed some contexts completely away, volcanic deposits have resulted in some of the most iconic contexts of archaeological preservation. The Roman towns of Pompeii and Herculaneum are probably among the most famous example of volcanic preservation. In AD 79, these towns were covered with thick deposits of volcanic ash that preserved artifact assemblages *in situ*. The plaster casts of the void spaces left by human bodies in the "Garden of the Fugitives" is a nearly unique snapshot of a shocking moment in human history,

FIGURE 9.18 A well-fired slate ware ceramic vessel depicting a Maya scribe from the site of Yaxuná, Mexico (ca. AD 750–900).

Source: Travis Stanton

one that has captured the imagination of public since its discovery. Ironically, this incredibly preserved context is actually one that represents quite poor preservation of the actual human remains inside the void space, stressing the fact that some conditions preserve certain data well and others poorly. In another important case of volcanic preservation, the 3.7 million-year-old footprints of three hominin ancestors, most likely of the species *Australopithecus afarensis* were found by Mark Leakey in Tanzania in 1978 (See also Chapter 8). At the time of their discovery, these footprints provided key evidence for the antiquity of **bipedalism** in our ancestral line, or put another way, when our hominin ancestors began to habitually walk on two feet. Although even earlier evidence of bipedalism has been found since the discovery of the Laetoli prints, they remain a captivating moment of a human history recording three of our ancestors walking across a field of wet volcanic ash.

FIGURE 9.19 The casts of human bodies at Pompeii, Italy. Although the organic remains of these people have long since deteriorated, the volcanic matrix which surrounded the bodies has preserved their forms, allowing archaeologists to capture their moment of death during the AD 79 eruption of Mount Vesuvius.

© balounm/Shutterstock.com

Other natural disasters can be variable in their impact on archaeological preservation. Landslides, for instance, have destroyed many sites. Yet, in the case of Ozette in the state of Washington, a landslide resulted in spectacular preservation of organic materials when a landslide covered the community in thick mud around five hundred years ago, effectively creating an anaerobic environment. Spectacular artifacts such as wooden toy canoes and effigy whale fins were recovered by archaeologists in the 1970s after this coastal site was exposed by a storm. Another landslide that covered the site of Lajia, China, around 2000 BC created contexts in some ways similar to the Garden of the Fugitives at Pompeii with skeletal human remains huddled together for protection against the force of the sediment.

The Role of People in Preservation

A final consideration of conditions of preservation concerns the role of humans. Human action can result in either the destruction or preservation of archaeological contexts. As we mentioned in some detail in Chapter 2, humans today are responsible for a vast amount of destruction of archaeological contexts through activities ranging from looting to agricultural practices to modern construction projects (we mentioned the issue of plow zones in Chapter 6). People in the past also played roles in such destruction, although as we mentioned in Chapter 7, destructive activities in the past can change archaeological contexts in ways that are also of great interest, informing archaeologists of peoples' interactions with even older material culture.

Despite all of the negative associations of people with the destruction of archaeological contexts and materials, people can also play critical roles in their preservation. Cultural heritage management is prime example of modern efforts focused on preservation. However, **curation**, or care and management, of sites and material culture is not just a modern phenomenon. Many libraries throughout the world have taken care of ancient manuscripts for centuries. The Vatican, for example, has a large collection of ancient manuscripts. The community of Timbuktu, Mali, is also famous for the large number of preserved manuscripts in diverse languages such as Arabic, Sonhay, and Tamasehq, passed down from generation to generation between the thirteenth and twenty-first centuries.

Bibliography

Aitken, Martin J., and Stephen Stokes. "Climatostratigraphy." In *Chronometric Dating in Archaeology*, edited by R. E. Taylor and M. J. Aitken, 1–30. Advances in Archaeological and Museum Science, Vol. 2. New York: Plenus Press, 1997.

Aston, Michael. *Interpreting the Landscape: Landscape Archaeology in Local Studies*. London: B.T. Batsford, 1985.

Barber, Elizabeth W. *The Mummies of Ürümchi*. New York: W.W. Norton & Company, 1999.

Battarbee, R. W. "Diatom Analysis." In *Handbook of Holocene Palaeoecology and Palaeohydrology*, edited by B. E. Berglund, 527–570. London: Wiley, 1986.

Baumer, Christoph. *Southern Silk Road: In the Footsteps of Sir Aurel Stein and Sven Hedin*. Bangkok, Thailand: Orchid Press Publishing, 2006.

Beach, Timothy, Nicholas Dunning, Sheryl Luzzader-Beach, D. E. Cook, and Jon Lohse. "Impacts of the Ancient Maya on Soils and Soil Erosion in the Central Maya Lowlands." *Catena* 65 (2006): 166–178.

Behre, Karl-Ernst, ed. *Anthropogenic Indicators in Pollen Diagrams*. Boston, MA: Balkema, 1986.

Bradley, Raymond S. *Quaternary Paleoclimatology: Methods of Paleoclimatic Reconstruction*. London: Allen & Unwin, 1985.

Brenner, Mark, Michael F. Rosenmeier, David A. Hodell, and Jason H. Curtis. "Paleolimnology of the Maya Lowlands: Long-Term Perspectives on Interactions among Climate, Environment, and Humans." *Ancient Mesoamerica* 13 (2002): 141–157.

Brinkhuizen, D. C., and A. T. Clason, eds. *Fish and Archaeology: Studies in Osteometry, Taphonomy, Seasonality, and Fishing Methods*. British Archaeological Reports International Series 294. Oxford: BAR, 1986.

Bryant, Vaughn M., Jr., and Richard G. Holloway. "The Role of Palynology in Archaeology." In *Advances in Archaeological Method and Theory 6*, edited by M. B. Schiffer, 191–224. New York: Academic Press, 1983.

Bryant, Vaughn M., Jr., and Stephen A. Hall. "Archaeological Palynology in the United States: A Critique." *American Antiquity* 58 (1993): 277–286.

Burroughs, William J. *Climate Change in Prehistory*. Cambridge: Cambridge University Press, 2005.

Byers, Douglas S, ed. *The Prehistory of the Tehuacan Valley, Vol. 1: Environment and Subsistence*. Austin: University of Texas Press, 1967.

Clottes, Jean, and Jean Courtin. *The Cave beneath the Sea: Paleolithic Images at Cosquer*. New York: Harry N. Abrams, Inc., 1996.

Contreras, Daniel A, ed. *The Archaeology of Human-Environment Interactions: Strategies for Investigating Anthropogenic Landscapes, Dynamic Environments, and Climate Change in the Human Past*. New York: Routledge, 2017.

Cooper, Jago, and Matthew Peros. "The Archaeology of Climate Change in the Caribbean." *Journal of Archaeological Science* 37, no. 6 (2010): 1226–1232.

Cronin, Thomas M. *Principles of Paleoclimatology*. New York: Colombia University Press, 1999.

———*Paleoclimates: Understanding Climate Change Past and Present*. New York: Colombia University Press, 2010.D'Andrea, William J., Yongsong Huanga, Sherilyn C. Fritz, and John N. Anderson. "Abrupt Holocene Climate Change as an Important Factor for Human Migration in West Greenland." *Proceedings of the National Academy of Sciences* 108, no. 24 (2011): 9765–9769.

Davies, Paul. *Snails: Archaeology and Landscape Change*. Oxford: Oxbow, 2008.

David, Simon J. M. *The Archaeology of Animals*. New Haven, CT: Yale University Press, 1987.

Deem, James M. *Bodies from the Ice: Melting Glaciers and the Recovery of the Past.* Boston: Houghton Mifflin, 2008.

Dimbleby, Geoffrey W. *The Palynology of Archaeological Sites.* New York: Academic Press, 1985.

Dincauze, Dena F. *Environmental Archaeology: Principles and Practice.* Cambridge: Cambridge University Press, 2000.

Evans, John G. *An Introduction to Environmental Archaeology.* London: Paul Elek, 1978.

Fieller, N. R. J., D. D. Gilbertson, and N.G.A. Ralph, eds. *Paleoenvironmental Investigations: Research Design, Methods, and Data Analysis.* British Archaeological Reports International Series 258. Oxford: BAR, 1985.

Fitch, Simon, Ken Thomson, and Vince Gaffney. "Late Pleistocene and Holocene Depositional Systems and the Palaeogeography of the Dogger Bank, North Sea." *Quaternary Research* 64 (2005): 185–196.

Flaux, Clément, Nick Marriner, Mena el-Assal, David Kaniewskim, and Christophe Morhange. "Late Holocene Erosion of the Canopic Promontory (Nile Delta, Egypt)." *Marine Geology* 385 (2017): 56–67.

French, Charles. *Geoarchaeology in Action: Studies in Soil Micromorphology and Landscape Evolution.* London: Routledge, 2003.

Fritts, H. C. *Tree Rings and Climate.* New York: Academic Press, 1976.

Gaffney, Vincent, Simon Fitch, and David Smith. *Europe's Lost World: The Rediscovery of Doggerland.* London: Council for British Archaeology, 2009.

Geib, Phil R., and Susan J. Smith. "Palynology and Archaeological Inference: Bridging the Gap between Pollen Washes and Past Behavior." *Journal of Archaeological Science* 35 (2008): 2085–2101.

Gornitz, Vivien, ed. *Encyclopedia of Paleoclimatology and Ancient Environments.* New York: Springer Publishing, 2009.Hiura, Isamu. "The Fundamental Study of Environmental Reconstruction at Archaeological Sites through Insect Remains (Konchū itai gunshū ni yoru iseki kankyō no fukugen ni kansuru kiso-teki kenkyū)." In *Scientific Conservation of Ancient Cultural Properties, Humanities, and Natural Science (Ko bunkazai ni kansuru hozon kagaku to jinbun shizen kagaku): The Final Report of Japan Society for the Promotion and Science,* edited by N. Watanabe. Tokyo, Japan: Teikyo University, 1984.

Iacumin, P., H. Bocherens, A. Mariotti, and A. Longinelli. "An Isotopic Paleoenvironmental Study of Human Skeletal Remains from the Nile Valley." *Paleogeography, Paleoclimatology, Paleoecology* 126, no. 1–2 (1996): 15–30.

Janusek, John W. *Ancient Tiwanaku.* Cambridge: Cambridge University Press, 2008.

Kibblewhite, Mark, Gergely Tóth, and Tamás Hermann. "Predicting the Preservation of Cultural Artefacts and Buried Materials in Soil." *Science of the Total Environment* 529 (2015): 249–263.

Kipfer, Barbara A. *Encyclopedic Dictionary of Archaeology.* New York: Kluwer Academic/Plenum Publishers, 2000.

Kolata, Alan L. *The Tiwanaku: Portrait of an Andean Civilization.* New York: Wiley-Blackwell, 1993.

Lambeck, Kurt, and Edouard Bard. "Sea-Level Change along the French Mediterranean Coast for the Past 30 000 Years." *Earth and Planetary Science Letters* 175 (2000): 203–222.

Lowe, J. J., and M. J. C. Walker. *Reconstructing Quaternary Environments.* 2nd ed. New York: Routledge, 1997.

MacNeish, Richard S. *The Origins of Agriculture and Settled Life.* Norman. OK: University of Oklahoma Press, 1992.

Madella, Marco, Carla Lancelotti, and Manon Savard, eds. *Ancient Plants and People: Contemporary Trends in Archaeobotany.* Tucson: University of Arizona Press, 2014.

Masud Alam, A. K. M., Shucheng Xie, Dilip Kumar Saha, and Sifatul Quader Chowdhury. "Clay Mineralogy of Archaeological Soil: An Approach to Paleoclimatic and Environmental Reconstruction of the Archaeological Sites of the Paharpur Area, Badalgacchi Upazila, Naogaon District, Bangladesh." *Environmental Geology* 53, no. 8 (2008): 1639–1650.

Moore, Peter D., J. A. Webb, and Margaret E. Collinson. *Pollen Analysis.* 2nd ed. Oxford: Blackwell Scientific Publications, 1994.

Myhre, Sarah E., Kristy J. Kroeker, Tessa M. Hill, Peter Roopnarine, and James P. Kennett. "Community Benthic Paleoecology from High-Resolution **Climate** Records: Mollusca and **Foraminifera** in Post-Glacial Environments of the California Margin." *Quaternary Science Reviews* 155 (2017): 179–197.

Nakagawa, Takeshi, Katsuya Gotanda, Tsuyoshi Haraguchi, Toru Danhara, Hitoshi Yonenobu, Achim Brauer, Yusuke Yokoyama, Ryuji Tada, Keiji Takemura, Richard A.Staff, Rebecca Payne, Christopher Bronk Ramsey, Charlotte Bryant, Fiona Brock, Gordon Schlolaut, Michael Marshall, Pavel Tarasov, and Henry Lamb. "SG06, A Fully Continuous and Varved Sediment Core from Lake Suigetsu, Japan: Stratigraphy and Potential for Improving the Radiocarbon Calibration Model and Understanding of Late Quaternary Climate Changes." *Quaternary Science Reviews* 36 (2012): 164–176.

O'Connor, Terry. *The Archaeology of Animal Bones.* College Station: Texas A&M Press, 2008.

Olivier, S., C. Blaser, S. Brütsch, N. Frolova, H. W. Gäggeler, K. A. Henderson, A. S. Palmer, T. Papina, and M. Schwikowski. "Temporal Variations of Mineral Dust, Biogenic Tracers, and Anthropogenic Species during the Past Two Centuries from Belukha Ice Core, Siberian Altai." *Journal of Geophysical Research* 111 (2006): D05309.

Panagiotakopulu, Eva, and Paul C. Buckland. "Insects from Archaeological Sites in Egypt." In *Beyond the Horizon: Studies in Egyptian Art, Archaeology, and History in Honour of Barry J. Kemp,* edited by S. Ikram and A. Dodson, 347–361. Cairo, Egypt: American University of Cairo Press, 2010.

Pearsall, Deborah M. *Paleoethnobotany: A Handbook of Procedures.* New York: Academic Press, 2013.

Piperno, Dolores R. *Phytoliths: A Comprehensive Guide for Archaeologists and Paleoecologists.* Lanham, MD: AltaMira Press, 2006.

Pişkin, Evangelia, Arkadiusz Marciniak, and Marta Bartkowiak, eds. *Environmental Archaeology: Current Theoretical and Methodological Approaches.* New York: Springer Publishing, 2018.

Raban, Avner, ed. *Archaeology of Coastal Changes: Proceedings of the First International Symposium "Cities on the Sea-Past and Present", Haifa, Israel, September 22–29, 1986.* British Archaeological Reports International Series 404. Oxford: BAR, 1988.

Renfrew, Colin, and Paul Bahn. *Archaeology: Theories, Methods, and Practice.* Seventh edition. Thamks & Hudson, London, 2016.

Richards, David A., and Jeffrey A. Dorale. "Uranium-Series Chronology and Environmental Applications of Speleothems. *Reviews in Mineralogy and Geochemistry* 52, no. 1 (2003): 407–460.

Robinson, David E, ed. *Experimentation and Reconstruction in Environmental Archaeology: Symposia of the Association for Environmental Archaeology, No.9.* Oxford: Oxbow, 1990.

Samadelli, Marco, Marcello Melis, Matteo Miccoli, Eduard Egarter Vigl, and Albert R. Zink. "Complete Mapping of the Tattoos of the 5300-year-old Tyrolean Iceman. "*Journal of Cultural Heritage* 16, no. 5 (2015): 753–758.

Schweingruber, Fritz H. *Tree Rings and Environment Dendroecology.* Berne: Paul Haupt Publishers, 1996.

Sheets, Payson D, ed. *Before the Volcano Erupted: The Ancient Cerén Village in Central America.* Austin: The University of Texas Press, 2002.

Singleton, Brent D. "African Bibliophiles: Books and Libraries in Medieval Timbuktu." *Libraries & Culture* 39, no. 1 (2004): 1–12.

Smith, A. G. "Pollen Analytical Investigations of the Mire at Fallahogy Td., Co. Derry." *Proceedings of the Royal Irish Academy* 59, no. B (1958): 329–342.

Stanley, Jean-Daniel, Franck Goddio, and Gerard Schnepp. "Nile Flooding Sank Two Ancient Cities." *Nature* 412 (2001): 293–294.

Tiesler, Vera, Andrea Cucina, Travis W. Stanton, and David A. Freidel. *Before Kukulkán: Maya Life, Death, and Identity at Classic Period Yaxuná.* Tucson: University of Arizona Press, 2017.Van Andel, Tjeerd H. "Late Quaternary Sea Level Changes and Archaeology." *Antiquity* 63, no. 241 (1989): 733–745.

Van de Noort, Robert. *Climate Change Archaeology: Building Resilience from Research in the World's Coastal Wetlands.* Oxford: Oxford University Press, 2013.

Van der Sanden, Wijnad. *Through Nature to Eternity: The Bog Bodies of Northwest Europe.* Amsterdam: Batavian Lion International, 1996.

Weide, D. Marie, Sherilyn C. Fritz, Christine A. Hastorf, Maria C. Bruno, Paul A. Baker, Stephane Guedron, and Wout Salenbien. "A ~6000 yr Diatom Record of Mid- to Late Holocene Fluctuations in the Level of Lago Wiñaymarca, Lake Titicaca (Peru/Bolivia)." *Quaternary Research* 88 (2017): 179–192.

Whitfield, Susan, ed. *The Silk Road: Trade, Travel, War, and Faith.* Chicago: Serindia Publications, Inc, 2004.

Making Sense of Things: Materials and Artifact Analysis

Archaeologists have a wide range of techniques at their disposal to analyze different kinds of materials and objects. Some of these techniques, such as seriation (not reviewed again in this chapter, see Chapter 8) and typology, are applicable to different kinds of artifacts. Others, such as fiber identification, are much more limited in their scope and application. In this chapter, we describe some of the techniques and methods available to archaeologists to employ in materials and artifact analyses. Although our discussion is by no means inclusive of all of the techniques available, we attempt to embrace a wide spectrum of methods more commonly utilized by researchers. This chapter includes both specific discussions of artifact classes (e.g., ceramics, lithics, and metal), as well as treatment of broader methods that are used for different kinds of material remains.

Typology

Once archaeologists have a collection of artifacts, the first step is to organize them into categories that can be compared to each other. Depending on the samples available to researchers, the amount of material can vary. In some cases, such as Paleolithic figurines, a relatively low number of examples are known throughout the world. Yet in most cases, the number of artifacts directly available to researchers through their own research can be overwhelming; this number is compounded greatly when considering similar artifacts available in already extant collections. For example, the existing collections of Upper Paleolithic tools contain a staggeringly large number of artifacts, far more than any one research team could analyze. Given this situation, creating classificatory systems, or **typologies**, that combine variation in artifacts into more inclusive categories, is a necessity to deal with large collections. But, typology is not just borne out of necessity due to large sample sizes. It also serves as a **heuristic device** (an imperfect practical method to help with immediate goals) to look for patterns in archaeological data (no matter the size of the sample), patterns that might not be readily visible to researchers if they were to treat each artifact as unique.

The idea of typology dates back to the beginning of systematic archaeological analysis (see Chapters 3 and 4) and underlies seriation (Chapter 8); Johann Winckelmann's study of ancient Greek and Roman sculpture being a pioneering example (Chapter 3). Regardless, archaeologists have always based some level of interpretation on the fact that things vary; we use the term "things" here as typologies can apply to a large range of material culture as small as artifacts and as large as cities. They vary in color, size, shape, material, and a host of other factors that we call **attributes**. To make sense of this variation, archaeologists employ typology. This method of categorizing things, however, does not take into account all

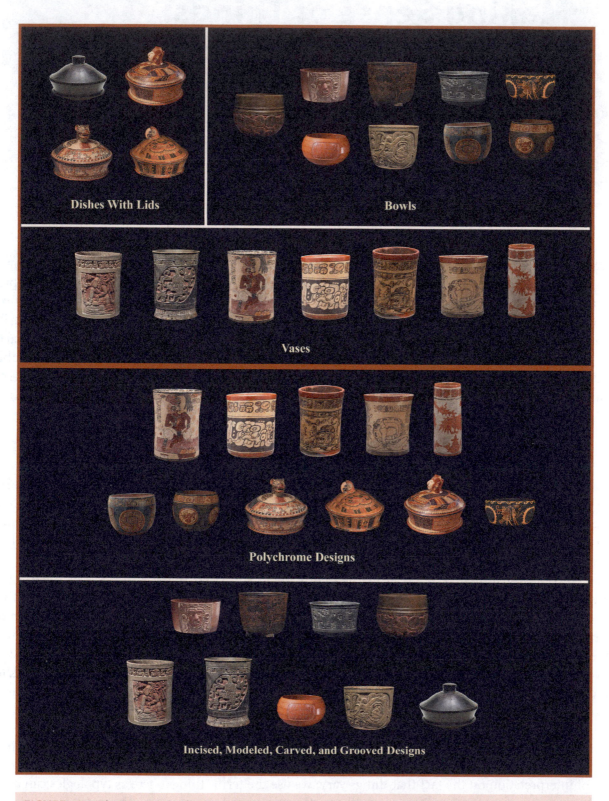

FIGURE 10.1 This image of Classic period Maya pottery from the Los Angeles Museum of Art shows how artifacts can be categorized based on different attributes; in this case form (top) and decoration (bottom).

Source: Los Angeles County Museum of Art & Justin Kerr collage of images (LACMA credit lines found on page 215.)

the variability that things have. To create manageable categories, researchers choose a limited set of attributes to define each type; and, these attributes must be distinctive enough to differentiate other types (e.g., how certain shapes of artifacts will be separated, or how to distinguish colors that may run along a continuum, never forget your Munsell Color book!). Given that it is the researcher who chooses which attributes structure the typological system, typologies must be understood as heuristic devices that do not necessarily reflect the way that people in the past ordered the things in their world. Typologies are arbitrary creations of archaeologists that help us make sense of the bewildering variability in material culture from archaeological contexts.

For example, a researcher may choose to order pottery vessels by slip color. By doing so, certain patterns of color distributions in pottery may become apparent. Maybe the red ceramics predate the orange pottery. Or, maybe the painted polychrome vessels are found more frequently in contexts associated with palaces and monumental architecture. Thus, this typology has helped researchers understand the material data. However, maybe another researcher comes along and chooses to arrange the pottery by vessel shapes, placing the dishes, jars, and basins all in separate categories. In this study, maybe the basins are found more in areas thought to be for storage and the jars in areas that have evidence of being kitchen spaces. This alternate typology has also contributed to a greater understanding of the past through the identification of different patterns using the same material data. And, both of these typologies, as heuristic devices, are irrespective of the way the people who actually produced and used the pottery probably chose to organize them conceptually.

In large part, typology is based on the concept of style (see also Chapter 3). **Aesthetic styles** are those that create sensory patterns (we often think of them as visual or auditory, but can really encompass any of the five senses) that we recognize as being distinct from others (again, using the idea of typologies). When we see the columns on the Lincoln Memorial in Washington, DC, we associate them with Greco-Roman architectural styles, as this shape of column is defined in our society as a particular kind of aesthetic category. Not all styles, however, are aesthetic. Archaeologists also talk about **technological styles**. For example, the way a person knapping stone tools creates a particular shape of projectile point may vary. One person

FIGURE 10.2 This early colonial mural from the convent at Cuauhtinchan, Mexico, depicts a lion, an animal not native to the New World, in an art style that dates previous to the arrival of Europeans; illustrating the malleability of styles.

Source: Travis Stanton

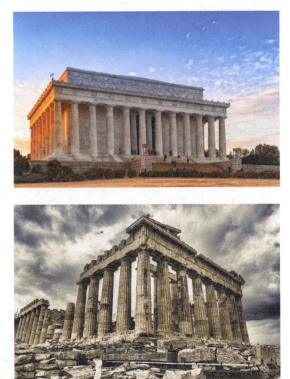

FIGURE 10.3 The architectural style of the Lincoln Memorial in Washington, DC, is modeled after ancient Greco-Roman styles like that found on the Parthenon in Athens, Greece, showing again the flexibility of styles over space and time.

© Anastasios71/Shutterstock.com
© Arthit Kaeoratanapattama/Shutterstock.com

may use direct percussion, whereas another may use pressure flaking. The general shape of both points may result being the same, but the techniques are different and identifiable with trained eyes; hence, technological styles. Regardless, the concept of style very much structures typological analysis.

Analogy and Interpretation

Analogy is an important tool for archaeological interpretation. Our understanding of the world today serves as a critical guide to interpret the material data that remains of past human behavior. Analogy serves as a cognitive framework that makes the relatively unknown more comprehensible through comparison of similar things. The use of analogy, however, does not come without pitfalls. The danger of using analogy is that the patterns archaeologists see in their data, although materially resembling something similar, something understandable today, may actually have been something different. In short, that the experiences we draw on from our own lives, lives that are situated in a particular cultural context, may color our interpretations and that we may miss alternative interpretive possibilities, drawn to seeing materially similar things in light of what we are familiar with. For example, an archaeologist may find a small, hafted lithic point. Based on previous experience with arrowheads, this researcher may draw an analogy to lithic projectile points. In reality, however, this artifact might have been used as a hafted cutting tool, not as a projectile at all. With these kinds of issues in mind, archaeologists have developed two primary methods to strengthen reasoning based on analogy; ethnoarchaeology and experimental archaeology.

Ethnoarchaeology

Archaeologists have used ethnographic data for interpretative purposes for a very long time. However, around the time of the rise of processual archaeology (early 1960s) ethnoarchaeology began to crystalize as a more formal method. It was about at this time that theoretical discussions of the use of analogy began to heat up, and by the time that Schiffer began focusing on formation processes and Binford proposed his middle range theory (see Chapter 4), ethnoarchaeology had become a widely employed method in the field. In the words of William Longacre (1991, 1, emphasis in original), a pioneer in ceramic ethnoarchaeology: "ethnoarchaeology is the study *by archaeologists* of variability in material culture and its relation to human behavior and organization among extant societies, for use in archaeological interpretation." In short, **ethnoarchaeology** is the ethnography of modern material culture by archaeologists to help them understand the material culture they collect through their archaeological research. Ethnoarchaeology provides data from modern contexts for archaeologists to use through analogy to better frame archaeological data. So, if a researcher sees modern people using a hafted lithic point as a cutting tool rather than as a projectile point in a particular region, that observation might be taken into consideration when similar points are found in archaeological contexts dating to 500 BC. The reason that Longacre (1991) emphasizes the phrase "by archaeologists" is that archaeologists see the material world differently than other researchers, such as cultural anthropologists. As archaeologists collect ethnoarchaeological data,

FIGURE 10.4 A local Maya potter from Yucatan, Mexico, manufacturing a ceramic jar for study by archaeologists.

Source: Travis Stanton

they pay attention to details that other researchers might not, thinking about the archaeological consequences of certain behaviors, those that have material outcomes.

Ethnoarchaeology has been employed in a wide variety of cultural contexts and on a great range of material culture. Ethnoarchaeologists have studied how all sorts of material culture is produced, used, stored, and discarded; from the construction of houses and butchering of animals to the manufacture and use of ceramic and lithic artifacts. Some researchers dedicate their entire careers to ethnoarchaeology, whereas others perform ethnoarchaeology in passing, in the time frames allowed by their other research commitments. Regardless of the amount of time invested in this research, archaeologists must remember that ethnoarchaeology, just like ethnography, requires an **institutional review board** (IRB) approval. IRB committees review research projects that include living human subjects as part of their work to ensure that ethical standards are followed and that people will not be harmed in any way.

Experimental Archaeology

Experimental archaeology is another method that archaeologists have in their toolbox to help strengthen arguments based on analogies; in this case **experimental archaeology** is the use of modern materials to create and use material culture that replicates their counterparts in the archaeological record. Archaeologists have experimented with all sorts of materials, from creating relatively simple engineering devices to show how Stonehenge was built with Neolithic technology to stone tools that are then used to butcher animals or to harvest crops, taking

FIGURE 10.5 Experimental work replicating lithic sickle blades from the Neolithic site of Ain Gazal, Jordan, has demonstrated the kind of wear that reaping wheat would have produced on these tools.

© Philip J. Wilke

FIGURE 10.6 These experimental ceramic test tiles from Yucatan, Mexico, have been subjected to different kinds of physical tests to understand the properties of particular clays and tempers that the Maya in the past would have used to make their own pottery.

Source: Travis Stanton

note as to how these activities transform material culture. Experimental archaeology shows researchers how things could have been done and what kinds of material remains or clues they would have left behind. In a study of ancient Maya pottery, one of the authors of this book has collaborated with Yucatec Maya potters to create ceramic test tiles using different combinations of local clays and tempers that were utilized by their ancestors. By experimenting with these tiles (burning, breaking, etc.), the researchers have been able to demonstrate that by adding certain amounts of locally available calcite crystals to the clay, cooking jars resist the tendency to fracture when exposed to the normal kitchen conditions of extreme heating and rapid cooling. Petrographic analysis (see below) of jars from archaeological contexts, jars that resemble modern cooking vessels, show that these same crystals were used for temper. These data suggest that this archeological pottery was also used for cooking and that past Maya potters were well aware of the thermal properties of calcite crystals.

General Methods for Artifact Analysis

There are several methods available to archaeologists that are virtually applicable to all kinds of artifacts, such as residue and use-wear analysis. Other kinds of analyses, such as source analysis, can be used across only a subset of artifacts types, but are applicable to a range of materials. In this section, we review some of these more generalized techniques.

Residue Analysis

Artifacts can have different kinds of residues on them that reflect activities they were used in, as well as certain kinds of postdepositional processes; residues are also a research focus for floors and soils, a topic we will cover in Chapter 12. Although the kinds of residues can vary widely, archaeologists tend to focus on certain general categories. For example, certain chemical residues might remain on artifacts long after their discard. In studies of chemical residues of pottery in Mesoamerica and the American Southwest, several research teams have identified theobromine, an alkaloid of cacao (chocolate plant), on ceramic vessels. This research demonstrates that production and consumption of chocolate products occurred in the New World at least 3,000 years ago and was more widespread than originally thought. Care must be taken with these kinds of studies, however, as chemical signatures are often shared among different products. It is only in some cases, like chocolate, that a unique chemical signature can be recovered for a particular substance.

Other kinds of residues that might be found on artifacts include a range of organic materials including pollen and phytoliths (discussed in Chapter 9). Plant and animal proteins and lipids can be identified, in some cases even to the level of genus or species. For instance, in a study of protein residues on early Paleoindian points from the site of Wally's Beach, Canada (dating to 11,000–11,300 BP), researchers found that the blood of horse and most likely bison was present on the artifacts, indicating that these animals were hunted by early Native Americans. Other organic residues include starches, which are polymeric carbohydrates that are found in plant tissue. Importantly, starches preserve very well and can survive grinding and some burning and boiling. They are also usually identifiable to species when examined under a high-power microscope. Even DNA material can be recovered if the conditions of preservation permit.

Use-Wear Analysis

Another type of analysis that crosscuts numerous artifact classes is **use-wear analysis**; the study of the wear on artifacts. The idea is that wear can appear on an object as a result of its use, and that different kinds of uses have the potential for causing different kinds of wear patterns. For example, lithic scrapers can be used for a variety of different tasks including working hides, wood, and bone.

Using experimental archaeology to perform scraping on these different kinds of materials using a stone tool manufactured to resemble archaeological examples (e.g., same material, size, and shape), researchers can observe the different kinds of wear (e.g., polishing, chipping, etc.). By matching the wear patterns of these experimental tools with archaeological artifacts, an inference can be made that the activities performed by the artifact were similar.

Compositional Analysis

Chert, clay, metal, and obsidian, among many other materials used by past peoples, are often materially and chemically variable. Mapping the variability in their composition across a landscape can help researchers determine where the materials used by past peoples came from; thus, bettering our understanding of how things moved around as well as how some things, such as ceramics, were manufactured (we will discuss this last point further along in this chapter). For example, using a petrographic microscope researchers have confirmed that the Stonehenge bluestones were quarried some 225 km away from the stone circle itself by comparing the composition of the stones to outcrops in the Preseli Hills of Wales. This confirmation had led to renewed discussion of how the nearly two-ton stones were transported; either completely overland, or in large part by the sea. Another important finding

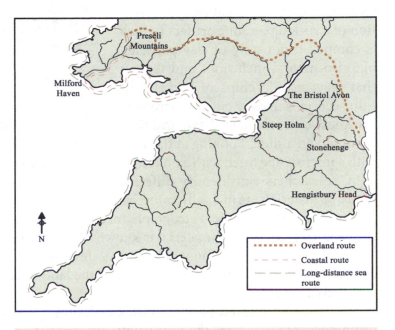

FIGURE 10.7 Possible routes for transporting the bluestones from the Preseli Hills to Stonehenge.

© Belem Ceballos Casanova, drawn after Parker-Pearson et al. 2015

of this research is that the stones appear to have been quarried at least half a millennium prior to being transported to Stonehenge, leading researchers to suggest that they were used for a monument in the local Welsh area before being dismantled and then taken to the location of Stonehenge to the east. Regardless of the discrepancy between the date of quarrying and the date they were erected at Stonehenge, this example shows one of the applications of **compositional analysis**, a series of methods that has become essential for archaeological research.

Archaeologists have several techniques at their disposal for performing compositional analysis. One popular technique just mentioned, petrography, is at a more "macro-level". Although performed under a microscope, this method is at a larger scale than the others we will discuss; measuring materials like quartz rather than elements such as hydrogen. Other techniques measure chemical composition at the atomic level; in particular, for materials such as lithics, ceramics, glass, and metals. For example, **mass spectrometry** measures the abundance of both commonly occurring and trace (rarely occurring) elements in a material by ionizing (a process changing the electrical balance of an electrically neutral atom or molecule to an electrically charged counterpart, an ion) material and then separating the ions according to mass-to-charge ratios; in short, it is a molecule weighing machine that can tell researchers how much of different elements are in a material. We have already touched on several mass spectrometry techniques in this book and will not repeat those here; accelerator mass spectrometry (AMS) radiocarbon dating, potassium–argon dating, uranium series dating, and a range of stable isotope analyses (see Chapters 8 and 9).

In this section, we will review some of the other more commonly utilized techniques for performing compositional analysis starting with petrography.

Petrography is the description and classification of rocks using thin sections analyzed under a microscope. This technique works by creating a thin section of a rock or ceramic artifact (which is composed not only of clay particles, but also natural inclusions and temper that may include chips of rocks). The thin section is usually cut 30 microns in thickness by a specialized saw and then mounted on a slide. Looking at the slide with a microscope fitted with a polarized light, researchers can identify different kinds of materials, principally minerals

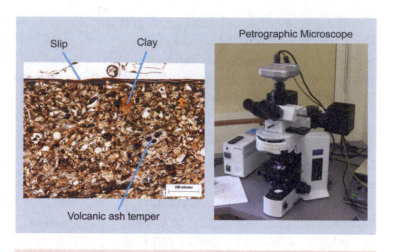

FIGURE 10.8 The slip, clay, and temper of a fragment of pottery can be identified using a petrographic microscope.

Source: Kenichiro Tsukamoto

that compose the sample. Petrography may aid in distinguishing different lithic or clay sources. If the original source of the material is known (like the Stonehenge bluestone example above), as with any of the other compositional techniques described below, researchers can discuss then begin to model how the material was moved around the landscape (e.g., trade, exchange, and other forms of materials acquisition).

Inductively coupled plasma atomic emission spectrometry (ICP-AES) is a part of a family of techniques that measures the wavelength of radiation emitted by a material through an inductively coupled plasma (ICP) mass spectrometer (MS); this family of mass spectrometry more or less replaced several others techniques (which we will not cover in detail here), such as optical emission spectrometry (OES), thermal ionization mass spectrometry (TIMS), and atomic absorption spectroscopy (AAS), which were utilized with more frequency several years ago. Given their sensitivity to trace elements, ICP methods tend to be the techniques of choice for elemental analysis today, although they are destructive. ICP-AES is a technique that uses inductively coupled argon plasma to excite the atoms in a material. When in an excited state, these atoms emit light, the wavelengths of which can be measured. Different materials emit different wavelengths. This technique is fairly reliable for charactering both major and trace elements in a material. A similar, but more expensive technique is **multi-collector inductively coupled plasma mass spectrometry** (MC-ICP-MS). This technique divides the samples by their isotopes and is able to detect trace elements with more accuracy. **Laser ablation inductively coupled plasma mass spectrometry** (LA-ICP-MS, or often referred to as just laser ablation) is another related technique that employs a laser to ablate a sample (reduce it to fine particles) prior to beginning the ionization process in the ICP-MS instrument. This technique is becoming much more popular in compositional analysis given its high sensitivity to trace elements.

X-ray fluorescence (XRF) is a technique that calculates the chemical composition of a material by measuring the fluorescent x-rays emitted by a substance when it is bombarded with gamma rays. The wavelengths of the fluorescent x-rays are a reflection of the elements contained by the material. There are two different XRF methods. The first is called **wavelength dispersive spectrometry**, which entails grinding the material into a powder. The second method is termed **energy dispersive spectrometry**, which is nondestructive and can analyze the surface composition of a material; in some cases, it is recommended that the surface be cleaned prior to analysis. Energy dispersive spectrometry is a relatively rapid technique that has been facilitated in archaeology by the development of portable handheld devices.

There are several X-ray scattering techniques that are used by researchers to analyze the crystal structures and chemical compositions of different materials. In archaeology, **x-ray diffraction** (XRD) has been implemented with some frequency. Instead of measuring wavelength of fluorescent x-rays, XRD measures how the electrons of certain materials spherically scatter waves of electromagnetic radiation when they are bombarded by X-rays. The way these waves are scattered reveals information concerning the crystal structure of the material, and hence its chemical composition.

Particle-induced X-ray emission spectrometry (PIXE) is a technique that bombards a material with an ion beam from a particle accelerator, causing electromagnetic radiation to be emitted. By measuring the wavelength of the electromagnetic radiation, which is particular to different elements, researchers can assess the chemical composition of the material. PIXE analysis is nondestructive and is increasingly used in archaeological research.

Scanning electron microscopy (SEM) is a technique that provides highly magnified imagery as well as compositional data. SEM uses a beam of electrons that creates a map of the surface of a sample using secondary electrons. Using backscattered electrons that are bounced off the surface, researchers can also get an idea of the chemical composition of a material. How the electrons are "ricocheted" off of the surface is related to the atomic number of the element it strikes. Maps of the surface are produced that show darker and lighter areas that respectively correlate with lower and higher atomic numbers. Although SEM is nondestructive, it is not particularly sensitive to trace elements.

Neutron activation analysis (NAA) is a highly sensitive and precise technique for measuring chemical composition that has a proven track record in the field. The method works by bombarding the sample with neutrons. This process leads the elements in the sample to form radioactive isotopes, the gamma emissions from which are unique to each element. By measuring the emissions, researchers can determine the elemental composition of the sample. In contrast to techniques such as SEM and LA-ICP-MS (which provide ways of analyzing different parts of the materials composing a sample), one drawback of instrumental neutron activation analysis (INAA) is its nature of a bulk analysis method, meaning that different materials that may compose a sample cannot be separated; they are all analyzed together. This is an issue for materials like ceramics that are not just composed of one homogenous clay (at *least* one source of chemical variability), but other materials such as temper that introduce a complex mixture of chemical sources. In some cases, tempering materials may come from areas hundreds of kilometers away from the source of the clay. Further, some elements such as lead (Pb), an important component to some materials such as ceramic glazes, metal alloys, and glass colorants, cannot be measured by INAA. Regardless, INAA analysis remains a highly sensitive and robust method for analyzing the composition of materials in archaeology.

Refitting

Piecing back together broken and fractured objects and artifacts can also be a highly useful activity in the laboratory. In many cases, the artifacts that archaeologists recover are broken. In some of those cases, pieces from the same object can be identified and the archaeologist attempts to piece them back together. Although this process can be hampered by formation processes (all of the pieces have weathered so that their points

FIGURE 10.9 Refitting a ceramic vessel from El Palmar, Mexico.

Source: Kenichiro Tsukamoto

of contact no longer match), in some cases the fragments begin to take shape and the object, or at least some larger part of it, becomes more understandable morphologically and the spatial distribution of the pieces can be analyzed. Lithic specialists have gone as far as to refit the waste from stone tool production to recreate the sequence of how stone tools were produced; recreating the *chaîne opératoire*, or operational chain of production. In the end, refitting can produce valuable data, but hinges upon the recovery of contiguous fragments from the same object, a situation that does not always present itself in archaeological research.

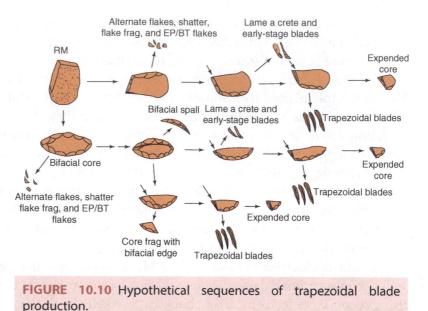

FIGURE 10.10 Hypothetical sequences of trapezoidal blade production.

From Archaeological: An Introduction, Laboratory Methods, 6/e by Mark Q. Sutton and Brooke S. Arkush. Copyright © 2014 by Kendall Hunt Publishing Company. Reprinted by permission.

Artifact Biographies

As we have seen, archaeological contexts are not static. This idea is the basis behind formation processes; material things can change their physical properties as well as their spatial and social contexts over time. Archaeologists have taken this point beyond the study of the formation processes of archaeological contexts, employing the idea of "biographies" to the study of material things like artifacts. The idea is that material culture, such as an artifact, or even a feature (e.g., a structure) or a place (e.g., by the spring), can be tracked over time. In terms of artifacts, archaeologists have argued that there are particular stages in their "life histories" that can be reconstructed; raw materials acquisition, production, use/reuse, and discard. Let's take, for example, a lithic scraper. The first part of the scraper's life history would have been the acquisition of the stone used to produce it. The second stage would have been the manufacture of the tool, although in this case maybe it was not a scraper, but a biface. This tool might have been used for a variety of purposes, such as a spear point and a cutting tool. These uses would have constituted part of the use/reuse of the object. But, maybe at some point the object broke and was reworked into a scraper by someone who recycled the material. A number of other uses, including scraping of hides and other materials, could have been associated with this stage in the artifact's life history. Then, the artifact was buried in the grave of the individual who used it (discard, where it was "used" as a grave good), where it stayed for three hundred years before the burial was disturbed by later peoples who took the object and continued to use it as a scraper (reuse), before tossing it into a rubbish heap (second discard event), where it was eventually found by archaeologists. By looking at different aspects of the artifact, archaeologists might be able to reconstruct several of the events just described. For example, source analysis might pinpoint where the original raw material acquisition occurred. Morphological analysis of the artifact might reveal certain areas where the biface was left intact (e.g., the scraper being manufactured using 90 percent of the original biface's edge). Use-wear and residue analyses might be able to identify different kinds of activities that the scraper was used for. Although it would be very unlikely that the archaeologist would be able to recover the entire biography of the artifact, certain snapshots of its life history might be able to be reconstructed, helping us to better understand the changing place of that object in past societies.

Artifact Classes and Analysis

There are two general techniques that produce artifacts: **reductive** and **synthetic**. Reductive techniques produce artifacts by subtracting from the original raw materials. Lithic, shell, wooden, and copper artifacts are those that are typically produced by reduction techniques. In contrast, synthetic techniques produce artifacts through addition. Ceramic, bronze, and glass artifacts are the products of synthetic techniques. These specific approaches and materials are often used to group artifacts into classes. Instead of grouping artifacts by other attributes such as shape (e.g., stone and ceramic bowls in the same artifact class), materials that are generally separated along the lines of reductive and synthetic techniques are commonly used (lithics, ceramics, glass, etc.). Given that certain materials provide similar opportunities for analysis (e.g., petrography can be conducted on all ceramics), we will divide our discussion of further kinds of artifact analyses by material type beginning with lithics.

Lithics

Humans and our hominin ancestors have used stone tool technologies for millions of years. Although other materials were certainly used as well, **lithics** (derived from the Greek term *lithos*, meaning stone) preserve extraordinarily well, allowing researchers to trace this artifact class back to its origins. The earliest known stone tool technology dates back to at least around 2.6 million years ago in East Africa, where researchers have defined the Oldowan tradition (also known as Mode 1); composed of relatively crude "choppers" (which could be cores as they

FIGURE 10.11 Middle Acheulian handaxes recovered from Al-Jafr Basin in Jordan (between 400,000 and 225,000 B.P.); the upper handaxe is early-stage bifacial cleaver that shows grip attributes, expendable midsection, and tranchet bit. The lower is late-stage handaxe that represents grip attributes and bifacially flaked bit, but a lack of midsection.

© Philip J. Wilke

FIGURE 10.12 Examples of the variety lithic artifact forms can take (from left to right): projectile points from Troyville, Louisiana; ground-stone tools from Troyville, Louisiana; flint lamp from Ain Gazal, Jordan; carved stone celt from the Guanacaste-Nicoya area of Costa Rica.

Projectile points and ground-stone tools: Copyright © Earth Search, Inc.
Carved stone celt: LACMA credit line FORTHCOMING FROM TAMMY.
Flint lamp: Kenichiro Tsukamoto
Avian Axe-God Pendant. Costa Rica, Guanacaste-Nicoya area, Guanacaste-Nicoya, 100 B.C. – A.D. 500. Jewelry and Adornments; pendants. Jade Height: 5 5.8 in. (14.29 cm). The Phil Berg Collection (M.71.73.312). Art of the Ancient Americas. Photo © Museum Associates/LACMA

Source: Kenichiro Tsukamoto

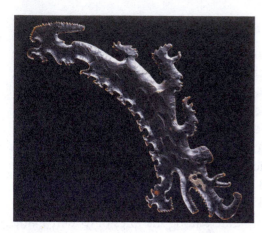

FIGURE 10.13 A complex flint eccentric depicting the Maya Maize god and two companions in a canoe shaped in the form of a crocodile. Pieces from the Classic period such as these represent an unmatched skill level of knapping.

Eccentric flint depicting a crocodile canoe with passengers, c. A.D. 600–900 (flint), Mayan/Dallas Museum of Art, Texas, USA/The Eugene and Margaret McDermott Art Fund, Inc., in honor of Mrs. Alex Spence/Bridgeman Images

FIGURE 10.14 Examples of pecked and abraded lithic material (beginning at the top left): the closely fitted andesite blocks of the Inka fortress of Saksaywamán, Peru (ca. thirteenth to fifteenth centuries AD); a limestone *mano* and *metate* (grinding tools) from the Maya site of Caracol, Belize (ca. seventh to ninth centuries AD); a New Kingdom calcite jar from Egypt (ca. 1550–1196 BC,); a chlorite and limestone figurine from Bactria, Afghanistan (ca. 3500–1500 BC,); a jade corpse plug (to keep the deceased person's vital essence from escaping from holes in the body) in the shape of a locust from Han Dynasty, China (ca. 206 BC to AD 220,

Top left: © SL-Photography/Shutterstock.com
Top Right: © Kara Grubis/Shutterstock.com
Los Angeles County Museum of Art credit lines on page 215.

are basically small cobbles or pebbles with just a few flakes knocked off of one side), flakes, and hammerstones. Although some researchers suggest that cut-marks on some bones and some proposed evidence for another crude stone tool tradition (Lomekwi) suggest an even earlier date for the manufacture of stone tools (possibly around 3.3 million years ago), the Oldowan tradition lasted for quite some time before another widespread tradition, the Acheulian (characterized by "axe-shaped" tools), was adopted, spreading to areas outside of Africa with the dispersal of hominins into Asia and Europe.

Over the course of time, people have used stones for a great variety of purposes including hunting, cutting, scraping, and drilling activities, use as building material, linings for fire pits and hearths, grinding stones, jewelry, weapons, and art. Some stones of interest to archaeologists are as simple as fire-cracked rocks that indicate the existence of a hearth or stones heated up and dropped into a container filled with water to boil a meal. Others are tremendously complex, such as the spectacular Maya eccentrics knapped (**knapping** is the process of knocking pieces off a rock by striking it with another object) in the shape of supernatural beings. When archaeologists speak of lithics, what they are usually referring to are materials that were worked in **chipped stone** (involving knapping of the material) or **ground stone** (manufactured through abrasion) traditions. However, there are a series of manufacturing techniques that go beyond this dichotomy. All kinds of rocks and minerals were used by past peoples. For example, materials such as hematite, mica, and pyrite were used for symbolic activities in Mesoamerica, often in forms that are not considered to be artifacts. In this section, we will discuss some of the basic concepts in lithic analysis keeping our focus more on artifacts.

Lithics can be produced with four primary techniques; pecking, grinding/abrading/polishing, sawing, and flaking. Although some lithics are produced by only one technique, others are the result of a combination of manufacturing methods. Pecking techniques involve processes of battering a stone with a hard material to shape it. Many architectural stones around the world, such as the precisely fitted Inka wall stones at the fortress at Saksayhuamán, were shaped by pecking, as were a wide variety of other objects such as grinding stones such as *manos* and *metates*. Grinding, abrading, and polishing are a series of related techniques that involve rubbing an abrasive material such as sand to slowly wear away at the stone. The kinds and sizes of abrasives can vary from different kinds of stones, sands, and powders resulting in different kinds of effects. Mesoamerican greenstone figures were often painstakingly manufactured using these kinds of techniques. Sawing was also a technique sometimes implemented in the manufacture of lithic objects, by way of employing materials such as abrasive stones and metal tools to cut.

Flaking is one of the most commonly encountered and ancient techniques found in the archaeological record. Flakes are small pieces of lithic materials that are broken off a larger

FIGURE 10.15 Blades and flakes from El Palmar, Mexico.

Source: Kenichiro Tsukamoto

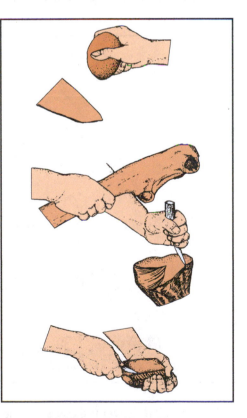

FIGURE 10.17 Direct percussion, indirect percussion, and pressure flaking.

From Archaeological: An Introduction, Laboratory Methods, 6/e by Mark Q. Sutton and Brooke S. Arkush. Copyright © 2014 by Kendall Hunt Publishing Company. Reprinted by permission.

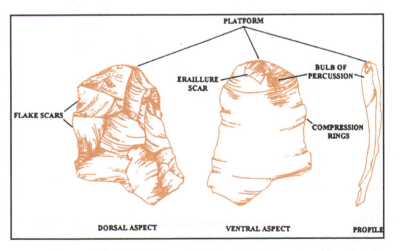

FIGURE 10.16 Basic morphology of a lithic flake.

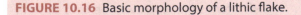

From Archaeological: An Introduction, Laboratory Methods, 6/e by Mark Q. Sutton and Brooke S. Arkush. Copyright © 2014 by Kendall Hunt Publishing Company. Reprinted by permission.

core (mass of rock prepared to detach flakes) or **nodule** (natural rock). Archaeologists categorize these pieces by their size, shape, and role in the production process. For example, the term **flake** is often reserved for a relatively thin piece whose length is less than two times the size of its width. When the length passed two times the size of the width and the lateral edges are roughly parallel, the piece is often referred to as a **blade**; both flakes and blades have a system to classify their morphologies. The small chunks and fragments that are generated from separating flakes and blades from the core are often referred to as **shatter**; **debitage** is a term utilized more generally for the waste generated by lithic production.

FIGURE 10.18 Lithic bifaces from El Palmar, Mexico.

Source: Kenichiro Tsukamoto

There are several general techniques used to produce stone tools using a chipped stone technology. **Direct percussion** (sometimes divided into hard and soft hammer techniques) involves striking the core with a hard object, often a hammerstone or antler. An anvil, such as a large stone, can also be used, called a **bipolar technique. Indirect percussion** involves placing an intermediate tool, or **punch**, on the core. By striking the punch, the shock waves can often be better controlled to create the desired effect on the core. **Pressure flaking** is a final technique whereby a pointed flaking tool is applied to a specific spot

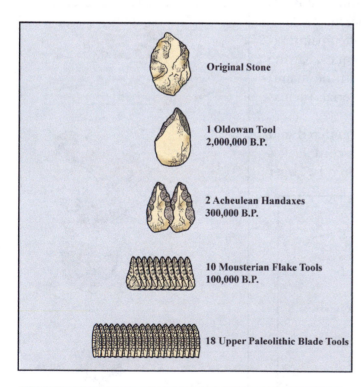

FIGURE 10.19a Over the course of the Paleolithic stone tool technology became much more efficient. By the time blade tool technology was invented during the Upper Paleolithic the amount of cutting edges that a single stone core could produce had greatly increased over the much earlier Oldowan tools.

© Belem Ceballos Casanova, drawn after Fagan and Durrani (2012).

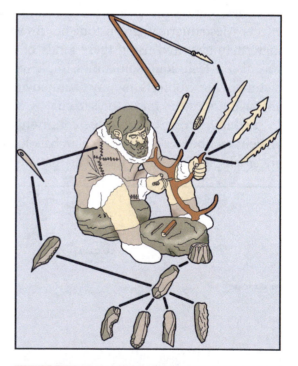

FIGURE 10.19b Not only was blade technology more efficient, but it also signified an important advancement in tool diversification. Blades were able to be shaped into a wide varied of forms that could also be used to work other materials such as bone and antler

© Belem Ceballos Casanova, drawn after Fagan and Durrani (2012).

on the core; gradually increasing the pressure on the tool and then pop off a flake or blade. Pressure flaking can be the final stage in the production of tools such as **bifaces** (a tool with two worked faces that create a single edge circumscribing it), tools such as projectile points that are worked on both sides of the original **blank** that was taken off the core. Pressure flaking can also occur during earlier production stages; however, the separation of blades from the core using a crutch is a good example. Once tools are in use, their edges may become dull and need to be **retouched** by taking off small flakes again to regain a useful edge.

The efficiency in producing chipped stone tools from a nodule increased significantly throughout human history. For example, early hominins produced only one chipped stone tool from a nodule using the Oldowan tradition. In the Acheulian tradition, *Homo erectus* usually produced two hand axes, which were sometimes resharpened over time, increasing their use-life. By 35,000 BP, *Homo sapiens* or anatomically modern humans invented **blade technology** that produce hundreds of blades from a single nodule, which were in turn used for making a variety of tools such as backed blades, burins and scrapers. The blade technology continued to be used over many millennia in certain parts of the world.

FIGURE 10.20   A Middle Jomon period vessel (ca. 3000–2000 BC) left and a Western Han Dynasty funerary sculpture (206 BC to AD 25) right. Given their plasticity, ceramics can be used to make a large range of different kinds of objects.

Flame-Style Vessel. Japan, Middle Jōmon phase, circa 3000–2000 B.C. Coil-built earthenware with incised, modeled, and applied decoration. 22 × 10 in. (55.88 × 25.4 cm). Los Angeles County Museum of Art, The William T. Sesnon, Jr. Bequest (M.81.62.1). Photo © Museum Associates/LACMA Funerary Sculpture of a Noble Lady. China, Western Han dynasty, 206 B.C.-A.D. 25. Molded earthenware with slip and traces of paint. 20 × 15 × 8 1/2 in. (50.8 × 38.1 × 21.59 cm). Los Angeles County Museum of Art, Gift of Nasli M. Heeramaneck (M.73.48.122). Photo © Museum Associates/LACMA

Ceramics

Ceramic technology is a relatively late invention of human history; its earliest appearance occurring in Jomon period contexts in Japan at a mere 16,500 years ago. Although ceramics were not invented or adopted by all past societies, this technology became increasingly utilized throughout the world during the Holocene (11,650 BP to the present) and, given its generally good preservation (as we shall see there is a lot of variability in terms of the preservation of ceramics) compared to many other artifact classes, is one of the most widely studied materials in archaeology.

Ceramics are a plastic medium, meaning that they can be easily manipulated and molded, although this **plasticity** is only

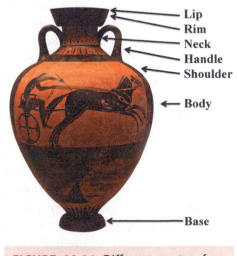

FIGURE 10.21 Different parts of an ancient Greek ceramic vessel.

© Kamira/Shutterstock.com

present prior to the firing stage of production. Given its plasticity before firing and its nonplasticity and hardness after firing, ceramics can be manufactured into an extremely large range of useful objects including drains, pipes, architectural features, figurines, personal adornments, musical instruments, and a vast array of cooking, serving, and storage vessels, among others. Although some ceramic artifacts are untempered, meaning that other substances have not been added to the clay, most ceramics are composed of both a clay component (which often has natural inclusions from the clay source) and **temper**, organic and/or inorganic materials that have been added to the **paste** (the ceramic mix prior to firing) aid in the production process (e.g., plasticity, workability, firing, and drying, among others). Tempers can range from organics like grass, blood, and eggs to inorganics like quartz, calcite, volcanic ash, and even old sherds.

Once the paste is created, it can then be manipulated into different shapes using a variety of different techniques. The simplest method is that the paste can be shaped by hand, often resulting in very simple objects like basic figurines and "pinch pots." Other pottery techniques include coiling and paddle and anvil techniques as well as the use of the potting wheel and molds; additions such as appliques can also be placed on the pottery. Once the shape has been made and the pottery dries, the surface can be subjected to different kinds of techniques. In some cases, a **slip** is applied to the surface, composed of a thin layer of clay and water. In other cases, different slips can be applied to make designs on the pottery. In some contexts, archaeologists have recovered ceramics with ornate decorative designs that are the product of techniques such as incisions, paints, and slips. Designs can also be created by placing a material over parts of the surface to shield it from the heat of the kiln, causing variations in color (called **resist designs**) or by molding or incising patterns. The surface of the pottery can be smoothed or **burnished**, often with a smooth stone and other kinds of substances can eventually applied after firing, such as stucco, paint, and even wax to help pottery retain liquid contents better.

The firing process turns clay into pottery; in technical terms, the plastic paste is fired into a hard nonplastic **fabric**. There are many different kinds of firing technologies that were used in the past. Some were rather simple, such as open pits that did not reach high temperatures. Others were very sophisticated constructions that produced well-crafted and durable pottery such as porcelain. Kiln technologies had an impact on some decorative styles as well. For example, Athenian potters produced red- and black-colored designs by controlling the amount of oxygen let into the kiln during the firing process. By creating oxidizing and reducing environments, the potters were able to provoke different reactions

FIGURE 10.22 (F) The red and black color tones of Athenian pottery.

© Lefteris Papaulakis/Shutterstock.com

FIGURE 10.23 A Mississippian incised shell gorget depicting an individual holding a severed head (ca. AD 1000).

Shell gorget depicting a flying shaman with a death's head in one hand and a ceremonial mace in the other/Werner Forman Archive/Bridgeman Images

of ferric oxide in the clays, producing the distinctive contrast between red and black colors. Although firing technologies can have a great impact on the durability of ceramics, the raw materials used are also very important. And, in the end, the environmental conditions in which the ceramics were deposited have a great impact on their survival over time. Thus, although ceramics tend to preserve well in certain archaeological contexts due to factors such as their manufacture and favorable conditions of preservation, in many cases they do not preserve well.

Shell

As with many other materials, shell can be worked into all sorts of objects, such as jewelry and a wide variety of tools. It is hard and generally durable, preserves relatively well (although is sometimes fragile), and can be directly dated. Residue and use-wear analyses are also applicable to shell artifacts. Even climatological data can be recovered from shell. However, when it comes to sourcing, shells are a bit different than other materials. Because they are from living beings that can reflect the oxygen and strontium signatures of the surrounding environment, the shell of certain species (e.g., land snails) can be subjected to stable isotope analysis (see Chapter 9), although this becomes somewhat complicated for marine species. Therefore, archaeologists often rely on the known distributions of mollusk species to determine the place where they were originally collected by past peoples.

FIGURE 10.24 The relationships between animals and people are complex and not all animal bone found in archaeological sites is there due to intentional human action (shown: Assyrian carved relief showing an individual carrying a goat).

© Radiokafka/Shutterstock.com

Bone and Antler

Bone and antler are materials that are often recovered in archaeological sites. Much of this material can be ecofacts,

FIGURE 10.25 A Paleolithic reindeer horn carved with shapes of a human, horse heads, and a snake (left, ca. 17,000–12,000 BP) and an ivory comb from Pakistan (right, ca. first-century AD).

Paleolithic reindeer horn carved into shapes of man, horse heads and snake, dating back to Magdalenian. From La Madeleine in the surroundings of Tursac, Aquitaine/De Agostini Picture Library/G. Dagli Orti/Bridgeman Images
Comb. Pakistan, Taxila region, 1st century. Ivory. 3 1/4 × 5 1/2 × 3/4 in. (8.25 × 13.97 × 1.9 cm). Los Angeles County Museum of Art, Christian Humann Asian Art Fund (M.86.255). Photo © Museum Associates/LACMA

remains of creatures (e.g., rats or lizards) that lived and died alongside the people who lived and worked at these sites. Others might be the remains of organisms that lived long after archaeological contexts were deposited, being introduced by some later formation process. Still others may be the remains of meals, such as wild deer or domesticated goats, showing signs of processing (e.g., cut-marks, boiling, see Chapter 12), but no evidence of being turned into what we might call an artifact. All of these materials are of interest to archaeologists. They can all yield important insights into how to interpret the past. Further, human bone can be abundant at some archaeological sites, often located in culturally significant contexts such as tombs, cemeteries, ritual offerings, and even middens (see Chapter 12). Regardless of whether it is human or animal, bone (and antler for animals) can also be modified into artifacts; other parts of animals such as skins and sinew (which can also fall under the category of fibers) can as well, although they usually do not preserve well and we will not treat them here. Artifacts made from these materials can range from weaving and leather-making tools to fish-hooks and objects used in ancestor worship. One advantage of working with bone specifically is that it can be directly dated via radiocarbon dating if enough collagen is preserved. Stable isotope analyses can also be run on this material. So, in addition to being able to identify the species the material once pertained to, other kinds of information can be extracted from artifacts made from these materials.

Metals

Metal technologies developed in various parts of the world and different times. In the grand scheme of archaeological time, however, all of the dates for early metal use are relatively late and we can consider metal a fairly new technology, one that has had a tremendous impact on the development of modern societies. **Archaeometallurgy** is the study of the manufacture and use of metals in the past. Metals are generally divided into two broad categories; nonferrous (those not containing iron, such as copper, silver, gold, and lead) and ferrous (those containing iron such as steel). As we have reviewed previously in this chapter, metals, such as some other materials, can be subjected to compositional analysis; the chemical composition of metals is dependent on both the raw materials used to manufacture the metal objects as well as the technologies implemented.

Past peoples worked different kinds of metals, depending on the availability of raw materials and existence of different kinds of metal-working technologies. For instance, in the Great Lakes area of the United States, peoples worked copper from nuggets of raw material that were locally available, potentially cold-hammering or even smelting the copper into objects as early as the fourth-millennium BC. Copper is one of the few metals that can occur in a "native" form and was worked by peoples in several parts of the world, including at sites in Turkey and Iran as early as the seventh-millennium BC.

Beyond working native copper, other technologies for manufacturing metal products were developed by past peoples at different times throughout the world. These technologies include the following:

- **Annealing.** Annealing is a form of heat treatment of metals to increase their workability (e.g., hot-working or forging). Although hard, metals can be brittle. By heating the metal up, it can become more pliable, decreasing the potential of fractures during the hammering process. This heating can also cause changes to the chemical composition of the metal.

FIGURE 10.26 Metal objects can take many forms: starting with the upper left: part of the Cuerdale silver hoard buried about AD 905 in Lancashire, England; "Agamemnon's mask" dating to the sixteenth-century BC, Mycenae, Greece; Tutankhamun's gilded sarcophagus, Valley of the Kings, Egypt (ca. fourteenth-century BC); Bronze dagger, Luristan, Iran (ca. 2600–2350 BC); decorated copper axe head, Dongson Culture, Sumba, Indonesia (ca. 100 BC to AD 300, courtesy of the Los Angeles Museum of Art); copper wine flask, Late Eastern Zhou dynasty, middle or late Warring States period (ca. 400–221 BC, courtesy of the Los Angeles Museum of Art).

Top left: © Tony Baggett/Shutterstock.com
Top middle: © Svineyard/Shutterstock.com
Top right middle: © Sean M Smith/Shutterstock.com

Source: Los Angeles County Museum of Art. Credit lines on page 216.

- **Smelting**. Metals can be extracted from ores (rocks and minerals that are mined) by heating the material to a temperature where the metal melts and can be separated from the rest of the materials in the ore.
- **Casting**. Casting is the process of placing liquid metal into a mold, where it cools and takes the desired shape. Lost-wax casting is one of the most complicated casting processes, whereby wax is molded into the desired shape and encased with ceramic material which is then fired, melting the wax away, but keeping its shape in the ceramic mold. Liquid metal is then poured into the mold to make

FIGURE 10.27 Native copper.

© Arturo Limon/Shutterstock.com

the metal object. The earliest known use of lost-wax casting comes from the Chalcolithic period Near East at around 6000–5500 BC. Loess soils (windblown, very fine sediment with a high clay content, see Chapter 9) also made it possible for craft artisans of the Shang Dynasty (1600–1046 BC) in China to produce elaborate bronze objects. They utilized loess soils of the North China Plain to make elaborate molds into which they casted melted bronze; complex molds that cannot be produced by wax. Skilled Shang artisans to make complex molds that cannot be produced by wax. Thus, as we can see, the study of geology provides insight into the availability of resources that ancient peoples utilized.

- **Alloying**. The processing of alloying involves the mixing of metals or a metal and another element whereby bonding occurs. Brass, for example, is an alloy of copper and zinc that is dated to the third-millennium BC in the Aegean. Other important alloys include pewter, bronze, and steel.
- **Plating**. Plating is a technique used to deposit a metal onto a conductive surface and was utilized in both the New and Old Worlds for well over 1,000 years.

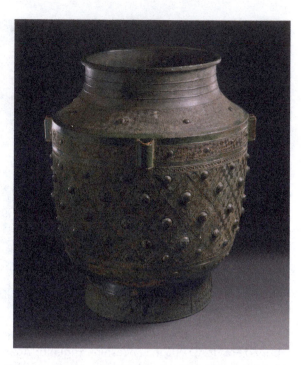

FIGURE 10.28 A Shang Dynasty cast bronze wine storage jar (ca. 1500–1200 BC,).

Ritual Wine Storage Jar with Dragons, Lozenges, and Triangles. China, Middle Shang dyn., Transitional phase, or late Shang dyn., early Anyang phase, about 1500-1200 B.C. Cast bronze. 13 3/4 × 11 3/4 in. (34.93 × 29.85 cm). Los Angeles County Museum of Art, Gift of Mr. and Mrs. Eric Lidow (AC1998.251.1). Photo © Museum Associates/LACMA

Much archaeological work on metals comes from research on production sites. Just like the production of ceramics was variable, so was the production of metal, including raw material extraction (e.g., mines) and production technologies (e.g., furnaces). **Metallography**, the study of the physical structure and composition of metals, is often employed by researchers to determine the composition of metals as well as the technologies that were employed by past peoples and the extent of corrosion of the material. Even the by-products of metal production, such as **slag** (or scoria, which is composed of silica and oxides formed during the smelting process), are also important to study and can reveal much concerning the manufacturing process of metals.

FIGURE 10.29 A copper slag sample from Itziparátzico, west Mexico (ca. AD 1350–1520),

© Blanca Maldonado

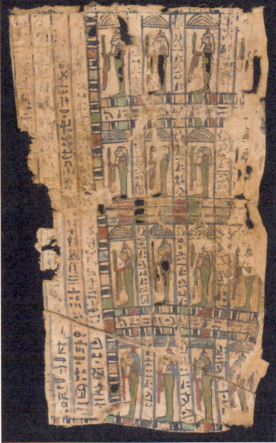

FIGURE 10.30 Fabrics do not tend to preserve well in archaeological contexts, but when they do can provide important data for study: a textile fragment from the Tarim Basin (upper left); a camelid fiber and cotton tunic from Wari culture, Peru (lower left, ca. AD 600–850); a fragment of a funerary cloth inscribed with a passage from The Book of the Dead, Ptolemaic period Egypt (right, ca. 305–31 BC).

© Elizabeth Barber
Man's Tunic. Peru, South Coast, Wari, 600–850. Camelid fiber and cotton, interlocked tapestry. 37 5/8 × 42 1/4 in. (95.57 × 107.32 cm). Los Angeles County Museum of Art, Los Angeles County Fund (70.3.1). Photo © Museum Associates/LACMA
Funerary Fragment of Cloth Inscribed with a Passage from The Book of the Dead. Egypt, Ptolemaic Period (305–31 BCE). Cloth with polychrome. 17 1/2 × 10 1/2 in. (44.45 × 26.67 cm). Los Angeles County Museum of Art, Gift of Mr. and Mrs. Ronald Berger (M.80.144.2). Photo © Museum Associates/LACMA

Fibers and Leather

Fabrics (made from animal fibers such as wool or plant fibers such as cotton), leather, cordage, and basketry were likely used very early on in human history, although their preservation is usually poor to nonexistent. Although organic materials like these do not have a tendency to preserve in most archaeological contexts, there are some environmental conditions where they preserve with more frequency, in arid and anaerobic environments in particular (see Chapter 9). For example, on the Paracas Peninsula of Peru and the Tarim Basin of western China, both dry environments, spectacular textiles have been recovered in burial contexts, wrapping the mummified remains of the people buried there.

Beyond species identification (e.g., to what plant or animal the material came from), researchers working with these kinds of materials focus on technologies such as looms and technological (e.g., type of

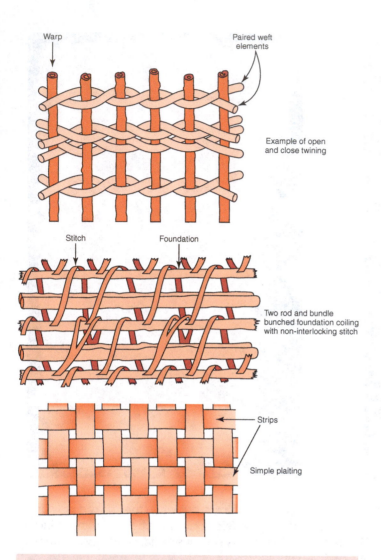

FIGURE 10.31 An important aspect of textile analysis is the study of the kind of weave that was used; here are a few examples of weaves that can be found among archaeological samples.

From *Archaeological: An Introduction, Laboratory Methods*, 6/e by Mark Q. Sutton and Brooke S. Artush. Copyright © 2014 by Kendall Hunt Publishing Company. Reprinted by permission.

FIGURE 10.32 These reed flutes from Egypt (ca. 1537–31 BC) demonstrate that more plant materials than just fibers and wood were used to make material culture by past peoples.

Flutes and Pipes. Egypt, 1537–31 BCE. Reed. Lengths range: 6 7/16 to 9 15/16 in. (16.3 to 23 cm). Los Angeles County Museum of Art, Gift of Robert Blaugrund (M.80.196.27). Photo © Museum Associates/LACMA

FIGURE 10.33 Tree species identification can sometimes be conducted at the microscopic level. Here, we see possible red mulberry (*Morus rubra*) from the site of Troyville, Louisiana

Copyright © Earth Search, Inc.

weaves or knots utilized) and aesthetic styles (e.g., woven designs or patterns of dyes). In some cases, implements for fiber working such as spindle whorls or awls may preserve where the fibers themselves do not. In other cases, the existence of unpreserved fibers is recorded as impressions in other kinds of materials such as clays. Iconographic data can also be a rich source of indirect information regarding materials made out of fibers. When the actual fibers do preserve, however, they can be directly analyzed that can include morphological analysis, direct dating, and analyses of use-wear and residues.

Wood

Wood is another organic material that can preserve better under particular environmental contexts. Although not a plastic material like clay, wood can be worked into a tremendous amount of shapes. It was used for elaborately carved architectural features such as lintels and doors as well as very small portable objects. It was probably one of the most, if not the most, utilized materials in the past, although like other organic materials does not tend to preserve well in the archaeological record. In addition to being able to directly dateable (wooden objects from Egypt were used to confirm the applicability of radiocarbon dating, see Chapter 10), wooden objects can be subjected to a wide range of studies including use-wear and residue analyses.

Glass and Faience

Glass objects are found with quite some frequency at historic sites, and at many sites dating to the last couple of centuries they can make up a rather large part of artifact assemblages. As a technology, however, glass is fairly recent. The origins of glassmaking appear to be traced back to northern Mesopotamia, where a glaze (a vitreous or glassy substance) was used to cover soapstone (steatite) and ceramic (where it is called **faience**) objects during the fifth-millennium BC. Some glass beads have been recovered in Sixth Dynasty (ca. 2345–2181 BC) tombs in Egypt, but it was not until

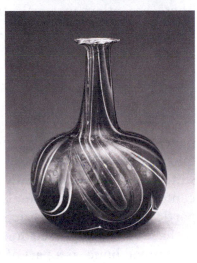

FIGURE 10.34 A wooden sarcophagus from Egypt (likely Thebes, mid-Twenty-first Dynasty, ca. 1000–968 BC.

Coffin. Egypt, likely Thebes, mid-21st Dynasty (about 1000–968 BCE). Wood, gesso, polychrome and yellow varnish. Base: 73 3/4 × 21 1/2 × 13 in. (187.33 × 54.61 × 33.02 cm); Outer Lid: 74 1/4 × 21 3/4 × 14 in. (188.59 × 55.24 × 35.56 cm); Inner Lid: 69 1/8 × 16 5/8 × 4 1/4 in. (175.58 × 42.23 × 10.79 cm). Los Angeles County Museum of Art, Purchased with funds provided by Mr. and Mrs. John Jewett Garland (M.47.3a-c). Photo © Museum Associates/LACMA

FIGURE 10.35 A small painted core-glass unguent container in the form of a tilapia fish from Tell el-Amarna, Eighteenth Dynasty Egypt (top, ca. 1352–1336 BC) and a glass bottle from the eastern Mediterranean or Italy (bottom, ca. first-century AD).

A small painted core-glass unguent container in the form of a tilapia fish which was a symbol of rebirth/Werner Forman Archive/Bridgeman Images Bottle. East Mediterranean or Italy, 1st century. Opaque glass. 3 7/8 × 2 7/8 in. (9.8 × 7 cm). Los Angeles County Museum of Art, Gift of Varya and Hans Cohn (M.88.129.42). Photo © Museum Associates/LACMA

around 1500 BC that glass vessels appear in the archaeological record, this time back in northern Mesopotamia, from where they may have quickly spread to Egypt with the expansionistic conquests of the Egyptian Pharaoh Thutmose III in the first half of the fifteenth-century BC.

Studies of glass share many of the same approaches as other materials we have described above, including compositional analyses and studies of production sites that can, in the case of glass, include furnaces and other manufacturing tools such as blowpipes. Glass can be produced in different ways. For example, broad glass is produced by creating a cylinder of molten glass using a blowpipe; the cylinder is then flattened to make a pane. Other techniques include crown glass, which begins as a bubble of glass created by a blowpipe and then spun on a disk where the resulting centrifugal force flattens it.

Final Comments

There are other materials that people in the past worked that we have not touched on here, such as stucco and plaster, which in some cases were used to make artifacts and features (e.g., floor surfaces). Depending on the cultural contexts and preservation conditions in which an archaeologist works, some of these other materials will be quite common or completely nonexistent. It depends on the researcher to find and employ the most appropriate techniques suitable for the material culture found in the specific contexts that they work in. However, one material in particular requires much more discussion. Although we have briefly discussed bone in general in this chapter, human bone, as a part of the potential remains of the actual people of the past, can tell us an incredible amount of information concerning their lives. It is a longer discussion of human remains then to which we now turn.

FIGURE 10.36 There are other materials that archaeologists also analyze; shown is a ceramic vessel that was covered with stucco and painted from the site of Yaxuná, Mexico (ca. AD 700–900). Both the stucco and paint can be subjected to different kinds of analyses.

© Vania Carrillo Bosch

Bibliography

Barber, Elizabeth W. *The Mummies of Ürümchi.* New York: W.W. Norton & Company, 1999.

Barnard, H., L. Shoemaker, O. E. Craig, M. Rider, R. E. Parr, M. Q. Sutton, and R. M. Yohe, II. "Introduction to the Analysis of Protein Residues in Archaeological Ceramics." In *Theory and Practice of Archaeological Residue Analysis*, edited by H. Barnard and J. W. Eerkens, 216–228. Oxford: Archaeopress, 2007.

Birch, Thomas, Thilo Rehren, and Ernst Pernicka. "The Metallic Finds from Çatalhöyük: A Review and Preliminary New Work." In *Substantive Technologies at Catalhöyük: Reports from the 2000-2008 Seasons*, edited by I. Hodder, 307–316. British Institute at Ankara, Vol. 48, Çatal Research Project, Vol. 9. Los Angeles: Cotsen Institute of Archaeology Press, 2013.

Bishop, Ronald L., and M. James Blackman. "Instrumental Neutron Activation Analysis of Archaeological Ceramics: Scale and Interpretation." *Accounts of Chemical Research* 35, no. 8 (2002): 603–610.

Crown, Patricia L., and W. Jeffrey Hurst. "Evidence of Cacao Use in the Prehispanic American Southwest." *Proceedings of the National Academy of Sciences* 106, no. 7 (2009): 2110–2113.

Cullity, B. D., and S. R. Stock. *Elements of X-Ray Diffraction.* 3rd ed. New York: Prentice-Hall, 2001.

David, Nicholas, and Carol Kramer. *Ethnoarchaeology in Action.* Cambridge: Cambridge University Press, 2001.

Drooker, Penelope B., and Laurie D. Webster, eds. *Beyond Cloth and Cordage: Archaeological Textile Research in the Americas.* Salt Lake City, UT: The University of Utah Press, 2000.

Duma, G., and I. Lengyel. "Mezőcsát Pots Containing Red Blood Pigment (Haemoglobin)." *Acta Archaeologicae Academiae Scientiarium Hungaricae* 22 (1970): 69–93.

Ewen, Charles R. *Artifacts.* Archaeologist's Toolkit 4. Walnut Creek, CA: AltaMira, 2003.

Frahm, Ellery. "Scanning Electron Microscopy (SEM): Applications in Archaeology." In *Encyclopedia of Global Archaeology*, edited by C. Smith, 6487–6495. New York: Springer Press, 2013.

Frank, Susan. *Glass and Archaeology.* New York: Academic Press, 1982.

Glascock, Michael D., and Hector Neff. "Neutron Activation Analysis and Provenance Resaecrh in Archaeology." *Measurement Science and Technology* 14 (2003): 1516–1526.

Goffer, Zvi. *Archaeological Chemistry.* 2nd ed. Hoboken, NJ: John Wiley & Sons, Inc., 2007.

Harmand, Sonia, Jason E. Lewis, Craig S. Feibel, Christopher J. Lepre, Sandrine Prat, Arnaud Lenoble, Xavier Boës, Rhonda L. Quinn, Michel Brenet, Adrian Arroyo, Nicholas Taylor, Sophie Clément, Guillaume Daver, Jean-Philip Brugal, Louise Leakey, Richard A. Mortlock, James D. Wright, Sammy Lokorodi, Christopher Kirwa, Dennis V. Kent, and Hélène Roche. "3.3-Million-Year-Old Stone Tools from Lomekwi 3, West Turkana, Kenya." *Nature* 521 (2015): 310–315.

Haslam, Michael, Gail Robertson, Alison Crowther, Sue Nugent, and Luke Kirkwood, eds. *Archaeological Science under a Microscope: Studies in Residue and Ancient DNA Analysis in Honour of Thomas H. Loy.* Terra Australis, Vol. 30. Canberra, Australia: ANU Press, 2009.

Hauptmann, Andreas. "The Investigation of Archaeometallurgical Slag." In *Archaeometallurgy in Global Perspective: Methods and Syntheses*, edited by B. W. Roberts and C. P. Thornton, 91–105. New York: Springer Publishing, 2014.

Hedges, Robert, and James McCullagh. "Mass Spectrometry in Archaeology." In *Mass Spectrometry Handbook*, edited by M.S. Lee, 765–795. New York: Wiley, 2012.

Holmes, William H. "Prehistoric Textile Fabrics of the United States Derived from Impressions on Pottery." In *Second Annual Report of the Bureau of Ethnology to the Secretary of the Smithsonian Institution, 1880-81*, edited by J. W. Powell, 393–425. Washington, DC: Government Printing Office, 1881.

Ixer, Rob A., and Richard E. Bevins. "Craig Rhos-y-Felin, Pont Saeson is the Dominant Source of the Stonehenge Rhyolitic 'Debitage'." *Archaeology in Wales* 50 (2011): 21–32.

Jackson, C. M., P. T. Nicholson, and W. Gneisinger. "Glassmaking at Tell el-Amarna: An Integrated Approach." *Journal of Glass Studies* 40 (1998): 11–23.

Jenkins, Ron. *X-Ray Fluorescence Spectrometry.* New York: Wiley, 1999.

Johansson, Sven A. E., John L. Campbell, and Klas G. Malmqvist. *Particle-Induced X-Ray Emission Spectrometry (PIXE).* Chemical Analysis: A Series of Monographs on Analytical Chemistry and Its Applications, Book 184. New York: Wiley-Interscience, 1995.

Kaner, Simon, and Tatsuo Kobayashi. *Jomon Reflections: Forager Life and Culture in the Prehistoric Japanese Archipelago.* Oxford: Oxbow, 2005.

Keeley, Lawrence H. *Experimental Determination of Stone Tool Uses: A Microwear Analysis.* Chicago: University of Chicago Press, 1980.

Killick, David. "From Ores to Metals." In *Archaeometallurgy in Global Perspective: Methods and Syntheses*, edited by B. W. Roberts and C. P. Thornton, 11–45. New York: Springer Publishing, 2014.

Kipfer, Barbara A. *Encyclopedic Dictionary of Archaeology.* New York: Kluwer Academic/Plenum Publishers, 2000.

Kooyman, Brian. *Understanding Stone Tools and Archaeological Sites.* Calgary: University of Calgary, 2000.

Kooyman, Brian, Margaret E. Newman, Christine Cluney, Murray Lobb, Shayne Tolman, Paul McNeil, and L. V. Hills. "Identification of Horse Exploitation by Clovis Hunters on Protein Analysis." *American Antiquity* 66 (2001): 686–691.

Lechtman, Heather. "Style in Technology: Some Early Thoughts." In *Material Culture: Styles, Organization, and Dynamics of Technology*, edited by H. Lechtman and R. Merrill, 3–20. St. Paul, MN: West Publishing Co., 1977.

Lee, Mike. "Preface." In *Mass Spectrometry Handbook*, edited by M. S. Lee, 13–15. New York: Wiley, 2012.

Longacre, William A. "Ceramic Ethnoarchaeology: An Introduction." In *Ceramic Ethnoarchaeology*, edited by W. A. Longacre, 1–10. Tucson: University of Arizona Press, 1991.

Moorey, P. R. S. "The Chalcolithic Hoard from Nahal Mishmar, Israel, in Context." *World Archaeology* 20, no. 2 (1988): 171–189.

Neff, Hector. "Laser Ablation ICP-MS in Archaeology." In *Mass Spectrometry Handbook*, edited by M. S. Lee, 829–843. New York: Wiley, 2012.

Nicholson, Paul T. *Brilliant Things for Akhenaten: The Production of Glass, Vitreous Materials and Pottery at Amarna Site O45.1*. London: The Egypt Exploration Society, 2007.

O'Connell, James F. "Ethnoarchaeology Needs a General Theory of Behavior." *Journal of Archaeological Research* 3 (1995): 205–255.

Parker Pearson, Michael, Richard Bevins, Rob Ixer, and Joshua Pollard, Colin Richards, Kate Welham, Ben Chan, Kevan Edinborough, Derek Hamilton, Richard Macphail, Duncan Schlee, Jean-Luc Schwenninger, Ellen Simmons, and Martin Smith. "Craig Rhos-y-Felin: A Welsh Bluestone Megalith Quarry for Stonehenge." *Antiquity* 89, no. 348 (2015): 1331–1352.

Pleger, Thomas C. "Old Copper and Red Ocher Social Complexity." *Midcontinental Journal of Archaeology* 25, no. 2 (2000): 169–190.

Powis, Terry G., Fred Valdez, Jr., Thomas R. Hester, W. J. Hurst, and S. M. Tarka. "Spouted Vessels and Cacao Use Among the Preclassic Maya." *Latin American Antiquity* 13 (2002): 85–106.

Rice, Prudence M. *Pottery Analysis: A Sourcebook*. Chicago: University of Chicago Press, 1987.

Roberts, Benjamin W., and Christopher P. Thornton, eds. *Archaeometallurgy in Global Perspective: Methods and Syntheses*. New York: Springer Publishing, 2014.

Scott, David A. "Metallography and Microstructure of Metallic Artifacts." In *Archaeometallurgy in Global Perspective: Methods and Syntheses*, edited by B. W. Roberts and C. P. Thornton, 67–89. New York: Springer Publishing, 2014.

Skibo, James M. *Pottery Function: A Use-Alteration Perspective*. New York: Plenum Press, 1992.

Thornton, Christopher P. "The Emergence of Complex Metallurgy on the Iranian Plateau: Escaping the Levantine Paradigm." *Journal of World Prehistory* 22 (2009): 301–327.

———"The Emergence of Complex Metallurgy on the Iranian Plateau." In *Archaeometallurgy in Global Perspective: Methods and Syntheses*, edited by B. W. Roberts and C. P. Thornton, 665–696. New York: Springer Publishing, 2014.

Torrence, Robin. *Ancient Starch Research*. Walnut Creek, CA: Left Coast Press Inc., 2006

Trigger, Bruce G. *A History of Archaeological Thought*. 2nd ed. Cambridge: Cambridge University Press, 2006.

Tykot, Robert H. "Scientific Methods and Applications to Archaeological Provenance Studies." In *Proceedings of the International School of Physics "Enrico Fermi" Course CLIV*, edited by M. Martini, M. Milazzo, and M. Piacentini, 407–432. Amsterdam: IOS Press, 2004.

Figure 10.1

LIDDED VESSEL (2158765): Lidded Vessel. Guatemala, Maya, A.D. 300-500. Slip-painted Ceramic with Postfire pigment and incised decoration. Overall (Diameter): 38 cm (14 15/16 in.) 29 cm (11 7/16 in.). Los Angeles County Museum of Art, Purchased with funds provided by Camilla Chandler Frost (M.2010.115.893a-b). Photo © Museum Associates/LACMA

LIDDED VESSEL WITH MODELED MACAW (2156694): Lidded Vessel with Modeled Macaw, Guatemala or Mexico, Petén or Campeche, Maya, 250-500. Slip-painted ceramic. 18 × 19 × 19 in. (45.72 × 48.26 × 48.26 cm). Los Angeles County Museum of Art, Anonymous gift (M.2010.115.942a-b). Photo © Museum Associates/LACMA

LIDDED VESSEL WITH SUPERNATURAL JAGUAR (1903367): Lidded Vessel with Supernatural Jaguar, Guatemala or Mexico, Petén or Campeche, Maya, 250-500. Slip-painted ceramic with post-fire pigment. 12 1/2 × 14 1/2 × 14 1/2 in. (31.75 × 36.83 × 36.83 cm). Los Angeles County Museum of Art, Purchased with funds provided by Camilla Chandler Frost (M.2010.115.1024a-b). Photo © Museum Associates/LACMA

BOWL WITH RATTLES AND SERPENT DESIGN (2257740): Bowl with Rattles and Serpent Design, Northern Guatemala or Southeastern Mexico, Maya, 250-550. Slip-painted ceramic with post-fire pigment. Diameter: 6 in. (15.24 cm); 5 1/2 x 6 3/10 x 6 in. (13.97 x 16.002 x 15.24 cm). Los Angeles County Museum of Art, Purchased with funds provided by Camilla Chandler Frost (M.2010.115.721). Photo © Museum Associates/LACMA

BOWL WITH MALE FIGURE AND WATER LILY SERPENT (2257760): Bowl with male Figure and Water Lily Serpent, Mexico, Yucatán, Chocholá or vicinity, Maya, 700-900. Slip-painted ceramic. Diameter: 5 1/2 in. (13.97 cm); 4 7/10 x 4 3/10 x 4 3/10 in. (11.938 x 10.922 x 10.922 cm). Los Angeles County Museum of Art, Purchased with funds provided by Camilla Chandler Frost (M.2010.115.625). Photo © Museum Associates/LACMA

BOWL WITH SUPERNATURAL SERPENT (2257742): Bowl with Supernatural Serpent, Guatemala or Mexico, Maya, AD 600-900. Slip-painted ceramic. Diameter: 7 1/2 in. (19.05 cm); 5 x 7 1/2 x 7 1/2 in. (12.7 x 19.05 x 19.05 cm). Los Angeles County Museum of Art, Purchased with funds provided by Camilla Chandler Frost (M.2010.115.707). Photo © Museum Associates/LACMA

BOWL WITH MAIZE GOD AND CHAHK IN WATERY LOCALE (2257736): Bowl with Maize God and Chahk in Watery Locale, Guatemala, Petén, Maya, 250-550. Slip-painted ceramic with post-fire pigment. Diameter: 6 in. (15.24 cm); 5 1/2 x 6 x 6 in. (13.97 x 15.24 x 15.24 cm). Los Angeles County Museum of Art, Purchased with funds provided by Camilla Chandler Frost (M.2010.115.740). Photo © Museum Associates/LACMA

VESSEL WITH GLYPHIC TEXT (221629): Vessel with Glyphic Text, Guatemala or Belize, Northern Petén, Maya, 400-550. Slip-painted ceramic. Diameter: 8 1/2 in. (21.59 cm) Height: 7 in. (17.78 cm). Los Angeles County Museum of Art, Museum Acquisition Fund (AC1992.129.1). Photo © Museum Associates/LACMA

GLOBULAR BOWL WITH CARTOUCHES (2257732) : Globular Bowl with Cartouches, Guatemala, Petén, Naranjo or vicinity, Maya, late 6th Century. Slip-painted ceramic. Diameter: 7 1/2 in. (19.05 cm); 7 1/5 x 7 1/2 x 7 1/2 in. (18.288 x 19.05 x 19.05 cm). Los Angeles County Museum of Art, Purchased with funds provided by Camilla Chandler Frost (M.2010.115.756). Photo © Museum Associates/LACMA

BOWL WITH WATER BIRDS (2257711): Bowl with Water Birds, El Salvador or Honduras, Maya, AD 600-900. Slip-painted ceramic. Diameter: 6 3/10 in. (16.002 cm); 3 1/2 x 6 1/2 x 6 1/2 in. (8.89 x 16.51 x 16.51 cm). Los Angeles County Museum of Art, Purchased with funds provided by Camilla Chandler Frost (M.2010.115.885). Photo © Museum Associates/LACMA

FOOTED VESSEL WITH K'AWIIL (2257765) : Footed Vessel with K'awiil, Guatemala, Maya, AD 600-900. Slip-painted Ceramic with post-fire stucco and pigment. Diameter: 5 in. (12.7 cm); 7 x 4 1/2 x 4 1/2 in. (17.78 x 11.43 x 11.43 cm). Los Angeles County Museum of Art, Purchased with funds provided by Camilla Chandler Frost (M.2010.115.553). Photo © Museum Associates/LACMA

CYLINDER VESSEL WITH K'AWIIL IMPERSONATORS (2257734): Cylinder Vessel with K'awiil Impersonators, Guatemala or Mexico, Maya, AD 600-900. Slip-painted ceramic with post-fire stucco and pigment. Diameter: 6 1/2 in. (16.51 cm); 8 3/10 x 5 1/2 x 5 1/2 in. (21.082 x 13.97 x 13.97 cm). Los Angeles County Museum of Art, Purchased with funds provided by Camilla Chandler Frost (M.2010.115.741). Photo © Museum Associates/LACMA

DRINKING VESSEL (1903415): Drinking Vessel, Guatemala, Northern Petén, Maya, 650-800. Slip-painted ceramic. Diameter: 4 1/16 in. (10.32 cm) Height: 5 1/8 in. (13.02 cm). Los Angeles County Museum of Art, Purchased with funds provided by Camilla Chandler Frost (M.2010.115.7). Photo © Museum Associates/LACMA

VESSEL WITH SNAKE-LADY SCENE (1903420): Vessel with Snake-Lady Scene, Maya, A.D. 600-800. Slip-painted ceramic. Diameter: 5 5/8 in. (14.29 cm) Height: 6 1/2 in. (16.51 cm). Los Angeles County Museum of Art, Anonymous gift (M.2010.115.3). Photo © Museum Associates/LACMA

CYLINDER VESSEL DEPICTING CORMORANTS AND WATER SIGNS (1903382): Cylinder Vessel Depicting Cormorants and Water Signs, Maya, AD 600-900. Slip-painted ceramic. Diameter: 3 1/2 in. (8.89 cm) Height: 9 1/4 in. (23.5 cm). Los Angeles County Museum of Art, Purchased with funds provided by Camilla Chandler Frost (M.2010.115.573). Photo © Museum Associates/LACMA

Figure 10.14

JAR (228814): Jar. Egypt, New Kingdom, 18th or 19th Dynasty (circa 1550 - 1196 BCE). Calcite. Height: 3 1/2 in. (8.89 cm); Diameter: 7/8 in. (2.22 cm). Los Angeles County Museum of Art, Mr. and Mrs. Allan C. Balch Collection (M.45.3.493). Photo © Museum Associates/LACMA

SEATED FEMALE FIGURE (197476): Seated Female Figure. Northern Afghanistan, Ancient Bactria, circa 2500-1500 B.C. Chlorite and limestone. 5 × 3 1/2 × 2 1/2 in. (12.7 × 8.89 × 6.35 cm). Los Angeles County Museum of Art, Purchased with funds provided by Phil Berg (M.2000.1a-f). Photo © Museum Associates/LACMA

CORPSE PLUG (1267490): Corpse Plug. China, Han dynasty, 206 B.C.-A.D.220. Abraded jade. Los Angeles County Museum of Art, Gift of Carl Holmes (M.70.76.17b). Photo © Museum Associates/LACMA.

Figure 10.26

AXE HEAD (185087): Axe Head. Indonesia, Sumba, Dongson Culture, 100 B.C.-300 A.D. Copper alloy. 8 x 5 1/2 x 3/4 in. (20.3 x 14 x 1.9 cm). Los Angeles County Museum of Art, Gift of Daniel Ostroff in honor of Samuel Eilenberg (AC1997.136.2). Photo © Museum Associates/LACMA

WINE FLASK (BIANHU) WITH SPIRALS AND VOLUTES (241314): Wine Flask (Bianhu) with Spirals and Volutes. China, Late Eastern Zhou dynasty, middle or late Warring States period, about 400-221 B.C. Cast bronze with copper inlay. 12 1/4 x 12 1/4 in. (31.12 x 31.12 cm). Los Angeles County Museum of Art, Gift of Mr. and Mrs. Eric Lidow (M.75.111.3). Photo © Museum Associates/LACMA

COVERED DOUBLE SPOUT AND BRIDGE VESSEL (197367): Covered Double Spout and Bridge Vessel. Peru, South Coast, Paracas, Paracas, 800-100 B.C. Ceramic, incised and resin painted. 7 3/4 x 9 3/4 in. (19.68 x 24.76 cm). Los Angeles County Museum of Art, Purchased with funds provided by Camilla Chandler Frost and Lillian Apodaca Weiner (AC1999.59.1). Photo © Museum Associates/LACMA

DAGGER (226244): Dagger. Iran, Luristan, circa 2600-2350 B.C. Bronze, cast. Overall length: 6 1/2 in. (17 cm); Hilt length: 2 in. (5 cm); Blade length: 6 1/2 in. (16.5 cm). Los Angeles County Museum of Art, The Nasli M. Heeramaneck Collection of Ancient Near Eastern and Central Asian Art, gift of The Ahmanson Foundation (M.76.97.481). Photo © Museum Associates/LACMA

Face-to-Face with the Past: Osteological and Mortuary Analysis

Not only do archaeologists find and study the material culture that survives from past societies, but they are often confronted with the remains of the very people who comprised those societies. The study of human remains, whether they be fragments of bones and teeth or include well-preserved mummified soft tissue, as well as the contexts in which they are found can provide a wealth of information from the scale of a single individual to that of an entire society. A consideration of these kinds of data provides windows to see into the lives of past peoples in ways that the study of artifacts, architecture, and other material remains available to archaeologists simply cannot.

Attitudes toward the scientific study of human remains, however, can vary greatly and researchers should take special care when confronted with them. As we saw in Chapter 2, the recovery, curation, and study of human remains can be contentious. Bodies are important symbols and, especially, when an ancestral connection is made to remains recovered through archaeological work, researchers must engage with local and national stakeholders as to how to proceed with the research. In some cases, research is not allowed to go forward, or only certain types of research are allowed, but the remains are returned to descendant communities for reburial. In other cases, a certain level of ambivalence toward the scientific study of human remains exists or no claims to heritage are made (for a wide variety of historical reasons). Yet, it is vitally important for researchers to understand the proper protocol with how to proceed with the recovery, analysis, storage, and, in some cases, repatriation of human remains in the cultural context in which they work. With these issues in mind, in this chapter we will outline kinds of analyses that researchers can employ when studying human remains and their contexts as well as the broader implications for understanding past societies.

Who Studies Human Remains? Archaeology, Bioarchaeology, and Bioanthropology

The study of human remains is often undertaken by biological or physical anthropologists. Since this subdiscipline includes the study of both behavioral and biological facets of humans (see Chapter 1), many researchers in this area of anthropology are particularly well suited to the study of human remains found through archaeological research. Some archaeologists and biological anthropologists, however, specialize in the study of human remains from a biocultural lens, an increasingly common occurrence in the field. Known as **bioarchaeologists**, these researchers are trained in the methods, techniques, and theory of archaeology, but can perform many of the analyses undertaken by biological anthropologists. Thus, they straddle the interface between archaeology and bioanthropology as archaeologists who specialize in the study of human remains. This dual training means that bioarchaeologists are familiar with the techniques used by archaeologists to recover primary data in the field and it is increasingly the case that bioarchaeologists perform the excavations of human remains. Being involved in the primary data collection of human remains in the field is important for researchers as this involvement gives a better understanding of the taphonomic processes that impacted them, in contrast to just studying the remains in a laboratory setting and reading about their context from a field report. **Taphonomy** is the study of what happens to the remains of an organism after death, including both body processing and formation processes. **Archaeothanatology**, a method that employs detailed human taphonomic study as a central element to research, is becoming increasingly popular in bioarchaeological studies.

Paleodemography

One important set of analyses that are performed on larger samples of human remains revolves around trying to characterize demographic variables in an archaeological population. **Paleodemography** focuses on the analysis of a range of vital statistics, such as age-at-death and the biological sex of the individual, in a mortuary population to understand questions such as health and well-being, life spans, fertility, and population decline and growth. The patterns in the vital statistics can be compared to a host of other data that are often used as proxies for factors such as social class, gender, patterns of violence, and diet, among others (see further along in this chapter) to help researchers understand how the populations of past societies changed over time. For example, we might ask if the life expectancy of a population changed after the advent of agriculture, and if so, if life expectancy changed for males and females in the same way. Before we can answer such questions, the first step is to collect basic skeletal data that can indicate the biological sex of individuals and age-at-death. By roughly estimating the age at which a sample of individuals from a population died, researchers have traditionally created **life tables**, models of the life processes of a population. From these tables, calculations on variables such as life expectancy (taken from the mean age at death from a population) and infant mortality are often made. Although life tables have been criticized on several grounds, including that they indicate more about fertility than mortality, they are still employed in paleodemographic research. Yet, collecting the data to estimate the age-at-death of any given individual also presents challenges to creating life tables as the methods do not yield very precise results.

Age-at-Death

Although there is considerable debate in the field concerning the methods used to estimate the age of an individual at the time of death, age-at-death profiles have been a staple of paleodemographic research for quite some time. In a relatively complete skeleton, several areas can provide information on the age-at-death of the individual. These areas can be linked to patterns of growth or degeneration of the body. For example, the age of children can be roughly estimated from the degree of ossification and fusion of particular parts of the skeleton. In particular, the degree of fusion of the epiphyses, or the distal ends of long bones, is often employed. Tooth formation and eruption and long bone length are other widely utilized indicators of age-at-death in children. For adults, special attention is given to degenerative patterns on the pelvis and the fusion of cranial sutures, among some other skeletal elements, to assign age ranges to individuals. In some instances, the amount of dental wear is taken as a proxy for age. This inference follows the idea that the more you chew the greater chance your teeth have to be worn down. Special care must be taken using the amount of dental attrition, however, as the kind of food a person ingests can influence the rate of tooth wear; a diet composed of a lot of hard foods such as nuts can wear teeth more quickly than a diet composed mainly of softer foods such as gruels. In any event, all of these methods provide an estimated range of age-at-death, and some of them can be very restricted to certain age ranges (e.g., tooth eruption for children, but not for older adults). Therefore, researchers tend to employ a suite of different methods to estimate biological (which does not always exactly coincide with chronological age) age-at-death, which are usually limited to rather broad categories (e.g., fetus, perinatal, infant, child, adolescent, young adult, middle-aged adult, and elderly adult) that impact the preciseness of life tables.

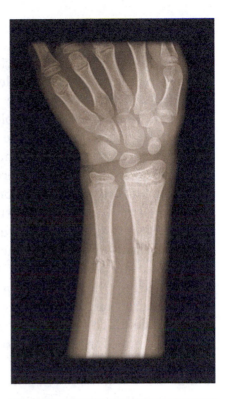

FIGURE 11.1 This x-ray of a child's arm shows the unfused epiphyses.

© Skyhawk x/Shutterstock.com

Biological Sex

Determining the biological sex (which is not the same as gender; gender being a social construct referring to roles in societies) of an individual can also present challenges. Although it is possible to link contextual data associated with a mortuary context to the biological sex of subadult skeletons (e.g., a written text in a burial indicating that its child occupant was biologically male or female), skeletons of individuals around the age of 14 and younger tend not to have clear physical differences based on sex as their secondary sexual attributes have not yet developed. For individuals 15 years or older, a determination of biological sex is made on the premise that **sexual dimorphism** exists between males and females. Sexual dimorphism means that there are physical differences between males and females that go beyond the reproductive system; sexual dimorphism exists along a spectrum, however, and varies among populations, meaning that researchers must take care using such data, especially with individuals who fall near the middle of the spectrum for a given population.

In general, there are two areas of the skeleton, the pelvis (especially the pubis) and, to a lesser extent, the skull, which are commonly used to determine biological sex. Although by no means the only areas of the skeleton that can be used, they generally provide the best data. Given that male skeletons tend to be more robust than female skeletons due to the tendency of males to have larger muscles, some parts of the cranium of males, such as the brow ridge, nuchal crest, and mastoid process, have a high tendency to be more pronounced; although cranial markers can differ by populations. The pelvis also tends to be more robust in males, but differences in the width of the pelvis also tend to occur based on biological sex, with females tending to have wider a pelvis with greater sciatic notches than males, among other differences. Additionally, the pelvis can provide evidence of females who experienced the process of vaginal birth. Parturition pits are formed on the pelvis where the ligaments connecting the pubic bones stretch during the birthing process. This stretching can cause damage that is often identified by researchers as remodeled bone forming the partition pits (also known as parturition marks or ventral pitting).

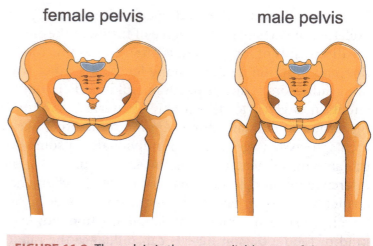

female pelvis   male pelvis

FIGURE 11.2 The pelvis is the most reliable area of the skeleton to determine the biological sex of an individual.

© Artemida-psy/Shutterstock.com

One of the major hurdles in using sexual dimorphism as a proxy for biological sex in humans is that there is some overlap in the range of traits common in males and those in females (e.g., height or muscle mass). This means that some individuals have measurements that fall into a gray zone between male and female estimations and cannot be determined. This means that some biological females could be misidentified as males and vice versa during analysis.

The most reliable method to determine the biological sex of a skeletal individual is through DNA analysis, also termed **archaeogenetics**. If sufficiently well-preserved DNA can be extracted from the remains, and this is a big if, the recovered genetic sequence can indicate the biological sex of the individual. In cases where the morphology of the bone material is ambiguous in terms of biological sex, such as with children and skeletal remains that fall into the gray area between male and female ranges, DNA analysis may be worth pursuing as an analytical tool. DNA analyses, however, are rarely used just to determine sex as they are quite costly and often unsuccessful. Further, DNA material does not preserve particularly well in many environments, but it tends to be more recoverable in colder contexts; it is often quite difficult to extract sufficient amounts of nuclear DNA from samples to confidently determine the biological sex of an individual

FIGURE 11.3 The site center of Tlatelolco, surrounded by Mexico City.

© Ulrike Stein/Shutterstock.com

regardless of the environment, but material from colder environments tend to produce better data. A good example of the use of DNA in the determination of biological sex comes from the Mexica (Aztec) site of Tlatelolco in Central Mexico. Researchers exploring a temple dedicated to Ehecatl-Quetzalcoatl, a god of wind and rain, found the sacrificed remains of thirty-seven children and six adults. DNA analysis of the remains of the children found them to be overwhelmingly, if not all, male, leading the researchers to suggest that boys were chosen to be impersonators (to be sacrificed as part of the performance) of this male deity.

Important Considerations When Working with Paleodemographic Data

Researchers very rarely work, if ever, with all of the individuals from a past population, and in most cases the numbers of individuals accessible for study represent a tiny fraction of the people who composed the population in the past. One of the main reasons that researchers do not work with complete, or at least nearly complete, populations has to do with how those populations are defined and the sheer numbers of people who would have composed them. If the population under study is large (e.g., the entire Nile Valley or all of Rome), there would be no feasible way to collect and study the remains of all of the millions upon millions of people who composed it, even if all of those people were still preserved in the archaeological record; which as we will see below, they usually are not. Thus, researchers are forced to use samples (see Chapter 5). And when samples are used, special attention must be paid to how well the data represent the large population and the kinds of contexts from which they come, as those contexts may bias the sample toward particular demographic data. For example, if the archaeological work is being performed in contexts associated with a particular social class (e.g., excavations in the large palaces rather than in the small houses thought to be of the lower classes), the demographic data will be skewed toward certain segments of past societies. This fact stresses the importance of a sampling strategy and how interpretations could potentially be biased if the data do not well-represent the larger population.

Yet, it is rarely the case that all of the people in a population are potentially accessible to researchers, even when the defined population is small, such as a single household or cemetery that could be potentially excavated in its entirety. As we have discussed previously in this book (Chapter 9), part of the issue here has to do with environmental conditions of preservation. Since human bodies are in large part composed of soft tissue, except in extreme dry, anaerobic, or cold conditions the great part of these bodies are reduced to bones and teeth relatively quickly, limiting the kinds of analyses that can be performed. For example, researchers interested in human brains (an important focus of research for paleoanthropologists interested in cognitive changes in our hominin ancestors) really never have the opportunity to study the brains themselves, but are forced to look at the brain case, which can provide information such as the size and shape of the brain. Actual brains have been found in archaeological contexts, but they are very rare. The earliest recovered brain material comes from the Windover site in Florida, where a series of individuals dating from 6000 to 5000 BC were found to still have preserved brain tissue, attributed to the waterlogged peat contexts in which they were found. But it is not just soft material that decays. Bones, and to lesser extent teeth, also fall victim to the impact of certain environmental conditions over time. Acidic soils or gnawing rodents can do great damage to bone material. Therefore, taphonomy is essential for understanding the skeletal population researchers have to work with. It is especially pertinent to note that certain individuals or parts of individuals in a population have taphonomic tendencies to preserve or not. For example, hard and dense parts of the body, such as teeth, have a greater tendency for preservation. Importantly, very young or old individuals are usually less preserved given a variety of biological factors that impact the durability of their remains. Therefore, a burial population tends to have fewer young children represented in comparison to young adults due to preservation, skewing the demographic analysis; a bias that researchers interested in paleodemography should be very mindful.

Cultural factors can also play a vital role in the preservation and recovery of human remains. The way bodies are treated by different societies impacts the potential for their being found, and the state in which they are found, by researchers in the future. For example, among the Classic period lowland Maya, it is common to find burials beneath the floors of houses. These burials tend to be placed below stucco floors and in prepared stone crypts (cists) that protect human bodies from rain and other elements. However, not all of the people who lived in any given household were actually buried in such contexts. Maya bioarchaeologists may only recover five to ten bodies from a household that was continuously occupied for over five hundred years. Many archaeologists have interpreted this pattern of only select people being buried underneath the floors as evidence on their cultural assignation as important ancestors. Regardless of the reason, however, the other bodies are not present, meaning that the sample of the individuals representing the population of the household is biased toward those who were selected for subfloor burial by the people who lived there. Such differential treatment of human bodies is an important consideration for researchers to keep in mind.

In other cases, human remains may be processed so that part or all of the body is intentionally modified or destroyed. Cremations, for example, are found in a wide variety of cultural contexts throughout the world. Although some remains may not be reduced completely to ash, cremains are notoriously difficult to analyze given their poor preservation. In Tibet, traditional mortuary practices include "sky burials," where the bodies of the deceased are disarticulated and fed to vultures. This practice virtually erases bodies from the material record, eliminating the possibility for their study. For all of these kinds of reasons, researchers need to pay special attention to the factors impacting the sample they have available for study.

Paleodiet

Another area of research concerning human remains (already discussed in Chapter 10) is **paleodiet**, what people in the past consumed for sustenance. Although, as we have seen, subsistence systems can be studied from different perspectives using a wide array of material data (e.g., food remains, iconography, agricultural features, and a variety of subsistence-related artifacts), data on foodways from human remains themselves provide a unique body-oriented perspective of past diets. In some extreme cases where the right environmental conditions have led to the preservation of parts of the digestive system, researchers are sometimes presented with the rare opportunity to study the actual food consumed by an individual in the short time before death. One of the most well-known of the Danish bog bodies, the Tolland Man, was subjected to a study of his stomach and intestines after the discovery of these Iron Age remains in 1950 (see also Chapter 9). Research revealed that the seeds of around forty different plants were in the Tolland Man's alimentary tract, including both domesticated plants such as barley and the seeds of wild plants such as knotgrass. Interestingly, no evidence of meat, fish, or fruit was discovered in the last few meals of a person who is widely thought to have been hanged prior to the deposition of his body in a bog around 400–200 BC. Since the plant remains were found in the intestine and not the stomach, researchers suggest that the Tolland Man had eaten some twelve to twenty-four hours prior to his death.

Most of the data available from human remains for paleodiets comes from stable isotope analyses. These kinds of analyses are based on the premise that "you are what you eat." What a person regularly eats and drinks can impact the chemistry of his or her body. Except for rare examples like the case of Tolland Man, researchers do not usually seek to study individual meals, but rather overall diet. In archaeological research, a **meal** refers to direct evidence of the things

FIGURE 11.4 A scene of food preparation from a carved relief at Angkor Wat, Cambodia.

© Lukiyanova Natalia frenta/Shutterstock.com

people ate at a particular time. In contrast, **diet** represents the pattern of consumption throughout peoples' lives. Stable isotope analysis reveals diet, not meals. In most cases, archaeologists have only bones and teeth to work with for stable isotope analysis, but other parts of the body, such as hair, can also be tested if they preserve. In particular, there are two primary stable isotopes that archaeologists rely on to identify people's diet, carbon (^{12}C and ^{13}C) and nitrogen (^{14}N and ^{15}N).

Analyses of $\delta^{13}C$ (δ = ratios of environmental isotopes, in this case ^{13}C over ^{12}C) in samples are reflective of the human consumption of C3, C4, and crassulacean acid metabolism (CAM) plants or animals that consume such plants. C3 plants include a wide range of plants that are found in both temperate and tropical environments. C4 plants are primarily tropical and subtropical grasses that include many domesticated grains such as tropical maize, sorghum, and millet. Identification of a high degree of consumption of C4 plants is often used to discuss a past population's reliance on domesticated grains as a staple

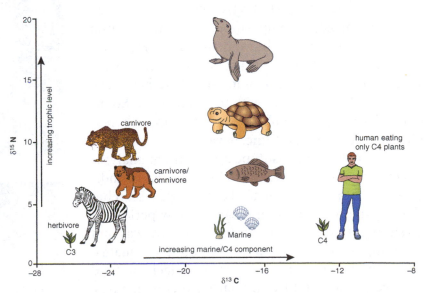

FIGURE 11.5 Different kinds of diets can result in different chemical signatures on bone materials.

© Kendall Hunt Publishing Company

food source. CAM plants include those which have adapted to arid environments, such as succulents; the values of the $\delta^{13}C$ of CAM plants generally fall between those of C3 and C4 plants. Bone collagen is commonly utilized as the material subjected to stable isotope analysis. For both carbon and nitrogen isotopes, bone collagen results indicate the diet for approximately the last ten years of an individual's life. Samples can also be taken from bone mineral, tooth enamel, dentine, and dental calculus. In the case of tooth enamel, which does not remodel like bone, the stable isotope values reflect the specific age-frame for an individual's diet when that tooth was being formed. Thus, the diet from the early part of an individual's life can be considered. In fact, the process of weaning children from breastmilk can be noted in stable isotope analyses of tooth enamel, in particular those of nitrogen.

Analyses of $\delta^{15}N$ (^{15}N over ^{14}N) are highly reflective of an organism's trophic (hierarchical) level in a food chain. The organism doing the consuming generally has a higher $\delta^{15}N$ value than the organism being consumed. Since legumes have a lower $\delta^{15}N$ value than nonlegumes, nitrogen stable isotopes can be used to identify the consumption patterns of these plant groups. Further, analyses of nitrogen stable isotopes can help identify the consumption patterns of terrestrial resources such as herbivorous or carnivorous animals and marine resources such as fish. Again, it is important to keep in mind that stable isotope analyses do not reflect individual items that were consumed, but are reflective of habitual patterns of consumption (diet) over the time frame revealed by the material being analyzed (e.g., bone collagen or tooth enamel). Occasionally, consumed items will not be reflected in the results.

Other elements, including strontium (Sr, its elemental, not isotopic composition), barium (Ba), iron (Fe), zinc (Zn), lead (Pb), and mercury (Hg) have also been used to research paleodiets, dietary deficiencies, and the presence of toxins. There have been some mixed results so far with these elements. Some, such as barium, have looked very promising, whereas others, such as iron and zinc, have not.

Apart from stable isotope and element analysis, aspects of subsistence can also be reflected by indicators of dietary stress. Instead of telling a researcher what a person ate, these indicators show periods of physiological disruption when a person was not receiving an adequate dietary amount or quality. For example, periods of substantial lack of food can result in low stature and flattened cranial bases, especially if the periods of nutritional stress coincide with infancy or adolescence. Pelvic deformation and bowing of the lower limb bones can occur in cases of severe vitamin D deficiency. Anemia, linked to

FIGURE 11.6 Indicators of dietary stress: (top) porotic hyperstosis, (middle) linear enamel hypoplasia, (bottom) cribra orbitalia.

© Vera Tiesler

iron intake, can cause the expansion of the marrow in the cranial vault that results in **porotic hyperstosis**, manifested on the cranial vault, or **cribra orbitalia** in the eye sockets; the impact of anemia can also be seen in **histological sections**, thin slices of the bone that are magnified to examine the inner structure of the tissue. Tooth enamel can also be a good indicator of dietary stress, specifically when parts of the enamel are absent, often in the form of visible grooves called **linear enamel hypoplasias**. Since enamel does not remodel over time, these linear defects remain throughout the entire life of the individual, a testament to episodes of early physiological stress. In many cases, researchers have used skeletal growth lines (also known as **Harris lines**)

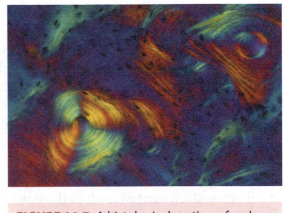

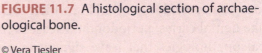

FIGURE 11.7 A histological section of archaeological bone.

© Vera Tiesler

as a proxy for dietary stress. These lines represent growth arrest (moment of stress) followed by growth recovery (after the stress ends) and can be found on different parts of the skeleton, including long bones, using X-rays. There is quite a bit of debate among researchers, however, regarding the usefulness of these lines as they do not present themselves in a clear pattern among children who have experienced stress and those who have not. Further, there are several causes for the development of these lines and, when they do develop, can fade as the individual reaches more advanced age. In older individuals, dietary stress has been linked to **osteoporosis** (bone loss), although other factors can greatly impact bone loss as well, including the reduction of estrogen during menopause in women. Oral pathologies (see more below) such as carious lesions (cavities) can also be an indicator of diet.

Although the focus of this section has been on diet, there are other substances beside food that people can ingest and can leave a trace on archaeologically recoverable human remains. For example, researchers working in the Atacama Desert of northern Chile have found that nicotine was widely consumed by the local population beginning at 100 BC. Traces of nicotine were found in thirty-five of fifty-six hair samples chemically analyzed from a series of mummified remains in this coastal Andean region. Evidence for coca leaf (from which cocaine is made) chewing in the Andes has also been found using hair samples.

Paleopathology

Evidence concerning diseases in past populations can come from many sources. For example, historic texts sometimes refer to epidemics. The Black Plague, which devastated Eurasia during the fourteenth-century AD, is mentioned in numerous historical documents. In other cases, evidence of diseases can come from iconography, such as the explicit ceramic figurines from the island of Jaina, Mexico. The study of disease in the past is termed **paleopathology** and one important source of data on this topic comes from the human remains themselves. In particular, researchers focus on the prevalence or frequency of pathological forms in past populations.

One of the most common paleopathologies identified among archaeological remains is **dental caries**, which is a disease process that results in the demineralization of teeth. Carious lesions, or what we commonly call cavities, are easily identifiable and tend to preserve very well given the durability of teeth. Dental caries is caused by the production of organic acids by bacteria that ferment carbohydrates like sugar and starches. Although dental caries may be found among the members of any past population, there has been a notable correlation of the incidence of this paleopathology and many agricultural subsistence systems; a correlation which is caused by the increase in carbohydrates and a decrease in proteins in highly agriculturally based subsistence systems. For example, studies indicate that populations living in the eastern woodlands of the United States prior to European contact had a lower degree of frequency of carious teeth during the early periods when their subsistence was based on foraging than in later periods when it was based on maize farming. This change in frequency is believed to be caused by the relatively high amount of sucrose in maize.

Periodontal disease, which often results in tooth loss, is another paleopathology that can be detected on skeletal remains. Inflammation of the gums due to plaque buildup can result in the loss of collagen attachment of teeth to the bone; leading to these teeth falling out out prior to death (**antemortem tooth loss** or AMTL, which can also be a result of severe caries). Studies indicate that, just like dental caries, periodontal disease is more common in farming-based subsistence systems. Other paleopathologies that leave signatures on skeletal remains include infections that manifest in the bones, like treponematosis (which includes syphilis, yaws, and pinta), tuberculosis, leprosy, scurvy (a metabolic disease resulting from a lack of vitamin C), and rickets (a metabolic disease that often results in the bowing of long bones).

We must remember that most diseases do not leave any evidence on the skeletal materials. Archaeologists will never be able to see the common cold, the flu, or even the bubonic plague through a macroscopic analysis of skeletal remains. Relatively new biomolecular analyses, however, are beginning to open up new insights into some diseases that have traditionally escaped notice on skeletal remains. In one particularly notable study, researchers were able to recover genetic evidence of the bubonic plague from skeletal remains; the disease had left its genetic footprint on the remains. In another case, researchers have argued that they have been able to identify malaria from skeletal remains through the identification of a particular protein. These kinds of studies will open new possibilities in the study of paleopathologies in the near future.

Trauma and Lifestyle Stress

There is a wide range of traumas that can impact the human body, and only some of those leave traces on skeletal materials. Many of those traumas are the results of accidents (e.g., falling and breaking a leg). Others are the results of intentional behavior, ranging from acts of malicious violence against a person (e.g., a blow to the head) to acts of body modification performed by a person to themselves (e.g., self-amputation of fingers). Even the ways in which some societies craft concepts of beauty on the body may result in traumas.

When addressing incidences of trauma on skeletal remains, researchers pay very close attention to the kinds of damage on the bones. Although it can be very difficult to pinpoint whether a trauma caused the death of an individual, if the area of trauma has evidence of remodeling of the bone, this indicates that some healing occurred and the trauma may not have been a factor in the person's death. For instance, trepanation, surgical removal of part of the skull cap, often shows remodeling of the bone, indicating that people regularly survived such surgical procedures. Healed areas of trauma are referred to as **antemortem** (before death) and, like in the case of trepanation just mentioned, can sometimes give insights into medical practices of past societies.

Other examples of trauma and damage to the body are classified as **perimortem** (around the time of death) or **postmortem** (after death). These kinds of damage do not show evidence of remodeling of the bone, and because of this shared trait can be difficult to distinguish. Therefore, careful scrutiny of both the bones (e.g., sharp, "fresh" breaks are common in perimortem trauma) and the taphonomy of the contexts is important. In terms of perimortem trauma, significant traumatic events can occur just prior to some other factor causing death or at some point soon after death. These small temporal differences are indistinguishable on the skeletal remains. A person might break an arm working, but falls off a cliff three days later; the broken arm having little or nothing to do with death. Alternately, a body may undergo damage after death has occurred. In some cases, that postmortem damage may quickly follow the time of death. For example, the discovery of the remains of King Richard III of England provided researchers with the opportunity to compare the remains with historical accounts of the king's death in the Battle of Bosworth field in AD 1485. Although the remains showed evidence of numerous areas of skeletal trauma, considering the historical context and the bones themselves researchers have argued that the king died from one of two blows to the head by bladed weapons, but that some of the other trauma present on the skeletal remains supported the historical narrative that his body was then stripped of armor and strapped to a horse to suffer further injury. Without this supporting historical information, however, it would have been difficult to distinguish between the perimortem or postmortem injuries. In other cases where the bones have been around for a long time prior to the trauma, postmortem damage can be more easily identified. Even archaeological work can damage the human remains (e.g., shovels or trowels during excavation). Again, special attention to the context often helps to separate perimortem and postmortem traumas.

FIGURE 11.8 Medical instruments, prescriptions, and two goddesses sitting on birthing chairs at the Temple of Kom Ombo, Egypt (second to first centuries BC). Past medical practices are of great interest to bioarchaeologists and can also be studied from a body-oriented perspective.

© Pecold/Shutterstock.com

FIGURE 11.9 Richard III of England (AD 1452–1485).
© Georgios Kollidas/Shutterstock.com

In cases of antemortem and perimortem trauma in particular, distinguishing between accidents and acts of violence is challenging. For instance, trauma to the mid-forearm (often called a parry fracture) is sometimes taken as evidence of someone protecting their head from an attacking blow, often with the left arm. However, some researchers are skeptical that all such breaks are the result of violence. In many cases, bioarchaeologists look to patterning in the ethnographic record to help distinguish between violent and accidental traumas. For example, head traumas (such as depressed cranial fractures) that occur above what is termed the "hat brim line" are more commonly associated with acts of violence than with accidents in contemporary societies. Special attention to the contexts in which the skeletal remains are found can also help to clarify, especially if the trauma in question was the cause of death. Recovering human remains with trauma from sharp objects on a medieval battlefield is highly suggestive of a violent rather than an accidental death. Such is the case of several mass graves dating to the Battle of Visby, which occurred in AD 1361 when a Danish king by the name of Valdemar attacked this city. Evidence from the graves not only shows a high frequency of traumas consistent with swords, axes, and projectiles, but many of the cutting traumas occurred in the area of the lower legs, indicating the use of shields and body armor to protect the trunk. Most cases of trauma are not as easily identified as having violent or accidental causes as the Visby materials and researchers should take care when making interpretations.

Violence can occur in many different kinds of cultural and behavioral contexts. Although warfare and other forms of organized violence in the past get a lot of sensational attention, other forms of violence were often much more impactful in ancient societies. For example, skeletal evidence of domestic abuse and child abuse can be traced back into the past. Another form of violence, common in the modern world, is structural violence. **Structural violence** occurs when social structural conditions prevent people from meeting their basic needs; thus, inflicting harm on them. This harm may not be in the form of physical violence against their bodies (such as cuts or blows), but can manifest in skeletal remains in other ways. For example, if the structure of a society prevented a certain social group (e.g., a lower social class) from having adequate access to meet dietary needs, evidence of malnutrition might occur with some frequency in skeletal remains from this group.

Another factor that can cause trauma on the body is the intentional modification of one's own body for the sake of identity and beauty; what we might term the manipulation of the "social skin." In contemporary western society, we are quite familiar with such modifications. Tattoos, scarification, piercings, and even branding are among the kinds of body modifications that people undergo today. Many people in the past also underwent such body modifications, although unless mummified remains, iconography or texts referencing such modifications, or jewelry associated with them (e.g., ear flares or lip plugs) are found, it is nearly impossible to identify such modifications as they impact the soft tissue (see Chapter 9 for some examples of preserved tattoos). In ancient Maya society, head-shaping and dental modifications were quite common, as were tattoos, scarification, and perforations of the earlobes for ear spools. Yet, researchers only have good burial evidence of the body modifications on the bones

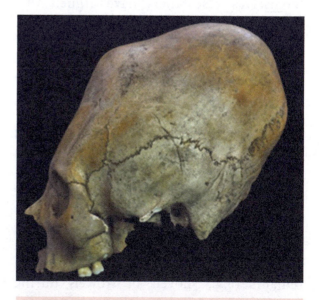

FIGURE 11.10 An example of head-shaping from Yaxuná, Mexico (ca. AD 600–800).

© Vera Tiesler

and teeth. We know about scarification and tattoos from iconography, but given the tropical environment we do not find this kind of data in the skeletal remains themselves.

One, often controversial, area of research into body processing that impacted skeletal material revolves around the question of cannibalism. Evidence from ethnographic and ethnohistoric sources indicates that cannibalism was a practice present in many parts of the world; occurring for a diverse number of reasons including funerary and medicinal practices as well as the use of human flesh as a starvation food. Archaeologically, cannibalism has been difficult to identify as many of the marks made on bones during the processing and consumption of the body can also be made for other reasons unrelated to consumption. For example, researchers working in the American Southwest have argued that certain cut-marks characteristic of butchering of game animals, in conjunction with other evidence such

as thermal modifications and "pot-polish" from the bones having been stirred around in a cooking vessel, indicate that some human remains were processed for consumption. However, there are other explanations for these patterns. For example, noncannibalistic funerary practices may result in all sorts of body processing. The Tibetan sky burials mentioned previously serve as a good illustration that bodies may be processed in ways that can cause great damage and that researchers should be very aware that a wide array of body processing, including intentional defleshing that would leave cut-marks, may have occurred in past cultural contexts. In a rather unique example of evidence of the consumption of human flesh, researchers working at the Ancestral Puebloan site of Cowboy Wash in Colorado discovered a coprolite containing human myoglobin (a protein found in muscle tissue). Given that the context of the abandonment of the site suggested violence and that the human myoglobin could have only been present in the coprolite if human muscle tissue had been consumed, researchers have argued that cannibalism occurred when the site was attacked.

However, most cases of possible cannibalism are not as clear cut, and in some cases, like the American Southwest, are considered an affront to descendant communities.

Moving on from trauma, the human skeleton can also be negatively impacted by stress from activities performed during a person's life. In particular, the excessive repetition of certain kinds of activities (conditioned by a person's lifestyle) can have a negative effect on the human body. We have all probably heard of carpal tunnel syndrome or tennis elbow. These are modern-day ailments suffered by people who perform certain tasks over and over again. This kind of **lifestyle stress** (or **occupational stress**) can be variable within and between populations depending on the presence/absence and distribution of certain kinds of activities in a society. For example, spondylolysis, which is a stress fracture of the vertebral arch, is sometimes caused by repeated hyperextension of the back and mechanically demanding labor.

Research on the island of Guam has demonstrated that both males and females had a high frequency of spondylolysis during the Latte period (AD 1200–1521), attributed to the moving of large megalithic *latte* stones. In another relevant study, research on an Early Neolithic (roughly 9500–8000 BC) sample, the skeletal remains of 162 individuals from the site of Abu Hureyra, Syria, demonstrated a pattern of degenerative damage to the knees, lower vertebrae, and the area of the big toe in females. Researchers argue that these areas of the skeleton receive a lot of stress during the process of grinding grains to eat. The Early Neolithic in the Middle East is when people began to move toward agriculture and grinding stones used to pro-

FIGURE 11.13 A study of skeletal remains from the site of Abu Hureyra, Syria indicate that degenerative damage to the knees, lower vertebrae, and the area of the big toe was caused by the daily use of grinding stones on the ground.

© Kendall Hunt Publishing Company, redrawn from Molleson (1994)

cess plants were found at Abu Hureyra. There are many other examples of lifestyle stress, including osteoarthritis. The difficult part of the research is sometimes not in identifying the stress on the skeletal remains, but explaining what repetitive activities caused this stress.

Migration

Human remains can also provide evidence of the movement of people across the landscape. There are three general methods that researchers utilize to test whether people were deposited in the same area that they spent the majority of their lives (i.e. they were local) or a considerable distance from it (i.e., they were foreign); dental morphology, DNA analysis, and stable and radioactive isotope analysis. Analysis of the **dental morphology** of individuals rests on fundamental ideas from evolutionary theory and population genetics. The shapes of teeth are sensitive to evolutionary change and tracking the changing distribution of certain morphological attributes of teeth might indicate movement of people. For example, certain attributes might be common in one population and absent in another at one period. During a subsequent period, those traits might be present in both populations. Citing **gene flow** (transfer of genetic material from one population to another), researchers use such evidence as a proxy for migration, not just the transfer of genetic material.

More recently, DNA analysis has been used to attempt to reconstruct the genetic similarity among individuals. In some cases, researchers have employed this analysis to determine whether a sample of individuals might have been related by blood (e.g., whether all of the bodies found in a single burial context were part of the same family). In other cases, archaeologists have compared the genetic relationship between populations to track gene flow. In this latter sense, the topic of migration is relevant. For example, researchers working with modern-day genetic data in Africa have suggested that they indicate a spread of people with Bantu Niger-Kordofanian ancestry from what is today Nigeria and Cameroon into eastern and southern parts of the continent over the past 5,000 years. Using archaeological DNA is more complicated, given the issues of recovery and preservation discussed previously. But, it is important to point out that regardless of whether the data come from modern or archaeological populations, what is being measured is **biological distance** (how genetically similar DNA samples are), not necessarily movement of people.

The most widely utilized data to infer migration come from stable isotope analyses; although one of the strontium isotopes sometimes utilized is radioactive rather than stable. As we have seen, stable isotope analyses can be used to reconstruct paleodiets. They can also be used to map movements of people. Although the stable isotopes utilized for studies of migration tend to be different from those used in dietary reconstructions, the fundamentals are the same; you are what you consume. In the case of migration, it is often the water that a person drank that is being measured, not the food. Water has particular chemical compositions in different regions. Certain isotopes in the water, such as strontium (Sr), are fundamentally determined by the surrounding bedrock from which it is taken; thus, linking the chemistry of the human body with a region. Oxygen isotopes are also commonly used for migration reconstructions, but, as we have seen (Chapter 9), are more an indicator of climate conditions and the source of the water (which, importantly, can vary from region to region) rather than the geology. Other stable isotopes, such as sulfur (S) and lead (Pb), are also utilized in migration studies, but have not proven as effective as strontium and oxygen as of yet.

Where the isotopes are sampled from can tell you different things concerning the whereabouts of an individual at different stages of his or her life. As mentioned previously, the enamel of teeth do not remodel; they signal the geological conditions during the time of their growth. Thus, using teeth researchers can estimate where individuals spent the early part of his or her life. But different teeth and even different parts of a single tooth can give different results if the person was moving around during

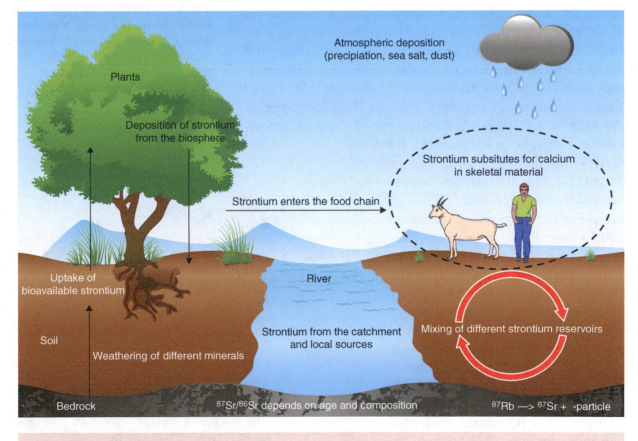

FIGURE 11.14 The strontium cycle.

© Kendall Hunt Publishing Company

these early years of life. For example, the enamel of first permanent molars develops during the first three years of life and therefore expresses the geology of the place of residence during early infancy. Other teeth develop a bit later.

In a study of an Early Classic (ca. AD 300–500) royal tomb at the Maya site of Yaxuná, Mexico, researchers used strontium isotopes data to identify the tomb's occupant as a foreigner, not fitting within the local variation of strontium values. Archaeological evidence suggested that this tomb was the earliest for a possible king at the site, fitting a pattern across some sites in Maya lowlands at the time whereby foreign individuals from the core central area of the lowlands migrated to sites nearer to the edges of the Maya area to found new dynastic lines, some of whom were commemorated for centuries in hieroglyphic texts and iconography.

Mortuary Contexts

Researchers studying the dead do not just focus their efforts on the study of the human remains themselves, but also on the contexts in which they were found. How the dead were treated can tell archaeologists a tremendous amount about past societies. Sometimes, mortuary contexts are simple, even consisting of a shallow hole dug into the Earth with a body and nothing more. In other cases, mortuary contexts can be sensational, such as a tomb with sumptuous offerings buried deep within a monumental structure, such as the Classic period Maya king of K'inich Janab Pakal's tomb at the archaeological site of Palenque in Mexico, or a royal cemetery like the Valley of the Kings in Egypt. Yet, regardless of how simple or complex mortuary contexts are, at some point in the past our ancestors began to form the first ideas of something beyond this world, something that required special treatment of the body after death. Such a cognitively important moment in human history this would have been, to be the first to contemplate death in the context that it might not be the end of the individual, that there might be some social life for the deceased beyond death. Such a realization has important existential implications for how we as humans situate ourselves in the broader idea of a cosmos. But, more practically for the

FIGURE 11.15 Mortuary contexts, as places of commemoration of the dead, are often focal points for social memory, such as this stone ship burial at Gettlinge, Sweden (such features date to both the first-millennium BC and AD).

© almgren/Shutterstock.com

FIGURE 11.16 The Temple of the Inscriptions at Palenque, Mexico; K'inich Janab Pakal's mortuary monument.

Palenque, Mexico. Temple of the Inscriptions, Aznar Cenamor, Fernando/ Private Collection/Bridgeman Images

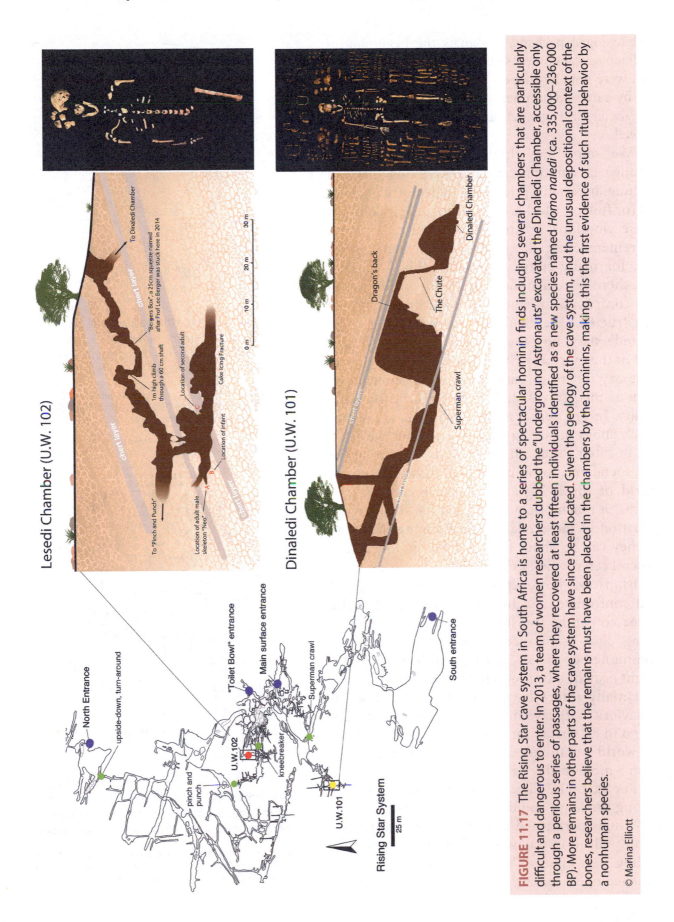

FIGURE 11.17 The Rising Star cave system in South Africa is home to a series of spectacular hominin finds including several chambers that are particularly difficult and dangerous to enter. In 2013, a team of women researchers dubbed the "Underground Astronauts" excavated the Dinaledi Chamber, accessible only through a perilous series of passages, where they recovered at least fifteen individuals identified as a new species named *Homo naledi* (ca. 335,000–236,000 BP). More remains in other parts of the cave system have since been located. Given the geology of the cave system, and the unusual depositional context of the bones, researchers believe that the remains must have been placed in the chambers by the hominins, making this the first evidence of such ritual behavior by a nonhuman species.

© Marina Elliott

archaeologist perhaps, it signals the beginning of archaeological contexts containing human remains that were not just shaped by taphonomic processes, but by a myriad number of social processes, including social class, gender, and identity construction, as well.

We sometimes think of death as eliciting a range of emotions among the living that can include anger and grief, and that mortuary rituals (or funeral rites) are ways that people confront those emotions, create closure, and create ways of remembering the deceased. In many senses and for many cultural contexts, this is correct. Yet, there is tremendous variability in how societies confront death and how the dead are socially constructed. The challenge for archaeologists is to understand how the material remains and context of the mortuary ritual (such as body position, funerary offerings, and "mortuary containers" such as pits, graves, and tombs) reflect this variability. In one sense, mortuary rituals are just as much about the living as they are about the dead. Death often results in momentous transitions in the social relationships among those left in the world of the living and mortuary contexts can be just a much a material reflection of the renegotiation of those relationships among the living as they can be about the dead. In another sense, funeral ceremonies are moments when social relationships can be renegotiated, grief is expressed and confronted, and in many societies when the deceased can be transformed into a new kind of being, such as an ancestor or ghost, that can be communed or socially engaged with; a being that might provide advice and protection, or that could potentially inflict harm. Whole hosts of social behaviors that leave material evidence of this are found in extremely varied expressions throughout the world and these can be difficult to understand from a modern-day perspective.

For example, Classic period mortuary rituals among the Maya could be prolonged, with different rituals performed at various times to transition the dead into new social entities, eventually ending in a kind of "posthumous" social death. Archaeologists know that many mortuary contexts

FIGURE 11.18 This stone altar from the Maya site of Tikal, Guatemala, shows the disinterment of a noble woman's bones from a tomb. The context carries a date of December 3, AD 711.

Schele Number: SD-2021, Drawing of Tikal Site, Maya Culture, Altar 5. Drawing by Linda Schele. Copyright © David Schele. Photo courtesy of Ancient Americas as LACMA.

FIGURE 11.19 Parading an ancestor mummy in Inka society; from Guaman Poma's early seventeenth-century indigenous manuscript detailing the injustices of colonial Spanish rule in the Andes.

Facsimile of a drawing by Felipe Guaman Poma from his "El Primer Nueva Coronica y Buen Gobierno"/Werner Forman Archive/Bridgeman Images

were reentered, in some cases centuries after the deposition of the body, and human remains manipulated for ancestor veneration and to transition the socially alive, but physically dead individuals toward new identities and roles in Maya society. In Inka society, mummified ancestors of ruler were not only brought out for public viewing for important occasions, they were actually continued to control landholdings through the empire. In these two cases, researchers know a great deal about the role of mortuary rituals from written sources and iconography. However, many mortuary contexts throughout the world lack such data, such as Bronze Age barrows in Europe where the **comingled** (mixed) remains of numerous individuals were sometimes placed together in a single context. In the end, human remains and their contexts provide a wealth of data for researchers, but arriving at inferences regarding their meaning can be challenging.

Bibliography

Angel, J. Lawrence. *Early Skeletons from Tranquility, California.* Smithsonian Contributions to Anthropology, Vol. 2, No 1. Washington, DC: Smithsonian Press, 1966.

Appleby, Jo, Guy N. Rutty, Sarah V. Hainsworth, Robert C. Woosnam-Savage, Bruno Morgan, Alison Brough, Richard W. Earp, Claire Robinson, Turi E. King, Mathew Morris, and Richard Buckley. "Perimortem Trauma in King Richard III: A Skeletal Analysis." *The Lancet* 385, no. 9964 (2015): 253–259.

Arriaza, Bernardo T. "Spondylolysis in Prehistoric Remains from Guam and its Possible Etiology." *American Journal of Physical Anthropology* 98 (1997): 37–45.

Berger, Lee R., John Hawks, Darryl J. de Ruiter, Steven E. Churchill, Peter Schmid, Lucas K. Delezene, Tracy L. Kivell, Heather M. Garvin, Scott A. Williams, Jeremy M. DeSilva, Matthew M. Skinner, Charles M. Musiba, Noel Cameron, Trenton W. Holliday, William Harcourt-Smith, Rebecca R. Ackermann, Markus Bastir, Barry Bogin, Debra Bolter, Juliet Brophy, Zachary D. Cofran, Kimberly A. Congdon, Andrew S. Deane, Mana Dembo, Michelle Drapeau, Marina C. Elliott, Elen M. Feuerriegel, Daniel Garcia-Martinez, David J. Green, Alia Gurtov, Joel D. Irish, Ashley Kruger, Myra F. Laird, Damiano Marchi, Marc R. Meyer, Shahed Nalla, Enquye W. Negash, Caley M. Orr, Davorka Radovcic, Lauren Schroeder, Jill E. Scott, Zachary Throckmorton, Matthew W. Tocheri, Caroline VanSickle, Christopher S. Walker, Pianpian Wei, and Bernhard Zipfel. "*Homo naledi*, a New Species of the Genus *Homo* from the Dinaledi Chamber, South Africa." *eLIFE* 4 (2015): e09560. doi:10.7554/eLife.09560

Bianucci, Raffaella, Lila Rahalison, Emma R. Massa, Alberto Peluso, Ezio Ferroglio, and Michel Signoli. "A Rapid Diagnostic Test Detects Plague in Ancient Human Remains: An Example of the Interaction between Archaeological and Biological Approaches (Southeastern France, 16th-18th Century)." *American Journal of Physical Anthropology* 136 (2008): 361–367.

Bridges, Patricia S. "Osteological Correlates of Weapon Use." In *A Life in Science: Papers in Honor of J. Lawrence Angel,* edited by J. E. Buikstra, 87–98. Scientific Papers, No. 6. Kampsville, IL: Center for American Archaeology, 1990.

Buikstra, Jane, and Douglas Ubelaker, eds. *Standards for Data Collection from Human Skeletal Remains.* Arkansas Archaeological Survey Research Series no. 44. Fayetteville, NC: Arkansas Archaeological Survey, 1994.

Buikstra, Jane E., and Lane A. Beck, eds. *Bioarchaeology: The Contextual Analysis of Human Remains.* New York: Routledge, 2017.

Campbell, Michael C., and Sarah A. Tishkoff. "The Evolution of Human Genetic and Phenotypic Variation in Africa." *Current Biology* 20, no. 4 (2010): R166–R173.

Cartmell, Larry W., Arthur C. Aufderheide, Angela Springfield, Cheryl Weems, and Bernardo Arriaza. "The Frequency and Antiquity of Prehistoric Coca-Leaf-Chewing Practices in Northern Chile: Radioimmunoassay of a Cocaine Metabolite in Human-Mummy Hair." *Latin American Antiquity* 2, no. 3 (1991): 260–268.

Cassidy, Claire M. "Skeletal Evidence for Prehistoric Subsistence Adaptation in the Central Ohio River Valley." In *Paleopathology at the Origins of agriculture*, edited by M. N. Cohen and G. J. Armelagos, 307–345. New York: Academic Press, 1984.

de la Cruz, Isabel, Angélica González Oliver, Brian M. Kemp, Juan A. Román, David Glenn Smith, and Alfonso Torre Blanco. "Sex Identification of Children Sacrificed to the Ancient Aztec Rain Gods in Tlatelolco." *Current Anthropology* 49, no. 3 (2008): 519–526.

Duday, Henri. *The Archaeology of the Dead: Lectures in Archaeothanatology.* Oxford: Oxbow Books, 2009.

Echeverría, Javier, and Hermann M. Niemeyer. "Nicotine in the Hair of Mummies from San Pedro de Atacama (Northern Chile)." *Journal of Archaeological Science* 40 (2013): 3561–3568.

Eriksson, Gunilla. "Stable Isotope Analysis of Humans." In *The Archaeology of Death and Burial*, edited by S. Tarlow and L. Nilsson Stutz, 123–146. Oxford: Oxford University Press, 2013.

Fischer, Christian. *Tollundmanden: gaven til guderne: mosefund fra Danmarks forhistorie.* Silkeborg: Silkeborg Museum, 2007.

Fornaciari, Gino, Valentina Giuffra, Ezio Ferroglio, Sarah Gino, and Raffaella Bianucci. *Plasmodium falciparum* "Immunodetection in Bone Remains of Members of the Renaissance Medici Family (Florence, Ital, Sixteenth Century)." *Transactions of the Royal Society of Tropical Medicine and Hygiene* 104 (2010): 583–587.

Frankenberg, Susan R., and Lyle W. Konigsberg. "A Brief History of Paleodemography from Hooton to Hazards Analysis." In *Bioarchaeology: The Contextual Analysis of Human Remains*, edited by J. E. Buikstra and L. A. Beck, 227–261. New York: Routledge, 2017.

Fujita, H., H. Hashimoto, S. Shoda, and T. Suzuki. "Dental Caries Prevalence as a Product of Agriculture and Subsistence Pattern at the Yean-ri Site, South Korea." *Caries Research* 45 (2011): 524–531.

Galtung, Johan. "Violence, Peace, and Peace Research." *Journal of Peace Research* 6, no. 3 (1969): 167–191.

Ingelmark, Bo E. "The Skeletons." In *Armour from the Battle of Wisby 1361*, edited by B. Thordeman, 149–209. Stockholm: Vitterhets Histoire och Antikvitets Akademien, 1939.

Lambert, Patricia M. "Violent Injury and Death in a Prehistoric Farming Community of Southwestern Colorado." In *The Routledge Handbook of the Bioarchaeology of Human Conflict*, edited by C. Knüsel, and M. J. Smith, 308–332. London: Routledge, 2014.

Lambert, Patricia M., Banks L. Leonard, Brian R. Billman, Richard A. Marlar, Margaret E. Newman and Karl J. Reinhard. "Response to Critique of the Claim of Cannibalism at Cowboy Wash." *American Antiquity* 10, no. 2 (2000): 397–406.

Larsen, Clark S. *Bioarchaeology: Interpreting Behavior from the Human Skeleton.* 2nd ed. Cambridge: Cambridge University Press, 2015.

Larsen, Clark S., Rebecca Shavit, and Mark C. Griffin. "Dental Caries Evidence for Dietary Change: An Archaeological Context." In *Advances in Dental Anthropology*, edited by M. A. Kelley and C. S. Larsen, 179–202. New York: Wiley-Liss, 1991.

Lovejoy, C. O. "Dental Wear in the Libben Population: Its Functional Pattern and Role in the Determination of Adult Skeletal Age at Death." *American Journal of Physical Anthropology* 68 (1985): 47–56.

Lovejoy, C. O., R. S. Meindl, T. R. Pryzbeck, and R. P. Mensforth. "Chronological Metamorphosis of the Auricular Surface of the Ilium: A New Method for the Determination of Adult Skeletal Age at Death." *American Journal of Physical Anthropology* 68 (1985): 15–28.

Lukacs, John R. "Dental Paleopathology and Agricultural Intensification in South Asia: New Evidence from Bronze Age Harappa." *American Journal of Physical Anthropology* 87 (1992): 133–150.

Martin, Simon, and Nikolai Grube. *Chronicle of the Maya Kings and Queens: Deciphering the Dynasties of the Ancient Maya*. 2nd ed. New York: Thames and Hudson, 2008.

McAnany, Patricia A. *Living with the Ancestors*. Austin: The University of Texas Press, 1995.

McNeil, William H. *Plagues and Peoples*. Garden City, NY: Anchor Press, 1998.

Milanich, Jerald T. *Archaeology of Precolumbian Florida*. Gainesville, FL: University of Florida Press, 1994.

Molleson, Theya. "The Eloquent Bones of Abu Hureyra." *Scientific American* 271, no. 2 (1994): 70–75.

Moore, James A., Alan C. Swedlund, and George J. Armelagos. "The Use of Life Tables in Paleodemography." In *Population Studies in Archaeology and Biological Anthropology: A Symposium*, edited by A. C. Swedlund, 57–70. Memoirs of the Society for American Archaeology, No. 30. Washington, DC: Society for American Archaeology, 1975.

Pennel, C. R. "Cannibalism in Early Modern North Africa." *British Journal of Middle Eastern Studies* 18, no. 2 (1991): 169–185.

Pezo Lanfranco, Luis, and Sabine Eggers. "The Usefulness of Caries Frequency, Depth, and Location in Determining Cariogenecity and Past Subsistence: A Test on Early and Later Agriculturalists from the Peruvian Coast." *American Journal of Physical Anthropology* 143 (2010): 75–91.

Sprague, Roderick. *Burial Terminology: A Guide for Researchers*. Lanham, MD: AltaMira Press, 2005.

Temple, D. H., and Clark S. Larsen. "Bioarchaeological Perspectives on Systemic Stress during the Agricultural Transition in Prehistoric Japan." In *Bioarchaeology of East Asia: Movement, Contact, Health*, edited by E. Pechenkina and M. Oxenham, 344–367. Gainesville: University Press of Florida, 2013.

Thordeman, Bengt. *Armour from the Battle of Wisby 1361*. Stockholm: Vitterhets Histoire och Antikvitets Akademien, 1939.

Tiesler, Vera, Andrea Cucina, Travis W. Stanton, and David A. Freidel. *Before Kukulkán: Maya Life, Death, and Identity at Classic Period Yaxuná*. Tucson: University of Arizona Press, 2017.

Tung, Tiffany. "Gender-Based Violence in the Wari and Post-Wari Era of the Andes." In *The Routledge Handbook of the Bioarchaeology of Human Conflict*, edited by C. Knüsel, and M. J. Smith, 333–354. London: Routledge, 2014.

Turner, Christy G., II, and Jacqueline A. Turner. *Man Corn: Cannibalism and Violence in the Prehistoric American Southwest*. Salt Lake City: University of Utah Press, 1999.

Wakely, Jennifer. "Identification and Analysis of Violent and Non-Violent Head Injuries in Osteo-Archaeological Materials." In *Material Harm: Archaeological Studies of War and Violence*, edited by J. Carman, 24–46. Glasgow: Cruithne Press, 1997.

Walker, Phillip L. "A Bioarchaeological Perspective on the History of Violence." *Annual Review of Anthropology* 30 (2001): 573–596.

White, Timothy. *Prehistoric Cannibalism at Mancos 5MTUMR-2346*. Princeton: Princeton University, 1992.

Wilson, Andrew S. "Hair as a Bioresource in Archaeological Study." In *Hair in Toxicology: An Important Bio-Monitor*, edited by D. J. Tobin, 321–345. Cambridge: RSC Publishing, 2005.

Settlement, Subsistence, and Exchange

As we have seen, archaeologists collect a wide range of primary data in the field. With these data, they can approach all sorts of research questions. Three important and interrelated topics that have been of primary interest to the field for quite some time concern settlement, subsistence, and exchange. All archaeological data have spatial components to them. **Settlement archaeology** is the study of human activities in space; it concerns situations as diverse as the organization of the small spaces of daily household activities to large-scale considerations of how populations were dispersed over substantial regions. Subsistence data also have a spatial component to them. How mobile foragers found food on a landscape (e.g., moving from place to place based on the availability of specific food items) or how sedentary farmers exploited resources (e.g., arable land or water sources) is inherently spatial and impacts how settlement was organized. Subsistence practices are also an important part of economic systems, but are not, by any stretch of the imagination, the only variable to consider how economies work. So, moving on to considering economic aspects of societies, exchange transactions, as we might surmise, also have a spatial component. Much more often than not, terms like trade and exchange imply the movement of things, information, and people across a landscape. And, to bring it back full circle, settlements, such as households and cities, are also critical components in how economic, social, and political systems work. Thus, in this chapter we will review these three topics together, although each may be studied on its own depending on the research questions of interest to the archaeologist.

Settlement Archaeology

As we just mentioned, settlement archaeology concerns the spatial aspects of human activities. And, as we saw in Chapter 6, human activities, and their material correlates, can be examined at different spatial scales, as small as the spatial arrangement of the objects on your desk (which is a small activity area) to the distribution of settlements throughout a region. In the history of the field, serious considerations of spatial questions really began at the regional level. In 1953, Gordon Willey, an archaeologist who worked throughout the Americas, published the first study of **settlement patterns** (which is the distributional study of material evidence for human occupation) by examining the surface evidence for occupations in region, in this case the Viru Valley of the coast of Peru. His groundbreaking work led to an explosion of settlement pattern archaeology beginning in the 1960s with the development of processual archaeology. Given the interest in past peoples' relationships to the environment among processual archaeologists (see Chapter 4), settlement pattern archaeology had great appeal; the natural environment could be taken into consideration in studies of how people distributed themselves and their activities over the landscape. Studies of smaller spatial scales, such as activity areas, soon followed and during the 1980s there was a more concerted focus on households. In this section, we examine settlement archaeology starting at the smallest of spatial scales (activity areas) and move toward increasingly larger scale analyses of human settlement; always keeping in mind that there is no better or more important scale than another. Archaeological research at any scale provides rich information on human activities and research questions or hypotheses are keys to address issues we want to better understand.

Activity Areas and Trash

The smallest scale of human activity that archaeologists examine is termed the **activity area**, a relatively small space where an activity or a specific set of activities were performed in the past. An activity area might have been the result of a onetime event; for example, a hunter stopping to sharpen a stone tool, leaving the material evidence of this fleeting moment in the lithic debitage left behind. It could also have been the product of generations upon generations of people using a space over time; for example, a kitchen space in a household occupied for centuries. Regardless of the time span for the activity area to form (which is important as it indicates whether or not the activity was repetitive), it represents a specific locus of human activity. Understanding where certain activities took place in space can help archaeologists answer all kinds of questions ranging from divisions of labor and social organization to how the economy was organized and people's experiences in the past.

Archaeologists usually demarcate past activity areas based on the spatial distribution of artifacts, ecofacts, features, and chemical data that reflect certain kinds of repeated activities. For example, food preparation areas can be associated with hearths, grinding stones, cooking jars and bowls (which are often blackened by fire), and certain chemical signatures in the soil, such as phosphates and proteins, which are good indicators of past organic material. Craft production in a workshop might be indicated in the trash expected for the manufacture of certain kinds of products (e.g., lithic debitage for stone tool production), as well as the tools needed to work the raw materials (e.g., hammerstones) and the raw materials themselves. In fact, trash is not only a critical element of activity area studies, but is one of the most important data sets that archaeologists have to work with. A person's trash can tell us an awfully lot about them, including things that have to do with consumption, socioeconomic status, health, age, education, and religion, among others, and it is worthwhile for us to discuss the topic trash in some detail here.

We often call archaeology the "science of trash." Regardless of whether you call it trash, rubbish, garbage, or refuse, archaeologists often find the most informative data in **middens** (trash deposits) or, more generally, in the things that past people threw away or left behind. Some middens are very large and highly stratified, often the result of dumping activities. Others are very thin and spread out, called **sheet middens**, often the result of the tossing of trash around a living space and/or activity area. Some middens were formed in relatively short amounts of time, whereas others were the result of depositional processes that occurred over centuries. And, the activities that generated midden materials can vary widely, affecting the kinds of materials that archaeologists find as well as the morphology of the trash deposits. Archaeologists have even gone so far as to create typologies of trash based on the kinds of activities that produced deposits. In one scheme, trash is divided into domestic (household trash), ceremonial (e.g., the remains of a ritual feast), and production (e.g., workshop debris) categories. Nonetheless, not all things left behind are the remains of trash. For example, some things left behind were forgotten or intentionally deposited as something highly meaningful. There are cases of artifacts, like heavy ground-stones, being cached in the ground by mobile peoples who did not want to carry them throughout the year, anticipating that they would return to dig them up the next time they passed through the area. This kind of behavior is called **curation**. Obviously, if an archaeologist finds a cache like this, for one reason or another the people never came back to reclaim the material culture. In other cases, material culture is deposited someplace as an offering. In such circumstances, there is often the assumption that there was never an anticipation of recovery, but that the past peoples intended to leave the material culture in a place forever. In Mesoamerica, it is quite common to come across such offerings, informing us of the ideology of past peoples. But, while all things "left behind" can be informative of activity areas, trash is particularly useful and is usually, however it is conceptualized (e.g., domestic, ritual, etc.), the most common data category with which archaeologists have to work.

Human refuse disposal is not a singular behavior. In fact, Michael Schiffer cautions that archaeologists should systematically study the formation process of refuse disposal because refuse activities vary greatly (see also Chapter 7). According to Schiffer, we can broadly divide refuse behaviors into five categories. Primary **refuse** refers to situations where people discard their items at its location of use, whereas **secondary refuse** means that the use and discard locations are different. **Tertiary refuse** refers to objects were twice removed from the location of use; moving the trash from a provisional trash area to a more permanent one. Because people seldom discard their objects at their activity area, most middens were the result of secondary or tertiary refuse disposals. **Provisional refuse** refers to broken or worn-out objects are not discarded, but stored for potential future use; basically saving borderline items that might be trash, but might also be useful. Finally, *de facto* **refuse** consists of the tools, facilities, structures, and other cultural materials that, although still usable, are left behind when an activity area is abandoned. *De facto* refuse deposition, in many cases, occurs in unusual situations such as volcanic eruptions, earthquakes, and warfare. Pompeii is one of the most prominent examples of *de facto* refuse. A sudden volcanic eruption in

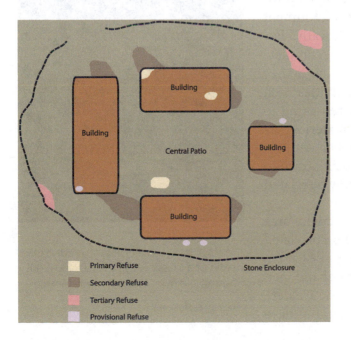

FIGURE 12.1 A schematic of a domestic complex showing where different kinds of refuse might be found. Primary refuse would be found in places where activities took place, such as inside structures and in the central patio (*de facto* refuse might also be found in these areas). The secondary refuse here is trash that has been swept off the central patio. The tertiary refuse areas are dumps where secondary refuse has been further removed.

Source: Travis Stanton

AD 79 covered the large part of the city that killed and buried its inhabitants, but simultaneously preserved most artifacts, ecofacts, and even people (primarily as void spaces) *in situ*. Nevertheless, Schiffer points out that archaeologists should not believe the "Pompeii Premise," an assumption that all floor assemblages straightforwardly reflect the organization of groups, differences among groups and individuals, and patterns of activities. In other words, even under unusual situations people still carry away certain items and not all the objects found in such contexts might reflect the total number of objects (those that might preserve at least) that were used in a space.

When thinking about activity areas, archaeologists must also be wary of the sequence of deposition. Refuse deposits can result from preabandonment (when the area was being initially used), abandonment (as people were leaving, which involves different activities and trash disposal patterns), or postabandonment (people who returned to leave things there, but who were not living there or using it as before) activities. For example, several ethnoarchaeological studies in the Maya Highlands indicate that refuse is differently treated according to size and type during preabandonment times. In these communities, most domestic vessels were discarded once a month, but sweat-bath rocks and ritual food preparation vessels were abandoned once or twice a year. Knives and machetes wore out once every three to five years. Finally, *metates* (stone tool for grinding grains) and axes were discarded only once per generation. Spatially, these studies suggest that preabandonment trash is deposited in five general areas:

- Objects lost in "artifact traps," such as under furniture.
- Artifacts swept to the edges of activity areas such as patios, called **maintenance disposal**.
- Damaged objects stored in out of sight areas where they could be potentially retrieved to be reused, **provisional discard**.
- Zone around the house where trash can be thrown, called a **toft zone**.
- Formal trash dumps.

Archaeological studies of trash at Maya sites like Chunchucmil confirm that these kinds of preabandonment disposal practices, although variable in time, also occurred prior to the arrival of Europeans to the New World. Abandonment processes, however, impact disposal practices greatly. For example, people generally begin to let trash accumulate in living areas and leave heavy objects of less value if they anticipate leaving an area. Postabandonment activities such as using an old living area as a trash dump or returning to perform ritual activities can also leave distinct material patterns of trash. Therefore, understanding the context, stratigraphy, and chronology of deposits is critical for using trash in archaeological interpretations, much of which may be related to activity areas.

Rapidly abandoned sites are often prized for activity area research as the artifacts are often assumed to be correlated with the specific areas in which they were used. Joya de Cerén, an archaeological site located in El Salvador, was abandoned rapidly because the volcanic eruption of Laguna de Caldera around AD 600. Unlike Pompeii, where people did not have

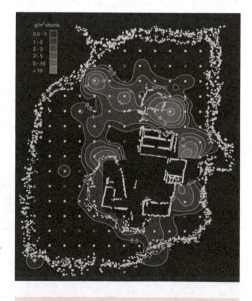

FIGURE 12.2 Density of trash around the patio of a Classic Maya (ca. AD 400–700) household from Chunchucmil, Mexico.

© Scott R. Hutson

time to escape from volcanic eruption, people at Joya de Cerén appear to have survived; their remains have not been found at the site and it is argued that they abandoned the site as the volcano, located a mere 1.4 km away, began to show signs of increased activity. However, they did not have time enough to bring their belongings with them, resulting in a situation where rich household artifact assemblages were left *in situ*. Payson Sheets and his team working at Joya de Cerén have discovered activity areas such as sleeping spaces, kitchens, storage areas, workshops, ritual spaces, and gardens throughout the site with most of the original artifact assemblage relatively intact; in many cases organic remains including maize plants left void spaces in the matrix much as the bodies at Pompeii. With these data, Sheets and his colleagues have been able to reconstruct many activity areas and have even discovered possible gender-oriented spaces. The gender division of activity areas in households has also been reported at other Mesoamerican sites such as Tierras Largas in the Oaxaca Valley of Mexico and Aguateca in the Petexbatún region of Guatemala. Nevertheless, care must be taken in assigning spaces to particular groups of people and we must always remember that spaces were never static; remember the idea of biography of space discussed in Chapter 10. For instance, Christine Hastorf, an archaeologist working in the Upper Mantaro valley of Peru, discovered out that the distribution of maize remains changed over time in this area; maize production having a gendered aspect to it. She concluded that the Inka conquest of the valley in AD 1460 provoked increase in men's control of women's activities for male-oriented public activities such as feasting.

Although the kinds of *in situ* artifact data found at sites like Joya de Cerén and Pompeii are tremendously informative to understand activity areas, they are also quite rare. In many cases, people constantly cleaned activity areas and the kinds of artifactual data that could be used to reconstruct the kinds of activities that took place in a space are no longer in association with the context. For example, when abandoning sites, people often took their valuable belongings with them, leaving few artifacts and ecofacts on the floor. What archaeologists find after excavations might be a relatively empty room. Given this situation, archaeologists have developed a variety of multi-scalar methods to reconstruct subtle traces on the surfaces on which people worked and lived. The most common methods that archaeologists employ concern the study of soil chemistry and micro-remains. By using techniques like fine-screening and flotation on a sample of excavated matrix, especially those associated with living surfaces, archaeologists can detect micro-remains from activities performed in spaces; things like micro-debitage and seeds that would escape normal screening methods. Studies of soil chemistry have become increasingly important in archaeology. Many activities leave residues on living surfaces. And, these residues can survive for long periods of time, being detectable in the chemical composition of the matrix or on a prepared floor surface. For example, storage rooms tend to contain grains and other food remains, which can be detectable through flotation and

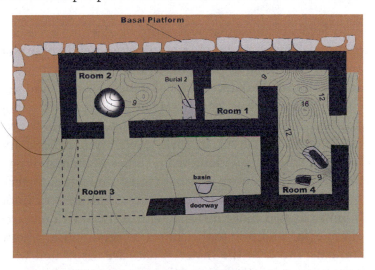

FIGURE 12.3 High phosphorus levels around two grinding stones in a Classic Maya domestic structure at the site of Chunchucmil, Mexico, suggest a food preparation function (in Room 4).

© Aline Magnoni

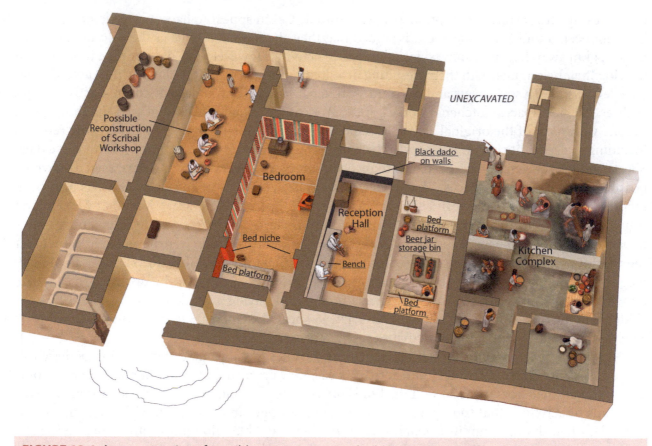

FIGURE 12.4 A reconstruction of possible activity areas in a building on the Giza Plateau of Egypt.

© 2018 Ancient Egypt Research Associates. Drawing by Wilma Wetterstrom. AERA_HouseUnit1.tif

high levels of phosphates. Resting or sleeping areas are usually generally poor in chemical compounds, whereas cooking areas are often rich in phosphates and have high pH values. Consumption areas are also rich in phosphates, but tend to have low pH values. These chemical signatures allow archaeologists to detect ancient kitchen, storage, and sleeping areas, as well as food preparation and consumption spaces, gardens, fruit tree areas, workshops, and staging areas that include preparation areas for farming, crop procession, or resource procurement. For instance, at the archaeological site of Çatalhöyük in Turkey, Wendy Matthews and her colleagues analyzed the microscopic layers in which they identified residues of animal dung. This evidence suggested to the researchers that some rooms were used as stables; important material evidence of early animal domestication.

In the end, the study activity areas can be very informative. But, there are a few issues to keep in mind as you move forward with activity area research. First, as with everything in archaeology, pay special attention to the context. Keep in mind whether you are looking at primary or secondary contexts and how the material data are associated with the space. Second, think about who may have been using the space. We have mentioned gendered-oriented spaces, but in reality there are all sorts of groups of people who might have been more associated with one space than another. Although identifying certain groups of people with particular spaces can be challenging, it is worthwhile to think about. Third, always remember that while you may identify certain activities in certain areas, this is not to say that those were the only activities that occurred in those spaces. Think about your kitchen. Archaeologists in the future might find the material evidence for the storage,

FIGURE 12.5 Popular culture has populated the spaces of Mesoamerican ballcourts with teams who are playing for survival (the losing team sacrificed according to these narratives). Yet, the ballgame was likely played in many different contexts; researchers know that in some instances gambling occurred, whereas in others the winning team given the ability to rob lingering spectators after the games. Here, we see a West Mexican ceramic scene (left) of the ballgame being played (ca. 200 BC to AD 500, courtesy of the Los Angeles County Museum of Art), juxtaposed with an actual ballcourt from the site of Cantona, Mexico (right) (ca. AD 600–900). It is rare that archaeologists get to see such spaces represented with people from a past point of view.

Source: Travis Stanton

Ball Court Model. Mexico, Nayarit, 200 B.C. - A.D. 500. Ceramic with slip and other pigments. 6 × 8 1/2 × 13 1/2 in. (15.24 × 21.59 × 34.29 cm). Los Angeles County Museum of Art, The Proctor Stafford Collection, purchased with funds provided by Mr. and Mrs. Allan C. Balch (M.86.296.34). Photo © Museum Associates/LACMA

preparation, and consumption of food there. But, maybe you also study in your kitchen, read this book, or watch television. Spaces most often have multiple functions, although the degree to which certain activities occur in them can vary. Fourth, some activities will not leave any material evidence; they are "invisible'" to the archaeologist. Maybe some of those activities are invisible because the material culture is no longer there; you take your books with you when you move. Other activities simply might not have any sort of materiality associated with them; for example, singing and dancing. Archaeologists need to be mindful that they will not have any chance of recovering certain activities; although sometimes iconography or epigraphy can help when other material evidence is lacking. Finally, as we mentioned previously, spaces can change over time. Your garage may have at one time had a car parked in it. Then it may have been turned into a workshop. After, it may have been even turned into a guest bedroom. Using the idea of the biography of place, archaeologists in the future might be able to reconstruct some of these changes using different kinds of data sets.

Households

The household is often considered the most fundamental social unit in archaeological research. It is the basic building block of societies; how most people begin to situate themselves in broader social contexts. But, what is the household? We often think of it as a synonym for a family or extended-family and in fact, anthropologists and archaeologists over half a century ago did not differentiate the term household from those of kinship and dwelling. However, more recent research based on accumulated ethnographic and ethnohistoric data from different parts of the world has demonstrated that bloodlines and lineages are not always the basis for households and that dwellings often hold people from different biological groups. Archaeologists have also realized that just because two houses share the same architectural design does not mean that the same activities necessarily took place in both, leading researchers to point out that anthropologists should study what people actually do in households rather than what their physical spaces look like. This is not to say that the way in which dwellings are spatially configured is not important. Living in an open longhouse is very different in some ways than living in a compartmentalized series of spaces like the cliff dwellings of the American Southwest. It means that just because two spaces were the same, that archaeologists should not assume that the activities performed in them were as well.

Following this anthropological approach, Richard Wilk and Wendy Ashmore, two pioneers in household research, define **household archaeology** as the study of a social group who shares certain activities that include production, distribution, consumption, pooling

FIGURE 12.6 A ceramic depiction of a household scene from West Mexico (ca. 200 BC to AD 500). The house is an important nexus of social identity for people and a critical scale of archaeological analysis.

House Group. Mexico, Nayarit, 200 B.C. - A.D. 500. Slip-painted ceramic. 12 × 10 × 8 in. (30.48 × 25.4 × 20.32 cm). Los Angeles County Museum of Art, The Proctor Stafford Collection, purchased with funds provided by Mr. and Mrs. Allan C. Balch (M.86.296.30). Photo © Museum Associates/LACMA.

of sources, transmission, reproduction, shared ownership, and co-residence. In this regard, **dwelling** means the physical setting within which activities take place and a **co-residential group** signifies those people who regularly share those physical settings. If a group regularly performs certain activities in a given place over time, the frequency of these activities leaves material traces. Therefore, in order to understand a household, people's activities need to be reconstructed. In this manner, household archaeology builds off of activity area research.

Neighborhoods

In societies that had substantial aggregations of people, the concept of **neighborhood** can be employed as an intermediate social unit that links households with broader sociopolitical contexts of entire sites (such as cities) and/or polities (e.g., states or empires). Using this scale of settlement study, archaeologists seek to understand social processes in which people negotiate processes of alliance and segregation through frequent face-to-face interaction. In a city, for instance, people from similar backgrounds (e.g., ethnic, cultural, educational, social, or economic) tend to share circumstances by living together in a residential area. In a landmark study of neighborhoods at an archaeological site, Elizabeth Stone combined textual records with artifacts, architecture, and spatial layouts at the Sumerian city of Nippur (Iraq) in Mesopotamia. Stone examined two adjacent domestic compounds (labeled TA and TB) which were located about 30 m from each other. Although the two compounds shared certain characteristics in spatial configurations, such as living, storage, workshop, and open spaces, there were distinctive differences as well. The houses in TA varied in size, shape, and quality of construction. In contrast, those in TA were generally large, uniform in plan, and well-constructed. Many of cuneiform texts found in TA concerned the buying and selling of houses, but these kinds of texts were absent in TB, which was characterized instead by the presence of administrative documents and temple accounts. These different lines of evidence suggested to Stone that TA was a residential compound of small property owners, whereas those of TB were generally officials tied to the temple bureaucracy.

In the case of Nippur, archaeologists were able to study neighborhoods, in part, because of the presence of written texts. This begs the question: can archaeologists identify ancient neighborhoods without textual data? Although studying neighborhoods without written texts is challenging, as neighborhoods do not always have easily visible boundaries that separate them, it can be done. For example, research at Teotihuacan (Mexico) has employed a multivariate analysis of artifacts to demarcate neighborhoods in this massive pre-Hispanic City. The spatial patterning of artifacts indicates that certain areas of the site were distinct in terms of their material culture. Thus, using material data, such as architecture and artifacts, archaeologists can attempt to piece together neighborhood organization without the luxury of written texts from which to draw.

FIGURE 12.7 A map of the city of Nippur, Iraq on a baked clay tablet showing researchers a past perspective of how this settlement should have been organized and envisioned.

Iraq: Map of the City of Nippur incised on a baked clay tablet, c. 14th century BCE/Pictures from History/Bridgeman Images

Sites

As we discussed in Chapter 6, archaeological sites refer to spatial clusters of artifacts, ecofacts, features, and/or structures. These can be as small as a handful of scattered artifacts or as large as a great metropolis such as Rome. Given this variability in scale, the treatment of sites in settlement archaeology can be very different. For example, the concept of the neighborhood can be applied to a city, but not for a small hamlet or a quarry. Further, archaeological sites can be variably defined, with some archaeologists using certain criteria to define their spatial limits that differ from the criteria used by other researchers (e.g., the density of material culture such as architecture); it is very rare that a site has a clearly understandable boundary marker that the archaeologist can read (e.g., "you are now entering the site"). With these issues in mind, the concept of the site is indispensable to settlement archaeology, as all settlements, one way or another, are sites.

One critical element of sites to consider in settlement archaeology is their spatial composition. **Site layouts** are both terribly variable and tremendously informative. Some sites may have particular functions, such as hunting camps, quarries, ritual temple complexes, or fortifications. Others may represent residential communities in some way or another, but may be characterized by certain kinds of activities that the archaeologist views critical for interpretive purposes (such as ports of trade, political capitals, or agricultural hamlets) despite the wide range of activities that may have actually occurred at them in the past. Regardless of how sites are defined, analysis of their spatial layouts can help archaeologists address of whole series of questions ranging from social organization and stratification to economic and ideological concerns. For example, assuming that social stratification is

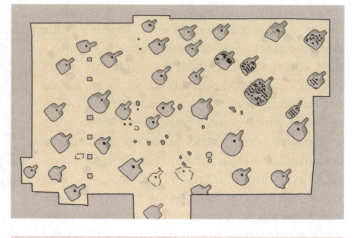

FIGURE 12.8 The plan of the site of Hamin Mangha, China (ca. 3000 BC) includes this area where the structures are similarly shaped and oriented. There may be many reasons to consider why this pattern occurred apart from political mandates from the community leaders. They may all point to a sacred point on the landscape or this orientation helps the houses to catch the sun in such a way to ideally regulate inside temperatures. Archaeologists must explore such varied possibilities when researching site plans.

© Belem Ceballos Casanova

reflected in spatial and material settings, archaeologists can examine the size and elaborateness of residences and their proximity to important administrative and religious structures as signifiers of social distinctions. These architectural differences may correlate with other indicators of wealth, such as sumptuous burials, the presence of luxury and prestigious materials, and/or quality and size of construction. Political variables can also impact site layouts. When political leaders intervene in the spatial layout of communities, the distribution, orientation, sizes, and architectural styles of houses can become relatively standardized (although such standardization does not always reflect such political processes). For instance, the ancient capital city of Chang'an in China was laid out as terrestrial representation Chinese cosmology involving cardinal directionality and gridded streets with an emphasis on the imperial palace located in the northern center of the city. The imperial palace is connected by the main gate and the entire city was walled as part of military system that guarded against invasion. Heijo Kyo, another ancient capital city, was founded in Japan in AD 710 by emulating the city plan of Chang'an, but not for the same reasons. Although the spatial layout of Hejio Kyo is almost identical to that of Chang'an, its function was weighted more on administration than on Chinese cosmology and defense against foreign invasion. There are many more examples of how site layouts can be interpreted, but suffice it to say that the spatial organization of sites can tell archaeologists a lot about past societies.

In talking about sites, we have mentioned the concept of residential community. Perhaps, it is easy for us to think of a spatially defined settlement, such as a hamlet or town, to represent a community. Although people who belong to those communities might not all see eye to eye, they all live together and share many of the same experiences. However, this is not to say that all communities are residential. In today's globalized and increasing online world, it is ever more apparent that communities are not restricted to specific spatial locations, but more broadly refer to groups of people who share an identity of belonging to a group (which *could* be based on spatial location) or whose interactions lead them to culturally construct communities. Communities in the past did not have to be strictly spatial either, and archaeologists use the term accordingly.

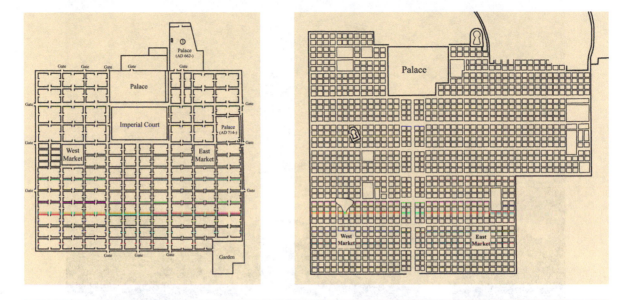

FIGURE 12.9 The site plans of Chang'an (left side) and Heijo-kyo (right side).

© Beletm Ceballos Casanova. Redrawn from http://www.drben.net/ChinaReport/Shaanxi_Province/Xian/Maps/Xian_Maps_All-Index.html and https://heritageofjapan.wordpress.com/tag/nara-city-changan-urban-design/

Regional Settlement Patterns

During the early portion of the twentieth century, archaeologists took a site-centric approach to their studies; usually meaning they tended to work at specific large and/or spectacular sites. This approach meant that the areas between these selected sites were relatively ignored, leaving the sites that *were* subjected to study to be considered in relative isolation to the cultural systems they were embedded within. Gordon Willey's (1953) initial work on settlement patterns over a region began to change this approach to archaeological data. Not only were places like cities (for sedentary societies) and home bases (for mobile societies) important, but now considerations of rural areas, places where raw materials were extracted and worked, and areas where subsistence or ritual activities occurred away from living areas could occur, envisioning all places where humans lived and worked as part of an integrated system. Willey's **regional approach** took into account a variety of settlements that interacted,

FIGURE 12.10 The sites created by mobile populations often have different kinds of material culture depending on the kinds of activities that were being performed in each place. To get a good sense of what life was like archaeologists should take a regional approach. Focusing only on one site gives a skewed view of the lives of these people.

© Belem Ceballos Casanova

FIGURE 12.11 Dún Aonghasa, Ireland, is stark example of how settlement is shaped by cultural factors such as anticipated violence. The builders of the site utilized the sheer cliffs of Aran Islands as a natural defense of the fortified position starting in the late second-millennium BC.

© National Monuments Service, Dept. of Culture, Heritage, and the Gaeltacht

competed, and complemented each other over time. He coined the term **settlement patterns** to describe his approach to understand the ways in which people disposed themselves over the landscape. During his landmark study of the Virú Valley of Peru, Willey recorded over three hundred sites during four months of fieldwork; classifying these as living sites, community or ceremonial structures, fortified strongholds or places of refuge, and cemeteries. Since the 1950s, archaeologists building on Willey's work have developed theoretical and methodological approaches to a better understanding of human settlements across the landscape. These studies have focused on questions such as how urbanization occurs (as the development of urban areas is a process that includes both a **core** area, such as a city, and its **periphery**, such as rural areas, that are equally important to the process), how and when mobile societies moved around the landscape, and how times of violence or peace impact the decisions concerning where people live.

Archaeologists apply a variety of spatial analyses to regional approaches. **Locational analysis** is a common analytic technique derived from economy and human geography. One of the models associated with this analysis is **Central Place Theory**. This model is predicated on the idea that when people locate their settlements, they seek maximum efficiency of exploiting natural and cultural resources with the minimum cost. Over time, people will come to fill the region, building their settlements that tend to be located evenly across the region. According to these kinds of models, central places perform the same functions, serving areas of the same size, but forming hierarchical locations from regional capitals to towns to small villages. Archaeologists represent this hierarchical pattern by drawing hexagonal lattices of different scales. These lattices are associated with three levels of material distributions; the distribution of local goods, centrally produced goods, and centrally administrated goods. Although central place theory can be useful for predicting site locations, a major criticism is its inflexibility in accounting for diverse sociopolitical organizations and change in settlement patterns over time. A similar, but slightly more flexible model uses so-called **Thiessen polygons**. The Thiessen polygon approach entails the drawing of perpendicular lines at the midpoints between settlements archaeologists have documented. The more perpendicular lines are drawn, the more complex polygons are created. The areas created by the Thiessen polygons are often considered the territory of each central place. Although more flexible, Thiessen polygons have also been criticized for not accounting enough for dynamic settlement systems.

FIGURE 12.12 The ideal polygon form of central place theory models. The central pyramid represents the primary center, the red triangles intermediate centers, the blue circles small centers, and the stars subcenters.

Source: Travis Stanton

As we discussed in Chapter 6, geographic information systems (GIS) have drastically improved spatial analyses, and in particular have been heavily applied to settlement archaeology. Through geodatabase creation, GIS manages the knowledge of locations and their associated attributes. By layering different archaeological, geological, and environmental data, GIS allows archaeologists to carry out spatial analysis, creating a variety of maps and other images such as viewshed, watershed, least-cost path, and predictive modeling. Nevertheless, GIS cannot directly offer interpretations of the past. Archaeologists still need to examine the outcomes of GIS and interpret patterns in the data. For example, by applying GIS archaeologists can conduct **network analyses**, integrating different environmental and cultural data into examinations of social, political, and economic networks at a regional scale and beyond. Barbara Mills and her team are pioneers of applying the **Social Network Analysis** in archaeological research. Using such analysis, they have demonstrated large-scale demographic changes such as migration and population aggregation in the American Southwest in the period AD 1200–1450. Mills and her colleagues have used decorated ceramics and obsidian as material signifiers of long-distance network relationships and identified a dramatic shift in network density and settlement centrality from the northern to the southern Southwest after AD 1300.

Landscape Archaeology

A related field of research in settlement studies is **landscape archaeology**, which acknowledges that people did not only adapt to the natural environments they lived in, but were active agents in the cultural construction of meaningful places. Bernard Knapp and Wendy Ashmore, pioneers in landscape archaeology, have divided landscape construction into three different areas. **Constructed landscapes** are those that are altered by human action. A city, for example, is a constructed landscape, and is layered with meanings. From the large monuments of the elites, which can be symbols of political authority and urban identity among other things, to the houses of the people living in the outskirts, meaning permeates urban environments. **Conceptualized landscapes** are considered to be "natural" environments that also have meaning. A mountain, for instance, may be known as a source of particular resources or a place where certain kinds of activities take place. **Ideational landscapes** are those that are imagined and/or emotional, and may have mythic qualities. So, in addition to being a source of water from the seasonal

FIGURE 12.13 The ideational landscape of the Island of the Sun on Lake Titicaca, Bolivia. The Inka believed that Manco Cápac, the first Inka and son of Inti (the Sun god), emerged from a crag on the island.

Source: © Creative Family/Shutterstock.com

melt of snow on its peak, a mountain may be a home to a deity or the place of some mythic event passed down from generation to generation. In the end, all places have meaning, and landscape archaeology acknowledges that it is worthwhile for archaeologists to consider them.

Subsistence

Archaeologists have a variety of methods at their disposal to reconstruct what people in the past ate, as well as how they obtained and processed their food. In Chapter 11, we discussed body-oriented approaches to subsistence, in particular stable isotope analyses of carbon and nitrogen. Dental wear can also give researchers an idea of the kinds of foods (soft or hard) that people ate with frequency; and pathologies, like caries, and other indicators of nutritional health, such as Harris lines and linear enamel hypoplasias, can also be informative. Methods for approaching subsistence were also touched on in Chapter 10, where we discussed artifact analyses. Some artifacts can be extremely helpful in understanding what people ate and how they processed their food. Projectile points, bone fishing hooks, lithic grinding stones, and ceramic storage, cooking, and serving vessels are all examples of artifacts whose morphology can be highly informative. The role of residue and use-wear analyses was also discussed in Chapter 10. Yet, although we have mentioned all of these analyses, as well as paleobotanical and faunal remains in Chapter 9, some further discussion of subsistence systems is warranted.

Beginning with plants, we know that particular species can be identified through the recovery of macro-remains, seeds, pollen, phytoliths, starches, and other kinds of chemical residues (e.g., the case of theobromine for cacao); these can be found in all kinds of contexts including living surfaces, associated with artifacts, and in coprolites. Plants can also be mentioned in epigraphic texts and shown in iconography. But, it is not only important to merely identify plants. Finding a handful of seeds at an archaeological site might indicate that its occupants utilized a particular plant, but it does necessarily say how important those plants were in the subsistence system. To study it, we should

FIGURE 12.14 Images of food production: a first-century AD relief of a Roman period butcher (left); a wooden sculpture of a woman grinding grain from Middle Kingdom, Egypt (ca. 2134–1991 BC, middle); a seated couple preparing food from West Mexico (ca. 200 BC to AD 500 right).

Butcher, bas-relief, Roman civilisation/Museo della Divilta Romana, Rome, Italy/De Agostini Picture Library/Bridgeman Images
Model of a Woman Grinding Grain. Egypt, First Intermediate Period - early Middle Kingdom, 2134–1991 BCE. Wood, gesso and pigments. 7 1/4 × 3 × 9 in. (18.42 × 7.62 × 22.86 cm). Los Angeles County Museum of Art, William Randolph Hearst Collection (51.15.10). Photo © Museum Associates/LACMA
Seated Couple Preparing and Eating Food. Mexico, Nayarit, Nayarit, 200 B.C. - A.D. 500. Red slip with cream and black painted slip decoration on ceramic. 8 × 4 1/2 × 4 1/2 in. (20.32 × 11.43 × 11.43 cm); 8 × 4 1/2 × 7 in. (20.32 × 11.43 × 17.78 cm). Los Angeles County Museum of Art, The Proctor Stafford Collection, purchased with funds provided by Mr. and Mrs. Allan C. Balch (M.86.296.18a-b). Photo © Museum Associates/LACMA

first understand the conceptual difference between meals and diet. As we discussed in Chapter 11, in archaeological research a meal refers to direct evidence of various kinds of what people ate at a particular moment. In contrast, diet means the pattern of people's consumption over a long period of time. Plant and animal remains in an archaeological site may represent either meals or diet of the past people, or both, although the stable isotope analyses of human bones can identify their diet. For example, archaeologists have known that maize was the staple of Mesoamerican diets for quite some time, tracing its domestication to at least the third-millennium BC. But, more recent evidence indicates that, although maize was consumed by people from this time onward, it became a staple element of the Mesoamerican diet only by the first-millennium BC; its importance changed over time. Thus, finding evidence for maize, although significant, is not enough. Researchers want to know how widely used plants like this were; how important they were at any period of time. The same can be said for animals, which are most often identified through their bones and teeth, or what is usually termed **faunal remains**, but which can also be gleaned through other preserved evidence such as hair and DNA as well in iconography and epigraphy.

Regardless of the frequency of use of particular species, their identification has implications regarding the nature of subsistence systems. For example, even in highly agricultural societies, wild species may continue to be exploited. Many societies actually practiced mixed subsistence strategies, whereby more than one strategy is used. In general, there are several kinds of subsistence strategies available to people that anthropologists recognize. Some common terms include the following:

- **Foraging** involves the collecting of food from "natural" sources, which are wild (uncultivated) animals and plants.
- **Cultivation** refers to an intentional preparation of fields, sowing, harvesting, and storing seeds or other plant parts.

- **Horticulture** is often defined as the small-scale planting of cultivates, often in fields that lie fallow (unused) for some period of time, allowing them to recover and nutrients to build back up (like **swidden** [slash and burn] techniques).
- **Pastoralism** is a subsistence system based on animal husbandry; pastoralism can include transhumance (moving animals from one place to another to graze) and usually involves domesticated species.
- **Agriculture** is often defined as people's commitment to their interdependence with domesticated plants and animals. Agriculture involves changes in the structure and organization of human society for the systematic exploitation of the Earth.

It is important to keep in mind that cultivation does not mean that the plants and animals need to be domesticated. Wild species can be cultivated as well as domesticated species. This brings up the question: what are domesticated species? **Cultivates** are species that are propagated and exploited by people. For example, you can take a fruit tree sapling out of the forest and plant it in your garden. You may be taking care of it and you may eventually eat its fruit, but that does not make it a domesticate. Likewise, if you take very young animals from the wild and then take care of them at home, those animals are **tamed**, not domesticated. **Domestication** is an evolutionary process that requires a genetic modification of a wild species through the interference by

FIGURE 12.15 Scene of a bovine being killed at Saqqara, Egypt.

© Anastasi Petrova/Shutterstock.com

humans, intentionally or unintentionally, in the reproductive process over multiple generations. Although other scientists may rely solely on DNA analysis or on morphological differences between archaeological and wild bones to identify domestication, archaeologists have further approaches at their disposal. They can examine changes in the material and spatial settings of subsistence, such as the appearance of ground stone tools and storage facilities, changes in land use, and new distributions of plants and animals found outside their natural range, as early signs of domestication. The selective breeding of some animal species can also be identified through paleodemographic analyses of the faunal remains. For example, if by controlling which individuals pass their genetic material on to the next generation (let's say just the trees with the largest fruit), you eventually wind up with bigger fruit on average from the trees in your garden, domestication has occurred. Even today, animal breeders often use just a few males who display the optimum characteristics being selected for. This selection often results in the **culling** of the population, whereby the other young males are killed and butchered for food while the breeding females (potentially used for milk as well) reach older ages. This pattern is identifiable in the faunal data by sexing and aging the remains as well as other archaeological evidence we just mentioned above.

Archaeologists also want to know what plants and animals were used for. Using the example of maize becoming a staple in Mesoamerican cuisine again, although we might assume that it was eaten prior to its adoption as a staple (e.g., third-millennium BC), and it surely was, some

FIGURE 12.16 Animals can have many uses in societies (e.g., food, companionship, wool, labor, and milk, among others): West Mexican ceramic dog with a human mask (left, ca. 200 BC to AD 500); a molded earthenware horse (middle) from the early Western Han dynasty (ca. 206–100 BC); a human figure (right) with a llama from the north-central highlands of Peru (Recuay culture, ca. AD 1–700).

Dog with Human Mask. Mexico, Colima, 200 B.C. - A.D. 500. Slip-painted ceramic. 8 1/2 × 15 1/2 × 7 in. (21.59 × 39.37 × 17.78 cm). Los Angeles County Museum of Art, The Proctor Stafford Collection, purchased with funds provided by Mr. and Mrs. Allan C. Balch (M.86.296.154). Photo © Museum Associates/LACMA.
Horse. China, early Western Han dynasty, 206–100 B.C. Molded earthenware with carved and painted decoration. 23 1/2 × 21 1/2 × 6 1/2 in. (59.69 × 54.61 × 16.51 cm). Los Angeles County Museum of Art, Gift of Richard Brustlin (M.2002.146.1). Photo © Museum Associates/LACMA.
Figure with "Moon Animal" Headdress and Llama. Peru, North-Central Highlands, Recuay, Recuay, AD 1–700. Slip-painted ceramic. 15 × 6 × 5 in. (38.1 × 15.24 × 12.7 cm). Los Angeles County Museum of Art, Purchased with funds provided by Camilla Chandler Frost (M.2010.115.102). Photo © Museum Associates/LACMA.

researchers have also argued that its initial domestication in Mesoamerica might not have been as a food resource, but as a base for a fermented beverage, a corn beer called *chicha*, a very widespread drink in the Andes at the time of the Spanish arrival. Other plants were never eaten, but were utilized for all sorts of other reasons including textiles, basketry, cordage, animal feed, and psychedelic drugs, as well as medicinal, ritual, and aesthetic purposes. And, just because a plant was edible does not mean that cultural preferences favored its consumption. Agaves are edible, but very few people in the American Southwest today actually consume them (outside of distilled tequila), preferring to use them as a way to decorate the landscapes surrounding their homes. The same goes for many animal species. For example, dogs, one of the first domesticated animal species (occurring over 10,000 years ago), can have many roles in a society; guarding the home, hunting, companionship, trash disposal, and even as a food resource. Camelids like llamas and alpacas in the Andes can be used for wool, as pack animals, for food, and are even found in ritual contexts as sacrificial offerings. Thus, just identifying a species is not enough, we have to understand the context in which it is found; being aware that in some cases species even enter archaeological contexts through natural formation processes

Beyond the actual evidence for food remains, archaeologists often find evidence of food acquisition and production on the landscape. In many cases, corrals, aqueducts, agricultural terraces, canals, raised fields, and other features preserve today. Such evidence can provide critical information to understand what kinds of food production systems were in place, which might give archaeologists clues as to how social, political, and economic systems were organized. Subsistence is a major, if not the major, part of any economy, and the vast majority of people who lived in the past participated in one way or another in the acquisition and/or production of food. However, in some more recent societies food production was an activity in which not everyone participated. In these societies, producing a surplus of food often freed up others to participate in other kinds of activities. Highly stratified societies, like those we term states and empires, are characterized by such situations. Industrial societies, like our own, are characterized by situations where most of the population is not directly involved in the food production process. Thus, it is easy to see how an understanding of subsistence systems is so important in archaeology.

Exchange

Exchange is a central concept in anthropology and is one of the fundamental bases for understanding economic systems, which revolve around patterns of production, distribution, and consumption. And, given that humans have been exchanging

FIGURE 12.17 A LiDAR image representing raised fields at the site of El Palmar, Mexico.

Source: Kenichiro Tsukamoto

things for a very long time, exchange is of great interest to archaeologists. But, as social exchange theory (coming out of work in sociology, psychology, and economics) holds, exchange fundamentally rests in the interpersonal relationships among people; it is not only goods and services that can be exchanged, but ideas and information as well. In some basic sense, all human interactions can be viewed as exchange. In a modern socioeconomic context, we often think about exchange being mostly about the product, the thing we are trying to obtain. Although exchange also has important social components today (e.g., birthday gifts), the social aspects of exchange in many past societies were often more fundamental to the exchange process than they are in contemporary societies.

This is an important point to keep in mind when researching this topic in past cultural contexts, especially those that focused more on nonmarket systems of production and distribution in nonmonetary contexts. Using the following example, we can see how the concept of exchange helps us to better understand not only economic systems, but also political, social, and ritual systems as well.

Let's say that there were two islands with different groups of people living on them. The kinds of resources on each island may have been relatively similar; food items like fruits, game, and fish as well as raw materials such as shell, wood, and stone. Regardless of the cultural similarities or differences (e.g., language and customs) between the two groups, they were in contact with each other and people on each island could have been reached from the other by boat, facilitating

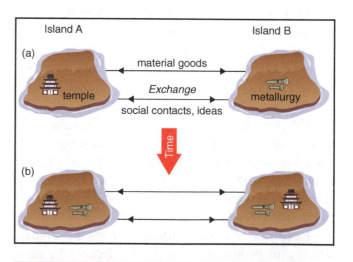

FIGURE 12.18 An example of how the distribution of material culture can change through exchange between two societies that originally had a difference in resources and cultural ideas.

© Kendall Hunt Publishing Company

the exchange of people, ideas, and material culture. Although it might not have been necessary to trade these kinds of resources between the two islands (as each island had similar resources), archaeologists might find, using techniques like the source analyses discussed in Chapter 10, that they *were* exchanged. How might archaeologists explain such a pattern, one that would not necessarily make sense using a modern capitalist logic of trying to minimize the costs of production and distribution? One hypothesis to explain the added effort might be to view the exchanged materials as a means to create and maintain long-distance social relationships, possibly through inter-island marriage patterns and/or gifting. Thus, the exchange pattern might reflect an important aspect of the social system. An alternative (and not mutually exclusive) way to think about the pattern would be to see the exchanges reflecting political alliances among communities; that their socioeconomic relationship was the basis to be able to call on the other islands aid in the event of, for instance, a conflict with a group on a third island. Further, the exchanges may have occurred on a ritual cycle, like each winter solstice, adding a ritual element to the exchange system. In the end, the study of exchange may inform us as several aspects of the societies under study.

Although archaeologists also use the term in this broader sense, they are particularly interested in the actual physical exchange of goods, things that can be materially traced in the archaeological record. Many cases of exchange, indeed, do involve some difference in the access to certain kinds of goods and materials. Although both areas might have had obsidian, for example, one had better obsidian (e.g., it was more easily worked, came from the "sacred mountain," was "cheaper," better prepared by the miners at the quarry, or just had a more appealing color). From very early on in archaeological studies, researchers have identified materials and goods that did not look local to the area in which they worked. The styles of artifacts were different, or the materials were not locally found. Early archaeologists talked a lot about trade, particularly long-distance trade of things that more easily identifiable as nonlocal. Over the years, archaeological studies of exchange have become more nuanced and have broadened to consider economic systems more generally. Thus, the study of economies can be complicated, but is a critical component to attaining a broader understanding of the people who lived in the past.

Broadly speaking, there are several modes of exchange that archaeologists study; in any cultural context these modes are not mutually exclusive and goods can move in different exchange networks that coexist in a society. **Reciprocity** is the exchange of goods or services among individuals considered to be social peers or equals. This type of exchange often involves debts and obligations on both parties. Although reciprocity is common among more egalitarian societies, it occurs in state-level contexts as well. If you give someone a birthday present this year, you may expect that the person will reciprocate with a gift on your birthday. Predicated on reciprocity, this gift-giving strengthens the social ties between the two people.

Another mode of exchange is called the **potlatch** (named for the events documented among indigenous groups of the Northwest Coast of North America), festive events where the hosts gave away things for prestige. The idea is that you invite people to the event, give them food and drink, as well as gifts; in the case of the Northwest Coast, wealth was also destroyed in competitive displays. Hosting a potlatch enhanced the person's or social group's prestige. The more lavish the event, the more prestige was accrued. By not matching or reciprocating such events, hierarchical relationships were formed and maintained by members of the society.

Barter is defined as a simple exchange (e.g., goods for goods, goods for services, services for services) through shared economic interests between parties. Although reciprocal exchange often happens over a period of time (using the example above, from one birthday to the next), barter is much more immediate (e.g., you exchange a blanket for a fishing net in one specific moment). Barter often occurs when monetary systems are absent or are in crisis. The question of money, however, brings up the issue of value. How is it that values are assigned to certain products and materials? It is one thing to think of an item of something that might be bartered; you really need the fishing net and you are willing to give up the blanket to get it. It is a bit different to think that you will pay three silver coins for the net. Monetary systems work because there is a widespread agreement that certain materials, such as gold or silver, have a certain value to them. The modern world economy is based on such logic. Some products today, such as oil, have a functional value to them. But others, like gold, are widely agreed on, and often scarce, materials that someone in the past convinced others was of a certain value despite not having the kind of functional value that a product such as oil has today. It is quite remarkable to think that a good portion of our modern economy is based on the cultural value of gold, which may stretch back all the way back to the Chalcolithic period (fourth-millennium BC) in the Levant area of the Middle East or Bulgaria where dates point to the fifth-millennium BC. Why not some other materials such as gemstones or shell? Although the reason most likely lies in the obscure historical circumstances of some areas of the Old World, creating money out of materials such as silver and gold (and paper bills that represent those materials being stored by some third party) changed how certain economies worked.

FIGURE 12.19 An animal figure in gold leaf from Varna, Bulgaria, a very early example of goldworking.

Bulgaria, Sofia, Natsionalen Istoritcheski Muzej, Gold leaf with animal figures from Varna/De Agostini Picture Library/A. Dagli Orti/Bridgeman Images

One mode of exchange that relies heavily on money today is **market exchange**. In this economic system, goods and services are bought and sold using some sort of monetary system; and as we are familiar with in today's globalized economy, the law of supply and demand is what drives this system. The system is greatly impersonal, with the participants seldom knowing each other on a personal level; thus, the system does not necessarily strengthen the social relationships between people like reciprocity does. Actual spaces, such as marketplaces, can exist and, in fact, archaeologists have identified such spaces at archaeological sites, although market economies can function without such spaces (e.g., travelling vendors who go door to door). Did past markets operate based on monetary systems? And, how impersonal were market exchanges in past cultural contexts? Although archaeological and historical evidence shows that some people in past societies used not only coins, but also shell, tobacco, cacao, and other objects as money, there appears to have been a lot of variability and flexibility concerning how markets, and materials of value, functioned. Further, it is very possible that some market exchange contexts in the past could have been more entangled in social relations than market economies today.

Redistribution is a centralized exchange controlled or heavily influenced by elites. Goods are accumulated by people with power (through systems such as taxation or tribute), which are in turn redistributed to other members of society. Such systems can function in official marketplaces, temples, or other redistribution centers. In some societies, archaeologists have documented centralized storage areas associated with monumental architecture. The term **palace economy** stems from the location of storerooms in centralized palace structures from the late Bronze Age like those found in Crete and Egypt.

In the end, archaeologists have several models to explore when researching economic systems in the past. And, as we saw in Chapter 10, they have a series of techniques to identify the movement of certain kinds of goods in the past. The issue is that these techniques, such as instrumental neutron activation analysis (INAA) or inductively coupled plasma (ICP) methods, usually indicate where the raw material was from. And, the context where the material was found only shows you where the material was left behind. The whole biography of movement between the moment of raw material acquisition (**provenance**, where the material was from) and discard (**provenience**, the archaeological context the material was archaeologically recovered) is usually not something that archaeologists can reconstruct. This is a very import thing to keep in mind when researching concepts like trade and exchange. Were the raw materials worked at the source of acquisition and exchanges as finished goods (e.g., lithic bifaces) or where the raw materials exchanged and worked elsewhere (e.g., exchange of the lithic cores that were eventually turned into bifaces)? Questions like these can be difficult to answer using chemical data alone, but can be approached using other material and contextual data, such as where the manufacturing debris for the production of the bifaces is found.

The organization of production is also an important topic for archaeologists to address. Continuing with the example of lithic bifaces, was their production done by full-time specialists laboring in workshops who dedicated their lives to this activity, having to then exchange the finished products for other things like food? Or, were they done by part-time specialists, working in cottage industries, maybe out of their homes, as a way to supplement their household economy, let's say, in addition to subsistence activities? Understanding the dynamics of craft specialization is important for understanding economic systems in the past.

The scale and intensity of exchange are other topics that are important for archaeologists to consider. Long-distance exchange is something that archaeologists discuss with some frequency, but in reality "long-distance" is a relative concept. For one researcher it may mean 100 km, but for another it may mean 1,000 km. Some exchange networks are incredibly large. The Silk Road, for example, connected societies from the Iberian Peninsula of westernmost Europe to Japan in the east; the Eurasian Steppes acting as a thoroughfare from Manchuria (China) to Hungary where goods were subjected to both direct (face-to-face exchanges between

FIGURE 12.20 The Palace at Knossos, Crete (Minoan culture, ca. second-millennium BC) with its storage areas is a prime example of a palace economy.

© Banet/Shutterstock.com
© Jaroslave Moravcik/Shutterstock.com

people from points A and C) and down-the-line exchanges (the product passes through the hands of middlemen [e.g., point B] and the people at points A and C never directly interact). This is not to say, however, that all important long-distance trade occurred over such distances. In considering distance, transportation methods are important to keep in mind. In Mesoamerica, long-distance trade occurred without the presence of pack animals or wheeled carts. In areas where water routes like rivers and seas existed, watercraft like canoes facilitated transport. In areas where such routes were lacking, all transport occurred by people carrying products. This is a very different kind of situation to those where horse-drawn carts existed. For example, relatively large boats existed in the Mediterranean, a body of water that greatly facilitated interaction and exchange for millennia. One of these boats, dating to the fourteenth-century BC, was recovered from the coast of Turkey back in 1982. The remains of the Uluburun shipwreck revealed products such as copper and tin ingots, amphorae filled with olives and glass beads, African ebony, elephant and hippo ivory, and Baltic amber beads. From these products, researchers were able to recreate the route to Uluburun, which, in turn, shed light on the scale of exchange in this part of the Mediterranean at this time. Yet one find, even a shipwreck like the Uluburun, although important, does not mean that exchange was particularly intensive, another important consideration. Archaeologists recovered one obsidian scraper at the site of Spiro, Oklahoma, that was sourced to a famous source of material in Central Mexico greatly utilized by societies like that found at Teotihuacan. Obviously, this find reveals that some sort of direct or indirect contact happened between these two areas at least once, but since no other obsidian from this source has even been reported, the exchange between these two areas was not intensive at all. These examples demonstrate that archaeologists need to be mindful of both scale and intensity in studies of exchange systems.

In today's globalized economy, the scale and intensity of exchange has reached levels never before seen in human history. This is not to say, though, that the process of globalization is relatively new. In fact, there have been many smaller attempts at globalization over the latter portion of prehistory and in the historic periods. The Inka, Aztec, Romans, Persians, and Han Dynasty Chinese are all famous examples of societies being driving forces in mini-globalized systems (but, by no means being the only forces driving those systems). Regarding this process of increasing scale and intensity of exchange, archaeologists often draw on **world systems theory**, a model created by American historian Immanuel Wallerstein. According to this model, the different parts of a widespread trading system can become so dependent on each other commercially that one can no longer think of them as independent entities. Today, globalization is conceived as an economic unit articulated by trade networks extending far beyond the boundaries of individual countries. Although a truly global system did

FIGURE 12.21 In pre-Hispanic Mesoamerica, there were neither pack animals nor wheeled carts. This West Mexican figurine captures a scene of a human porter using a tumpline around his forehead to carry a large ceramic jar (ca. 200 BC to AD 400).

Man Using Tumpline to Carry Vessel. Mexico, Colima, Colima, 200 BCE - 400 CE. Slip-painted ceramic. 15 × 7 1/4 × 12 3/4 in. (38.1 × 18.42 × 32.39 cm). Los Angeles County Museum of Art, The Proctor Stafford Collection, purchased with funds provided by Mr. and Mrs. Allan C. Balch (M.86.296.112). Photo © Museum Associates/ LACMA.

not exist before the modern era, people have been "globalizing," seeing beyond their local region, for a very long time, and in some cases, different areas did become so integrated economically that archaeologists can discuss the "process" of globalization.

Final Comments

Although there are many other topics of interest that go beyond settlement, subsistence, and exchange, this triad forms a nucleus of important issues that much archaeological work touches upon in one way or another. As we mentioned in the introduction, these topics intertwine with each other and many more topics, including political structures and forms of social organization. Moving on to the final chapter, we will discuss the idea of meaning in archaeology, one of the major contributions of a postprocessual archaeology.

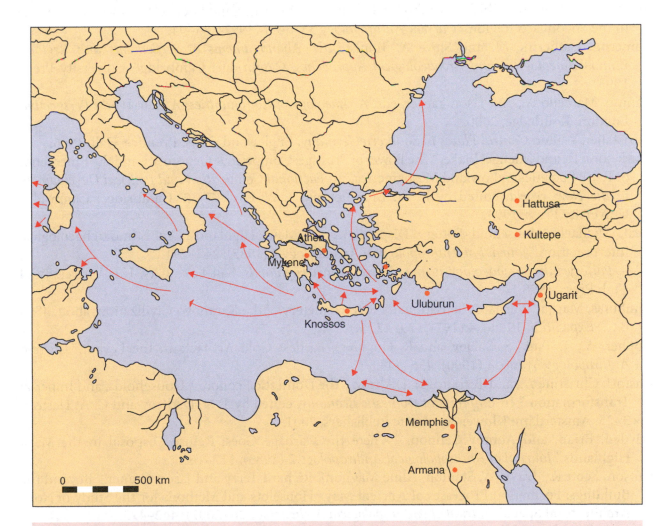

FIGURE 12.22 The trade routes archaeologists have proposed using data from the Uluburun wreck.

© Kendall Hunt Publishing Company, redrawn from Besserdich 2013.

Bibliography

Arnauld, M. Charlotte, Linda R. Manzanilla, and Michael E. Smith, eds. *The Neighborhood as a Social and Spatial Unit in Mesoamerican Cities*. Tucson: The University of Arizona Press, 2012.

Ashmore, Wendy A., and Richard R. Wilk, eds. *Household and Community in the Mesoamerican Past*. Albuquerque, NM: University of New Mexico Press, 1988.

Barker, Alex W., Craig E. Skinner, M. Steven Shackley, Michael D. Glascock, and J. Daniel Rogers. "Mesoamerican Origin for an Obsidian Scraper from the Precolumbian Southeastern United States." *American Antiquity* 67, no. 1 (2002): 103–108.

Besserdich, Rico. "Uluburun: The Oldest Wreck in the World." *X-Ray Mag* 55 (2013): 17–23.

Binford, Lewis R. "Dimensional Analysis of Behavior and Site Structure: Learning from an Eskimo Hunting Stand." *American Antiquity* 43 (1978): 330–361.

———"The Archaeology of Place." *Journal of Anthropological Archaeology* 1 (1982): 5–31.

Blake, Michael, Brian S. Chisholm, John E. Clark, Barbara Voorhies, and Michael W. Love. "Subsistence in the Soconusco Region." *Current Anthropology* 33, no. 1 (1992): 83–94.

Cameron, Catherine M. and Steve A. Tomka, eds. *Abandonments of Settlements and Regions: Ethnoarchaeological and Archaeological Approaches*. Cambridge: Cambridge University Press, 1993.

Canuto, Marcello A., and Jason Yaeger, eds. *Archaeology of Communities: A New World Perspective*. London: Routledge, 2000.

Christaller, Walter. *Central Places in Southern Germany*. Englewood Cliffs: Prentice-Hall, 1966.

Clark, John E., and Michael Blake. "The Power of Prestige: Competitive Generosity and the Emergence of Rank Societies in Lowland Mesoamerica." In *Factional Competition and Political Development in the New World*, edited by E. M. Brumfiel and J. W. Fox, 17–30. Cambridge: Cambridge University Press, 1994.

Deal, Michael. "Household Pottery Disposal in the Maya Highlands: An Ethnoarchaeological Interpretation." *Journal of Anthropological Archaeology* 4 (1985): 243–291.

———*Pottery Ethnoarchaeology in the Central Maya Highlands*. Salt Lake City, UT: University of Utah Press, 1998.

Gimbutas, Marija. "Varna: A Sensationally Rich Cemetery of the Karanovo Civilization, about 4500 B.C." *Expedition* 19, no. 4 (1977): 39–47.

Gopher, A., T. Tsuk, S. Shalev, and R. Gophna. "Earliest Gold Artifacts in the Levant." *Current Anthropology* 31, no. 4 (1990): 436–443.

Hastorf, Christine A., and Terrance N. D'Altroy. "The Domestic Economy, Households, and Imperial Transformation." In *Empire and Domestic Economy*, edited by T. N. D'Altroy and C. A. Hastorf, 3–25. Amsterdam: Kluwer Academic Publishers, 2001.

Hayden, Brian, and Aubrey Cannon. "Where the Garbage Goes: Refuse Disposal in the Maya Highlands." *Journal of Anthropological Anthropology* 2 (1983): 117–163.

Hutson, Scott R., Travis W. Stanton, Aline Magnoni, Richard Terry and Jason Craner. "Beyond the Buildings: Formation Processes of Ancient Maya Houselots and Methods for the Study of Non-Architectural Space." *Journal of Anthropological Archaeology* 26 (2007): 442–473.

Inomata, Takeshi, and Ronald W. Webb, eds. *The Archaeology of Settlement Abandonment in Middle America*. Salt Lake City, UT: The University of Utah Press, 2003.

Joyce, Rosemary A., and Susan Gillespie, eds. *Beyond Kinship*. Philadelphia, PA: University of Pennsylvania Press, 2000.

Kent, Susan, ed. *Method and Theory for Activity Area Research: An Ethnoarchaeological Approach*. New York: Columbia University Press, 1987.

————*Domestic Architecture and the Use of Space: An Interdisciplinary Cross-Cultural Study*. Cambridge: Cambridge University Press, 1990.

Knapp, A. Bernard, and Wendy Ashmore. "Archaeological Landscapes: Constructed, Conceptualized, Ideational." In *Archaeologies of Landscapes: Contemporary Perspectives*, edited by W. Ashmore and A. B. Knapp, 1–30. Oxford: Blackwell Publishers Ltd., 1999.

Kottack, Conrad P. *Mirror for Humanity: A Concise Introduction to Cultural Anthropology*. Boston, MA: Sixth edition. McGraw Hill, 2008.

Larson, Greger, and Dorian Q. Fuller. "The Evolution of Animal Domestication." *Annual Review of Ecology, Evolution, and Systematics* 45 (2014): 115–136.

MacNeish, Richard S. *The Origins of Agriculture and Settled Life*. Norman: University of Oklahoma Press, 1992.

Manzanilla, Linda and Luis Barba. "The Study of Activities in Classic Households: Two Case Studies from Coba and Teotihuacan." *Ancient Mesoamerica* 1 (1990): 41–49.

Marcus, Joyce. "Territorial Organization of the Lowland Classic Maya." *Science* 180 (1973): 911–916.

Matthews, W., C. A. I. French, T. Laurence, D. F. Cutler, and M. K. Jones. "Microstratigraphic Traces of Site Formation Processes and Human Activities." *World Archaeology* 29 (1997): 281–308.

Mills, Barbara J., John M. Roberts, Jeffery J. Clark, William R. Haas, Jr., Deborah Huntley, Matthew A. Peeples, Lewis Borck, Susan C. Ryan, Meaghan Trowbridge, and Ronald L. Breiger. "The Dynamics of Social Networks in the Late Prehispanic U.S. Southwest." In *Regional Network Analysis in Archaeology: New Approaches to Regional Interaction*, edited by C. Knappett, 181–202. Oxford: Oxford University Press, 2013.

Polanyi, Karl. "Ports of Trade in Early Societies." *The Journal of Economic History* 23 (1963): 30–45.

Poma, Huaman. *Letter to a King*. Translated by Christopher Dilke. E. P. Dutton, New York, 1978.

Pulak, Cemal. "Discovering a Royal Ship from the Age of King Tut: Uluburun, Turkey." In *Beneath the Seven Seas*, edited by G. F. Bass, 34–47. New York: Thames & Hudson, 2005.

Robertson, Ian G. "Investigating Teotihuacan through TMP Surface Collections and Observations." *Ancient Mesoamerica* 26 (2015): 163–181.

Sanders, William T., Jeffery R. Parsons, and Robert S. Santley. *The Basin of Mexico: Ecological Processes in the Evolution of a Civilization*. New York: Academic Press, 1979.

Schearn, Isaac. "Subsistence." In *Perspectives: An Open Invitation to Cultural Anthropology*, edited by N. Brown, L. Tubelle de González, and T. McIlwraith, 1–23. Washington, DC: American Anthropological Association, 2017.

Schiffer, Michael B. "Is There a "Pompeii Premise" in Archaeology?" *Journal of Anthropological Research* 41, no. 1 (1985): 18–41.

————*Formation Processes of the Archaeological Record*. Albuquerque, NM: University of New Mexico Press, 1987.

Schortman, Edward M., and Patricia A. Urban. "Modeling Interregional Interaction in Prehistory." *Advances in Archaeological Method and Theory* 11 (1987): 37–95.

————"Living on the Edge: Core-Periphery Relations in Ancient Southeastern Mesoamerica." *Current Anthropology* 35 (1994): 401–430.

Sheets, Payson D. *The Ceren Site: A Prehistoric Village Buried by Volcanic Ash in Central America*. Fort Worth: Harcourt Brace Jovanovich College Publishers, 1992.

————*Before the Volcano Erupted: The Ancient Cerén Village in Central America*. Austin: The University of Texas Press, 2002.

Smith, Michael E. "The Aztec Marketing System and Settlement Patterns in the Valley of Mexico: A Central Place Analysis." *American Antiquity* 44 (1979): 110–125.

Stanton, Travis W., and Aline Magnoni. "Places of Remembrance: The Use and Perception of Abandoned Structures in the Maya Lowlands." In *Ruins of the Past: The Use and Perception of Abandoned Structures in the Maya Lowlands*, edited by T. W. Stanton and A. Magnoni, 1–24. Boulder, CO: University Press of Colorado, 2008.

Stanton, Travis W., M. Kathryn Brown, and Jonathan B. Pagliaro. "Garbage of the Gods? Squatters, Refuse Disposal, and Termination Rituals among the Ancient Maya." *Latin American Antiquity* 19 (2008): 227–247.

Stone, Elizabeth C. *Nippur Neighborhoods*. Studies in Ancient Oriental Civilization 44. Chicago: The Oriental Institute of the University of Chicago, 1987.

Sullivan, Alan P., Philip B. Mink, and Patrick M. Uphus. "Archaeological Survey Design, Units of Observation, and Characterization of Regional Variability." *American Antiquity* 72, no. 2 (2007): 322–333.

Walker, William H. "Ceremonial Trash?" In *Expanding Archaeology*, edited by J. M. Skibo, W. H. Walker, and A. E. Nielsen, 67–79. Salt Lake City, UT: University of Utah Press, 1995.

Wilk, Richard R., and Robert M. Netting. "Households: Changing Forms and Functions." In *Households: Comparative and Historical Studies of the Domestic Group*, edited by R. M. Netting, R. R. Wilk, and E. J. Arnould, 1–28. Berkeley: University of California Press, 1984.

Willey, Gordon R. *Prehistoric Settlement Patterns in the Virú Valley, Peru*. Washington, DC: Bureau of American Ethnology Bulletin 155, Smithsonian Institution, 1953.

Meaning in Archaeology

The idea of "meaning in archaeology" can be understood in several different senses. On the one hand, this phrase can be taken to refer to the ways in which past peoples created an understanding of the world that they lived in; what the world, and the things in it, meant to them in an emic sense. This interpretation of the phrase "meaning in archaeology" touches on topics of ideologies and symbolism, facets of archaeological research that became more mainstream with the advent of postprocessualist interpretational frameworks in the 1980s (see Chapter 4). On the other hand, returning to the idea of the "past in the present" developed in Chapter 1, the phrase "meaning in archaeology" could be taken to signify what archaeology means for us today; in other words, what role the creation of the past has in contemporary societies. In this final chapter, we will touch on both of these ways of interpreting "meaning in archaeology" as a means of wrapping up some final thoughts.

Ideology and Symbolism

In 1965, a pair of children on the Gulf Coast of Mexico came across a spectacular greenstone figure dating to a very early period of Mesoamerican societies. Using a small part of the figure emerging from the ground to crack palm nuts, the children decided to dig up the stone to take it back to their home, revealing, to their surprise, that it was composed of a seated individual holding a baby-like figure with feline features. Dubbed the Señor de las Limas, this figure was quickly identified as having been carved in a style associated with early Olmec society (ca. 1000–400 BC). The seated figure had a number of etched carvings distributed across its face and body that quickly became the focus of study for iconographers grappling to study early Mesoamerican religious systems. In an early study of these designs, a researcher by the name of Michael Coe suggested that these images represented different gods within an Olmec pantheon, breaking with traditional academic belief at the time that early Mesoamerican societies did not have anthropomorphic gods. Primarily drawing on perceived iconographic similarities between the Olmec designs on the Señor de Las Limas figure and later Mesoamerica deities well known from ethnohistoric accounts, Coe argued that the infant-like figure was an early version of a rain god and that the four heads etched into the shoulder and legs of the seated figure were early representations of Mexica (Aztec) gods Xipe (God of Springtime according to Coe), the Fire Serpent, Quetzalcoatl (God of Wisdom and Life according to Coe), and the Death God.

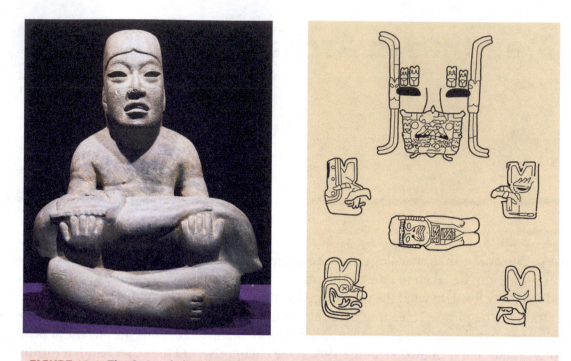

FIGURE 13.1 The Señor de las Limas figure (ca. 1000–400 BC) and the incised designs.

El Senor de las Limas, green stone statue depicting young man holding baby jaguar in his arms, Olmec civilisation/ Museo do Antropologia, Jalapa, Mexico/De Agostini Picture Library/Bridgeman Images. © Belem Ceballos Csasnova, drawn after Coe 1968, Tate 2012

Although the interpretations of the figures have changed since Coe's original work, using a similar method of relying on ethnohistoric and ethnographic data, archaeologists, iconographers, and epigraphers have drawn off of the Señor de Las Limas and other Olmec iconography to understand indigenous cosmovisions. The ethnohistoric and ethnographic records of Mesoamerica demonstrate that indigenous peoples throughout this world region shared a similar version of the cosmos, divided into four horizontal directions and one vertical direction; the vertical axis extending upward into the celestial realm and downward into the underworld. This cosmic directionality is replicated in different contexts by indigenous communities today. Towns are laid out in the four directions, as are agricultural fields, often leaving material evidence of rituals associated with the directions beyond just their spatial plans. Even the human body is a replication of the cosmos,

FIGURE 13.2 This Olmec greenstone celt from Rio Pesquero, Mexico, shows the five world directions of Mesoamerican cosmology; the four horizontal directions marked by maize stalks and the vertical center marked by the Maize god.

Schele Number: SD-4523, Drawing of Rio Pesquero, Maya Culture, Celt incised to form a quincunx pattern with corn plants on axial points and individual, whose legs form a serpent head, carrying a serpent in his arms. Drawing by Linda Schele. Copyright © David Schele. Photo courtesy of Los Angeles County Museum of Art.

with the arms and legs representing the four horizontal directions and the body and head representing the vertical direction.

Students of Precolumbian Mesoamerican societies have seen this kind of directional symbolism replicated in many different kinds of contexts. For example, early carved Olmec greenstone celts often show this symbolism quite explicitly, with four directional maize cobs surrounding an individual (often interpreted today as the Maize god) who represents the vertical axis. Dedication offerings in public plazas also replicate this pattern, marking the places where they are buried as cosmic centers. A famous example of such an offering from the site of Cival, Guatemala, was placed in a shallow cross-shaped pit carved into the bedrock below the most important public plaza of the city. Inside the pit were upright greenstone celts, four in each direction and one in the center, along with a large amount of greenstone pebbles and water jars; the jars also aligned to the five cosmic directions. Even the plans of many ancient cities replicate this fundamental pattern with causeways and temples marking the directions.

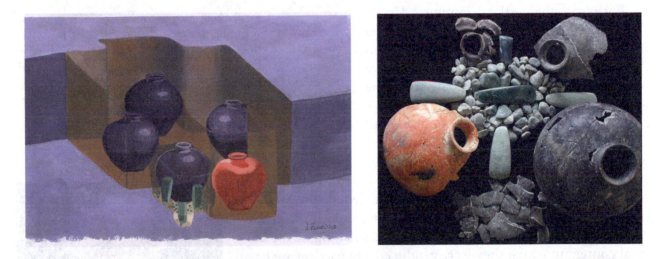

FIGURE 13.3 A cache of vessels and greenstone found in a cruciform hole cut in the bedrock at the Maya site of Cival, Guatemala (ca. 800–700 BC). Note how the greenstone celts and ceramic vessels are arranged based on Mesoamerican cosmic directionality.

© Francisco Estrada-Belli

Returning to the Señor de Las Limas figure, an understanding of the ethnohistory and ethnography of Maya societies helps researchers working on its iconography comprehend the figure better. The figure has directional iconography on its face, with the four horizontal directions marked as maize cobs on its forehead, the face representing the vertical direction. The body of the seated figure, also representing the vertical direction, is marked by four, still enigmatic figures that could represent directional deities (scholars are still at odds regarding the individual meaning of each figure). Fundamentally, the figure is a representation of the cosmos, showing a human body at its center. Thus, the study of the symbolism on the Señor de Las Limas figure, in conjunction with other Mesoamerican iconography, epigraphy, ethnohistorical documents, ethnographic data, and material contexts at archaeological sites, has given researchers a much more profound understanding of how Mesoamerican peoples culturally understood the world around them during Precolumbian times. The patterns in all of these data, of which the cryptic symbols on the Señor de Las Limas figure are but one small part, inform us of both **cosmology** (concerning peoples' conceptions of the origin, development, and nature of the universe) and **ideology** (a system of ideas; these ideas can be of a political, religious, social, or economic nature, among others, or even a combination). Yet, although research into the symbolism of this particular cultural context has advanced greatly due to access to relevant ethnohistoric and ethnographic data, not all research into past symbolism has the luxury to work with such evidence. These kinds of symbols, and cultural contexts, can be much more challenging to understand.

For example, the famous Upper Paleolithic Venus figurines, found across Eurasia but primarily in Europe around the period 26,000–21,000 years ago, have been variably interpreted. In particular, the voluptuous female examples of this figure class are the most famous; although not all the figures are female, and those that are female are not all carved in this voluptuous style. These figures specifically have been interpreted as representing mating alliances, erotic art, and the female life cycle, in particular hearkening to ideas that they were used in fertility rituals. Yet, without a more detailed understanding of the cultural context in which they were produced and used, as we have from the Olmec example above, it is difficult to have any level of certainty as to what the Venus figurines represented. The figures are so old that there are neither ethnographic nor ethnohistoric data that relate to them, illustrating the challenges in working with symbols.

The stone circle at Stonehenge is another relevant example of how little we can say with certainty about symbolic meaning in the past when a cultural context lacks ethnohistoric and ethnographic data to contextualize it. First constructed in the third-millennium BC, the famous stone circle is but part of a much larger Neolithic and Bronze Age complex of earthworks and burial contexts. Given the arrangement of the stones and other features, many researchers have proposed that the stone circle represents an astronomical observatory and/or calendar; calendrical calculations could be made using observations of the movement of celestial bodies through their alignment with certain stones. The famous Heel Stone and embanked linear features are aligned to the sunrise of the summer solstice and sunset of the winter solstice, indicating that this interpretation has great merit. Yet, studies of other

FIGURE 13.4 Symbolism such as this mosaic of Neptune's triumph in the frigidarium of Neptune's baths in Ostia Antica, Rome, Italy, is much easier to understand today due to knowledge of its meaning that has survived to modern times. If we knew nothing about Greco-Roman mythology, deciphering the significance of this scene would be much more difficult.

© mgallar/Shutterstock.com

FIGURE 13.5 The Venus of Willendorf, found in Austria (ca. 26,000 BP).

Modified from image © frantic00/Shutterstock.com

possible celestial alignments (other stones and pits filled with cultural materials) have been met with skepticism. The fact that cremated human remains are associated with the circular rings of small chalk-filled pits within the embanked area suggests that some sort of mortuary function was part of Stonehenge's repertoire. However, whether these remains indicate some sort of ancestor worship and that the emic meaning of Stonehenge included ideas about ancestors is also debatable. By citing the Venus figures and Stonehenge, we do not mean to suggest that the study of symbolism and meaning in contexts without reliable ethnographic and/or ethnohistoric data from which to draw is not worthwhile. On the contrary, testing hypotheses associated with symbolic patterns is an endeavor that scholars should embrace. Our point is that the study of meaning and symbolism can be ever more challenging in these kinds of contexts. Scholars should embrace the possibilities of studying symbolism and ancient meaning in all past contexts, but temper their interpretations by understanding the limitations

FIGURE 13.6 Some examples of iconography are easier to understand than others. The iconography shown on the walls of the tomb of Khaemteri, who lived during the time of Rameses II (1279–1213 BC), is more straightforward to understand than some of the other examples here; the analysis of this mortuary scene featuring the god Anubis facilitated in part by readable hieroglyphic inscriptions (top left). Examples such as the Newspaper Rock State Historic Monument, located in Utah, (top right) and this geoglyph from the Nazca Valle in Peru (colloquially named the "spaceman") (bottom left) are not so easy to interpret given the lack of written records and in some cases oral traditions. The petroglyphs at Valcamonica, Italy, (bottom right) have engendered considerable debate concerning their meaning. Although some researchers see hunting scenes and depictions of violence among the 300,000 images etched in the rock surfaces, others doubt these interpretations.

© Vladimir Melnik/Shutterstock.com
© Don Mammoser/Shutterstock.com
© Ron Ramtang/Shutterstock.com
© Pecold/Shutterstock.com

of the data available in any particular context. There is a widespread joke among archaeologists that every time someone finds a female figurine the first interpretative reaction is often that it represents "ritual" (which is such a broad concept that it means very little) or "fertility" (which is more likely a product of the researcher's cultural context more than anything else). Such figurines likely varied tremendously in their meaning in time, space, and cultural context. To tease out such meanings requires access to solid data. Although some iconography is very explicit, such as the depiction of captives on monuments in many parts of the world, we must remember that we cannot be in the minds of past peoples. So, although we may feel more comfortable identifying the figures in ancient Egyptian murals because we can now read the hieroglyphs, we must be careful with Bronze Age petroglyphs that retain great ambiguity. Some may seem obvious, but we must always be careful.

FIGURE 13.7 This mosaic found at the site of Pompeii, Italy, certainly invites one to think of it as a representation of a guard dog, but researchers must always keep their minds open to alternative possibilities, even when the answer may seem obvious.

© eFesenko/Shutterstock.com

Complicating the study of meaning and symbolism, researchers must keep in mind that not everyone in a cultural context "reads" symbols in the same way. Although we may be able to say that Mesoamerican peoples created art that reflected how they generally conceived the cosmos, there may have been many different kinds of readings of these symbols. Take monuments like the arches of Rome or the great pyramids of Gaza in Egypt. These monuments could have had specific meanings that were intended by their builders. The Arch of Titus of Rome was built as an honorific arch in AD 82 by Emperor Domitian to commemorate the military victories of his brother Titus. These victories included the siege of Jerusalem in AD 70. Although researchers may conclude that the meaning of this arch was to commemorate an important figure in Roman history and that it has served as a symbol of pride for many citizens of the empire, the monument was also probably viewed as a negative symbol of imperialism by people who were disenfranchised by the expansion of the empire, such as the residents of Jerusalem who suffered the sack of their city and witnessed the destruction of the Second Temple. Something similar could be surmised of the great pyramids at Giza, which would have been powerful symbols of pharaonic rule that some in Egyptian society would have applauded and others might have seen as symbols of oppression.

These examples serve to demonstrate that is no one way to interpret symbols and that while researchers may uncover the

FIGURE 13.8 The Arch of Titus, Rome, Italy.

© Marco Rubino/Shutterstock.com

meanings intended to be conveyed by their producers, we should always be aware of the potential for alternative readings. In many ways, this quote, often attributed to George Bernard Shaw, conveys this very point regarding symbols: "The single biggest problem in communication is the illusion that it has taken place." We might modify this to say that the single biggest problem in symbolic communication is the illusion that everyone reads the symbols in the same way.

Thinking about the concept of "reading," we also have to keep in mind that writing is also symbolic. Letters in our alphabet represent sounds that we speak. And, the words they form are also open to interpretation. What do you really mean to say when you say "funny"; "funny ha ha" or "funny hmmmm"? Regardless of the flexibility in meaning of letters and words, when written language was invented (and it appeared independently in various parts of the world), it represented a substantial change in the

way that information was communicated and stored, and many researchers view the appearance of writing as a momentous development. Although not all ancient script is fully understandable to epigraphers today, many systems of written communication are fairly readable to contemporary scholars. Some scripts include **ideographs**; symbols that represent a concept like the equal sign (=) in mathematics. Others use **logograms**, which represent actual words in a language rather than concepts. For example, the Classic period Maya used logograms like the symbol of a hand to represent the verb *ch'am* (to grab). They also used syllabograms, symbols that represent phonetic sounds, such as the word for jaguar, *bahlam* written **ba-la-m(a)**. This demonstrates that societies can use different kinds of systems of representing within a single written language.

Another issue that researchers working with meaning and symbols should keep in mind is that even the intended meanings of symbols can vary in time and space. Just because the intended meaning of a symbol in one area of the world during a specific period is successfully uncovered through careful research does not mean that when that symbol is found elsewhere, or at some of time, that it necessarily was created to have the same meaning. For example, Nordic runes have their origin in Greco-Roman writing systems. Some scholars have suggested that the early use of the runes in Scandinavia was for magic, rather than as an actual writing system; the meaning of these symbols being very different based on their cultural context.

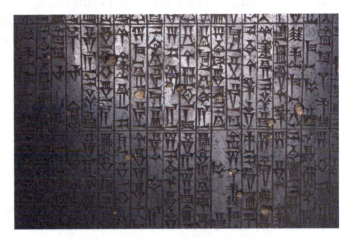

FIGURE 13.9 A detail of the cuneiform inscription from Code of Hammurabi stela, which details the laws set down by this Babylonian king in 1754 BC.

© jsp/Shutterstock.com

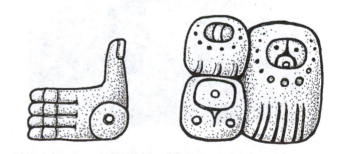

FIGURE 13.10 Examples of Classic Maya script: the logogram verb *ch'am* (to grab [on the left]); the syllabogram word *bahlam* (jaguar [on the right]).

© Karl Taube

The Past in the Present:
The Meaning of Archaeology in Contemporary Societies

We started out this book with a discussion of the importance of the past in the present. Although we will not review that discussion in detail here, the past is critical for identity formation, historical legitimation for the ways things are done today, and a host of political processes, among other things. What archaeology can mean to people today can be extremely varied, but one thing is certain; the construction of narratives of the past matters. Archaeology's own realization of this fact has grown in very important ways in recent years. Although there has been an understanding that the past can be used for political means for some time, archaeologists have only confronted their role in how the past can be used in more recent times. Stemming from this realization, researchers have begun to reflect on their own role in as active agents in contemporary societies, acknowledging that their work has an impact on the living world around them. It may seem strange to think this, but for years many archaeological projects did not engage with diverse stakeholders, preferring to "extract data" from an area of the world and create narratives that neither took into account local knowledge and interests, nor assessing the impact that their interpretations could have. Many archaeologists preferring to simply envision their work as focusing on the "dead," absolving themselves of any interactions or obligations with the living. This situation has changed.

FIGURE 13.11 Rök Runestone in Sweden (ca. ninth-century AD).

© Stefano Zaccaria/Shutterstock.com

FIGURE 13.12 People can have very diverse ideas of heritage and can interact with archaeological sites in different ways. Here we see two solstice events, one at Stonehenge (Great Britain) and the other at Tiwanaku (Bolivia).

Source: Travis Stanton

© 1000 Words/Shutterstock.com

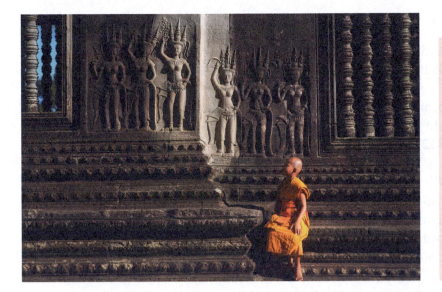

FIGURE 13.13 Archaeology today must engage with a variety of different stakeholders who may include descendent communities, tourists, government representatives, business owners, and landowners. An understanding that archaeology is just as much about social life in the present (and future) as it is about the past is critical for researchers in a modern archaeology; shown, a young monk at Angkor Wat, Cambodia.

© Pentium5/Shutterstock.com

Although some archaeologists critically engaged with stakeholders prior to the 1990s, it was in this decade that the field began to more greatly acknowledge its role in modern societies and challenge itself with finding ways to engage with living peoples who have diverse interests in the past they study. One outcome of these changes has been the development of **community archaeology**, a strategy of ethically engaging with local communities and stakeholders that runs parallel to archaeological research. Fundamentally, community archaeology is about a conversation. This conversation is between archaeologists and stakeholders in the past that archaeologists create through their research. Although this may sound simple, in most cases it is not. To start with, "stakeholders" are never a unified group. They can include descendant communities, landowners, developers, and government officials, among others. To begin and sustain a productive and healthy conversation with all of the potential stakeholders, archaeologists must listen and establish trust through transparency and mutual respect. A recognition of the impact of archaeological research in modern society places archaeologists in the role of primary stewards, not owners (see Chapter 2), of the past. In this role, archaeologists enter partnerships, in many cases with descendant communities. Descendant communities are sometimes composed of members who may do not agree among themselves about how to study and interpret the past. In some cases, **indigenous archaeology** may even be practiced, whereby members of a descendant community perform archaeological research. Regardless of who the stakeholders are, however, a modern archaeology engages in partnerships.

The partnerships that archaeologists enter with stakeholders may be simple. In many cases, they are complex. The variation in the social dynamics of such partnerships means that there is no one recipe for collaboration. But, if there is one fundamental ingredient to collaborating with descendant communities and other stakeholders, it is respect. Respect for nonarchaeological voices to be heard and alternative narratives voiced, even if those narratives are at odds with those generated through archaeological research. Each collaborative relationship will be composed of a unique set of conversations and negotiations. In a modern ethical archaeology, researchers must make attempts to engage. Gone are the days of when archaeologists could ignore living peoples and the impact of their work in the present. Today, we recognize that the past is in the present, and how we engage and construct the past matters for many people today.

Bibliography

Bernal, Ignacio. "Views of Olmec Culture." In *Dumbarton Oaks Conference on the Olmec, October 28th and 29th, 1967*, edited by E. P. Benson, 135–142. Washington, DC: Dumbarton Oaks Research Library and Collection., 1968

Bevan, Lynne. "Warfare, Violence, and the Construction of Masculinity in the Iron Age Rock Art of Valcamonica, Northern Italy." In *Warfare, Violence, and Slavery in Prehistory*, edited by M. Parker Pearson and I. J. N. Thorpe, 127–138. BAR International Series 1374. Oxford: Archaeopress, 2005.

Caroselli, Marlene. *Leadership Skills for Managers*. New York: McGraw-Hill Education, 2000.

Coe, Michael D. *America's First Civilization*. New York: American Heritage Publishing Co., Inc., 1968.

Dobres, Marcia-Anne. "Venus Figurines." In *Oxford Companion to Archaeology*, edited by B. M. Fagan, 740–741. Oxford: Oxford University Press, 1996.

Green, Dennis H. *Medieval Listening and Reading: The Primary Reception of German Literature 800–1300*. Cambridge: Cambridge University Press, 1994.

Jones, Brian W. *The Emperor Domitian*. London: Routledge, 1992.

Joralemon, David. *A Study of Olmec Iconography*. Studies in Pre-Columbian Art and Archaeology Number Seven. Washington, DC: Dumbarton Oaks Research Library and Collection, 1971.

———"The Olmec Dragon: A Study in Pre-Columbian Iconography." In *Origins of Religious Art and Iconography in Preclassic Mesoamerica*, edited by H. B. Nicholson, 27–71. Los Angeles: UCLA Latin American Center Publications, 1976.

Pool, Christopher A. *Olmec Archaeology and Early Mesoamerica*. Cambridge: Cambridge University Press, 2007.

Tate, Carolyn E. *Reconsidering Olmec Visual Culture: The Unborn, Women, and Creation*. Austin: University of Texas Press, 2012.

Zimmerman, Larry J., and Kelly M. Branam. "Collaborating with Stakeholders." In *Archaeology in Practice: A Student Guide to Archaeological Analyses*, edited by J. Balme and A. Paterson, 1–25. Oxford: Wiley Blackwell, 2014.